COMPUTER SIMULATION AND MODELING:
An Introduction

RICHARD S. LEHMAN
Franklin and Marshall College

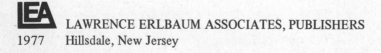

LAWRENCE ERLBAUM ASSOCIATES, PUBLISHERS

1977   Hillsdale, New Jersey

DISTRIBUTED BY THE HALSTED PRESS DIVISION OF

JOHN WILEY & SONS

New York   Toronto   London   Sydney

Lawrence Erlbaum Associates, Inc., Publishers
62 Maria Drive
Hillsdale, New Jersey 07642

Distributed solely by Halsted Press Division
John Wiley & Sons, Inc., New York

Library of Congress Cataloging in Publication Data

Lehman, Richard S
  Computer simulation and modeling.

  Includes bibliographies.
  1. Digital computer simulation.   I. Title.
QA76.9.C65L44   001.4'24   77-22124
ISBN 0-470-99296-4

Printed in the United States of America

Contents

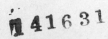

Preface

This is an introductory book about computer simulation and modeling in the social and behavioral sciences. Its major aim is to present simulation and modeling as a useful and exciting technique that can be applied in many areas of social science research and theory.

Computer simulation is being used in increasing numbers of ways by many scientists. The literature dealing with simulation is expanding rapidly. Almost paradoxically, however, no book has been written for the social scientists who wish to write a simulation but cannot conceive of how to begin. This book attempts to fill that need.

There are several other ways of viewing this book as well. Whereas it can serve as a textbook for a course in simulation, it can also be regarded as a second-level text in computer programming, the examples in which are simulations. Some of the topics presented here have not appeared in the literature that is readily available to social scientists. For example, we present an extended discussion of computer accuracy and efficiency. The intention in discussing such material is not to make the reader into an expert programmer. Instead, the hope is that by having their attention called to some areas that have been the exclusive province of computer science, social scientists can benefit from a wealth of material that they may not otherwise encounter.

An additional aim of the book is to deal with a body of material on computer simulation and modeling directly. We do not survey the literature of the field of simulation but do direct our attention to some of the metatheoretical considerations involved. An entire chapter is devoted to the problem of validating a simulation; another large section is concerned with the benefits, the whys, and the why nots of simulation.

A few assumptions are made about the reader of this book. In the first place, he or she is assumed to be an advanced undergraduate or graduate student in one of the social and behavioral sciences, or at least to have some knowledge of them. I am a psychologist, but it is hoped that this does not bias the book in any significant way. The three major examples developed throughout the book are drawn from psychology, sociology, and urban development. Incidental examples represent economics, political science, and business administration. In addition, the reader is encouraged to develop his or her own pet project mentally while reading the book and thus make the material even more individually meaningful.

A second assumption about the reader is that he or she has some familiarity with computer programming. The book is not intended to be an introduction to programming, and so some elementary computer understanding necessarily is assumed.

All of the illustrative computer material in the book is in Fortran. But it is not essential that it be the language with which the reader is acquainted. An algorithmic language, such as Fortran, BASIC, PL/I, or ALGOL, is probably the first language learned by most social scientists. With a background in any of those, the book and its examples should be easily comprehensible and beneficial.

Fortran is used not because I feel that it is in any sense the "best" language. In most respects, in fact, it is not the best for simulation. Indeed, it is far from a perfect language for many of the activities engaged in by social scientists. The fact remains, however, that it is the most widely available computer language, and the one probably familiar to most social scientists.

Two complete simulation programs appear throughout the book as a source of many of the illustrations of programming, coding, and validation. Major discussions of these examples are set in a type face different from the bulk of the volume, making it easy for the reader to follow their development. The complete listings of these example programs appear in appendices, along with examples of their input and output.

A third example simulation is also presented in an appendix; in contrast with the others, however, it is not discussed in the text. Instead, it serves as a source for suggested exercises in most of the chapters. If the reader faithfully completes this series of problems, by the end of the book he or she should have a simulation program that resembles the one given in the appendix.

Many of the topics presented in the text should be regarded as essential in gaining a full understanding of the discussion. Other topics, however, are somewhat more advanced and technical than is necessary to comprehend the important material. They are included for the more sophisticated reader, or for the student who wishes to explore certain topics in more depth. These sections of the text, and the exercises derived from them, are marked with an asterisk and can be omitted without any loss of continuity.

The author of any book feels a debt of gratitude to many people who have aided, directly or indirectly, in its preparation. In the final analysis, of course, it is the author who must accept the responsibility for the final product and any errors of commission or omission in it. Indeed, in some cases I have asked advice and then explicitly disregarded it.

Richard M. Steere and Martin D. Murphy both read parts of the manuscript and helped catch some major and minor errors and sources of confusion. Richard V. Andree commented in detail on some of the mathematical material in Chapter 6 and was good enough to allow me to paraphrase some of his own examples rather freely.

It is surprising how an author can overlook major faults in his or her work until they are pointed out by someone else, at which time they become painfully obvious. This book has benefitted greatly from a careful and detailed review given it by Professor N. John Castellan, Jr., of the University of Indiana. Professor Castellan put a 15-year friendship with me on the line to point out what should have been obvious but, of course, wasn't. There are imperfections still, but it is hoped that they are less serious now than before his critique. I am very grateful for his help in making this a better book.

The three example simulations were modified and reproduced here with the kind permission of:

James M. Sakoda, and Gordon and Breach Publishers, for Sakoda's program CHEBO.

The North Carolina Educational Computing Service, for the program CITY.

Douglas Hintzman, and Academic Press, for Hintzman's program SAL, which appears here as SIMSAL.

Without these three example simulations, this book would be vastly different and much less valuable; I owe the individuals and publishers just listed a great deal of appreciation.

Figures 1.1 and 8.1 in this book are modifications of an illustration in R. S. Lehman and D. E. Bailey, *Digital Computing,* and appear here by permission of the publisher, John Wiley and Sons, Inc.

Several of the subroutines presented in the book are based upon published algorithms. For permission to reproduce an algorithm, or to base a program on a published flowchart, I express my appreciation to:

The Association for Computing Machinery, Inc., for the use of the normal distribution algorithm described in J. H. Ahrens and U. Dieter, Computer methods for sampling from the exponential and normal distributions, *Communications of the ACM,* 1972, **15**, 873–882. Copyright 1972, Association for Computing Machinery, Inc.

Prentice-Hall, Inc., for a modification of an exchange sort flowchart, appearing as Figure 4.2 here, which originally appeared in D. U. Wilde, *An Introduction to Computing.*

John Wiley and Sons, Inc., for subroutines (Tables 3.1 and 3.2 here) based on flowcharts, and a modification of a flowchart of the tree traversal (Figure 4.9

here), which appeared in T. L. Booth and Y. T. Chien, *Computing: Fundamentals and Applications.*

The bulk of this book was written while I was on a sabbatical leave during the 1974–1975 academic year. I must express my appreciation to Franklin and Marshall College for granting me that leave. The College also supplied all of the computer time and facilities necessary to write and test the example programs.

Mary Ann Russell handled the typing of the entire manuscript with her usual aplomb. Her frequent requests that I quit editing so that she could have something to do were appreciated and kept the book more nearly on schedule than it might otherwise have been.

Although the name of Daniel E. Bailey does not appear here as a reviewer or other contributor, he influenced the work in a strong but indirect way. In the first place, it was Dan who first introduced me to the computer and its use in psychology. Second, it was through my involvement with him in a series of summer institutes that I first became aware of a need for a book such as this. Finally, Dan's personal encouragement provided a necessary impetus to begin writing. I owe him a great deal.

Perhaps the most important contributors to this book include a town and a family. To my parents and the small town of Idyllwild, California, I must say thank you; I can hardly conceive of a sabbatical retreat more appropriate for writing than the one they provided. My wife Jean contributed mightily by her support and encouragement, her recognition of a writer's need for solitude, and her tolerance of the inevitable bouts with irritability and frustration that accompany putting words on paper. My daughter Barbara learned quickly not to "bother Daddy," even when I was in the next room. She provided some amusing distractions when she proudly displayed flowcharts that she had drawn, using one of my templates.

And finally, it is you, the reader, who has provided the most guidance during the writing. My perception of the unseen and abstract audience for the book directed the entire effort. But that is as it should be; the book is for you.

1
Introduction and Overview

The earliest of the formal speculative approaches to the study of the behavior of mankind began as a branch of philosophy. In the late nineteenth century the modern scientific method began to be applied to the study of behavior and various disciplines in the social and behavior sciences emerged as separate entities. Throughout the relatively short history of the social science fields, the empirical techniques for investigating behavior have become progressively more refined. Careful observation replaced speculation, controlled experimentation supplanted observation, and criteria for theoretical explanation matured. Among the most recent developments has been the use of the computer as an instrument, and sometimes as an analogy, in the development and testing of explanatory theory. Such use of the computer is known as computer simulation.

Simulation as a technique is not new, and even computer simulation has been with us since the first days of the computer itself. In the earlier history of the computer, however, simulation was regarded as an esoteric enterprise and was not widely used or appreciated. Partly because of an increasing familiarity with the computer as a research instrument and partly in recognition of some of its unique characteristics, computer simulation is becoming a much more widely applied research tool for the social and behavioral sciences.

Apart from its obvious use in experimental control and data analysis, the computer fills two general roles in scientific research. In the first, the computer serves as an analogy to some aspect of the real world of behavior. An operating computer is under the control of a program that directs all of its activities. Likewise, behavior in living organisms, whether it be at a microscopic cellular level or at the level of international relations, is governed by sets of laws that direct it. The task of the social and behavioral scientist is to understand those laws. Because the computer and real behavior proceed in a dynamic fashion over time, and because both are governed by sets of potentially decipherable rules, the computer can become an analogy for the real world.

1

A second general kind of role for the computer is in the use of a computer program to express a theory about the operation of the real process. Here the computer is more than an analog. The computer can actually be said to simulate the real process, at least under certain circumstances and within certain kinds of assumptions and definitions.

The discussion of these two general roles of the computer in scientific research is an important emphasis in this book. Our focus is primarily on the computer as a research tool for the social/behavioral scientists — a device that aids in the construction and testing of theoretical statements about behavior.

MODELS AND SIMULATIONS

Let us begin our discussion of the logic of computer simulation and modeling with an example. Consider a simple social situation involving two easily identifiable groups. If we observe the spatial distribution of people at a cocktail party, we may notice that the members of the two groups (men and women, in this case) tend to organize into pairs. Of course, there would be interaction among just men, or just women, but the predominant organization might be mixed sex pairs.

A different set of groups might produce a different organization. Members of labor and management, for instance, would most likely arrange themselves into two groups and show very little interaction across group lines.

Pursuing the example further on a descriptive level may suggest that we should seek to quantify the observations, perhaps by measuring the actual distances between individuals at different points in time, plotting rates of approach and avoidance, and so forth. However, that is of little interest to us in the present context, because the scientist does not remain content with observation, no matter how precise, for very long. The goal of science is not only to describe but also to explain.

Most modern social scientists ascribe the differences in the two social situations to attitudes. An attitude is an assumed property of the individuals in the situation and governs their propensities to approach or avoid members of their own and other groups. A positive attitude toward another group would cause an individual to approach a member of the other group, whereas a negative attitude would have the opposite effect. In the first example, members of each sex might be conceived as having a strong attraction to the other group and only a weak attraction to their own group. In the second illustration, positive intragroup attitudes and negative intergroup attitudes could be inferred.

Theories and Models

The preceding discussion of the process of social attraction in terms of the explanatory characteristics of attitudes is an instance of a simple theory. A theory is a general statement of a principle abstracted from data and observation that purports to explain the behavior under consideration. In this case, the theory ascribes certain properties to the individuals involved (specifically attitudes) and uses those properties to explain the behavior.

Theories have four distinctive features that are important to our discussion. First, they are related to data, meaning that they are tied closely to observations of the phenomenon. Second, they attempt to offer an explanation of the observed behavior, at least at one level. Note that saying that individuals tend to approach those others to whom they have a positive attitude does not really explain the behavior at any level other than that intended — it says nothing at all about a possible physiological mechanism, for example. Third, the theory offers the possibility of making testable predictions. If, for example, we know that two groups have mutually positive attitudes toward each other, we can predict that their members are going to approach each other given an opportunity. Finally, theories often make use of hypothesized processes or features of the participants that are not directly observable by themselves — the attitudes in this example.

A scientist interested in exploring attitudes and social attraction in detail has several possible courses of action open to him or her. A direct procedure builds on the predictive nature of the theory. If the theory indicates an approach by groups with known attitudes, a reasonable experiment is to find groups with the appropriate attitudes and determine whether or not they actually behave as the theory suggests. This is the traditional theory-testing kind of experiment that has served as the cornerstone of the scientific method.

Another procedure would be to abstract the essential elements of the situation and theory into a simpler form. For example, one might draw a square and, letting rocks and twigs represent the two groups, move them around in patterns dependent on some hypothetical attitudes. Likewise, if one were mathematically inclined, one might develop a precise formula relating strength of attitude to attraction and then to rate of approach or retreat.

A third kind of representation of the theory is more to the point of this book. We might write a computer program expressing some of the essentials of the social situation and the associated theory. A two-dimensional array might represent the social field or room in which the action was to take place. Different symbols could be located in the array to indicate the locations of members of the two different groups. Attitudes could be represented by values in the program and the individual characters moved about in the array as a function of the group attitudes.

These three different forms of representation of the situation and theory are called models. In this case, we have a physical model (the rocks and twigs), a mathematical model, and a computer model. In each, the model is a representation of the theory where the individual actors are represented in some way, and elements of the theory govern the rules by which the model is manipulated.

A model, then, is a representation of a theory. The theory itself typically is expressed verbally, but the model may be represented in any of several different media.

There are several important differences between a theory and a model which should be clarified. In the first place, the model is only a representation of the theory; it is not the theory itself (there are exceptions, as we discuss later). A model is a useful extension of the theory in that it is typically more concrete and easier to grasp. Objects and variables can be manipulated and their effects observed in the model. To some extent, the model allows us to observe the theory in action — the theoretical variable of attitude can be observed as having an effect on the movement of the representations of the interacting individuals. In this way the model allows one to check some of the predictions of the theory and permits quick exploration of some new hypotheses that may present themselves during the operation of the model.

A model is typically an application of a theory to a specific situation. Theories are usually stated in broad terms and are applicable in many different specific instances. A model is more restricted in its intent, applying only to a subset of the phenomena addressed by the theory. The simplification required by the model makes it less generally applicable than the full theory; but, at the same time, is usually much more specific than the theory can be with regard to the actual processes involved. To this extent it strengthens and extends the specificity of the theory while not attempting to speak to the full range of processes covered in the theoretical statement.

The model, however, is not an explanatory statement. The model is only a simplification and abstraction of certain key elements of the theory. It is the theory that makes the predictions and the statements of cause and effect. The model allows us to explore the consequences of the theory but not to explain the behavior.

The computer model, and to some extent the physical model, presents an element of the real situation that is not present in the mathematical model; and that is the element of time. Real processes in the real world unfold over time in a dynamic and changing fashion. The mathematical model deals with time as well in that it may be represented as a variable. In the physical and computer models, however, the process actually occurs over time when the model is operated. In some sense, the treatment of time is illusory, in that time in the operation of the models does not necessarily correspond to the actual clock time required by the real phenomenon. Nevertheless, the dynamic, operating nature of these two kinds of models set them apart in some ways from the more static mathematical model.

Simulations

If a computer model is a model expressed as a computer program, what then is meant by computer simulation? At times, the terms "computer model" and "computer simulation" may be regarded as interchangeable. But there are subtle differences. For example, Schultz and Sullivan (1972) define simulation as "... the modeling of a process by a process" (p. 7). Simulation is thus seen as itself a process – the operation of a model – but a process that is in some sense a copy of or parallel to a real process, the latter being the real-world process that is of interest in the theoretical context. In our example, the real process is the observed social interaction; the theory is the explanatory statement in terms of attitudes and approach and avoidance tendencies. The computer program, or some other representation, is the model; the actual operation of the model is the simulation. Stated in another way, simulation is the model in operation.

Nothing in our discussion so far limits the use of the term "simulation" specifically to computer simulation. Indeed, much simulation does not involve the computer at all. The game of Monopoly, for example, is really a simulation. It contain a representation (a model) of a real system, and playing the game constitutes a simulation according to our definition.

Simulations are sometimes grouped into several types; the Monopoly game would usually be called a "man–man" simulation, because no machine is involved. Many games fall into the "man–man" category, as do a large number of other simulations where human participants take various roles in order to gain an understanding of the simulated system. Such simulations include playing roles, such as participants in community decision making, considering international relations problems, and so on. Guetzkow (1962) surveys a number of man–man simulations.

Another common kind of simulation is called "man–machine." Here both computer and human participants are involved. For example, in a simulation known as the Executive Game (Henshaw & Jackson, 1966), human participants are formed into groups, each group representing the management team of a small manufacturing business. Each team makes decisions about allocating resources (that is, raw materials, new production facilities, research and development). The decisions are made independently by the teams and are submitted to a computer program. The program embodies a simplified model of the economic system for a group of competing companies and computes sales figures, income, profit and loss, and other business figures. The output is distributed to the players, who make their decisions for the next simulated business period, and so forth.

Several man–machine simulations have been developed around the process of community planning and politics. In one such simulation (Duke, 1964), participants play the roles of city planners, politicians, and real estate speculators. A computer program makes numerous computations based on a model of community growth, the results of which are distributed to the players, who then make decisions for the next period of play, and so forth.

Man–man and man–machine simulations usually have either or both of two purposes. One is primarily instructional in that the participants are expected to gain an understanding of the process simulated to a greater extent than is possible by other means of education. In a simulation, the participants can come to understand the complexities of, for example, international relations, more thoroughly and quickly than by reading or lecture.

The second purpose of these simulations is similar to those we shall note for simulation in general — research and exploration. The simulation offers a small-scale, simplified situation in which various aspects of human behavior can be investigated. Many take the form of laboratory games, such as the city planning simulation just mentioned.

A third class of simulation, the all-machine simulation, is the concern of this book and is what is generally meant by the term "computer simulation." In the all-machine simulation, the computer program is the model of the system being simulated, and the operation of the program is the simulation. Human participants do not enter into the actual simulation process itself.

Abelson (1968) defines the term simulation as "... the exercise of flexible imitation of processes and outcomes for the purpose of clarifying or explaining the underlying mechanisms involved" [p. 275]. This definition introduces several new elements into the meaning of simulation that need some additional discussion.

In the first place, we note the use of the phrase "processes and outcomes" in Abelson's statement. This is our first explicit mention of the results of a simulation — the output of a computer. We should certainly expect the results of a simulation — the output — to resemble or imitate the outcomes of a real process. Consideration of results, in fact, is an important element in the assessment of the validity of a simulation exercise. Equally important, however, is the imitation of process by the simulation. Note that the terminology is "flexible imitation" and not "exact copy" or something similar. This suggests that although the process is to be regarded as similar or parallel, no one to one correspondence need be implied. This is an important distinction, at least in the history of some kinds of computer simulations. Among early workers, there was an attempt to draw an analogy and to build a simulation on the fact that both the computer and the human nervous system are made up of a large number of individual binary devices. This parallel has not served well in the development of simulations. The concern is not with functional identity of elements but with parallelism in process. A computer program causes the computer to carry out certain processing operations, and the human nervous system also carries out certain operations. The important element in the simulation is the similarity of process, and not any presumed similarity of structure.

The second important point to note in Abelson's definition is that of the purpose of simulation — to clarify or explain. Clarification is one of the elements of simulation that we have noted earlier, but explanation has been reserved until now for theory and not for simulation. And here we come upon one of the important distinctions and ongoing debates in the literature of computer simulation.

We may interpret the meaning of explanation in the definition in two general ways that seem to fit with contemporary views on the subject. One position holds that the computer program is actually the theory. In the view of some writesr (see, for example, Gullahorn & Gullahorn, 1965) a computer program is an adequate medium for expressing the theory. A theory need not, in this viewpoint, exist in any other form. The program is the theory, and the theory is the program. In this instance then, the program may be said to have explanatory powers; it is a theoretical statement, and such statements are explanatory in nature.

Such an extreme view is not often found in the social and behavioral sciences. It is more characteristic of a branch of computer science known as artificial intelligence, about which we will say more shortly.

A more reasonable approach, and that taken by most contemporary simulation workers, is that theory and computer models are inseparable but different. The simulation program represents the theory, and the theory represents the simulation program. The simulation is a test of the theory, and the theory is regarded as the parent to the program. However, changes in the program necessitated by lack of fit to the data are interpreted as changes to the theory itself.

As an example, Simon and Hayes (1976) present a theory and program that attempts to explain and predict the behavior of humans in a problem-solving task requiring substantial understanding. A formal theory was developed and embodied in a simulation program. The theory and the program, taken together as a single unit, offered several predictions that were put to empirical test. As a result, both theory and program were revised, resulting in a new theory and accompanying computer model.

Using the theory and the model together in this fashion avoids a perplexing problem that arises when the program is treated as the sole expression of the theory — the program bug. A theory can be perfectly sound but its embodiment in the model can be flawed by an imperfect program. As anyone with experience in programming can appreciate, program errors are a constant problem. However, the presence of a few flaws in the program does not necessarily imply that the theory expressed by the program is incorrect. Indeed, Simon and Hayes indicated that many of the predictions and results of their program were based on "hand simulation," because the program had not been completely modified to deal with the particular problem types that were required by the theory.

In the latter instance, we see that the computer model can be a useful expression of a theory even though the program itself cannot operate. The nonoperating computer model has become extremely popular in psychology where much current theory is of an information processing sort. An information processing theory in psychology is concerned with explanation in terms of the processes and subprocesses that intervene between a stimulus and a response. In the information processing theory, the theory consists of a conceptual "program" which may never be realized as an operating simulation. It is still a model, however, and a very useful one at that. The general information processing approach in psychology has become so widespread that at least one introductory textbook (Lindsay & Norman, 1972) uses it for its entire theoretical orientation.

The information processing theory illustrates that the computer can serve as an analogy even when it is not being used in simulation. Information processing theories make use of computer terminology (input, output, subroutines, and so forth) but also typically describe an active process, just as a program does for a computer. The computer as a processor of information, controlled by a program made up of a series of discrete subprocesses, is science's current analogy; we return to this point again in Chapter 9.

The information processing approach need not be limited to psychology. Every social and behavioral science studies active, ongoing processes that can conveniently be represented as a process model of the kind we are discussing. Figure 1.1 illustrates the overall representation that is central to our discussion of modeling and simulation. The top half of the figure illustrates a simplified conceptualization of natural phenomena as studied by the scientist. The process is initiated by some input or stimulus, ultimately causing observable output. The exact nature of the process may not be directly observable, and so theories are constructed about it. Theory is generally developed from a study of the relationships between the system's inputs and outputs. In an experimental setting, the theory is typically put to test by providing specially constructed inputs (the independent variables) and observing the outputs (the dependent variables).

The computer simulation of the phenomenon shows the same relationships; the lower part of Figure 1.1. Here, the process is replaced by a representation of it, the operating computer program. In contrast to the real process, the inner workings of the program are known, if not directly observed. Experiments can be conducted with the simulation program and inferences made about the adequacy of the program by comparing the input and output of the real and the simulated phenomena.

Simulation is thus viewed as the operation — from input through output — of a computer program. The program is a process model of the operation of some real occurrance and is based on, and perhaps indistinguishable from, a theory concerning it. A computer model and a simulation are tools in attempting to understand the nature of the laws governing behavior; they help in prediction and explanation, which are the central elements in science.

Artificial Intelligence

Artificial intelligence is a branch of the rapidly growing discipline of computer science. Because of the similarity between many of its activities and those of social and behavioral science simulation, we must be careful to make the distinction between the areas clear.

In artificial intelligence, research and programming are directed toward the development of computer systems that exhibit behavior which, if observed in humans, are likely to lead one to say that the individual is showing intelligence. The most common research areas include pattern recognition, problem solving, theorem proving, and game playing. All of these general problems are recognized as requiring intellectual effort — hence the designation artificial intelligence.

Artificial intelligence has a great deal of superficial similarity to the problems

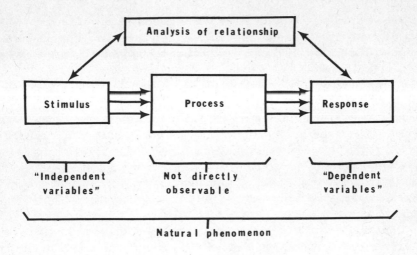

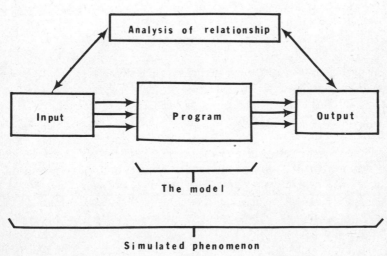

FIGURE 1.1 Conceptualizations of natural and simulated phenomena. (Modified from Lehman and Bailey, 1968, p. 219.)

that we are discussing here. The task is to create a computer system that mimics human behavior and may thus be mistaken for a simulation effort. However, there is an important distinction between simulation and modeling and the work in artificial intelligence.

Artificial intelligence shows comparatively little concern with the actual human processes involved with, for example, problem solving. There is no attempt to make an artificial intelligence program serve as a model of human problem solving, which is in turn based on a theory about the nature of human problem solving. Frequently no theory is involved at all, but only a conception of how to make a computer solve a problem. If there is a theory of human problem solving, it usually takes the form of an extrapolation from the program; if the computer does it in such and such a way, then the human must do likewise.

Another way of stating the distinction is based on the overall goals of the effort. For the social and behavioral scientist, the purpose is to better understand, on the level of scientific discourse and theory, the actual process being studied. In artificial intelligence, in contrast, the aim is not understanding but merely producing a program that can deal with a particular kind of task. The fact that the same task can be handled by humans frequently provides the only source of contact between the behavioral sciences and the artificial intelligence workers.

All this is not to say that there can be no benefit to the behavioral sciences from artificial intelligence. On the contrary, much can be gained. Work in pattern recognition, of which Selfridge (1959) is an early example, can feed back into perceptual psychology to aid in identifying and exploring the processes by which humans receive, process, and respond to sensory input. Attempts to develop artificial intelligence programs to translate from one language to another have forced linguists to recognize that they really have a very limited understanding of human languages. Indeed, most of the advances made in recent years in the areas of linguistics and language behavior have come from artificial intelligence workers. Schank and Colby (1973) present several excellent recent papers in the area.

Apart from the similarity of many task areas, and the possibility of fruitful interchange, artificial intelligence remains an effort quite separate from simulation as we view it here. Apter (1970) applies two different terms to the two different approaches to making the computer do what seem similar tasks. He refers to "simulation" in the sense that we have been using it here — a scientific tool to assist in the development and testing of theory. For artificial intelligence, in which the aim is making the computer exhibit "intelligent" behavior regardless of mechanism and with no effort at modeling, Apter suggests the term "synthesis." Because that word implies the combining of separate elements to obtain a desired result, as opposed to starting with a tentative understanding and deriving an operating consequence, we shall frequently use his terms as well.

WHY SIMULATE . . .

The decision to use any particular scientific technique in pursuing a problem is determined by a large number of factors. The appropriateness of the method is one consideration, the potential to advance theoretical understanding is another, and economy is yet a third. In this section, we discuss the various advantages of computer simulation in scientific research.

Theoretical or Metatheoretical Benefits of Simulation

Among the most compelling reasons for simulating are the theoretical considerations. Computer models and simulations are often the outgrowth of theory, and developing a simulation from a (usually verbal) theoretical statement has several potential advantages.

An important benefit is the clarification of theoretical statements. Most theories, at least in the social and behavioral sciences, are verbally expressed and can often be described as "loose." A loose verbal theory, be it of personality, social interaction, urban growth and development, or whatever, is frequently riddled with gaps in logic, contradictions, relationships left unspecified, unknown parameters, and a host of other difficulties. The simulation writer must make the functions relating variables explicit, define initial values and parameters, and resolve contradictions, or the simulation cannot function properly.

Simulation may also be a critique of a theory. A theory may be so loosely stated as not to be amenable to simulation at all without extensive modification, or without the addition of so many restrictive assumptions as to vitiate the theory as a useful scientific device. In the social and behavioral sciences it is not at all uncommon for theories to have an appearance of completeness and logical consistency. Their weaknesses may not be apparent until an investigator attempts to put them to a critical test, to draw firm inferences and predictions from them, or to build a model based on them. The use of a computer simulation frequently can reveal their flaws by highlighting their inconsistencies or lack of complete specificity.

A computer simulation often leads to a more complete expression of a theory than may otherwise be possible. This is primarily because of the ability of the computer program to deal with great complexity, both in terms of its own variables and in terms of its data. A verbally stated theory, or indeed a mathematically presented one, often becomes incomprehensible when it attempts to deal with large numbers of variables and parameters simultaneously. The computer model does not generally suffer from such difficulties. (However, see the discussion of Bonini's paradox, below.)

Perhaps the most important theoretical benefit to be derived from a computer simulation approach is that of using the program and theory to generate and explore new hypotheses and implications of the theory. It is here that the distinction between theory and model becomes the most blurred, but the benefit is the greatest. A model is developed from a theory, perhaps giving the theory greater clarity than before. However, the model is then implemented as an operating simulation, thus allowing the consequences of the theory to be explored directly. Less than optimal agreement between simulation and real data may cause modifications in the programmed model, and consequently in the theory itself. Conversely, exploration with the simulation may suggest relationships that can be explored in a real experiment. The net result of this complex interconnection between theory, simulation, and experimentation is an advancement in the theoretical understanding of the processes that is all important in science.

Finally, because a computer simulation is a model of some real process, the program's activities can be made to parallel the actual processes to a greater degree than is possible with other forms of models. This is of benefit even in simple and well-specified theories — it allows the theory to be more easily understood because it is possible to "watch" the process unfold over the course of operating the program, as we have noted previously.

Practical Benefits of Simulation

An operating computer simulation in many respects provides an ideal experimental subject for research. Once the program is operating correctly (and we shall have a good deal to say about how you can decide that it is), it is a relatively simple matter to run many experiments quickly. It suffers none of the practical problems that plague behavioral researchers — it does not need to be fed, housed, or paid; it does not require a massive survey effort; it usually keeps appointments with researchers; and it does not object to having things done to it that you could not do with real subjects.

In a computer model, it is easy to represent randomness and to deal with random variables. It is not difficult, for example, to make several simulation runs of a program assuming that a variable has the rectangular distribution, and then to change the program slightly to sample the same variable from a normal distribution, or from an exponential distribution, or from any of a number of theoretical distributions.

Several authors have pointed out that a computer simulation program forms a kind of archive for storing some kinds of data. This is particularly true in the case of the General Problem Solver (Newell, Shaw, & Simon, 1958; Newell & Simon, 1972) or Feldman's (1971) simulation of the behavior of a single subject in a binary choice experiment. In both of these efforts, the major aim was to develop a program that would match the protocol produced by an actual subject during the course of an experiment. The storage and representation of the actual subject's protocol forms a kind of archive for that subject. The archive might also be a large data base of public opinion material, voting records, or any of a variety of other sorts of data instead of results for a single subject. Such a data base, although perhaps initially developed only for the simulation, could serve as a valuable, and computer accessable, store of information for use in a variety of other ways.

Finally, a computer model and simulation is frequently an economical approach to the development of a theoretical position. With modeling, a new minitheory can often be developed rather quickly; certainly much more quickly than by the traditional approach of a series of experimental studies to explore a new explanatory conception. The model can serve as a kind of rough draft of a theory, allowing a quick preliminary check on many of the consequences of a theory. If the model makes predictions that are obviously incorrect, that difficulty can often be uncovered in a less painful and time-consuming fashion when simulating.

Other Benefits of Simulation

Computer simulations as forecasters of behavior are probably most obvious to the public in predicting elections. In such cases, the goal is the prediction of the outcome without regard to the specific mechanisms and processes involved. Election prediction programs typically make use of a large multiple regression equation. The vote totals from a large number of key precincts are entered into the equation, along with coefficients determined on the basis of past elections. The "model" in this simulation is the regression equation which simplifies and abstracts the results of many individual voters over the past several elections into a single mathematical expression. Although a simulation involving the individual attitudes of thousands or millions of individual voters would probably be of more interest to the behavioral scientist, it would require such a large amount of computing time that the television network would certainly lose the race to "call" the election first.

Forecasting need not be limited to elections, of course. A highly accurate simulation model of personality could be an invaluable aid to a psychotherapist who wanted to know which therapeutic approach to apply. Likewise models of attitude structures could aid in determining effective advertising and sales strategies.

In a closely related area, simulation programs can be extremely useful training aids in a variety of fields. The psychotherapy example just cited could serve as the basis for a training program for therapists. A few such simulations are already in existence, as are programs to aid the training of physicians in diagnostic procedures.

Finally, model building and computer simulation has a benefit beyond the purely scientific and scholarly; it can be an exciting, challenging, frustrating, rewarding, and enjoyable enterprise. As Apter (1970) states: "And, let's admit it, model building of all kinds gives a scientist some of the pleasure of being a creative artist" (pp. 26–27).

. . . AND WHY NOT SIMULATE

A major difficulty with any computer simulation project is determining the validity of the simulation. That is, does the model as operated in the simulation really reflect the real-world system it is intended to parallel? This topic is of great importance; we address it briefly in the following section of this chapter and again in Chapter 8.

There is a seductiveness about computer simulation that is frequently a major disadvantage. It is dangerously easy to become so involved in the programming task that the importance of the scientific enterprise becomes secondary. It is so easy (and often such fun!) to elaborate a program to add new little features that the program often is never really finished. As a consequence, the potential for scientific advancement inherent in simulation may be negated. Certainly many worthwhile simulation studies have never seen the light of print because the researchers became so enamored of their program that nothing of scientific worth ever comes of it. Simulation is best engaged in when there is a clear goal in mind and when there is sufficient self-discipline to prevent the project from continuing endlessly.

There are other serious problems as well. A very critical one has to do with the amount of simplification and specificity introduced into the model in the process of developing the simulation program. The risk here is twofold: lack of faithfulness to the theory being simulated and loss of generality. The first is related to the problem of validity and is deferred until later. Regarding the second, we merely point out that it is entirely possible that the model can be so simplified as to have no relevance to anything other than the specific situation, and perhaps even the specific data sets used.

In interpreting the results of a simulation study, it is all too easy to overlook the simplifications and necessary assumptions that have been made and to treat the results as if they are the "gospel" about the subject. This difficulty is not lessened by the ability of the programmer, given a little skill and care, to produce highly convincing output that fairly cries out to be believed.

Finally, the simulator must beware of what Dutton and Starbuck (1971) term "Bonini's paradox," and we describe the paradox in their words:

A model is built in order to achieve understanding of an observed causal process, and the model is stated as a simulation program in order that the assumptions and functional relations may be as complex and realistic as possible. The resulting program produces outputs resembling those observed in the real world, and inspires confidence that the real causal process has been accurately represented. However, because the assumptions incorporated in the model are complex and their mutual interdependencies are obscure, the simulation program is no easier to understand than the real process was. (p. 14)

Bonini's paradox is an extreme, but unfortunately all too common, problem of simulation. It frequently results from a programming project that is over-elaborated, most often as a result of the appeal of the programming aspects of the research. The message should be clear — understand what is being attempted and stop when the goal is achieved.

THE VALIDATION PROBLEM

Validating a computer simulation is one of the most difficult, and most important, aspects of the simulation process. We introduce the topic briefly here and later devote Chapter 8 to a more complete view of validation.

Validation is the determination of how adequately the simulation reflects those aspects of the real world it has been designed to model. The need for validation, and its logic and procedures, have received a great deal of attention from scholars since simulation studies were first begun. Despite this history, generally agreed on criteria have not yet been developed. There has not evolved a single set of rules and tests which, if satisfied, results in a simulation that is uniformly regarded as valid. A large part of the difficulty may be caused by the failure to recognize that there may in fact be multiple criteria for validity, and that validity is heavily dependent on the purpose for which the simulation is intended.

To illustrate the problem of multiple criteria, let us return to an example that we have used earlier — that of predicting the outcome of an election. The usual television network programs make their predictions on the basis of carefully selected key precincts which in the past have served as excellent presagers of election results. It would also be possible to construct a simulation program based on hundreds, thousands, or indeed millions of individual voters, each with his or her own attitudes toward candidates and issues. Indeed, this has been accomplished on a small scale during several recent elections (e.g., see McPhee, 1961, 1963; Pool, Abelson, & Popkin, 1964) but never nationally. However, there is no reason why, in principle, it cannot be done.

Suppose that there are two such programs to predict election outcomes — one based on a multiple regression formula relating key precincts, and the other based on very large numbers of simulated individual voters. Suppose, furthermore, that the two programs make identical predictions about the outcome of an election — predictions that coincide with the actual election result. That is, both programs appear equally valid with respect to the predicted outcome. Which program is more valid? Are they equally valid? If you must choose one as a theory of the behavior of the electorate, which should you choose?

These are difficult questions, and the answers are in part dependent on the aims and needs of the investigator. If only the prediction of the outcome is desired, then either program can suffice, and a television network is well advised to choose the fastest and most economical.

But are the programs equally valid as expressions of theories of behavior? Here the question is considerably more difficult. We must consider the nature of theory in scientific explanation and the criteria for evaluating theoretical statements. If the researcher's aim is for a theory predicting voting behavior of the electorate, he or she is now confronted with two formulations leading to identical predictions. The choice of the theory here must be based on the other considerations traditionally applied to scientific theory, such as simplicity, generality, and flexibility, because the criterion of accuracy of prediction has already been met. In this case, simplicity would probably prevail and the multiple regression model be selected.

However, that decision may not be satisfactory to an investigator whose concern was more with individuals than with groups. Indeed, the process represented by the multiple regression procedure in no way resembles the actual process by which voters decide how to vote. Voting is a highly individual matter. The final outcome is determined by the particular attitudes and beliefs of a large number of individuals. If the theoretical interest is at the individual level, the multiple regression model may be entirely inappropriate. In the terms often applied in evaluation of theory, the explanation is at the wrong level of analysis; it deals only with mass behavior and not with individual behavior.

The distinction drawn here may sound familiar — between artificial intelligence with its tendency to avoid process representation and "true" simulation — but it is not quite that simple. To the mass behavior theoriest, the use of the multiple regression model may well be an entirely appropriate simplification for his or her purposes. His or her interests are at an entirely different level and he or she may be perfectly content to approximate the behavior of large numbers of individuals with a mathematical expression. Indeed, a simulation of election behavior may be only a part of a much larger model of, say, international relations where national election returns are but one small subprocess.

At some point in any simulation program, simplifications are made in the way of representing components of the system. If this were not the case, every model in social and behavioral science would have to be built up of representations of biochemical processes in individual neurons, connected into specific subsystems to make up individuals, in turn formed into groups of individuals, and so forth up to the level of theoretical interest. This approach, of course, is patently ridiculous. The appropriate level of analysis and simulation for one purpose may be inappropriate for another. The usefulness of a simulation as an adjunct to scientific theory must be considered within the larger context of the level of analysis, the purposes of the simulation, and often the costs involved.

Another problem in validation relates to the utility of the simulation and its model in generating testable hypotheses. A good theory must make predictions that can be tested by experiment and observation in the arena of real behavior. No less can be said for a computer model. The model, and its associated theoretical framework, must be capable of being empirically tested. If it is not, it stands as nothing but a possibly interesting exercise, unfortunately of no scientific value.

Validation of computer simulations and models hinges on two different, but closely related, topics that may have been apparent to the careful reader. The first is in the relationship between the output of the real and simulated systems. It should be almost painfully obvious that if the program produces results that are at variance with the data from actual behavior, then the simulation cannot be regarded as valid. This side of the validation coin has received extensive treatment in the literature of simulation, but only recently has serious attention been paid to its equally important counterpart.

The other aspect of validation is that dealing with the theory, its status as a legitimate scientific statement, and its relationship to the model and the simulation. Fridja (1967) was among the first to argue for careful attention being paid to the correspondence between program and theory. In Chapter 8 we return to these topics in more detail and outline some of the procedures that have been proposed for judging the validity of a simulation.

THE ORGANIZATION OF THIS BOOK

In this chapter we have attempted to establish a general framework for discussing computer simulation and modeling. The computer model and simulation is viewed as an important tool in scientific research. It offers a technique for developing, clarifying, expressing, and evaluating theory. There are particular strengths and weaknesses associated with simulation and modeling; it is a relatively new technique and many of its potentialities and pitfalls have not yet been fully explored.

The following five chapters (Chapters 2–7) deal with writing computer simulation models in detail. In some respects, they constitute a second-level text in Fortran programming in that they presuppose a certain familiarity with programming and computer use. They are more than a programming text in that they are oriented specifically to the writing of computer models. They do not attempt to teach Fortran programming but illustrate how to use it in model building. Specific hints, techniques, and procedures will be discussed and illustrated by using three example programs.

The programming chapters offer an approximate parallel to the temporal sequence in writing a simulation program — starting with planning the simulation, continuing to the data representation, then writing random processes, coding the program in Fortran, and finally documenting the program.

Following these technical chapters, we return to the theoretical discussion begun here with a more extended discussion of validation in Chapter 8. There we elaborate on the two principal emphases noted previously — the similarity of the real and simulated results and the worth of the model as a theoretical statement.

The final chapter offers some last comments on a number of ideas that recur at various points in the discussion and suggests some topics for additional study.

For the reader who has skipped the Preface and jumped immediately into Chapter 1, a few words are in order. First, this book is not intended to be a high-level treatise on computer simulation. Instead, it is meant for the advanced student, graduate student, or professional who knows a little about computers and programming but who does not understand the logic of modeling and wants to know how to go about writing a simulation. Several higher level texts are included in the Suggested Readings at the end of this chapter.

By the same token, this book is not a survey of computer simulation developments and theory. Reference has already been made to several such surveys; they and a few others are listed at the end of the chapter.

An essential element in learning the kind of material presented here is a selection of examples and problems. Three complete simulation programs appear in this book. Two of them, which we preview in the next section of this chapter, provide the major source of illustrative material throughout the book. The third program is developed in stages throughout the following chapters as a continuing exercise. This simulation topic is offered in the hope that the reader, in addition to working on the other suggested exercises, will develop his or her own program while working through the book. A finished simulation program that may result from completing the exercises is presented in Appendix C. The reader's own program may, of course, differ in many ways from the one offered. This fact should present no particular problem; no programming project offers but a single "correct" solution. Indeed, for most programming problems, there is probably at least one correct solution for each person who solves it! In addition to the continued problem, each chapter, except the first and the last, offers a set of exercises that should prove helpful to someone learning the techniques to be described.

A PREVIEW OF THE EXAMPLES

The two programs introduced here continue throughout this book as examples and illustrations. These example materials have been selected for several reasons that should be stated at the outset. I claim no originality in the simulations. Indeed, the first program (CHEBO) was written originally by someone else and modified for use here; the second (SIMSAL) was based on an existing program but rewritten in Fortran by me.

The first criterion used in selecting the examples was that they should be relatively simple; not so simple as to be worthless as models, but elementary enough to be readily explained and understood. At the same time, they are complex enough to be interesting, and perhaps to serve as the basis for additional independent study.

A second criterion was that the examples should represent two different fields of the social and behavioral sciences.

Third, the examples had to represent several different programming techniques and data organizations.

Extremely large programs were excluded as a fourth criterion, because not all readers are likely to have access to very large computers.

Finally, the programs had to be written in, or at least amenable to (as in the case of SIMSAL), the Fortran programming language. Fortran is in many ways a poor choice for writing simulations, but it is also true that it is probably the closest thing that we have (or are likely to get for some time) to a universally available computer language. As an additional consideration, most people learn Fortran or a closely related algorithmic language, such as BASIC or ALGOL, as their first language. Because this book is directed at the relative novice in simulation, he or she should stay with a familiar language rather than have to learn an entirely new sort of language, such as LISP, as well.

CHEBO — The Checkerboard Model of Social Interaction

This model and simulation allow the investigation of the relationships between two groups of social entities, usually people. The relationship is represented graphically, as on a checkerboard. Various parameters can be manipulated in the simulation, the most important being two sets of attitudes — the attitude of group members toward themselves and the attitude of group members toward members of the other group. The checkerboard model is the work of James Sakoda, a sociologist at Brown University, and has been described by him (Sakoda, 1971). (It is no coincidence that CHEBO resembles our earlier example of group attitudes.)

SIMSAL

This program is the more complex of the examples but deals with what is superficially the simplest situation — the learning of a paired-associates list of items by a single subject. The simulation program is based on the doctoral dissertation of Douglas Hintzman (Hintzman, 1968). Hintzman called his program, which was probably written in a dialect of LISP, SAL, for Stimulus and Association Learner. Our version, in Fortran, is a simplification of SAL, hence the name SIMSAL. SIMSAL comes from a distinguished family tree, being closely related to the Elementary Perceiver and Memorizer (EPAM) of Feigenbaum and Simon (Feigenbaum, 1963).

SUGGESTED READINGS

Apter, M. J. *The computer simulation of behaviour.* New York: Harper & Row, 1970. An excellent summary of a large number of simulation efforts; also contains a concise introduction to some of the metatheoretical considerations in simulation.

Dutton, J. M., & Starbuck, W. H. *Computer simulation of human behavior.* New York: Wiley, 1971. This exceptional volume contains 38 papers dealing with a great variety of simulations from individual cognition studies through a model of the United States economy. Of special note is a bibliography that the authors estimate contains 71–84% of the literature on simulation through 1969, and an extensive section on methodological issues.

Feigenbaum, E. A., & Feldman, J. *Computers and thought.* New York: McGraw-Hill, 1963. This collection of 21 papers and essays deserves a place on the shelf of anyone seriously interested in computer simulation of cognitive processes. Several of the papers are classics in this young field.

Green, B. F. *Digital computers in reserach.* New York: McGraw-Hill, 1963. An excellent introduction to computers in behavioral research. The chapter on models summarizes much early work.

Guetzkow, H., Kotler, P., & Schultz, R. L. *Simulation in social and administrative science: Overviews and case studies.* Englewood Cliffs, N. J.: Prentice-Hall, 1972. This excellent survey presents a bakers' dozen carefully selected papers and studies. The organization is in terms of an overview of an area followed by a specific case example paper, usually a "classic" study.

Loehlin, J. C. *Computer models of personality.* New York: Random House, 1968. This paperback provides an excellent survey of four personality simulations, set into a context of the logic, strengths, and weaknesses, of simulation.

Newell, A., & Simon, H. A. *Human problem solving.* Englewood Cliffs, N. J.: Prentice-Hall, 1972. This is the definitive description of the General Problem Solver (GPS), written by its originators – two towering figures in the field of computer simulation.

Nilsson, N. J. Artificial intelligence. Paper presented at IFIP Congress 74, Stockholm, August 5–10, 1974. (Also available as AI Center Technical Note 89, Stanford Research Institute, Menlo Park, Calif. 94025.) An up to the minute summary of the artificial intelligence (AI) field. Difficult reading but worthwhile; excellent bibliography.

Schank, R. C., & Colby, K. M. *Computer models of thought and language.* San Francisco, Calif.: Freeman, 1973. The most recent of several survey books cited here, this is also at a higher level – nearly one-half of the book is artificial intelligence papers. Probably of interest mainly to psychologists.

Weizenbaum, J. *Computer power and human reason: From judgment to calculation.* San Francisco, Calif.: Freeman, 1976. This brilliant and outspoken book by an outstanding computer scholar is a "must read" for anyone concerned with the impact of the computer on society. In the context of this chapter, Weizenbaum's discussion of theories and models (Chapter 5) is highly recommended.

2
Planning and Organizing the Simulation Project

Beginning programmers often jump directly into writing Fortran with little consideration of what they are trying to accomplish. In writing simulation programs, so direct an approach is a dangerous mistake. Simulation, and indeed all programming, is a several-step process, with writing computer code among the last things to be done. Starting to write too soon nearly always results in wasted time and effort, for poorly conceived programs are best remedied by scrapping them and starting over.

PLANNING THE PROJECT

Any research effort, and simulation is no exception, is really a poorly ordered process. Our discussion lists principal kinds of activity instead of describing a fixed and unchanging order. The simulation process must begin with a decision that simulation is an appropriate means of study of some phenomenon. Perhaps this decision is reached by a desire to explore an existing theory; or it may be that no theory really exists and modeling is undertaken to aid in developing one. For whatever reason, the next step is the consideration of the operations involved in the process and how they may be represented in a simulation program. The project may proceed to writing the program next and let its internal structure develop incidentally. Even better would be to spend considerable time planning the program organization first. The process of coding itself often necessitates changes in the conceptual model, and therefore changes in the conceptual representation of the theory. Once the program is in use, it is most likely to be revised, again indicating changes in the model and the theory. In fact, the simulation process is typically a never-ending loop of activity, as indeed is all research. Most simulations, like most other research efforts, are probably never really finished but only described at various stages of incompleteness.

This chapter deals with the initial step in the simulation – planning the model and the simulation. We begin by clarifying the purpose of the entire project and then continue to identify the elements in the process that are relevant to the simulation and theory. At that point we find the first real introduction to the two major examples that are to become more familiar throughout the book. Next comes an important thrust of this chapter — the development of the conceptual model, that representation of the theory that is to form the basis of the simulation program. After that, we briefly consider the problem of data representation and then turn to the second major discussion, the overall organization of the simulation program.

THE PURPOSE OF THE SIMULATION

A simulation may serve a number of different purposes. We have mentioned several already but we should now look directly at the question of purpose and see how it relates to planning the simulation program. Clearly, purpose is also important in assessing validity, but we discuss that aspect of purpose later.

Simulation as Prediction

As we have already mentioned, much prediction can be accomplished by computer programs that really represent synthesis rather than "true" simulation. Television election prediction is an easy to understand and almost classic example. In such a program, there is very little concern with process modeling at all; the important thing is to get the best prediction in the shortest time. Process parallelism is of utterly no concern — just get a prediction. In this case, probably none of the usual benefits accrue to the simulation writers. It is doubtful that they clarify or explore any substantive theoretical position, nor do they attempt to simulate other situations to collect experimental data.

Closely related, however, is the previously cited work of Abelson and his associates (Pool *et al.*, 1964) and of McPhee (1961). The purpose of these election simulations was both to predict and to explore. They allowed a number of experiments to be conducted in order to assess the impact of various campaign strategies on certain groups of the electorate. The results, in the sense of prediction, were certainly of practical benefit to campaign strategists. More importantly, the simulations themselves were more than just predictors; they were sophisticated theoretical statements concerning voter behavior, attitudes and attitude change, and so forth.

If a straightforward prediction is the aim of the project, then a synthesis is satisfactory; use any appropriate computational scheme. Although prediction is certainly a benefit that may be derived in any simulation, it is not the purpose in the effort that we are describing here. We are concerned with deriving scientific benefit from our efforts as the primary aim; if good forecasts present themselves as well, so much the better.

Instructional Simulations

In addition to simulations the principal aim of which is simple prediction, another group of models that will be of little concern are those designed entirely for instructional purposes. In many ways an instructional model is an entirely different kind of simulation. The aim of the instructional simulation is to demonstrate some particular phenomenon or relationship. Typically there is little concern with representing a subject area in careful detail, and the entire model is generally greatly simplified. Input and output are often minimal, especially in the programs where students are expected to operate the programs themselves. An excellent example of an instructional simulation can be found in the EXPER SIM system (Main, 1972; Rajecki, 1972). Additional discussion of using instructional simulations can be found in Lehman, Starr, and Young (1975) and Lehman (1977).

Scientific Simulations

The focus in this book is simulation as a scientific tool. Simulation is, in this context, a technique for expressing, testing, and exploring the relationships and consequences implied by a particular theory. If the program also happens to predict elections or other events, or can be used in teaching, those outcomes are incidental benefits; we are not attempting to write simulations for those purposes.

Our aim in planning the simulation, then, is to maximize the scientific benefit that we may hope to derive from the exercise. In order to gain any benefit, we must be prepared to think carefully about the scientific substance of the problem and not become unduly distracted by the mechanics of the programming task confronting us. Much of simulation is detailed coding of computer instructions, but that effort must be kept in perspective. The aim is not primarily to write an elegant, or efficient, or complex program, although we shall devote a large portion of this book to those topics. Our purpose is somewhat more lofty — we are really trying to advance our understanding of the laws governing behavior.

An early decision in writing a simulation, although often not a conscious one, is the degree to which the simulation is to be founded on existing theory. In some cases, the effort begins as a straightforward attempt to represent a theory in a program. This approach is more characteristic of some of the earlier work in simulation. The efforts of Gullahorn and Gullahorn (1965), for example, fall into this mold.

A second general approach is represented by our CHEBO example. Here, two existing theories were combined and the program was written in an effort to apply them in a specific situation.

SIMSAL illustrates a third method for relating simulation and theory. The general information processing approach utilized in SIMSAL derived from previous work, but there really was no direct theoretical predecessor for the theory represented by the program. The theory was in effect developed during the writing of the program. Although the theory now exists in a separately stated verbal form, it was developed primarily during the simulation process. In contemporary usage, this approach is quite common. The simulation writer, in developing the conceptual model of the process, is breaking new theoretical ground. Most likely there are relationships to other research, but the specific application is new and unique.

Whatever the overall relationship to previous theoretical work, the simulation project is certain to result in a better understanding of the process, and a clarification of the theoretical structure itself. If that is not the result, then there is little benefit to be gained from using a simulation.

SUMMARIZING THE PHENOMENON

An appropriate starting point in planning a research simulation is with the careful study of the phenomenon to be represented in the operating model. In such a review, some elements will stand out as being important to a theoretical understanding, and some will appear to be relatively unimportant. One task in the first review of the phenomenon and the related research literature is to determine what is relevant and what is irrelevant to the theory.

Theory relevance is closely related to the matter of the level of analysis chosen for the problem. We have mentioned this matter in Chapter 1 and now return to it again. In an investigation of human learning, for example, it is reasonable to assume that the true basis of learning is to be found at the biochemical level. Yet, for many purposes, that is an entirely inappropriate starting point for a theoretical understanding of the learning process. Our understanding of the most elementary processes in the nervous system is at present so incomplete that any attempt to understand complex learning in those terms is doomed to failure. However, learning processes can be studied at entirely different levels of analysis.

Theories are profitably constructed at any of several possible levels of analysis, and the best level for a particular problem is a prime consideration in devising a theory, model, and simulation. These comments are made by way of introduction to the study of two areas that are to serve as our examples throughout the book, and we turn to them now.

Elementary Social Interaction

The cocktail party of the example introduced in Chapter 1 will serve as a useful format in which to discuss the first example simulation, CHEBO. The cocktail party illustrated a social situation with two easily identifiable groups of individuals. In one scenario, over a period of time, members of the two groups — men and women, perhaps — tended to arrange themselves into mixed pairs, one from each group. Another possible situation — labor and management was the previous example — might show a different arrangement after a period of interaction. In the latter case, the two groups might tend to segregate themselves in different parts of the room.

What kinds of theoretical interpretations can be placed on the cocktail party situation? In his initial presentation of the simulation, Sakoda (1971) considered two general approaches, field theory and attitude theory. Attitude, usually conceived as a positive or negative attraction toward some individual, object, or concept, is a prime motivating force in current social psychology. Attitudes direct the approach to or avoidance of other people, depending on the degree of similarity of attitude.

The social field or arena where behavior occurs is another common element of modern sociology and social psychology. One way of representing the social field might be in terms of a sort of game board, with the interacting individuals being the pieces on the board. This way of representing the social field, along with the use of attitudes, was utilized by Sakoda (1971) in developing the checkerboard model of social interaction.

As a first attempt to develop the model of the situation presented in the cocktail party in terms of attitude and field theory, we must ask what is theory relevant. Clearly, the attitude conception itself is, as is some indication of approach and avoidance. Real people have a great many attitudes, both toward other people and toward abstract ideas; freedom, abortion, invasion of privacy, and taxes are but a few examples. Will it be necessary to deal with all of those kinds of considerations, or will it be possible to simplify the theory in attempting to build a model? Certainly, an approach between two people can be caused by many different attitudes simultaneously. For a simple exploration of attitude theory all of the possible reasons for approaching an individual can be collapsed into a single "attraction score" or attitude. In order to make the situation slightly more realistic, each individual can be assumed to have two attitudes — one representing an attraction toward (or perhaps away from) members of the opposite group, and the other representing the attraction toward members of one's own group. The theory-relevant concept of the attitude can be represented rather simply, therefore, with some attendant loss of full generality because a single "attitude" in the model can really represent the sum total of all of the attitudes that may be present in a human.

In addition to attitude, the theoretical background chosen by Sakoda speaks of the social field. Is the social situation represented by a cocktail party in a room theory relevant? It is not, in that social movement and attraction need not be conceived as taking place in physical space. A convenient simplification and abstraction is the representation in the model of the checkerboard. Movement on the board certainly can be interpreted as being parallel to physical movement in real space, but it need not be restricted to physical space. People can be socially "close" even though they are widely separated in physical space. Sakoda's checkerboard is a representation of a social field, and distances on it can be interpreted as social distances and not just physical distances.

Several other theoretical implications can be drawn from the field and attitudes theories that are important in planning a simulation. In the first place, modern measurement theory as applied to attitudes suggests that attitudes may be positive, negative, or neutral; additionally, positive and negative attitudes may differ in strength. These considerations suggest that attitudes can be represented numerically in the program. Theory, however, does not suggest a clear function by which attitude is related to movement; Sakoda found it necessary to devise that function and thus clarify and explicate the theory.

Another suggestion that derives from, and is important to, the theoretical background of CHEBO is the effect of distance. There is intuitive appeal to the notion that the closer you are to another person, the stronger becomes the influence of your attitudes toward that person on your behavior. That idea, too, is present in field theory; again, Sakoda dealt with it explicitly in developing the conceptual model of CHEBO.

What have we accomplished so far in our discussion? We have isolated several elements of the situation that are theory relevant — attitudes, space, and distance, particularly — and several that are not — notably physical space and multiple attitudes. In addition, we have suggested a few ways in which the situation, and its theory-relevant characteristics, may be represented in a computer program. We shall return to CHEBO in more detail later and see how these considerations enter into the conceptual design of the model.

Paired-Associates Learning

Now consider our second example, a typical human paired-associates learning experiment. Outwardly, the situation appears simple. An experimenter presents a syllable to a subject who responds in some way, typically with another syllable or, in our case, a number. The experimenter tells the subject whether or not he or she has been correct by supplying the correct response syllable or number, presents the next syllable, and so on until he or she has completed a list of syllables. Then the experimenter begins again, typically with the order of the syllables randomly changed. The process continues until some criterion is reached, for example, one complete run through the list without error. Then the experiment may end, or the subject may be asked to learn another list or to engage in some other task depending on the specific experimental hypothesis to be tested.

What is the subject doing all this time? He or she is said to be learning the list of syllables, each paired with a particular response item. But what is the subject really doing? At first, he or she probably makes random guesses at responses. The first time through the list, there certainly is no better strategy than to guess.

The second time through the list, he or she might remember and try to use some information such as "There's a syllable that begins with C that has a response of 8." In this way, if the syllable CYJ appeared, the subject would be more likely to guess "8" than some other number. If the guess is incorrect, then perhaps the subject will have to learn that there are several "C" syllables and that he or she must pay attention to the second or third letter. [In a similar kind of study on probability learning, Feldman (1971) had subjects give the reason for each guess. A simulation program then attempted to reproduct the protocol of guesses and reasons.]

Psychologists typically observe several things in a paired-associates task. One simple measure is the number of trials to criterion. Another common dependent variable is the number of errors per trial, a trial usually being defined as one complete presentation of the list. Several aspects of the situation can be varied, such as the difficulty of the list of items. A list made up of highly similar items, such as XYR, XYB, YXB, is harder to learn than such a list as COQ, MIZ, KIG. Interference studies can be conducted by having a subject learn one list, learn a second list, and then relearn the first list. Subjects perform differently on the second learning depending, among other things, on the similarity of the two lists.

What is of theoretical interest in this situation? Certainly not the behavior of the experimenter. All he or she must do is to present syllables, record responses, and give the correct answers. At the end of each trial, he or she shuffles the list of syllables, and must recognize when the subject has reached the specified criterion. Then he or she does whatever is needed in the experiment — sending the subject home, running a second list, or whatever. In any case, the experimenter's work is purely routine and mechanical; he or she could be replaced by a machine. Indeed, in an increasing number of laboratories, the experimenter is being supplanted by a small computer, but that's not the concern of this book.

The subject is another matter. He or she begins the experiment by making random guesses but gradually comes to associate a single response with each unique stimulus. In other words, the subject learns.

Learning in humans, or in animals for that matter, is a very complex and mysterious phenomenon. After many years of study, psychologists still do not understand the basic processes involved — those of forming bonds between items, or just how "memories" are actually stored. Investigators have established many other things about learning, however. We referred to some of those findings in the paired-associates task earlier. In addition, much human learning appears to be associative in nature in that learned items are not stored and retrieved purely at random. In studies of free recall, presenting a single item often will trigger the recall of a whole string of items, generally in the same order from trial to trial. Memory is therefore a highly structured storage medium. Indeed, if we questioned subjects after they had learned a list, they might be able to produce a whole set of stimulus—response pairs if we asked them to, for example, "Give me all the items that begin with 'N.'"

Our learning example, SIMSAL, is based on the theoretical and experimental work of Hintzman (1968). The major effort there was to explore the role of simple discrimination among stimuli in learning. At the time, much of human learning theory tended to minimize discrimination as an important part of the learning process, and Hintzman sought to demonstrate that it was not unimportant. His approach was to develop a conceptual model of the process, implemented in a program, which could accomodate many of the common human learning paradigms, and then to simply investigate how much of the learning literature could be accounted for by the model.

The level of analysis chosen by Hintzman suggested that several elements in the learning processes were important, and that several others were not. In particular, the model makes use of a data storage form known as a "tree"; trees appear to be reasonable approximations to the kinds of memory organization shown in human studies. Specific input and output processes are really unimportant in the level of analysis used in SIMSAL and so may be handled in any convenient manner in the model.

Finally, forming individual learned associations between stimuli and responses does not appear to be an all-or-none phenomenon in the human literature. The reason is probably at a much more detailed level of explanation than has been desired for the model. For example, we will find in the conceptual model several subprocesses (forming a particular stimulus—response bond, for example) that are governed by a simple probability function. This is another simplification, just as is the use of two attitudes in CHEBO, but this time for the purpose of preserving the desired level of theoretical discourse.

SIMSAL is constructed to model primarily the discrimination process in human learning. The choice of that phenomenon, and level of analysis, was dictated by the scientific interests of the investigator. There are simplifications, of course, just as there were with CHEBO. However, we have now suggested many of the considerations necessary in summarizing the learning situation, and are now ready to proceed to developing the most important element in the simulation — the conceptual model.

THE CONCEPTUAL MODEL

The next step in planning the simulation is the detailed specification of the conceptual model of the process. A conceptual model is a concise, systematically organized statement of the process, including the specification of the input and the output, the processes and the subprocesses involved, the variables and constants, and the data organization. In order that a conceptual model result in a successful simulation, it must meet three general criteria proposed by Abelson (1968).

First, as should be clear by this time, the process to be modeled must be a dynamic one – that is, something must take place over time. Although static theories certainly have their place in science, they are seldom simulated. A theory of long-term human memory organization, or of social organization at a particular time, is a valuable scientific statement. However, it is not amenable to simulation because nothing changes.

Second, the process should be what Abelson refers to as a "closed system," meaning that all inputs and variables are completely specified. Such assumptions as "other things remaining constant" are incompatible with a closed system and must be made explicit. We earlier referred to theories not meeting this requirement as being incomplete, or as having "gaps" in them. Ideally, as we have noted, the original theory represents a closed system. Realistically, it is often up to the simulation writer to insure that the system is indeed closed.

A closed system, in Abelson's terminology, is an unusually rare occurrence in the social and behavior sciences. Most complete theoretical systems are markedly open in that far too many operations are incompletely specified, inputs undefined, and functions poorly defined. This "closing" of the system is, in fact, one of the major benefits of a simulation approach to a problem. A simulation forces the necessary completeness, but often at the expense of simplifying the situation and thus the scope of natural occurrences to which the theory can address itself. Yet the requirement is present in a simulation, and the social and behavioral sciences must benefit from the constraint that it places on theory construction.

Abelson's final requirement of the conceptual model is that it be "well specified." In order that a model be well specified, careful attention must be directed to six individual elements: units, properties, inputs, processes, sequencing, and consequences.

Units. By units we mean that the conceptual model must identify a group of entities or elements of some sort to be operated on by the process. The choice of the units is usually dictated by the level of analysis of the theory and may be, for example, individuals, social groups, or neurons. All of the units are often at the same level of analysis but not necessarily. In the checkerboard, for example, the units are of several sorts and at two different theoretical levels. In one case, we have the interacting individuals themselves (called "pieces"), represented by two sets of attitudes (to their own group and to the other groups), and also by indicators of current positions on the board. At another theoretical level is the checkerboard itself, which represents the social field in which interaction takes place.

At one level of analysis, SIMSAL has but a single unit; the memory structure or tree. The tree holds individual stimuli and responses and is really the "carrier" of the entire action of the model. At another level, however, SIMSAL's units are individual elements in the tree itself. It is the latter conception that becomes the most helpful in additional analysis of the conceptual model.

Properties. Properties are sets of values and constants attached to the units. At any point in the simulation the properties of a unit define its status in the system. In CHEBO, each of the pieces or individuals has four properties – location (row and column), type (is it a "square" or a "cross"), attitude toward the other group, and attitude toward own group.

In SIMSAL, the units and their properties reside in a memory tree. The reason for the name and the exact nature of the data organization are discussed later; for now we note only that each unit in SIMSAL's memory has four properties. The first is the symbol or literal representation of the letter being stored. The second property of a letter is its position in the syllable being learned (1, 2, or 3, because a syllable may have only three letters). The final two properties are called pointers and are discussed later. In essence, however, they indicate where to locate both the next letter in the syllable and the next syllable or perhaps the response. SIMSAL has several other properties as well, but they attach to the process itself rather than to individual letters and they govern various aspects of learning.

Inputs. Every process has input to initiate and direct it. The nature and extent of the input will vary a great deal according to the process being modeled. There is always a certain amount of "housekeeping" necessary in a simulation program, and often in the input specifications are to be found several control parameters that deal with the printing or suppressing of certain kinds of information, where to direct output, and termination criteria. It is not with these input functions that we are concerned now; they usually result from the actual coding of the program. Important in planning are only those inputs that start the process and perhaps govern it while it is in motion.

CHEBO has very simple input demands. It requires the attitudes of the two groups toward each other and themselves, a power parameter to govern rate of movement, and a distance exponent to specify the influence that individuals have on each other. Starting board positions may be input as well but are usually determined randomly by the program; an option such as input versus generated starting positions or values is a useful and helpful feature to build into a program and should be included whenever possible.

Input to SIMSAL is of two sorts, that for the experimenter and that for the subject. Because the subject is programmed as a subprocess, its input comes primarily from the experimenter, but we consider the two elements of the system separately here. For the experimenter, the required information is the number of lists to be presented, the syllables and correct responses for each list, and the termination criterion and/or number of trials to be conducted. In addition, in our version of the program, the experimenter is also told how many different subjects to run, but that is one of the mechanical elements of the input. As for the subject, it is initially provided with several learning rate parameters (actually, probabilities). Apart from those values, other input to the subject consists of the presentation of syllables by the experimenter, one at a time, each followed by feedback from the experimenter giving the correct response.

Processes. What is required here is a detailed specification of the actual processes and subprocesses involved in the simulation. These are the "working parts" of the simulation; the functions and procedures that relate the systems' units to one another and that change their properties. Instead of detailing the processes involved in our examples here, we shall delay it until later and merely identify some of the important functions now.

The major process in CHEBO is moving each piece to a new location during each cycle. Moving, however, involves the subprocess of deciding where to move, which in turn entails the further subprocess of comparing the present position with all other possible positions in order to select the best. There are several "housekeeping" functions as well, including initialization and output.

For SIMSAL, most of the key processes have been described previously. For the experimenter, they include randomizing and presenting a list, recognizing a learning criterion, and keeping and reporting records. For the subject, the important steps are responding to a presented syllable, learning, and reporting the contents of memory when requested.

Sequencing. Processes and subprocesses are organized into a temporal sequence. In some simulations, the sequencing is of the "start at the top and go until you finish" variety. More commonly, the exact succession of processes and subprocesses in any given execution of a simulation program is contingent on the outcome of the processes themselves and cannot be specified exactly in advance. The sequencing is most conveniently expressed in a flowchart, a topic to which we direct our attention briefly later in this chapter.

Consequences. The consequences of the simulation are those results that we should like to see — the output of the program. Usually the consequences are the final or intermediate properties of the units of the system, although occasionally other features are of interest as well.

CHEBO is a model of movement in the social field. The most important consequence is the board position of each piece after each cycle of the program. In addition, various summary statistics about the two interacting groups are output — the program computes the centroid or average position of each group, the distance between the two centroids, and the dispersion of each group. Of somewhat less importance are the individual moves made by each piece on each cycle; their printing is an option in the program.

In SIMSAL the memory tree of the subject is certainly of interest. This structure, which has grown or developed during the learning process, shows the final properties of the letters and the overall memory organization. The tracing of the experiment or protocol kept by the experimenter is frequently of interest as well. Indeed, in human research, only the protocol is regularly available in a standardized form — introspective records are notoriously nonstandard and difficult to compare across subjects. In order to compare SIMSAL's performance with that of humans, the protocol is the most important consequence of the simulation.

Certain values in each simulation program are fixed throughout and need be printed only once. That output is usually done at the beginning of the program as a part of the "header" material that identifies the run and its parameters. Examples of this kind of output — not really a consequence of the simulation — are the three learning parameters in SIMSAL and the group attitudes in CHEBO.

Whatever the nature of the output, the consequences are those aspects of the simulation that are the predictions of the model. They are what you really want to see and are the elements of the model that are important in appraising the validity of the simulation.

Our discussion of these six features of well-specified models has grouped together the multiple considerations necessary in planning of the conceptual model of the simulation. It is very difficult to make general statements that can assure the simulation writer of having a workable conceptual model at the end of the process. Several of the six criteria may be reasonably easy to specify in any given case, and others may be difficult. Indeed, any of the six may well become a major stumbling block in the course of simulation. Particularly difficult are often the identification and specification of the processes and subprocesses, and the decisions related to sequencing the operations. Major theoretical considerations enter into each decision made in planning the conceptual model; those considerations are particularly evident in the processes and sequencing.

In order to illustrate the six elements of the conceptual model more fully, let us consider the example models carefully. We will here present the descriptions of the units and properties, inputs, processes, and consequences of CHEBO and SIMSAL. We will defer the discussion of the sequencing of the processes briefly, until we present the flowcharting techniques that allow a pictorial representation of sequencing.

CHEBO

The basic unit in CHEBO is the individual piece in a social field. In general we speak of the two groups of pieces as "crosses" and "squares," although in any specific example there may be men and women, or labor and management, or any other two distinct groups.

The representation of the social field is a two-dimensional data arrangement in the program — the checkerboard from which the model derives its name.

Each unit in the simulation has three major properties: its type (it is a cross or a square), its current row location, and its current column location. These properties are stored in the array MAP; the program listing provides specific information about their representation. Four additional properties — the attitudes — pertain to groups of pieces and are stored separately. Two pairs of values are maintained in the program. One set applies to all of the squares and gives their attitudes toward members of their own and the opposite groups. Because all members of a group are assumed to have identical attitudes, these values need not be stored as properties of each piece. A second pair of attitude variables holds the corresponding values for the crosses.

The inputs to the program include, of course, the inter- and intragroup attitudes, as well as parameters controlling the evaluation of each piece's position on the board and the speed with which the pieces can move. A variety of mechanical information is supplied to the program as well, including the size of the board and number of pieces, termination criterion, and so forth.

The processes embodied in CHEBO fall into two major groups. The first deals with "housekeeping" functions and includes input, output, and computation of various group statistics. Provision is made for randomly generating starting positions for the pieces or accepting them as input.

The most important process in the program is the simulation of social interaction. Because interaction is represented in the program by changed positions of the pieces on the board, the process that accomplishes the movement is the embodiment of the theory. In Sakoda's model, approach to another individual is governed entirely by attitudes and distance. In its simplest terms, an individual will tend to move in a direction that will result in his or her being closer to those to whom he or she holds a positive attitude and away from those toward whom a negative attitude prevails.

As the process is represented in CHEBO, pieces are moved individually. For a single piece, there is a range of possible positions into which it may move. Those positions are defined by the "rules of the game." One rule states that a move outside the social field (beyond the checkerboard) cannot be considered. A second rule indicates that only adjacent squares on the board can be moved to, and then only when they are vacant. In some cases, when all of the adjacent squares are full, a piece may be allowed to consider a jump of one row or column, but never more.

The decision of where to move, or even whether to move at all, is based on a comparison of the current location to all other possible ones. Each possible location is given a value, computed by a formula taking account of the distance between a location and all other pieces, as well as the attitude toward each other piece. When the location with the greatest value is found, the piece is moved there. The process is repeated until all pieces of the board have had an opportunity to move, and then the board positions are output. The process repeats until a termination criterion is satisfied.

The evaluation of positions to which a move may be made is an important one. It is the core of the model, for it specifies how interpersonal attitudes and social distance combine to determine whether to move and, if so, to what new position. It is this formulation that is the precise statement of the loose suggestions from field and attitude theory that Sakoda has added in clarifying and extending the theories.

The value of a position is based on the location of the position relative to all pieces of the board. Suppose that we wished to find the value of the position occupied by piece A. As a first step, another piece, B for example, is found and its distance from A computed as the sum of the squares of the differences between the pairs of X and Y coordinates. For example, if piece A is located at Row 5, Column 3, and piece B is at Row 2, Column 4, then the distance is defined as

$$D = (5 - 2)^2 + (3 - 4)^2 = 10;$$

or if we let X be the row coordinate and Y the column,

$$D = (X_A - X_B)^2 + (Y_A - Y_B)^2.$$

The general formula for the distance D between any two pieces, i and j, is

$$D = (X_i - X_j)^2 + (Y_i - Y_j)^2.$$

The distance is next weighted by two factors — the attitude of piece i toward piece j, and a program parameter called "distance weight." The resulting values are summed over all pieces on the board to obtain the value of a position:

$$\text{Value} = \Sigma \left(\frac{V}{D^{1/w}} \right),$$

where D is the distance between two pieces as defined above, V is the attitude of piece i toward piece j, and w is the distance weight.

In the previous example, if the attitude of piece A toward piece B is $+3$ (moderately strong attraction) and the distance weight is 2, then the contribution of the relationship between piece A and B to the total value of A's position is

$$\frac{3}{10^{1/2}} = \frac{3}{\sqrt{10}} = .949.$$

The complete value is computed by making this computation for all other pieces on the board compared with piece A. The partial results are summed and the total is the value of position A.

The effect of the distance weight is to vary the relative effect that close and distant positions have in determining the value; the greater the distance weight, the stronger is the influence of relatively distant pieces on the board.

CHEBO's consequences follow directly from the rest of the conceptual model. As we note in our discussion of flowcharting, CHEBO proceeds in cycles. Each cycle represents an opportunity for each piece on the board to move to an adjacent square if the evaluation function indicates an "advantage" in so doing,

In order to observe the process in action, the board positions must be output after each cycle. Several other outputs are available as well, including measures of group location and dispersion as discussed earlier.

SIMSAL

The conceptual model identifies two important elements in the simulation — the experimenter and the subject. The experimenter is in complete charge of the learning experiment. This component of the program accepts as input several control parameters (for instance, the number of subjects, number of items on each list, and so forth) and the lists of stimuli and responses. The experimenter then conducts the experiment by presenting each subject with the stimulus items, waiting for a response after each, and then giving the correct answer. The experimenter keeps a record of each stimulus and response on each trial of the experiment and prints it when each subject has reached criterion.

The subject in the experiment is more complex than the experimenter. The subject must learn to associate stimuli and responses. In doing so it uses a memory tree, or discrimination net in Hintzman's terminology. The memory tree contains as its basic unit the letter of a stimulus syllable. Each letter has four properties — its position in the syllable, its value (what character it is), and two pointers to succeeding elements in the tree.

There are two kinds of input to the subject. The first consists of three probabilities supplied as input. These probabilities serve in Bernoulli events, as is to be discussed in Chapter 5, to influence the rate of learning. The second form of input to the subject consists of stimulus syllables presented by the experimenter during the operation of the program.

There are four subprocesses in the subject segment of the model. Two of these are primarily housekeeping in nature; one erases the memory to insure a naive subject for the experiment, and the second performs a limited introspection of a kind only possible with a program — a complete printing of the memory tree.

The other two subject subprocesses could be designated as "learning" and "responding." In the first, the subject may (or may not, depending on an input probability) add a new unit to its memory. This action, which is explained in later chapters dealing with trees in detail, constitutes the simulation of learning. The final subprocess requires that the program trace through its memory tree, comparing elements of a presented stimulus with stored elements of previous stimuli in order to discriminate among them, until an appropriate response is located.

A Last Comment on the Conceptual Models

As we conclude this discussion of the formulation of the conceptual model, one cautionary note is in order.

In the writing of this book, the examples were coded first, and if the development of the conceptual models appears relatively painless, it is because the finished product was already in hand. Do not be deceived — the development of the examples was preceded by the careful analysis of the situations and development of the conceptual models nevertheless, but you are not privileged to see that sketchy and informal work. The presentation here is more like seeing a finished research report than observing the scientist in action in his or her laboratory.

Indeed, the reader should keep in mind the two laws of research propounded by Bachrach (1962); they apply equally to writing computer simulation models. Roughly paraphrased, Bachrach's first law is: People don't do research the way that people who write books on how to do research say that they do. In other words, the real process is always "messier," less formalized and rigid, and certainly less clear as to the form of the result than you are led to believe by seeing either the final product or the "formula" for conducting research. There is no magic formula for successful research; and there is none for computer simulation either.

Bachrach's second law has to do with time; real time on the clock and calendar, not computer time: Things take longer than they do.

DATA REPRESENTATION AND ORGANIZATION

The computer is a binary device. Inside the computer everything is represented in a binary fashion whether it is numeric data, alphabetic information, or program instructions. Fortunately, a high-level programming language, such as Fortran, relieves much of the burden of processing binary data and allows us to do most of our own thinking in terms of decimal numbers, alphabetic characters, and Fortran program statements. Nevertheless, the fact that we are dealing ultimately with a binary machine, and in a highly stylized language, forces certain constraints on the way we organize programs and data.

Programs are expressed in a special language; in this book that language is Fortran, although we discuss a few others in Chapter 9. The language imposes certain limitations on the way in which we organize and express both the data and the simulation programs themselves.

Fortran, and indeed virtually all computer languages, are sequential in nature. This is a clear constraint and must be dealt with carefully in developing the model and program. Of course, in a social situation, individuals make their "moves" not sequentially but in parallel. But in CHEBO, as we have noted, the moves are made in order.

The language places other constraints on the model builder as well. Computers operate entirely on binary representations of information. This makes some sorts of operations difficult to represent in the computer, and also places constraints on the degree of accuracy that we can expect, as we discuss in Chapter 6.

In addition, a particular data organization is implicit in any language. In Fortran, the basic data arrangement is the subscripted variable or array. In many instances that is exactly what we need, as for example with CHEBO's checkerboard. In other programs, we must develop procedures for using Fortran's arrays to write an entirely different form of data structure, the tree in SIMSAL for example.

It is not the intention of this section to develop the Fortran techniques for dealing with various data structures. We devote Chapters 3 and 4 to those topics. The point here is to indicate that planning the simulation must take into account both the characteristics imposed by the language and those demanded by the phenomenon being modeled. In SIMSAL, in order to simulate the process adequately, we are forced to develop a tree functionally similar to human memory, even though it is not Fortran's usual data structure.

The representation of data is often the most troublesome aspect of the simulation to the beginning model writer. How does one represent personality, for example, or memory, or voter attitudes? The answer is "by numbers," but that clearly is not a satisfactory response.

Part of the difficulty is in the question. The way to approach the problem is by a careful analysis of what is meant by personality, and how it is relevant to the process to be simulated. CHEBO deals with an aspect of personality, namely interpersonal attitudes. It is true that attitudes are represented by numbers; the numbers enter into a formula which determines whether or not a particular piece on the board is to be moved into an adjacent square. Once the board is represented as a two-dimensional array in Fortran, individual pieces are represented as values in the array, the formula for evaluating a position is developed as a function of the numbers called "attitudes," and the criterion for comparing two board positions as a function of their evaluation is specified, much of the mystery of representing attitude vanishes. The attitude is only a number which enters into a computation, and as a result of the computation, either a number in an array remains where it is or it is moved to an adjacent cell and its former location set to zero. Phrased in those terms, the problem is a computer problem — how to program the formulas and processes. The computer doesn't "care" that we regard one of the numbers as a peculiarly human attribute called an attitude; it is merely a number.

This is not meant to minimize the difficulty. Representing the data and other aspects of the system is one of the most knotty conceptual problems in planning the simulation.

Again, there is no magic formula that can be offered to aid in solving the representation problem. Careful study and review of the conceptual models will give some hints. As the discussion of the examples proceeds, their representational techniques become more apparent and may be of help to the reader in developing procedures for his own problem.

A few suggestions may be helpful. First, don't be overwhelmed by the problem. When the solution is reached, its simplicity is usually surprising. Second, look at related simulations. How did someone else solve the problem? Can his or her methods be adapted? If not, what is different about your problem? Third, work on some other aspect of planning the simulation. Start with the specification of the processes instead of the units, or consider what properties are essential to your model. Do those properties suggest a way they can be represented? If you can list them, an array may suffice. Is a branching arrangement possible? If so, maybe a tree or a list data organization is suggested. Finally, take a list of verbal descriptions of the processes or parts of them and see what you can quantify. If you have written "Person A likes Person B," try "Person A is attracted to Person B with a strength of 7.0 on a scale of 10."

PICTURES OF THE SEQUENCE — FLOWCHARTING

If a picture is worth a thousand words, then a flowchart certainly must be as well. A flowchart provides an easy to grasp representation of the action of the process involved in a simulation program. It specifies the sequences much more succinctly than can words and makes the various choice points and branches readily apparent.

Many programmers are taught flowcharting when they first learn to code. If you are among this group, you can probably skip over this section. If you are among the many who program by starting with Fortran code, however, now is the time to start changing your habits.

Flowcharts, like theories, may deal with any of several levels of analysis. At the broadest level, they are little more than the chapter headings in a book, only hinting at the contents within. At the other extreme, every minute operation occupies a space in the flowchart, and a minor change in the program requires revision of the flowchart if it is to be kept current. Although flowchart devotees may disagree, it is rare that an extremely detailed flowchart is either necessary or helpful in planning a simulation program. Highly specific flowcharts are usually the results of after the fact analysis rather than a tool employed in writing the program.

Our intent here is to present flowcharting as a helpful tool in planning a program. A flowchart may also be a part of the description of the finished product; we have a few more words to say about flowcharts as documentation in Chapter 7.

A standard set of flowcharting symbols has evolved over the years and has been formalized by the American National Standards Institute (ANSI) (1970). The most commonly used symbols are defined in Figure 2.1. We use the ANSI

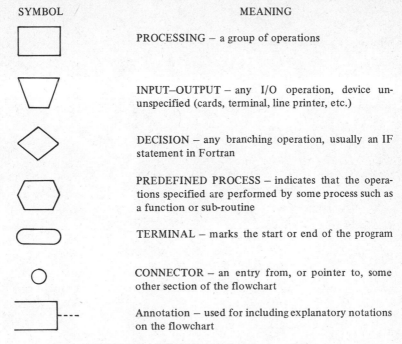

SYMBOL   MEANING

PROCESSING – a group of operations

INPUT–OUTPUT – any I/O operation, device un-unspecified (cards, terminal, line printer, etc.)

DECISION – any branching operation, usually an IF statement in Fortran

PREDEFINED PROCESS – indicates that the operations specified are performed by some process such as a function or sub-routine

TERMINAL – marks the start or end of the program

CONNECTOR – an entry from, or pointer to, some other section of the flowchart

Annotation – used for including explanatory notations on the flowchart

FIGURE 2.1   ANSI Standard flowchart symbols.

standard throughout this book, although most programmers develop their own idiosyncratic symbols and usages for the planning stages of programming. What is important in the planning is of course the flowchart as an aid, not the flowchart as a formal entity. The programmer should feel free to adapt the symbols to his own style in planning and perhaps use the ANSI form only for the final version of the flowchart.

Figure 2.2 presents the sequencing of CHEBO in flowchart form. The processes were discussed earlier; here we see them connected indicating the sequential and cyclic nature of the process. Although there are many details left unspecified in the figure, the overall flow of the process is clear. Among the missing particulars are the source of the board positions and the termination criterion ("Done?" in the figure). In the program, the initial board configuration can be either input or randomly generated. The termination criterion for the program is normally a fixed (input) number of cycles or a specified number of cycles during which no pieces have been moved, thus indicating a stable social organization.

At a somewhat finer level of analysis, the "move all pieces" process appears in Figure 2.3. Here again, much detail is omitted. The "pick a piece randomly" box contains a subprocess for randomly selecting from among the pieces on the board that have not yet been moved. Likewise, the "pick an adjacent position"

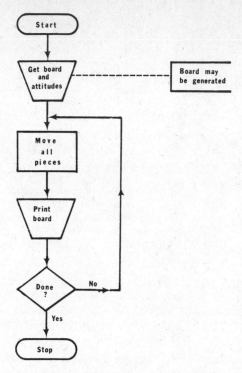

FIGURE 2.2   Overall flowchart of CHEBO.

operation represents a systematic procedure for searching around some location on the board. The "get a value" process refers to a function that embodies the evaluation of an adjacent position as described earlier. It would be possible, of course, to describe the "get a value" process in flowchart form as well. In this case, however, it is probably clearer to use the verbal—mathematical description. The flowchart would be precise and would probably include an operation box for nearly every Fortran statement in the evaluation function. Such detail may be valuable in the final descriptive documentation of a simulation program, but even that is doubtful. Certainly in planning, the level of flowchart detail in Figure 2.3 is adequate. It clearly shows the sequences in the process and gives broad hints at the sorts of coding details that must be present.

Figure 2.4 presents the flowchart of SIMSAL. The level of detail is about the same as in Figure 2.3; it is adequate for illustrating the general nature and order of the processes but does not attempt to show all of the procedural and computational detail.

This presentation of both flowcharts marks the end of the parallel development of the examples. Until Chapter 8, only selected aspects of them will be used to illustrate specific points.

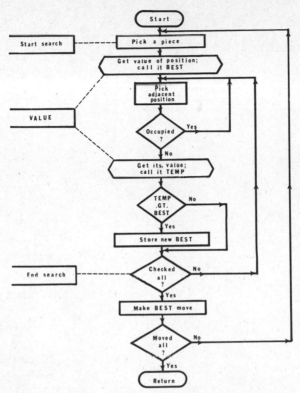

FIGURE 2.3 The 'move all pieces' routine (MOVE) in CHEBO. (Annotations give the names of the separate routines in the program.)

PROGRAM ORGANIZATION AND STRUCTURE

Throughout the discussion of the conceptual model, the terms "process" and "subprocess" have occured frequently. The processes that are being simulated are conceived as being made up of subprocess, and perhaps subsubprocesses. In a similar manner, the flow charts for the example simulations identified a number of different subprograms, each incorporating one or more of the subprocesses in the conceptual model.

It is an unusual computer routine, let alone a simulation, that is made up of a single program. Most programs are divided into a single controlling program and a series of subprograms that are called upon by the "master" or "main program." In this section we address the topic of programs and subprograms, their advantages and disadvantages, and some considerations in using them. It is at this point that we begin to discuss programming detail and leave, for the time being, the consideration of higher level metatheoretical problems in simulation and modeling.

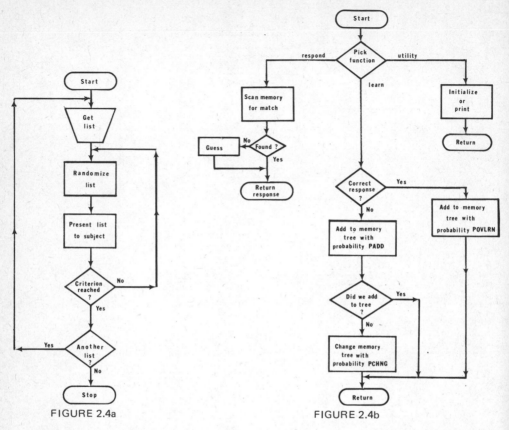

FIGURE 2.4a

FIGURE 2.4b

FIGURE 2.4   (a) Overall flowchart of SIMSAL experimenter. (b) Flowchart of SIMSAL subject.

The division of a program into a set of small, self-contained subprograms is an element of what has become known as structured programming, regarded by some as the first major revolution in the history of computer programming. We consider the essentials of structured programming briefly and then progress to a detailed presentation of subprograms in Fortran.

The Elements of Structured Programming

We will not attempt to summarize either the history of structured programming or all of its details. The reader is referred to one of the sources in the Suggested Readings, for example Knuth (1974) or Dahl, Dijkstra, and Hoare (1972), for good discussions. The literature on the topic is vast, often technical, and growing rapidly. We can but scratch the surface and draw some important implications for simulation programming in Fortran.

Before we look at structured programming, we should reiterate a point made several times earlier. Programming is not just coding, but the entire process of program design and writing. Developing the conceptual model or choosing an algorithm is just as much a part of the programming process as is writing Fortran code. Structured programming is a set of guidelines imposed on the simulator throughout the entire process of program development.

The usual guidelines of structured programming can be expressed in two short phrases: program in short, well-defined modules; and avoid the GO TO statement.

The first rule implies that a program should be written as a set of short subroutines and functions, linked together by a main program which itself does little more than issue CALLs. A good guideline for the meaning of "short" is about one output page of code. Although it is not always possible, many subroutines and functions can indeed be expressed in about 50 lines, the length of a typical page of program listing.

By a "well-defined" module we mean one with a single entry, a block of operations, and a single exit. Insofar as allowed by the algorithm, the operations are executed sequentially with little if any branching. Figure 2.5 illustrates two hypothetical flowcharts, only one of which follows the structured programming rule.

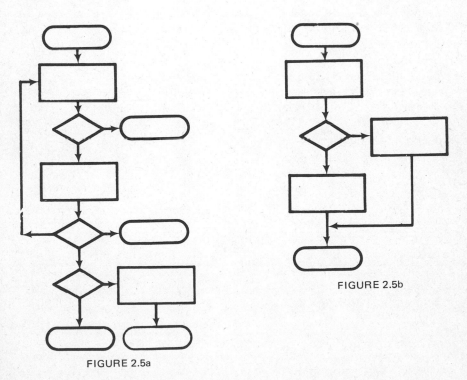

FIGURE 2.5b

FIGURE 2.5a

FIGURE 2.5 (a) A poorly defined module with multiple returns and branches. (b) A well defined module with a single entry and exit.

Most of the controversy surrounding structured programming revolves around a supposed banning of the GO TO statement. Technical discussions of structured programming, such as that by Knuth (1974), are often couched in non-Fortran languages, principally ALGOL or one or its close relatives. Such languages offer a richer vocabulary of control statements than does Fortran, primarily a construction known as the IF—THEN—ELSE. The Fortran programmer is more limited, having available only the IF, the DO, and the GO TO itself. The Fortran programmer cannot avoid the GO TO entirely, but minimizing its use is usually valuable. Knuth (1974), not a strong advocate of structured programming himself, argues for the occasional use of the GO TO even in an ALGOL-type language.

Benefits of structured programming.   A number of benefits accrue when the guidelines of structured programming are followed. Certainly, structured programs are more readable; they are generally short and comprehensible, and the elimination or reduction of branching statements reduces the task of tracing multiple paths through a program.

Less obvious perhaps, but no less real, is a general increase in programmer efficiency. Being forced to drastically reduce branching leads to the development of concise algorithms that are not only readable but easier to debug when trouble develops. Because the individual routines also are short and have single, clearly defined entries and exits, locating the source of an error is often simplified.

An additional benefit appears in future modification of a program. Rarely is a program, and especially a simulation program, so perfect that it will never be revised. A structured program, with its neatly concise modules, is simpler to modify. Usually only a single routine needs to be changed, eliminating a potential source of many new errors.

In many computers it is possible to store the object versions of subprograms, linking them together only when execution is required. This is a clear advantage when either debugging or modifying, because typically only one or two routines need be involved at a time. All the remaining modules can be left in a compiled form, saving a good deal of compilation time.

Fortran does not allow all of the requirements of structured programming to be followed completely; the language has too few control commands. However, many of its recommendations can be followed with benefit. In Chapter 7 we discuss the overall structure of our example programs and illustrate how the strictures of the discipline are incorporated (and violated, in one case) in them.

Programming Subprograms

Fortran recognizes four different categories of subprogram — statement functions, supplied functions, FUNCTIONs, and SUBROUTINEs. The first three, collectively called simply "functions," differ from the SUBROUTINE in several important ways and share some characteristics, although they are all different from one another.

Supplied Functions

The supplied functions are a part of the Fortran language and serve a convenient and familiar example to introduce some of the important concepts of functions as a group. The function most often used by social and behavioral scientists is that for computing a square root. The Fortran statement

$$SD \ = \ SQRT(VAR)$$

computes the square root of the value VAR and stores it as SD. As compared with an ordinary Fortran arithmetic expression, such as

$$X \ = \ Y+Z$$

the square root statement is not translated directly into machine language when the program is compiled. Instead, the compiler inserts a prewritten sequence of instructions — a subprogram — into the machine code. That prewritten sequence embodies an algorithm for extracting the square root of whatever expression appears in the parentheses in the original Fortran statement.

The quantity inside the parentheses, VAR in the example, is known as the "argument" to the function; it gives the value on which the function is to operate. Many of the familiar supplied functions in Fortran, such as SIN, COS, and TAN, have a single argument. Some other functions have more than one argument. The function AMAX1, for example, accepts as arguments any number of real values, constants, or variables. The function returns as its value the largest of the arguments.

An important point to note here is that functions — and this holds for all kinds of functions — are known as "single valued." They return a single value to the program in which they are called upon.

Also note the way that functions are used. They appear in an arithmetic expression; this mode of referring to a subprogram is called an "implicit" reference, as it is implied by the use of the function name in an expression. All functions in Fortran are implicitly referenced; SUBROUTINEs, in contrast, are referenced in an explicit way, by the CALL statement which we consider later.

Every Fortran system supplies a number of functions as a part of the compiler. The functions vary in name and also in type of argument and value returned. There are, for example, several "MAX" functions in most Fortran systems; one common set includes AMAX1 for real arguments returning a real value, AMAX∅ for integer arguments with a real return, MAX∅ for integer arguments and return, MAX1 for real arguments and an integer return, and so forth. (Note also that we use the convention of ∅ indicating a "zero" and O representing the letter "oh" when there is any possibility of confusion.)

Statement Functions

The supplied functions are, as the very name suggests, supplied with the Fortran language. Fortran also has provision for programmer-defined functions as well. The simplest form of programmer-written subprogram is the statement function; it is adequate for defining a function that can be written in a single Fortran expression. More complex functions, requiring more than a single line, are known as FUNCTIONs and are discussed after statement functions are considered.

Both forms of programmer-defined functions are single valued, require at least one argument, and may vary in type of both argument and returned value, just as was the case with the supplied functions.

A statement function is defined by writing the function definition before the first time it is used. The usual practice is to define functions at the beginning of the program. As an example of a statement function, suppose that the computation

$$X = (A**3+B**3+C**3)/15.65$$

was needed at one point in a program, and

$$Y = (AX**3+BX**3+CX**3)/15.65$$

at another point. Because the computations are identical except for the particular values involved, there may be an advantage to defining a function to perform the operation. The statement

$$SUMCUB(X,Y,Z) = (X**3+Y**3+Z**3)/15.65$$

defines a function named SUBCUB. Later in the program, we can write

$$X = SUMCUB(A,B,C)$$

$$Y = SUMCUB(AX,BX,CX)$$

with exactly the desired results.

This example illustrates several important elements of the statement function. First note the name of the function. Naming functions follows the usual Fortran convention; SUMCUB is a REAL function, meaning that its value — that is, the value returned — is a REAL value. The type of functions is established by the first-letter code, unless there is an explicit definition in a type statement elsewhere in the program.

Note also that the function is defined by writing the name of the function, followed by parentheses enclosing the names by which the function refers to the arguments. This is an important point. The argument names used in the function definition are known as "dummy" variables and have meaning only in the function definition. When the function is actually used, those dummy variables are replaced with the actual values presented in the function reference. This allows the same variable name to be used − as X is in the example − in both the function definition and in the program itself without confusion. Suppose that the first function reference is executed in the program with the values of A, B, and C to 15.8, 9.87, and 1.005, respectively. The function is therefore referenced as before,

$$X = SUMCUB(A,B,C)$$

and the value of

$$\frac{15.8^3 + 9.87^3 + 1.005^3}{15.65} = 313.536$$

is computed by the function. After the function reference, the value of the program variable X is 313.536; the fact that an X appeared in the function definition is immaterial.

The dummy variable illustrates an additional important concept in functions. In general the variables in the function definition have no relationship to the variables in the program that uses the function. This fact makes it possible to write completely general functions, such as those supplied by Fortran, with no concern about possible confusions between variables with the same name.

There is a slight exception to this rule in the case of the statement function. If a variable is used in the definition of a statement function that is not a dummy variable, that variable is assumed by the compiler to refer to the same variable in the program in which the function definition occurs. For example, a statement function defined by

$$AOVERX(A) = A/X$$

takes a single argument, A, and divides it by a program variable called X. Thus, the program segment

$$X = 55.93$$

$$RESULT = AOVERX(166.8)$$

will give the RESULT = 2.982 = 166.8/55.93.

Statement functions can be defined by an arithmetic statement of virtually any complexity, with the restriction that it must be only a single statement. Of particular note is the ability to use functions in defining other functions. The function definition

$$IRAND(N) = INT(RNDM(DUMMY)*N+1)$$

occurs in SIMSAL. It specifies a function named IRAND, and in doing so it refers to two additional functions, INT and RNDM. INT is a supplied function the result of which is the integer part of its argument. RNDM is another programmer-defined function, to be presented fully in Chapter 5, which returns a random number; IRAND itself returns a random number in the range 1—N.

As with the supplied functions, some care must be exercised in the argument types for statement functions. When an INTEGER variable is used in the dummy argument list, each function reference must also have an INTEGER argument in the corresponding position. For example, a function defined by

$$\texttt{MIXDUP(X,N) = X**N+X**(2*N)}$$

must always be referenced with two arguments, the first REAL and the second INTEGER. The following references are permitted to MIXDUP:

$$\texttt{I = MIXDUP(A,N)}$$
$$\texttt{KK34 = MIXDUP(WXYZ,3)}$$
$$\texttt{M9 = MIXDUP(17.99,8)}$$

but

$$\texttt{JJ = MIXDUP(I,4)}$$

would result in an error, because the first argument in the function reference is an integer. Note also that MIXDUP is an INTEGER function, assuming that it has not been defined to be REAL (or something else) in a type statement previously.

FUNCTIONs

A FUNCTION is a separate subprogram in every sense. It begins with the statement

$$\texttt{FUNCTION name(arg}_1\texttt{, arg}_2\texttt{, ...)}$$

where "name" is the name given to the FUNCTION subprogram and arg_1, arg_2, ... are the arguments. The general rules for statement functions apply here as well, except that the function is not defined on a single line. In particular, the types of the arguments must agree with the calling sequence, the arguments are dummy variables, and the first letter of the function name defines the type of the function.

The first-letter type coding can be overridden by placing a type designation in front of the word FUNCTION. For example,

$$\texttt{REAL FUNCTION ISUB(...)}$$
$$\texttt{INTEGER FUNCTION XMARK(...)}$$
$$\texttt{LOGICAL FUNCTION LTEST(...)}$$
$$\texttt{REAL FUNCTION HMEAN(...)}$$

are all acceptable FUNCTION lines. Note that the last one is redundant since a function named HMEAN would be typed as REAL without the REAL specification.

Following the FUNCTION statement that marks the beginning of the function definition may appear any legal Fortran statements needed to define the function, except SUBROUTINE, BLOCK DATA, or another FUNCTION. Therefore, a FUNCTION may define its own subscripted variables, use any type or other specification statements, or do input and output or any other permissible operation.

A FUNCTION must physically end with an END statement, just as a program must. At least once before the END, the name of the function must appear on the lefthand side of a replacement statement. This assigns a value to the function to be returned to the calling program. Once that is done, a RETURN statement causes a return of control to the calling program.

Table 2.1 presents an illustrative FUNCTION. The complete logic and purpose of this function is discussed in Chapter 5; for now, we note several mechanical elements of a FUNCTION. The FUNCTION returns an INTEGER value as a FUNCTION of two arguments, one INTEGER and one REAL. The FUNCTION physically terminates with the END statement, but there are two RETURNs. The FUNCTION follows one of two alternative courses, depending on the value of N, the first argument. Each of the ways of computing the value of BIN terminates in a RETURN to the calling program. Note also that the name of the FUNCTION, BIN, occurs at least once before each RETURN in order that a value may be assigned to the FUNCTION. The FUNCTION BIN itself returns a binomial random value from a population with parameters N and P.

In contrast to the statement function, the FUNCTION has no access at all to variables in the program from which it is called. (We consider a possible exception by the use of COMMON below.) Any variables in the FUNCTION are completely unrelated to any variables in the calling program, except that values are communicated to the dummy arguments in the function reference. The variables I and BMEAN in Table 2.1, for example, are local to the FUNCTION. They have no meaning elsewhere and can in fact be the same as variable names in the program that refers to BIN.

FUNCTIONs are extremely useful elements of Fortran programming. Because they are completely independent of any program in which they might be used, they can be written in very general form and widely used in various applications. The next several chapters contain several algorithms that can be used in a number of ways; many of them are presented as FUNCTIONs.

The FUNCTION, although a very general and flexible form of subprogram, has two important limitations. First, the arguments to the FUNCTION must be only single variables or constants; they cannot be arrays. The second weakness is that a function, in general, is single valued — it returns a single value to the referencing program. In some cases, using a FUNCTION, with its single-valued

TABLE 2.1
An Example FUNCTION Subprogram

```
      INTEGER FUNCTION BIN(N,P)
C
C     GENERATES A SAMPLE FROM A BINOMIAL DISTRIBUTION
C        WITH PARAMETERS N AND P.
C
C     A NORMAL DISTRIBUTION ROUTINE (RNORM) IS NEEDED
C
C
C     SELECT APPROPRIATE ALGORITHM
C
      IF(N.GT.25) GO TO 100
C
C     DIRECT COMPUTATION METHOD FOR SMALL N
C
      BIN = 0
      DO 1 I = 1,N
      IF(RNDM(DUMMY).LE.P) BIN = BIN+1
    1 CONTINUE
      RETURN
C
C     NORMAL APPROXIMATION METHOD FOR LARGE N
C
  100 X = RNORM(DUMMY)
      BMEAN = N*P
      BIN = INT(X*SQRT(BMEAN*(1.0-P))+BMEAN+.5)
      IF(BIN.LT.O .OR. BIN.GT.N) GO TO 100
      RETURN
      END
```

implicit reference, is awkward. A SUBROUTINE subprogram overcomes both of these weaknesses of the FUNCTION.

SUBROUTINEs

In many ways, a SUBROUTINE is similar to a FUNCTION — it is a completely separate routine, all of its arguments are dummys, and it may contain virtually any permissible Fortran statement. There are some important differences, however. A SUBROUTINE is referenced explicitly in a CALL statement of the form

$$\text{CALL name}(\text{arg}_1, \ldots)$$

where "name" is the name of the subroutine being CALLed, and "arg" is an argument, if any. SUBROUTINEs need not have any arguments and need not return any value(s) to the calling program. The arguments in a CALL may be anything that is required by the SUBROUTINE, including variables, constants, array names, and even the names of other subprograms.

A SUBROUTINE begins with a statement of the form

$$\text{SUBROUTINE name } (arg_1 \ldots)$$

where "name" is the name of the SUBROUTINE. The argument list and its enclosing parentheses may be omitted if the routine has no arguments. The name of a subroutine can be any series of one to six characters, the first being a letter, just as with a FUNCTION or statement function. The first letter coding of type is irrelevent in a SUBROUTINE; because the name is not used to return a value, a SUBROUTINE has no type.

Like a FUNCTION, a SUBROUTINE terminates with an END statement and must contain at least one RETURN, marking the point at which control is returned to the calling program. Any legal Fortran statement is allowed in a SUBROUTINE, except FUNCTION, BLOCK DATA, and SUBROUTINE.

A major distinction between the FUNCTION and the SUBROUTINE is in the manner of communication with the calling program. Any values returned to the calling program must be assigned to an argument in a SUBROUTINE, where the FUNCTION name is used in the FUNCTION. For example, the following simple code will find the mean of an array:

```
SUBROUTINE MEAN(X,N,XBAR)
DIMENSION X(1000)
SUM = 0.0
DO 1 I = 1,N
SUM = SUM+X(I)
1 CONTINUE
FN = N
XBAR = SUM/FN
RETURN
END
```

A CALL to the subroutine might take the form

```
DIMENSION DATA(500)
    .
    .
    .
CALL MEAN(DATA,500,AVERGE)
```

A dummy array (X) is established in the subroutine to hold data communicated by the calling program. In this example, 1,000 locations are assigned to X, but all of them need not be used. The CALL communicates two arguments, the array containing the actual data — it is known as X in the SUBROUTINE but as DATA in the calling program — and the number of data values actually present — N. The third argument is used to pass the computed mean back to the calling program. The subroutine computes the value of the mean and assigns it to the dummy variable called XBAR. When the RETURN is executed, the third argument contains the returned value in the variable AVERGE of the calling program. (Arguments in FUNCTIONs may also be used in this fashion but they rarely are.)

Another feature of the SUBROUTINE can be illustrated by a slight modification to this example. A SUBROUTINE is allowed to use a variable name in a DIMENSION statement. For example, we might write

```
SUBROUTINE MEAN(X,N,XBAR)
DIMENSION X(N)
```

which allows a variable allocation for the array X in the SUBROUTINE depending on the value of the argument N.

SUBROUTINEs are extremely useful programming tools. Like FUNCTIONs, they are completely transportable and can be written in very general forms. In addition, they do not have some of the restrictions that are found in FUNCTIONs. A brief glance at the listing of the example simulations in Appendices A and B will illustrate a number of SUBROUTINEs, some that have no arguments at all. Such routines are very useful for output operations, among other purposes.

The Use of COMMON Storage

Throughout the discussion of subprograms until now, we have stressed the point that communication between subprogram and calling program is by means of the argument list or, in the case of the functions, by function-assigned value. The emphasis has been on the independence of variables between subprogram and calling routine, with the same variable names being entirely separate. It is this separation of the locations used by the calling program and all subprograms that gives subroutines and functions their flexibility and generality. However, there are many cases when passing all of the information needed by a subprogram through an argument list is extremely cumbersome and often error producing. In such cases, it may be desirable to make the same variable names actually refer to the same storage locations in the calling program and in a subprogram. Fortran provides for such a facility through the use of a common storage area, usually referred to as COMMON because of the Fortran declaration required.

The reason that storage of variables is completely independent among subprograms is that they are treated by the compiler as, in effect, completely separate programs. Each is compiled separately, and the storage for variables needed by each routine is thus separate as well. Correspondences among variables mentioned in argument lists is established later, usually just before the program is finally executed, or perhaps during execution, depending on the particular computer system.

The compiler can produce a storage area, separate from all programs and subprograms, that can be shared by a number of routines. This storage area is known as COMMON, and only variables that are explicitly listed as belonging there are located in COMMON. Once there, a variable can be referenced by any routine and by the same or alternative names.

CHEBO uses COMMON extensively but is much too complex to serve as a simple example. Consider instead the subroutine for computing the mean that we just presented. In it, the data array was communicated to the subroutine by argument. Instead, we might place the array in COMMON; then it could be removed from the argument list. If we write

```
DIMENSION DATA(500)

COMMON DATA
```

in the calling program, and

```
SUBROUTINE MEAN(N,XBAR)

DIMENSION X(500)

COMMON X
```

in the subroutine, we have established a COMMON area containing a 500-element array. The calling program uses the name DATA to refer to the array, and the subroutine uses X, but it refers to the same locations because the variables are stored in COMMON. Note that in this case the arrays must be the same length, where in the first example they could be different.

Dimensioning information can be established in the COMMON statement instead of using two statements; thus,

```
COMMON DATA(500)
```

in the calling program and

```
COMMON X(500)
```

in the subroutine accomplish exactly the same result as before.

A COMMON statement can list any number of variables, and they are assigned to common storage in the order mentioned. The statement

```
COMMON W(100),X(500),Y(10,5),Z,A,B,C
```

established a COMMON area of 654 locations — 100 for W, 500 for X, 50 for Y, and one each for Z, A, B, and C. A parallel declaration in the subprogram might be

```
COMMON W(100),THIS(500),Y(10,5),ZSUB(4)
```

Note that the same variable name can be used, as in the case of W. Indeed, to avoid confusion on the part of the programmer (not the compiler!), the use of the same variable names is recommended as a good programming practice.

A second feature of the COMMON statement is also illustrated in these examples. The first statement establishes four single locations — for Z, A, B, and C. In the subprogram, those same four locations are used by a subscripted variable ZSUB. The equivalence between them is established in the order in which the locations are assigned, so that Z in the calling program is the same as ZSUB(1) in the subprogram, A is equivalent to ZSUB(2), and so forth. The COMMON statement therefore can be used to establish synonomous names for locations between subprograms, just as the EQUIVALENCE statement can establish synonyms in a single program.

Perhaps the most important, and most easy to break, rule about COMMON is that the block of common established in the calling program and in each subprogram must be the same length. The reason should be clear. The COMMON statement establishes a separate storage area that is accessable by all routines that contain the appropriate COMMON statements. To have different lengths implied by the COMMON statements in separate routines is contradictory. The most frequent reason that the rule is broken stems from the ability of the different routines to use different variable names for referring to the same location, coupled with the ability for each routine to subdivide the COMMON area in different ways. The difficulties can be minimized by keeping COMMON relatively simple by always using the same variable names and COMMON subdivisions in all routines that are to access COMMON.

The use of COMMON is frequently error prone for another reason as well — it is treated differently by different compilers and computer systems. Standard Fortran (ANSI, 1970) defines the characteristics of the Fortran language but does not address the implementation of the language. Most features of Fortran are comparatively straightforward to implement in a compiler; it is not hard to define what must be done to compile an arithmetic expression, for example. But COMMON poses a very different problem. The expectations about COMMON are stated in the standard, but providing COMMON is not a simple matter of writing a Fortran to machine language translator. COMMON must be dealt with by such other system functions as the routines that link together programs for execution, and those that load linked programs prior to execution. The complexity of the system-level operations surrounding COMMON frequently cause difficulties that are difficult to diagnose and highly specific to computer installations. The listing of SIMSAL in Appendix B, for example, includes a COMMON statement that is required to circumvent a known error in the handling of certain kinds of programs by the Univac 70/46 computer on which all the examples in this book were written.

Despite its occasional difficulties, COMMON is a very valuable feature of Fortran when large numbers of subprograms, and/or large argument lists, are involved. In some instances, though, even COMMON as we have discussed it so far is not enough. There are times when COMMON profitably can be subdivided in a different way than into just variables and arrays. We turn now to the concept of COMMON blocks.

Labeled COMMON.[1] A simple COMMON declaration, such as those il-lustrated previously, establishes a single COMMON area or block, known as "blank" or "unlabeled" COMMON, containing the variables listed in the state-ment. It is also possible to establish multiple blocks, give each block a name or label, and allow access to some blocks by some routines and not by others. This technique is not widely used but has great benefit in complex programs consist-ing of a large number of separate subprograms.

A labeled COMMON block is established in a COMMON declaration by naming a block and then listing the variables that are to be stored in it. For example, the declaration

```
COMMON /BLOCK1/X(100),Y(50)
```

establishes BLOCK1 containing two subscripted variables, X and Y. A number of blocks can be established in the same statement, for example,

```
COMMON /BLOCK1/X(100),Y(50)/BLOCK2/A,B(75)
```

This statement defines two blocks; BLOCK1 is the same as before, and BLOCK2 contains the single variable A and the array B. Unlabeled COMMON is just another block, except that it has no name. To define an unlabeled COMMON block, we could write

```
COMMON ISUB,J/BLOCK1/X(100),Y(50)/BLOCK2/A,B(75
```

and define BLOCK1 and BLOCK2 as before, with the addition of an unlabeled area containing ISUB and J.

COMMON declarations are cumulative throughout a program or subprogram. Variables are assigned to blocks in the order that they are listed in the declara-

---

[1] A section or problem marked with an asterisk is a more advanced topic that can be omitted without loss of continuity.

tions, so that

```
COMMON ISUB/BLOCK1/X(100)/BLOCK2/A
        .
        .
        .
COMMON J/BLOCK1/Y(50)/BLOCK2/B(75)
```

has exactly the same effect as the previous declaration.

The real advantage of labeled or named COMMON is in the case where several subroutines need some of the COMMON area, and other routines need other parts of COMMON. We might write a main calling program with the declaration:

```
COMMON ISUB,J/BLOCK1/X(100),Y(50)/BLOCK2/A,B(75)
```

as before. This gives the main routine access to all of the COMMON areas. Now suppose that there is a group of subprograms, either FUNCTIONs or SUB-ROUTINEs, that need only the unlabeled and BLOCK1 areas. Each of their declarations might be:

```
COMMON ISUB,J/BLOCK1/X(100),Y(50)
```

thus establishing an access to only the blank and BLOCK1 areas. Another group of subprograms could use the statement:

```
COMMON /BLOCK2/A,B(75)
```

and be allowed to obtain the values in only the BLOCK2 area. Likewise, if access to the blank and BLOCK2 COMMON regions were needed,

```
COMMON ISUB,J/BLOCK2/A,B(75)
```

will establish it.

An example of blank and labeled COMMON can be found in Appendix C, where the simulation resulting from the series of chapter exercises is presented.

*Multiple Entries and Returns

In this final section of our discussion of program organization, we make a slight exception to the policy of presenting only ANSI Standard Fortran to discuss briefly a very useful feature of SUBROUTINEs that is supported by many compilers. Because it is nonstandard Fortran, we cannot be as explicit in the rules as may be desired, for individual compilers vary somewhat in their requirements.

Many compilers allow multiple entries to SUBROUTINEs and FUNCTIONs. In such cases, the first entry is by way of the normal SUBROUTINE or FUNC-TION statement. Subsequent entries to the subprogram are at a statement known as the ENTRY. The usual application of this feature is in the case where a first CALL to a subroutine is made to do some initial work, such as establishing constants. Thereafter another entry is used to accomplish some procedure that must first be initialized. We will see an example of the optimal use of the multiple entry in Chapter 5 in presenting a random number function. The overall appearance of the FUNCTION, with a number of omissions, is as follows:

```
FUNCTION RANDOM(XYZ)

  .
  . }  Statements to initialize the generator
  .

RETURN
ENTRY RNDM(WXYZ)

  .
  . }  Statements to generate a single number
  .

RETURN
END
```

The initial entry to the routine is made in a function reference, such as

$$DUMDUM = RANDOM(ANYARG)$$

This usage starts a random number generation sequence by picking (or reading as input) an initial value or "seed" for the generator. This step must be accomplished or the subsequent use of the random number function does not operate properly. Once the function has been initialized, however, obtaining a single random number is a simple matter of writing a statement, such as:

$$RANDNO = RNDM(XXX)$$

This function reference uses the second entry point defined by the ENTRY statement in the function definition.

Many Fortran systems allow statement numbers to be communicated as arguments to SUBROUTINEs. In this case, the return to the calling program may be to some other point than the statement immediately following the CALL. Because this multiple RETURN feature is highly variable across compilers, we do not discuss it further here.

CONCLUSIONS

This chapter has ranged over several topics, yet there is an integrating theme — processes and subprocesses. Real phenomena can be represented in terms of various levels of subprocesses; their identification is an important part of planning the simulation program. The course of planning the simulation program includes a careful analysis of the critical elements of the real process that must be represented in the theory and in the model. Many theory-relevent aspects of the process can be represented conveniently as subprocesses in the model as well. The all-important formula relating the evaluation of a board position in CHEBO, for example, is implemented in FUNCTION VALUE in the actual program. It is not without good reason, then, that we consider planning the program and its structure in the same chapter in which the overall planning of the entire simulation is discussed. These are rather high-level concerns in the mechanics of simulating. In the next several chapters we consider more specific elements of simulation programming.

EXERCISES

2.1 Consider the process by which an urban area expands as the population grows. The expansion and various uses to which available land is put is not a random process. As population grows, new housing, industrial, and business areas are required, but they do not appear helterskelter. The policies established by various councils and zoning boards not only control the location of new housing and business areas but also often provide guidelines by which various kinds of property can be built. For example, there may be an overall desire to have a certain percentage of the population live in single dwelling, another percentage in apartments, and so forth. In addition, there are frequently priorities established that govern the taking over of existing space – vacant land converted to housing before any slum area is razed, and so forth. Give some thought to the problem and then write down the critical processes as well as the theoretical assumptions that underly your thinking. (This is the first statement of our third example simulation; it continues in these exercises and in the following chapters.)

2.2 Draw a rough flowchart expressing the sequencing of the processes in Problem 2.1. You might consider time as being represented by a large loop in the program, with each circuit around the loop indicating some time period, such as 10 years.

2.3 SIMSAL is structured into two routines – a main program that serves as the "experimenter" in the learning situation, and a subroutine that represents the "subject." Writing the program in this way violates the recommendation of structured programming that all the individual routines be small. Draw a rough flowchart of a program that would accomplish the same process as that shown in Figure 2.4 but with much smaller routines.

2.4 What kinds of data representation may be implied in the urban growth simulation discussed in Exercise 2.1? In other words, what may be appropriate units and properties for the simulation? (Hint: there may be two kinds of things – the city itself and various sorts of priorities.)

2.5 Before you get too far into simulating a city, what are you trying to accomplish by the simulation?

2.6 Modify SUBROUTINE MEAN so that it finds a standard deviation as well. Test it with some data.

2.7 Rewrite SUBROUTINE MEAN as a FUNCTION. (Hint: be careful how you communicate the data array.)

2.8 Suppose that your city simulation has a main program that uses a number of arrays, for example MAP(50,50),ROTOT(50,9),COTOT(50,9),PERCEN(9). There are several subroutines that need MAP, ROTOT, and COTOT but not PERCEN. In addition, there is another group of subroutines that need PERCEN but none of the others. Write the necessary COMMON statements for the main program and for both sets of subroutines.

SUGGESTED READINGS

Abelson, R. P. Simulation of social behavior. In G. Lindzey & E. Aronson (Eds.), *The handbook of social psychology*. Vol. 2. *Research methods*. (2nd ed.) Reading, Mass.: Addison-Wesley, 1968. An excellent survey of simulation and modeling. Covers many of the topics of this chapter, often in greater depth. Also briefly summarizes several important (indeed classic) models.

Chapin, N. Flowcharting with the ANSI standard: A tutorial. *Computing surveys*, 1970, 2, 119–146. A good overview and introduction to flowcharting using the standard symbols.

Dutton, J. M., & Briggs, W. G. Simulation model construction. In J. M. Dutton & W. H. Starbuck (Eds.), *Computer simulation of human behavior*. New York: Wiley, 1971. A detailed step by step discussion of developing simulation models. The exposition is built around two examples – materials inventory control and a baseball game.

Emshoff, J. R., & Sisson, R. L. *Design and use of computer simulation models.* New York: Macmillan, 1970. A good introduction to simulation methodology; its examples are primarily management science.

Martin, F. F. *Computer modeling and simulation.* New York: Wiley, 1968. A useful reference book for a number of modeling techniques and basic algorithms. Discusses planning and conceptualization, statistical procedures, and using models. Examples are primarily business.

Nilsson, N. J. *Problem-solving methods in artificial intelligence.* New York: McGraw-Hill, 1971. An excellent presentation of many of the techniques developed in problem-solving research. Of particular note is the careful attention to the problem of representation which Nilsson identifies as a major conceptual difficulty.

3

Data Requirements
and Structures

Chapter 2 presented the broad view of planning the simulation program. This and the next three chapters discuss the inner workings of simulation programs in detail. Chapter 3 deals primarily with defining the data requirements for the simulation and with the organization of the data within the program. Chapter 4 focuses on several common operations that are performed on data — primarily sorting, searching, and retrieval. Chapter 5 concerns itself with random processes, and coding for accuracy and efficiency are confronted in Chapter 6.

Data Storage Media

Anyone familiar with digital computers recognizes that there are several kinds of physical media within which the data for any program may reside. The obvious examples are punched cards, magnetic core, magnetic tape or disk, and so forth. In some simulations, the use of such auxiliary storage is an absolute necessity. Some programs require a large base of data for operation — opinion surveys, voting records, or research protocols, for example. Often this material is of a magnitude such that it cannot be kept "in core." External storage is often mandatory, depending on the size of the data base, how often it is needed during the simulation, and the size of the main memory allocation available to the simulation programmer.

The management of auxiliary storage is unlike that of main storage; getting data to and from tape or disk is different, and sorting and searching present unique problems. The Suggested Readings in Chapter 4 offer sources of general procedures for dealing with external storage. The specific details differ according to the medium, the computer, the executive system, and the operating policies of a particular computer center. To attempt to deal with such a tangle of imponderables would confuse more than clarify, and we won't pursue the matter further here. The simulation writer who suspects that he or she is placing excessive demands upon his or her computer's main storage is best advised to seek out competent help at his computer center before proceeding further.

Our topic for this chapter is main memory — core, fast store, or whatever it is called locally. Main memory is that storage medium in which data are directly accessible by the program; indeed they reside within the program itself in space allocated by the arithmetic and declaration statements.

The physical arrangement of memory is not generally of concern to the programmer, although in some cases that we discuss later it is very important. Our interest in this chapter is with the defining and use of the storage area as the programmer sees it. The first consideration is with the data requirements of the program — what is required by the model, and what is necessary for the operations that we are to perform. Next we turn to a presentation of several kinds of organizations for the data. This topic is usually found under the heading of "data structures" and deals with arrays, stacks, lists, and trees, among other topics. Finally, we make a few comments and suggestions about managing data organizations in Fortran.

THE DATA REQUIREMENTS

There are three major determinants of the data storage procedures used in simulation: the units and properties of the model, the parallelism between the program and the real world, and the program's own processing requirements.

Units and properties. If the conceptual model of the simulation has been developed with care and in some detail, many of the considerations in data organization are already likely to be apparent. CHEBO, for example, must have a representation of the checkerboard — perhaps suggesting a two-dimensional array with characters denoting different pieces. In SIMSAL, on the other hand, a simple array will not suffice for representing the subject's memory. However, a simple array would do nicely for the experimenter segment of the program to maintain the list of syllables and responses, and to tally responses from the subject.

The delineation of the units and their properties in the conceptual model usually defines the content of storage; processing and parallelism considerations often determine its form.

Parallelism. There are at least two ways in which a simulation program may be said to parallel an actual process. At one level, the flow of action in the program, and perhaps the organization of the program itself, mimic the real process. In SIMSAL, for example, the program contains two separate routines, one simulating the experimenter and the other the subject.

The second kind of parallelism is in data organization, and that is the concern here. Humans learn in a way that often reveals an underlying memory organization. When an item is learned, it is not randomly placed into memory; it is located so that there is a connection between the new element and other things already stored. When asked to retrieve items, subjects do so in a way that suggests an underlying associative network. Syllables do not appear randomly in subjects' reports; they are highly organized.

In light of what is known about human memory organization, it is unlikely that a simple Fortran array could serve as an adequate computer representation. The human associative memory suggests a different kind of data storage structure for the simulation, namely the tree. The tree is a well-known and widely used data organization in many computer applications. Its characteristics make it highly appropriate as the procedure selected to model human memory organization.

Processing requirements. A major determinant of the storage organization is the processing to be done by the simulation program. Here again, the importance of a carefully developed conceptual model must be stressed. The model will specify the kinds of operations to be carried out by the program, and that in turn will often dictate, or at least suggest, an optimal data arrangement.

CHEBO, for example, treats individual pieces as the basic units of the model. The pieces are placed into a two-dimensional array named BOARD which represents the playing field; a zero entry indicates no piece, −1 a "square," and +1 a "cross." That symbolism is adequate for some processing, but for other operations individual "squares" and "crosses" must be identified. For those cases, an alternative representation of the pieces is used. In the program, an array named MAP contains the row and column coordinates for each individual "square" and "cross."

In SIMSAL, the data organization must grow over time. In the course of "learning," SIMSAL's subject must add new information to its memory storage, and also retrieve previously "learned" items. In addition, because there are several trials in a typical learning experiment, and on each trial the syllables come in a different random sequence, additions and retrievals from "memory" occur in an unpredictable order. In Chapter 4 we discuss search and retrieval procedures more carefully, but it should be clear that a sequential search through an array may be inefficient. For example, if the subject has identified the first letter as an "M," there is no need to pursue any item in memory whose first letter is anything other than an "M." The tree used in SIMSAL not only shows an organization parallel to human memory but makes the search operation considerably more efficient than do other storage arrangements.

Other processing procedures place other requirements on storage. In order to arrange for a random presentation of syllables in SIMSAL, or to randomly order the sequence of CHEBO moves, two processing options present themselves. First, whenever the list of syllables (or the pieces, for that matter) is randomized, the entire list can be scrambled. However, that would entail the inefficiency of moving a number of data elements (three letters and a response for SIMSAL) each time. Instead, the items are kept in a fixed order, and a one-dimensional array giving only syllable numbers (or piece numbers) is shuffled each time; the values are then used as pointers to indicate which syllable (or piece) is to be presented or moved next.

The reader should be alert to similarities in the processing and data representations of the examples, although they deal with quite different phenomena. Both CHEBO and SIMSAL use a pointer vector for a component of the ordering process. CHEBO employs a maplike representation of spatial arrangements; both involve search procedures, although SIMSAL has a tree search whereas CHEBO uses a concentric-squares approach.

Other simulations may make different demands. In some processes, lists of items are produced, and the lists may shrink and grow during the operation of the program. Depending upon the way items are placed into and removed from the lists, the data storage may be a stack, a queue, or a linked list; we shall explore these forms of data structure shortly.

Besides adding and deleting items, the nature of any searching to be done has an important impact on defining the data organization. SIMSAL's tree is ideally suited for the search employed, because the search is determined by the order of the letters in the presented syllable. In other instances, though, the search might be for a specific numeric or alphabetic value. In such a case, a binary search as discussed in the next chapter might be best and would dictate that the data be maintained in a simple array in numerical or alphabetic order.

In short, the general requirements as to what must be stored in the data are dictated largely by the units and properties of the conceptual model. The choice of the data structure to store the properties is most often determined by the processing requirements of the model, with a careful eye on parallelism. In order to select from among the variety of data structures available, the programmer must understand their organization and operating characteristics. The remainder of this chapter introduces the structures, and Chapter 4 discusses their use.

DATA STRUCTURES

Fortran is an algebraic language. This means that it lends itself easily to writing expressions that are algebra-like in their construction. Because an important element of algebra is the variable, the fundamental or primitive data representation in Fortran is the variable. The data required by a Fortran program — properties of units, constants and parameters, housekeeping arrays, and I/O areas — are all defined by the programmer as single or subscripted variables.

Other languages offer different kinds of data representation as primitives. SNOBOL, for example, takes as its primitive a string of alphameric characters of indefinite length. We introduce a few of these other languages briefly in Chapter 9.

In Fortran as with other languages, any data organization must be embedded within the primitive data type. CHEBO's board, for example, is readily represented by a two-dimensional Fortran array. However, the tree in SIMSAL is a different data organization. In order to use a tree for the subject's memory, it must be incorporated into Fortran's subscripted variable notation. To do so is not difficult, as we shall see, but it does involve more effort than may be required in some other languages. Conversely, other languages are not able to accomplish what Fortran can do easily. In SNOBOL, for example, it is extremely cumbersome to code even very simple arithmetic expressions.

In this section we discuss ways of representing several different data structures within the constraints of Fortran. In some cases, Fortran is perfectly suited for the required data arrangement; in others, a way must be found to make the structure fit into an array.

In passing, we should note that we are not concerned here with yet another element of Fortran's data storage. We will assume that the type of the variable (REAL, INTEGER, LOGICAL, etc.) is appropriate for the kind of information to be stored in it. Our interest is at a higher level; namely the use of and interrelationships between the data, regardless of their type in Fortran.

Variables and Arrays

A great deal of simulation programming can be accomplished in Fortran without recourse to any storage organization other than the primitives of the language — single variables and arrays. In general, Fortran's primitives are used in one of two different ways. For convenience, we may designate them as "value" variables and as pointers. In the first, the value of the variable is actually the value of interest. The variable named 00 in CHEBO, for example, gives the attitude of the "circles" toward each other as a signed integer number.

The other way to use arrays in Fortran is as pointers. If a variable is a pointer, then its value is not the quantity sought but indicates where that final value is to be found. Pointer variables and arrays are extremely powerful tools in programming. Indeed, the more complex data structures to be discussed in this chapter can be programmed only by using pointers.

The idea of a pointer array was introduced briefly for randomly ordering the presentation of syllables in SIMSAL. A more thorough discussion of the SIMSAL procedure will illustrate the use of a pointer array.

The SIMSAL main program (the experimenter) reads syllables and responses into two arrays. The three-letter syllables are placed into the two-dimensional array LIST. Each row of LIST contains a single syllable, one letter in each of the three columns of the array. The responses are stored in the array RESP. Positional information associates syllables and responses — the response for the syllable in LIST(1,1), LIST(1,2), and LIST(1,3) is found in RESP(1), and so forth. The syllables and responses remain in LIST and RESP in their input order throughout the program.

For some SIMSAL experiments, there are two separate lists. Each list may have up to 20 elements; both LIST and RESP therefore contain space for 40 items. A special pointer, IJUMP, is maintained to indicate the end of the first list. If there are two lists of eight items each, Locations 1–8 of LIST and RESP contain the syllables and responses for List 1, whereas List 2 occupies Locations 9–16. IJUMP would have the value 8, indicating that the first list ends at Location 8, and that List 2 begins at Location IJUMP+1.

A 20-element one-dimensional array, ORDER, holds pointers. It is initially set to the integers 1, 2, . . . , 20 by the statements

```
        DO 1104 I = 1,20
   1104 ORDER(I) = I
```

As the SIMSAL experimenter sets up each trial of the experiment, it randomly permutes the elements in ORDER, following a shuffle algorithm to be presented in Chapter 5. For now it is sufficient to note that the shuffle results in ORDER containing the values 1 . . . NSYLAB in random order. (NSYLAB is the number of elements in the list to be presented.) The sequence of item numbers in ORDER controls the presentation of syllables to the subject; if ORDER(1) contains a 5, then the first syllable to be given is in LIST(5,1), LIST(5,2), and LIST(5,3).

The next step is to actually present the syllables to the subject. This is accomplished in the following loop (only the sections of the program dealing with the pointer array are reproduced here). For this illustration, assume that IJUMP is zero, indicating a single-list problem:

```
        DO 1202 J = 1,NSYLAB
        ITEMP = ORDER(J)+IJUMP
        ICORR = RESP(ITEMP)
C       ICORR IS THE CORRECT RESPONSE
C       ITEMP IS THE STIMULUS NUMBER
C       NOW FILL THE STIMULUS ARRAY (QUE)
        DO 1203 K = 1,3
   1203 QUE(K) = LIST(ITEMP,K)
          .
          .
          .
        CALL SUBJCT(QUE, ...)
          .
          .
          .
   1202 CONTINUE
```

In this listing, we see the use of the pointer array ORDER clearly. The variable ITEMP holds a value from ORDER, a number between 1 and NSYLAB. ITEMP then becomes a pointer into the arrays RESP and LIST. RESP(ITEMP) is the correct response and is called ICORR. The stimulus presented to the subject is a three-element vector called QUE. QUE is filled from LIST; specifically, it is the entries in the ITEMPth row of LIST. The entries in LIST and RESP are never moved, but they are extracted in a random order to be used in ICORR and QUE.

Note the advantage in using the pointer array. If the actual list were randomized, for every random interchange in the shuffle there would have to be four data elements moved — the three letters in the syllable plus the correct response. With the pointer array, the shuffle involves but one item, the pointer.

The four-to-one gain in computer time may not seem consequential until it is noted that the shuffle is repeated NSYLAB times for each trial, that it typically requires five to ten trials for SIMSAL to learn a list to criterion, and that there may be more than a single list to be learned, as well as many different "subjects" in any single execution of the program.

Note also the effect of the pointer IJUMP in this process. If there are two lists, IJUMP is set to zero to select from the first list and the computation of ITEMP involves only selection the Jth element from ORDER. In contrast, suppose that List 2 is being presented, and List 1 has eight elements. Now IJUMP would have a value of 8. In this case, a pointer is taken from ORDER, 8 is added, and an element from the second list is selected. In this context, IJUMP is not technically a pointer but is usually called a "displacement." In effect it displaces the origin of the addressing in the array from the first location upwards IJUMP places.

It is important to note in this example that the pointer refers to a row in the array LIST, and that there are three elements (all in row ITEMP) indicated by the single pointer value. As we become more familiar with pointers, we will often refer to the fact that they frequently lead to more than a single value.

Many details were omitted from the large loop (DO 1202 . . .) in the example. The complete program listing in Appendix B shows the intervening steps. In essence, within that loop, there are two CALLs to SUBJCT, once to present the syllable in QUE and receive a response and a second to give SUBJCT the value contained in ICORR and cause the subroutine to "learn."

Following the loop, the experimenter performs a check for learning criterion, determines whether "overlearning" trials (additional presentations after criterion is reached) are to be given, prints a protocol, and continues to the next simulated subject.

The preceding example of a pointer array and displacement variable is just their first introduction. They will continue with us as we move on to the discussion of other kinds of data structures.

Stacks and Queues

Many simulation programs involve the formation of lists of units or properties that change during the operation of a program. As one example, a simulation of a turnpike toll plaza might have several lanes of traffic, each with a line of vehicles waiting to be served. If the vehicles were the units in the simulation, each might be represented by such properties as type (for example, car, truck), weight, distance traveled, etc. A simulation program might be written to have some particular mix of vehicles arrive for service, wait for a time in a line, and then continue on.

An important element in this kind of simulation is the waiting line. Such a line is usually called a queue and is characterized by its first in—first out nature. The first unit into the queue is the first served, the second is served next, and so forth. Many kinds of computer simulation involve the formation of queues at one point or another.

A similar, but less complicated, data structure is the stack. Here elements are added to a list but are removed for processing in reverse order, in a last in—first out fashion. This kind of data structure is known as a "stack," or sometimes a push-down store. Anyone familiar with a cafeteria is also familiar with a stack — plates are often found on them. Adding a plate causes the entire stack to be pushed down. The first plate removed was the last added, and removing the top plate causes the stack to pop up. Indeed, adding to and retrieving from a stack are usually referred to as "pushing" and "popping," respectively.

Stacks

A stack is simple to implement in Fortran. All that is required is a one-dimensional array and a single pointer variable. The storage vector must be adequate to hold the largest number of elements that have to be kept in the stack at any one time.

If a push-down store is contained in the array STACK, then these statements initialize the storage procedure

```
DIMENSION STACK(100)

IPOINT = 0
```

assuming that 100 elements are enough.

The following coding will place an item contained in TEMP into the "top," thus pushing the stack:

```
IPOINT = IPOINT+1

IF(IPOINT.GT.100) GO TO 999

STACK(IPOINT) = TEMP

        .
        .
        .

999 error return--stack full
```

An error branch is provided in the event that the stack is full.

"Popping" the stack to retrieve the top element is equally simple:

```
IF(IPOINT.LE.0) GO TO 998
TEMP = STACK(IPOINT)
IPOINT = IPOINT-1
```

.
.
.

```
998 error return--stack empty
```

In both of these program segments, IPOINT is a pointer variable indicating the location of the last element placed in the stack. Adding a new element involves incrementing the pointer and storing the new value. Removing an element requires the inverse process — transfer the desired element to TEMP and decrement the pointer.

The data values contained in the stack may themselves be the required values (value variables), or they may be pointers, just as the elements in SIMSAL's ORDER indicated a row in another array.

A stack forms the basis of one of the most well-known and highly successful of the problem-solving programs, the General Problem Solver (GPS) of Newell and Simon (1963, 1972). The strategy employed by GPS is to develop goals and subgoals, the final goal being to solve some problem. In its first studies, GPS was applied to problems in symbolic logic, the goal being to transform one side of an expression into the opposite side by applying a set of rules. The ultimate goal was an expression of equality. However, that goal is always "pushed down" on a stack, and a subgoal set. Often that subgoal is itself placed in the stack, and a subsubgoal established. That goal accomplished, the stack is "popped" and the next higher goal worked on, and so forth until the stack is empty and the problem solved.

Stacks may also be used for less grand simulations and, indeed, find many applications in computing. A stack is an essential ingredient in any language compiler for decoding algebraic statements. Stacks are also used in conjunction with various operations on other data structures, most particularly in some tree searching procedures.

A very important application of the stack in Fortran is the programming of recursive functions. A recursive function is one which, in its definition, calls itself. An easy to understand, if somewhat overworked, example is that of a factorial. As most behavioral scientists know, the factorial of n is defined as

$$n! = n \times (n-1) \times (n-2) \times \cdots x 2 \times 1 .$$

Another form of the definition makes the recursive nature of the factorial more apparent:

$$n! = 0, \qquad n < 0$$

$$n! = 1, \qquad n = 0$$

$$n! = n(n-1)!, \qquad n > 0$$

This definition states that to find $n!$ we may multiply n by $(n-1)!$ which can lead to a recursive function definition very easily.

Recursive functions are extremely useful and powerful tools in programming and are of particular usefulness in writing simulations. Many languages allow recursion; unfortunately, Fortran does not. But the fact is that recursive functions can be programmed in Fortran, not as simply as in other languages, but successfully nonetheless.

The secret to programming recursion in Fortran is the stack. A stack is used to hold the successive values that are needed in computing a function (n, $n - 1$, etc.) until the end of the recursion is reached. From that point, the stack is "popped" repeatedly until it is exhausted, using each successive argument as it is obtained. Day (1972) discusses programming recursive functions in Fortran and presents two coded examples.

Queues

The coding of a queue or first in—first out data structure is slightly more complicated than a stack, as two pointers must be maintained. One pointer indicates the "head" of the queue, the item to be retrieved next, and the other pointer indicates the "tail," the location for the next entry. When an item is removed from the queue, the head pointer is incremented to the next entry. Likewise, when an item is added to a queue, it is placed at the tail and that pointer is advanced by 1.

Figure 3.1a illustrates a queue containing five items; Figure 3.1b shows the same queue after three insertions and four retrievals have been made. Note that as additions and deletions occur, the region occupied by the queue moves farther down into the array, resulting in wasting of storage space. The way to alleviate the problem is to have the queue "wrap around" so that when the tail pointer passes the end of the array, it is set to 1, thus connecting the two ends of the array into a ring. In programming the wrap around, care must be taken that the array is large enough to contain all of the elements that may be in the queue at any one time, thus avoiding the possibility of the tail of the queue overwriting the head.

The coding of either stacks or queues can be accomplished directly in the simulation program. Because queue processing is slightly more complex than that for stacks, a pair of subroutines often makes life easier. The two subroutines presented in Tables 3.1 and 3.2 should aid the programmer in using queues as data structures. They can be used by any program and with any array with its

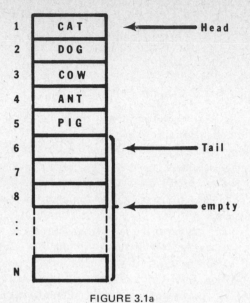

FIGURE 3.1a

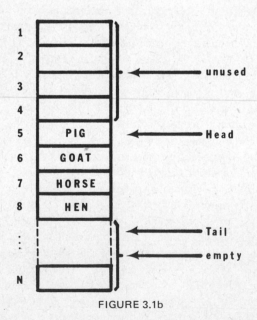

FIGURE 3.1b

FIGURE 3.1 (a) A queue containing five items. (b) The same queue after four deletions and three insertions.

TABLE 3.1
Subroutine to Insert a Value into a Queue (QUEPUT)

```
      SUBROUTINE QUEPUT(Q,VAL,IHEAD,ITAIL,N,IFULL)
C
C     ENTERS AN ITEM INTO A QUEUE
C     ARGUMENTS---
C        Q          THE ARRAY CONTAINING THE QUEUE
C        VAL        THE VALUE TO BE ENTERED
C        IHEAD      HEAD POINTER (NEXT ITEM TO BE REMOVED)
C        ITAIL      TAIL POINTER (PLACE TO PUT NEXT ITEM)
C        N          MAXIMUM DIMENSION OF Q
C        IFULL      RETURNS A 0 IF A NORMAL EXIT WAS MADE, A 1
C                       IF QUEUE WAS FULL AND ITEM WAS NOT STORED
C     IHEAD AND ITAIL SHOULD BE ZERO BEFORE FIRST CALL.
C
      DIMENSION Q(N)
C
C     IS QUEUE FULL?
C
      IF(IHEAD.NE.ITAIL) GO TO 1
      IF(IHEAD.EQ.0) GO TO 1
      IFULL = 1
      RETURN
    1 IFULL = 0
C
C     IS QUEUE EMPTY?
C
      IF(ITAIL.NE.0) GO TO 2
      IHEAD = 1
      ITAIL = 1
C
C     STORE VALUE
C
    2 Q(ITAIL) = VAL
C
C     DO WE WRAP AROUND?
C
      IF(ITAIL-N) 3,4,3
    3 ITAIL = ITAIL+1
      RETURN
    4 ITAIL = 1
      RETURN
      END
```

associated pointers. The programmer should, of course, check the error indicators returned by the subroutines after each CALL, and take appropriate action if necessary.

In a program containing a number of arrays used as queues, the necessity of maintaining pointers could become cumbersome. In that case, with slight modification the queue array can be defined so that the first two locations contain

TABLE 3.2
Subroutine to Retrieve a Value from a Queue (QUEGET)

```
      SUBROUTINE QUEGET(Q,VAL,IHEAD,ITAIL,N,IEMPTY)
C
C     ARGUMENTS ARE THE SAME AS QUEPUT, EXCEPT THAT IF
C     QUEUE IS EMPTY, IEMPTY RETURNS A 1.
C     OTHERWISE, IEMPTY = 0 AND VAL RETURNS A VALUE.
C
      DIMENSION Q(N)
C
C     IS QUEUE EMPTY?
C
      IF(ITAIL.NE.0) GO TO 1
      IEMPTY = 1
      RETURN
    1 IEMPTY = 0
      VAL = Q(IHEAD)
C
C     DO WE WRAP AROUND TO SET HEAD POINTER?
C
      IF(IHEAD-N) 2,3,2
    2 IHEAD = IHEAD+1
      GO TO 4
    3 IHEAD = 1
C
C     IS QUEUE EMPTY NOW?
C
    4 IF(IHEAD.NE.ITAIL) RETURN
      ITAIL = 0
      IHEAD = 0
      RETURN
      END
```

the head and tail indicators. Some minor changes in the subroutine coding would be needed, but it would eliminate the need for keeping the pointers separately and passing them as arguments.

A moderate additional change to the queue subroutines would allow a value to be entered at or removed from either end of the storage array. This modified form of queue is known as a double-ended queue or "deque." The same pair of subroutines could then maintain either a queue or a stack, depending on which end was used for adding and which for deleting. In fact, the same storage array can serve as either, depending only on the rules used in inserting and deleting.

Just as with SIMSAL's ORDER array, stack and queue elements may be made up of more than a single element. In this case, the actual datum stored in a stack or queue might itself be a pointer to the location where the actual values are stored. If ORDER in SIMSAL were a stack or queue instead of a sequentially processed array, its pointers would be of that sort. The elements that are moved around in storage — ORDER's values — are not the actual values of interest, but simply an indication as to where they can be found.

One final point that may be made about queues and stacks is that, because they are both retained in Fortran arrays, they can be processed as any array. For example, their contents may be printed out directly without reference to the head and tail pointers. The only feature that distinguishes a stack or queue from an ordinary array is the procedure used to insert and remove; aside from that, the information is as directly accessible as any array.

Linked Lists

Stacks and queues have the advantage of holding information in a fixed sequence, and allowing recovery of individual items as a function of their storage order. Although they are very useful data structures for many kinds of operations, they lack flexibility. It is impossible to insert items into the middle of the array without a cumbersome process of moving all elements either above or below the new item. The linked list overcomes this difficulty and introduces an extremely flexible and powerful data organization.

In a stack or queue, a pointer indicated the location of the next item to be recovered and, in the queue, the place to store the next element. A linked list carries the concept of the pointer to the level of the individual data item itself. Each element in a linked list contains two segments — the data and a pointer to the next sequential item. Figure 3.2 illustrates a linked list schematically. Each item in the list is shown as a pair of data cells, one called the "datum" and the other the "pointer." Together, the two are called a "cell," a "data element," or sometimes a "node."

Adding an element to a linked list involves storing the new datum in the first part of a cell, setting the pointer to the following element, and changing the pointer on the preceding node to indicate the new element. Figure 3.3a illustrates the organization of the list after an item is added to it. The new datum has the value HEN, and was inserted between CAT and DOG.

In order to delete an element from a linked list, only a single pointer need be changed — that of the preceding cell. Schematically, after deleting DOG, the list in Figure 3.3a appears in Figure 3.3b. Note that the deleted element still shows a pointer to COW; but because DOG can never be reached (there is no pointer to it), its pointer is meaningless.

A linked list is easily maintained in a pair of Fortran arrays, one containing the data values and the other the pointers. There is no particular reason, of course, why two arrays are needed. Two columns of a two-dimensional array could serve just as well, as could adjacent locations in a single array. In the latter case, it is

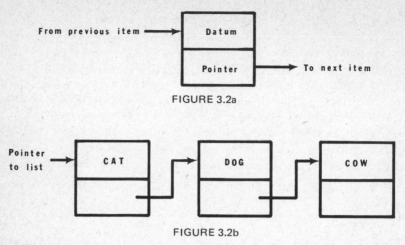

FIGURE 3.2a

FIGURE 3.2b

FIGURE 3.2 (a) Schematic representation of a single cell in a linked list. (b) A linked list containing three elements.

usually advisable to use one location as the datum and the next succeeding location for the pointer; location *n* is a datum and location *n* + 1 is its pointer.

With two arrays, assume that the data are in LIST and the pointers in LPOINT. Then the linked list in Figure 3.2 might appear as in Figure 3.4. Note the value of the pointer in the last entry; the usual procedure is to mark the end of the list by some special pointer value, often zero or a negative number. Using a zero as the end of list indicator allows negative values to be used as a part of the data or for other purposes. Because the example data here will be simple and always positive, a negative value will suffice for our purposes and will set off the marker value clearly.

Figures 3.5 and 3.6 illustrate the contents of the list arrays after the operations shown in Figures 3.3a and 3.3b, respectively.

If another insertion is to be performed on the list in Figure 3.6, there are two options as to where to place the new item. It can be stored in Location 5, immediately following HEN. More efficient use of the list array would be accomplished, however, by inserting a new element into a space left vacant by a previous deletion. In this case, the new item would be stored in Location 2, because DOG is no longer on the list.

The way to arrange for efficient storage is to maintain a second list, usually called the "availability" or "free list" in the same array. This list functions as a stack; whenever an item is deleted, its location is placed on the availability list. When a new item is to be stored, the first location on the free list is used.

In programming a list structure, the arrays are first initialized so that all locations are on the availability list and the head of list pointer is set to zero, indicating an empty list. A second pointer is maintained to the head of the free

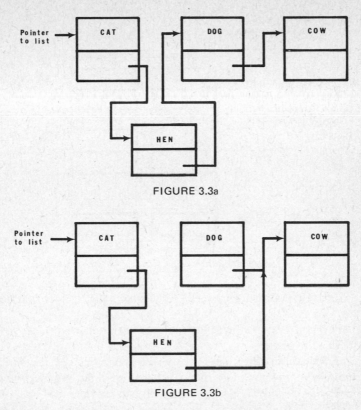

FIGURE 3.3a

FIGURE 3.3b

FIGURE 3.3   (a) The list after inserting a new item. (b) The list after deleting an item.

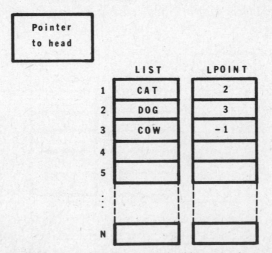

FIGURE 3.4   A linked list contained in a pair of arrays.

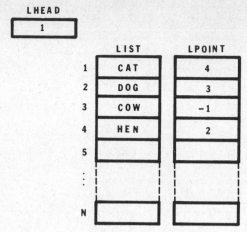

FIGURE 3.5   A list after one insertion.

list, and it is changed whenever an item is added or deleted. After the initialization, and before the first insertion, a 500-element list array might look as indicated in Figure 3.7.

After the initial items are stored, the contents of the array appear as in Figure 3.8. (Compare this figure with Figure 3.5; they are the same except for the availability list.) After DOG is deleted, the list appears as in Figure 3.9. Note that the availability pointer now dictates Location 2 for the next insertion. When Location 2 is used, its pointer value (5) becomes the new value for the start of the free list, and processing continues. Figure 3.9 contains the same list as does Figure 3.6, with the availability list added.

A linked list is an extremely useful and widely employed data structure. It offers the flexibility of easy insertion and deletion without requiring extensive

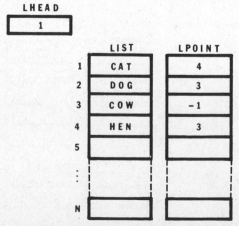

FIGURE 3.6   The same list after a deletion.

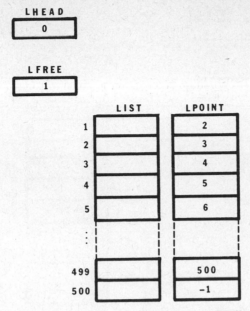

FIGURE 3.7 A list after initialization of the free list.

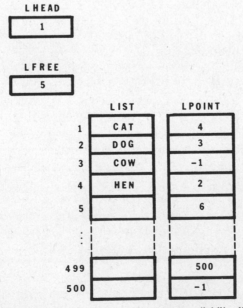

FIGURE 3.8 The list from Figure 3.5 with an availability list added.

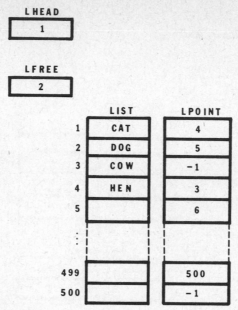

FIGURE 3.9   The list from Figure 3.6 with an availability list added.

changes in the organization. As we have noted with pointers, stacks, and queues, moreover, the data element in a list can easily be a pointer itself, thus allowing the list to indicate items not in the list itself.

But the flexibility and power of the list is purchased at the cost of doubling the total amount of storage required. Each data value requires two locations, one for the datum and another for the pointer. When the data and pointers assume only relatively small values, they can be placed in the same location through a packing operation, such as that discussed later in this chapter, but that also involves the added cost of packing and unpacking.

The linked list is such a versatile data structure that several programming languages have been developed using it as the primitive data structure, just as Fortran uses the array. For example, nearly all of the contemporary models of cognitive processes are programmed in the list processing language LISP or one of its dialects, which is discussed in Chapter 9.

Many higher level programming or computing science texts present algorithms for dealing with lists. The coding of them is probably best handled by a small set of subroutines, following the algorithms given in a good source. We will not develop the algorithms and code in detail; the reader should locate a set of algorithms, study them, and write the code her- or himself. Day's (1972) little book is an excellent and concise introduction to many Fortran programming techniques and deals with all of the data structures discussed in this chapter crisply and concisely, with examples in Fortran. Booth and Chien (1974) offer a thorough discussion of data structures and present their algorithms as flow-charts.

Other types of lists Before we address the topic of trees, we should mention two additional varieties of linked lists. A circular list is one where the pointer of the last element indicates the first item in the list. The list thus becomes endless and is sometimes called a "ring." The advantage of a circular list is particularly evident in searching, an operation to be discussed in Chapter 4. In effect, it enables a search to begin at any location on the list, because the first item can be reached from the last as well as from the first item pointer.

A second variety of list is the doubly linked list. In this form of list, each cell contains a datum and two pointers. One pointer designates the following item just as in the singly linked list and the other indicates the preceding item. The two pointers, often called the "forward" and "backward pointers," allow a list to be traversed in either direction. If, in addition, the list is circular, then any item can be reached from any other and going in either direction.

A major advantage of the doubly linked list is gained in the deletion operation. In order to delete an item, the following steps must be accomplished:

1. Locate its predecessor.
2. Change the predecessor's pointer to indicate the deleted element's successor.
3. Add the deleted element to the free list.

The difficulty is in Step 1. A predecessor can be recognized only because its pointer indicates the cell to be deleted, and an inefficient sequential search must often be employed to find that entry in a list. With a doubly linked list, a search is not required because the location of the preceding item is contained within the data element itself.

Trees

It is but a small step from the linked list to a tree. In a tree, each element has a datum and two (or more) pointers, each indicating a succeeding entry. A tree is therefore a structure where each element has two (or more) successors. A tree with exactly two pointers for each data entry (and thus two successors) is known as a "binary tree" or "bitree."

In a tree, data elements are almost universally called nodes. The succeeding elements are other nodes, and the connections between nodes are usually called "branches."

SIMSAL uses a tree as its subject's memory. The tree was selected because it parallels what is known of human memory, and because processing is facilitated by such a structure. The subject's data organization must be flexible so that it can grow as the subject "learns," it must be amenable to a random ordering of inputs and retrievals and it must hold data in an easily searched form. A tree is ideal for all of those demands. Indeed, trees are regularly employed when there is a large set of data, and many searches, additions, and deletions are involved. This is often the case in simulations as well as in such data processing applications as information retrieval, airline reservation systems, and so forth.

The SIMSAL tree has four segments in each node, two pointers and two data elements. The tree is contained in a 120 X 4 array called, appropriately, TREE. The number of rows in the array was established by determining the maximum storage that could reasonably be required, under the worst experimental conditions. The four columns of each row represent a single node. The tree is binary, with the two pointers representing what are called the "correct" and "error" branches.

SIMSAL's unit is the letter, and each letter has four properties. In the tree, each node stores a letter, and the four columns of TREE hold the properties. In terms of our present discussion, two of the properties are data values and the other two are pointers. The first two columns of each TREE row contain data values. Column 1 holds a single alphameric character from a syllable. Column 2 indicates the position of the letter in the three-letter syllable. An entry of D,1 in Columns 1 and 2 therefore identifies a letter D occurring in the first position in a syllable. Columns 3 and 4 are pointers to successor nodes the meaning of which can best be seen in an illustration.

Figure 3.10 shows a tree that resulted from a SIMSAL run, drawn schematically. The contents of the array TREE appear in Figure 3.11. This particular tree resulted from learning the list:

Syllable	Response
ABC	1
DEF	2
GHI	3
JKL	4

Apparently, the first syllable presented to SIMSAL was DEF, because the first node formed, the root of the tree, contains the letter "D." The entries in the first row of TREE, the contents of the first node, are interpreted as follows:

1. There is a "D" in Position 1 of the syllable.
2. When searching the tree for a response, if the first letter of the syllable is "D," then look in Node 2 for the next letter (this is the "correct" branch).
3. If the first letter is not "D," then try Node 3 next (the "error" branch).

At the end of every branch in a tree is a final node, usually called "terminal node." SIMSAL's tree has two kinds of terminal nodes, one holding a response and the other reserved for future expansion if needed. Node 16 in Figures 3.10 and 3.11 is a response terminal. A response node is easily identified; it is empty

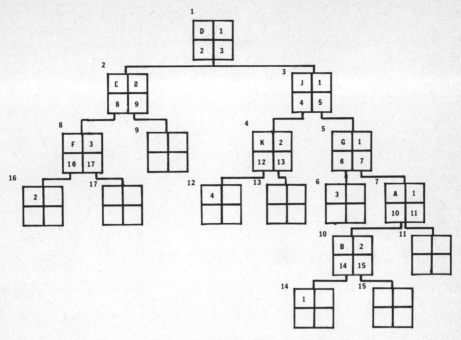

FIGURE 3.10   A tree from SIMSAL's memory.

except for Column 1. The value in Column 1 is the response for the syllable stored in the branch above the terminal.

The other kind of terminal in the tree is illustrated by Node 9, and it is completely empty. Although a response terminal can occur only at the end of a "correct" branch, an empty node will be found by tracing an "error" branch. An empty node is built whenever SIMSAL learns a letter; indeed learning generally establishes two nodes. A "correct" node is used to store the response, whereas the empty terminal is reserved for later use. For example, Node 9 would have been used had there been another syllable in the list the first letter of which was "D." In that case, the test of Node 2 ("Is 'E' the second letter?") would have failed. A new node would then have been formed in Row 9 containing an alternative letter for Position 2 in a syllable beginning with "D."

When SIMSAL's subject is presented with a syllable, it searches the tree for a response. By following the leftmost branch of the tree to its terminus, the entire syllable can be spelled, with the last node holding the response. It is interesting to note that SIMSAL learned all three of the letters in "DEF" although, because the four syllables in the list are completely unique, only the first letter is needed to discriminate between any two. This phenomenon of learning more than necessary is known as "overlearning." The amount of overlearning is influenced

Row (node)	Column 1	Column 2	Column 3	Column 4
1	D	1	2	3
2	E	2	8	9
3	J	1	4	5
4	K	2	12	13
5	G	1	6	7
6	3			
7	A	1	10	11
8	F	3	16	17
9				
10	B	2	14	15
11				
12	4			
13				
14	1			
15				
16	2			
17				
.				
.				
.				
120				

FIGURE 3.11   The array TREE from SIMSAL, showing the tree in Figure 3.10.

by one of the parameters input to the program. (In this example, the probability of overlearning was set at .50.)

The search algorithm is discussed in detail in Chapter 4, but a brief sketch here illustrates using the tree. The search begins by testing the first node against the first letter of the stimulus. If there is a match, the search proceeds to the node indicated by the "correct" branch (Column 3). Whenever there is a match, the "correct" (left) branch of the tree is followed until a terminal node is found. Then the response in Column 1 is made.

When a mismatch occurs the next node tested is indicated by the "error" branch (Column 4). If a complete righthand ("error") branch is traversed to an empty node, SIMSAL makes a random guess at the response.

When the list of syllables is high in intralist similarity (for example, many syllables can be differentiated only by comparing all three letters), the tree is a great deal "fuller." In that case, many new nodes are formed and learning the list requires more trials. An example of such a full tree is shown in Figure 3.12. The syllable beginning at the root of the tree is DEF and its response is 2. The reader may find it interesting and informative to trace the other seven syllables and responses in this tree of 33 nodes.

Adding a new node to SIMSAL's tree is reasonably simple. A node can be created only after a response has been made, and during the course of tracing

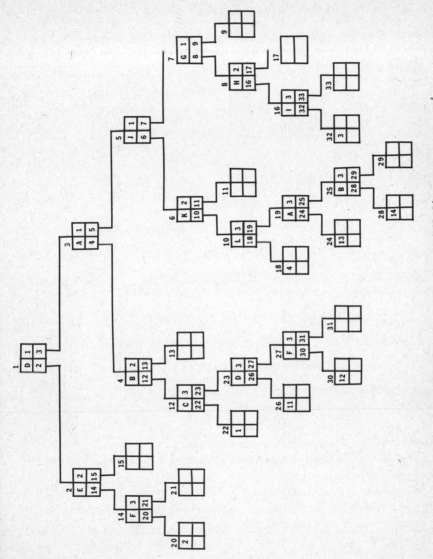

FIGURE 3.12 A fuller tree from SIMSAL's memory.

through the tree to respond, SIMSAL sets several necessary pointers. In particular,

IZ: indicates which position in the syllable (1, 2, or 3) has shown a mismatch between the stimulus and the syllable being traced in the tree.

IPOINT: the next available row in TREE, that is, the node to be created.

I1: the last (highest numbered) occupied node.

The stimulus is contained in the three-element array STIM and the correct response is in ICORR. The actual node building statements are these:

$$TREE(IPOINT,2) = IZ$$

This stores the position of the letter.

$$TREE(IPOINT,1) = STIM(IZ)$$

This stores the character from the syllable.

$$TREE(IPOINT,3) = I1+1$$

$$TREE(IPOINT,4) = I1+2$$

These statements store the correct and error pointers, indicating that the next two available locations in TREE are to be used for the nodes.

$$TREE(I1+1,1) = ICORR$$

This stores the correct response in a terminal node on the left branch.

$$TREE(I1+2,1) = 0$$

This establishes an empty "error" node.

$$I1 = I1+2$$

This advances the pointer to the last node used.

In Chapter 4 we discuss several other important tree operations, including searching and maintaining trees in specific orders.

So far, we have discussed only binary trees, those in which each node leads to exactly two additional nodes. In principle, a node can have any number of successors. In such a case, the programming is somewhat more complex; usually it is necessary to maintain a count of the number of successors as a part of each node. In addition, the Fortran coding is best accomplished by using a single-dimensional array. That procedure avoids having to allocate a number of columns equal to the largest number of successor nodes that can be anticipated. The sketch in Figure 3.13 illustrates a node with three successors in a one-dimensional array. This example assumes that there is but one datum in each node. The second entry in the node, located at the node address+1, is the number of successor nodes, and their pointers are located in the succeeding locations.

The maintenance of a generalized tree with multiple branches is a complex

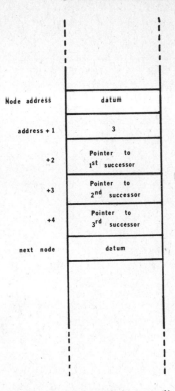

Node address	datum
address + 1	3
+2	Pointer to 1st successor
+3	Pointer to 2nd successor
+4	Pointer to 3rd successor
next node	datum

FIGURE 3.13   A generalized tree node in a one dimensional array.

matter, especially if nodes are added and deleted frequently during the operation of the program. In SIMSAL, nodes were never deleted from the tree. If they were, some additional "housekeeping" operations would be required to establish a "free" list. The management of additions and deletions in trees is discussed in Chapter 4, along with a number of other operations.

With the discussion of trees, we complete our overview of the most commonly used data structures in simulation programming. As should be clear, not all simulation programs use all of these procedures. Indeed, some of the data structures are not represented by our examples.

STORAGE MANAGEMENT IN FORTRAN

In this section, we shall discuss two topics in Fortran programming — the use of declarations in managing and allocating storage, and the process of packing several data elements into a single location and unpacking them to obtain the correct values. These two topics are technical. They have very little to do with the actual development of simulation programs but are aids in Fortran programming.

Fortran Declarations

Most Fortran programmers are familiar with the declarations required in allocating storage; DIMENSION, COMMON, EQUIVALENCE, and the several "type" declarations, such as INTEGER and REAL. This section offers a few comments and observations that may make programming easier, and perhaps more elegant, and that facilitate debugging.

Aside from FORMAT statements, no single section of a Fortran program offers a more fertile ground for careless errors than the declarations. Many program bugs can often be traced to such errors as different variable types between main program and a subroutine, dimensions too small so that subscripts advance beyond the array into some other storage area, arrays of different sizes between parts of the program and subroutines, incorrectly overlapping arrays because of errors in EQUIVALENCE statements, and so forth.

Here, in list form, are some suggestions for the programmer. Even the author does not always follow his own advice — some of these suggestions are contradicted in the example programs:

1. Order the declarations in the same way in all routines. In the examples, the order is always type statements, followed by DIMENSION, COMMON, EQUIVALENCE, and finally DATA.

2. Within each declaration, arrange the variable names in alphabetical order, unless there is good reason not to do so (and some reasons are presented in Chapter 6).

3. Avoid type statements unless inconvenient. It is always much easier to remember the Fortran rule for typing by first letters (I-N are INTEGER) than to run the risk of forgetting which variable is what type. In programs with logical variables, begin them all with the same letter (L, for example).

4. Use only the DIMENSION statement for all array declarations. It is easier to look only at the DIMENSION statements to track down errors than to inspect the type, COMMON, and other statements as well.

5. Unless space is at a premium, allow the precision of variables to be defined by the compiler; that is, try to avoid INTEGER*2 or DOUBLE PRECISION kinds of statements.

6. EQUIVALENCE statements can be useful but should be used only when necessary to conserve space or when an array is to be referenced by both single and multiple subscripts.

*Packing and Unpacking

Fortran normally assigns a single value to each of its variables or array locations. Packing refers to placing more than one value in a single location; unpacking is the retrieving of the packed values.

Packing and unpacking procedures are often employed in alphabetic problems but are useful in other applications as well. Packing is a valuable technique for conserving space; if a large number of locations are required for storing relatively small arithmetic values, or if a large amount of alphabetic data is being processed, only a small amount of each computer word is used to store the data and the remainder of the word is wasted.

The problem is especially conspicuous in alphabetic processing. Reading al phabetic data with an A1 FORMAT specification results in storing a single alphameric character in each location. On most computer systems, however, a computer word is capable of storing at least four characters, and some computers allow up to 10 characters per computer word. Clearly, a single character per computer word results in wasting 75–90% of the available space.

Reading alphabetic data with an A4 specification results in more efficient use of storage. In that case, the data are "packed" four characters per word as they are read. The problem arises when the program must process individual characters from packed storage. Fortran permits the comparison of storage locations with the IF statement, but it compares the entire word. If a comparison of single characters is required, the IF cannot handle the problem when more than one character is present; the words must be unpacked first.

Packing of storage locations can also be very useful in programming for the data structures discussed previously. An important element in all of the structures is the pointer which is a part of each list element or tree node. The pointer is usually a comparatively small arithmetic value because it gives only another row number. In the generalized tree, the count of the number of successor nodes is also a small value. Packing pointers and counters can often conserve a surprising amount of storage, at the cost of usually fairly simple packing/unpacking operations.

Many computer centers have developed generalized pack/unpack routines for their users. If one is not available, either of two general strategies can be followed in developing the procedures.

A simple pack/unpack algorithm takes advantage of the variable precision option available in some Fortran compilers. In particular, the declaration

$$\text{LOGICAL} * 1$$

is permitted by some Fortran implementations. (This procedure has been tested on the IBM 360/370 series and the UNIVAC 70/46 compilers.) Because a LOGICAL variable typically is used for but a single binary digit – interpreted as .TRUE. or .FALSE. – only a single 8-bit character need be allocated for each value.

Using a LOGICAL*1 array and overlapping it with a variable that contains packed characters, it is possible to extract single characters by referencing an element of the LOGICAL array. Figure 3.14 shows the overlapping storage arrangement. A Fortran subroutine for the pack/unpack operation is presented in Table 3.3.[1] A similar procedure is presented by Hanson (1974).

---

[1] This subroutine was originally programmed by Richard M. Steere.

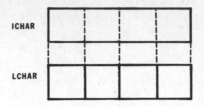

Declarations to obtain the overlap:

INTEGER*4 ICHAR
LOGICAL*1 LCHAR (4)
EQUIVALENCE (ICHAR, LCHAR(1))

FIGURE 3.14   Overlapping an array and an integer variable to allow packing and unpacking.

In the event that the procedure in Table 3.3 violates the rules of the local Fortran compiler, and assuming that a pack/unpack routine is not available in the local library, a second algorithm can be employed. The key to packing and unpacking is the shift operation. Someone familiar with assembly programming can easily write a routine using the assembly shift commands; but the same result often can be accomplished with standard Fortran code. Only the general procedure is sketched here because the exact operations depend on the word length of the computer being used.

If single-digit numbers are to be packed, they can be multiplied by successive powers of 10 and added together. That is, if the numbers 1, 3, 5, and 7 are to be packed into a single value, then the operation

$$1*1000 + 3*100 + 5*10 + 7 = 1357$$

does nicely. If the numbers are at most two digits, then multiplication by successive powers of 100 suffice. For example, to pack 15 and 23, we make the following computation:

$$15*100 + 23 = 15*100**1 + 23*100**0 = 1523$$

Care must be taken to insure that the resulting sum in packing does not exceed the maximum allowed for integer numbers.

The unpacking operation is most conveniently programmed by using the standard MØD function in Fortran. (The MØD or modulo function of X,Y is the remainder when X is divided by Y.) If, for example, the four digits 1357 have been packed into IPACK, then the following Fortran statements can unpack IPACK into the four-element array IUPACK.

```
        DO 100 I = 1,4
        IBACK = 5-I
        IUPACK(IBACK) = MØD(IPACK,10)
100  IPACK = IPACK/10
```

TABLE 3.3
A Fortran Pack/Unpack Routine Using a LOGICAL∗1 Equivalence Algorithm (PACK)

```
      SUBROUTINE PACK(IWRD,ICHAR,IB)
C
C     A PACK/UNPACK ROUTINE USING A LOGICAL*1
C     EQUIVALENCE ALGORITHM.
C
      INTEGER*4 IWRD,NOTH,JWRD,ICHAR(4),IW(4)
      LOGICAL*1 BYTE(4),BYTE1(16)
      EQUIVALENCE (BYTE(1),JWRD),(BYTE1(1),IW(1))
      DATA NOTH/4H    /
C
C     IF IB IS NEGATIVE OR ZERO, UNPACK IWRD INTO ICHAR
.C
      IF(IB) 10,10,20
   10 JWRD = IWRD
      DO 11 I = 1,4
   11 IW(I) = NOTH
      K = 0
      DO 12 I = 1,13,4
      K=K+1
      BYTE1(I) = BYTE(K)
   12 CONTINUE
      DO 13 I = 1,4
   13 ICHAR(I) = IW(I)
      RETURN
C
C     SWITCH IS POSITIVE. PACK ICHAR INTO IWRD.
C
   20 DO 21 I = 1,4
   21 IW(I) = ICHAR(I)
      K = 0
      DO 22 I = 1,13,4
      K = K+1
      BYTE(K) = BYTE1(I)
   22 CONTINUE
      IWRD = JWRD
      RETURN
      END
```

The first value unpacked by the routine is IUPACK(4), the least significant digit. The first MØD operation results in the computation:

$$MØD(1357,10) = 7$$

which is stored as IUPACK(4). IPACK is then divided by 10 and returned to IPACK. Note that the division is an INTEGER computation, so that the new value of IPACK is 135. The operation then repeats, with the result

$$MØD(135,10) = 5$$

being stored as IUPACK(3). When the routine terminates, the array IUPACK contains

IUPACK(1)   1

IUPACK(2)   3

IUPACK(3)   5

IUPACK(4)   7

The integer division operation is used to accomplish a right shift, as done in assembly programming, after the rightmost digit in IPACK is "stripped off" by the MØD operation.

If the values were originally packed by powers of 100, then the modulus 10 must be changed to 100 in both the MØD reference and in the integer division.

The packing procedure may be generalized to dealing with characters by changing the scaling factor (10 or 100 in these examples) so that the resulting multiplication shifts a character far enough to the "left" in the sum to allow the next character to be added to the "right" or least significant part of the value.

The unpacking operation must be modified in the same way, so that a single character may be removed from the "right" of the packed word, and then the word shifted right by an integer division.

Although this discussion of packing and unpacking has been generalized, it is hoped it can provide a starting point for developing a pack/unpack function that can be used on any computer system.

EXERCISES

3.1 Draw a flowchart for a function that pops a stack. The array containing the stack should be stored in COMMON, the argument to the function should be a stack pointer, and the function value should be the element returned.

3.2 Write the Fortran FUNCTION corresponding to the flowchart in Exercise 3.1.

3.3 Write a subroutine that will initialize a linked list. The name of the array to contain the list should be the argument to the subroutine. You may wish the routine to return the value of the pointer.

3.4 Write a subroutine called NUHEAD to enter a new value at the head of an established list contained in an array named in an argument.

3.5 Write a subroutine named NUTAIL to accomplish the same goal as NUHEAD in Exercise 3.4, except that it adds a new tail.

3.6 Write a subroutine (NUMID) that inserts a new element into the middle of a linked list stored in an argument array. Be sure that you tell the subroutine where (that is, after which element) the new entry belongs.

3.7 Write a generalized delete subroutine to remove elements from any position on a linked list. Be careful — the head and the tail are slightly different than an item in the middle. Arguments to the subroutine should be a pointer to the item to be deleted and the name of the list array.

3.8 Write a subroutine to exchange two elements in a linked list. Again, the arguments should be the list array and a pointer to the item to be exchanged with its successor.

3.9 Write a function subprogram that accepts three arguments and uses them as a "stimulus" to produce a "response" stored in a terminal node in the tree described for SIMSAL.

*3.10 Modify the subroutine written for Exercise 3.7 so that it deals with a doubly linked list.

3.11 Suppose that the urban growth simulation deals with nine different land use types — single dwellings, apartments, highrise units, ghetto, business, factory, recreation, unbuildable (for example, rivers), and vacant space. If the needs of a growing city are met in a fixed priority order, then a stack could be used to hold those priorities. Write a subroutine to initialize the priority stack by reading an input series of property designations. Then write a function which, when called with any dummy argument, returns as its value the next priority item.

*3.12 Write a subroutine named UPACK which uses the MØD function to unpack a computer word into an array, each element containing a single character.

SUGGESTED READINGS

Booth, T. L., & Chien, Y. T. *Computing: Fundamentals and applications.* Santa Barbara, Calif.: Hamilton, 1974. This book is an excellent general text and can well be a reference in many programming applications. Of particular note is the extended coverage given to data structures and their use. Many algorithms are presented as machine-independent flowcharts.

Day, A. C. *Fortran techniques: With special reference to non-numerical applications.* Cambridge, England: Cambridge University Press, 1972. This slim volume is a masterpiece of conciseness and lucidity. Never slighting a subject, the author covers the topics of this chapter and the next, as well as numerous others, in a fashion that should serve as a model for any kind of technical writing.

Harrison, M. C. *Data-structures and programming.* Glenview, Ill.: Scott, Foresman, 1973. This high-level textbook is difficult going for social and behavioral scientists but is worth the trouble if a good coverage of the field is needed. It is a text for computing science courses in data structures.

Sherman, P. M. *Techniques in computer programming.* Englewood Cliffs, N. J.: Prentice-Hall, 1970. Chapter 12 contains a discussion covering much of the material of this chapter, but with a slant toward alphameric processing. Chapter 13 deals with storage allocation in some detail and is worth investigating when confronted with a large program.

4
Working with Data Structures

Depending on the demands of the conceptual model, simulation programs are called on to execute a wide variety of algorithms. Although many are straightforward and others are idiosyncratic to a particular problem, a few operations are encountered in many different kinds of programs. This chapter is devoted to one class of these frequently found algorithms, those dealing with the data structures presented in Chapter 3. The operations of sorting and searching occupy the bulk of this chapter, with a few less common procedures receiving somewhat less attention. In Chapter 5 we discuss another large group of algorithms; those for generating, testing, and using random numbers.

Sorting refers to arranging data values in either ascending or descending sequence based on their numeric or alphabetic order. Searching is the process of scanning a data structure to locate some particular item. Sort and search procedures are among the most thoroughly investigated topics in computer science, and it is possible for us to present only some of the highlights of this vast field. For additional detail, a wide variety of books and technical papers deal with sorting and searching; some of them are listed in the Suggested Readings for this chapter.

SORTING

There are a number of reasons for a simulation programmer to employ a sort procedure. For example, it may be desirable to print lists of items from smallest to largest. In some models, the logic may require that data be processed in a particular order — alphabetically, perhaps. In another case, the simulation program may compute various statistics on some results of the simulation; computing a median, for example, virtually requires that the data be at least partially sorted. But perhaps the major reason for using sorts in simulation writing is that having ordered data expedites search procedures. If a search is invoked frequently, it is often best to have the data in a sorted array so that the most efficient searches may be employed.

Outside of simulation programming, many data processing and record keeping procedures use sorts extensively. Because of the large amount of sorting done in commercial and business data processing, a great deal of attention has been paid to the development of efficient sort algorithms.

Only a few of the many sorts can be presented here. Some deal primarily with external media, such as tapes and disks. As in Chapter 3, we are concerned here only with sorting data that are "in core." Even with that restriction, there are many algorithms remaining to be considered. We discuss the most common, pointing out their advantages and disadvantages. Other procedures can be found by consulting the references in the Suggested Readings; the Knuth (1973) and Martin (1971) entries are particularly notable and quite exhaustive.

Library routines. Every computer center has a library of programs available to its users. Often a very efficient sort routine can be found there – computer manufacturers like to tout the efficiency of their sorts in advertising and sales meetings. A little time spent with a library manual often can save a lot of programmer effort, especially when very large arrays are involved or when external devices are required.

Exchange Sorts

The first sorting algorithm is also the easiest to understand and program. Although inefficient for more than about a dozen items, it provides a good introduction to sorting procedures.

The simple exchange sort can be described easily; in a one-dimensional array of n items, start with the first two. If they are in the correct order, that is, the first is smaller than the second, do nothing and go on to the second and third items. If the first pair is out of order, interchange them and then proceed to the next pair. Continue through the data until all pairs, ending with the $(n-1)$th and nth items, have been compared and interchanged if necessary. Then start again with the pair in Positions 1 and 2 and repeat the entire procedure until one complete pass through the array is made with no interchanges. At that point, the array is sorted.

As an example of this sort, consider the data shown in Figure 4.1a. The first pass through the array is represented by Figure 4.1b, where interchanges are indicated by arrows. The second pass through the array is shown in Figure 4.1c. Note that as the procedure advances through the array, the smaller values move upward while the larger move downward. This progressive movement is caused by the exchanges of adjacent items; hence the name of the sort procedure. At

Position	Value				
1	10	10	10	10	10
2	18	18	5	5	5
3	5	5	18	3	3
4	3	3	3	18	11
5	11	11	11	11	18

(a) Before sort   **(b) The first pass**

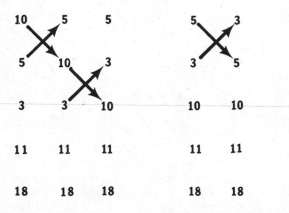

(c) The second pass   **(d) The fourth and final pass**

FIGURE 4.1 The contents of an array: before, during, and after an exchange sort. (a) Before sort. (b) The first pass. (c) The second pass. (d) The fourth and final pass.

the end of the third pass through the data (Figure 4.1d), the array is in order; the next pass will have no interchanges and the sort will be complete.

On each scan through the data array, the largest remaining item is moved to the bottom of the unsorted part of the data. For this reason, after the first pass, the largest element is in the nth position; on the second pass, the next-largest in the $(n-1)$th place, and so forth. Once these elements have reached their correct positions, there is no need to look at them again. On the first pass, therefore, the comparison must be made for items n and $n-1$. On the next pass, however, item n can be ignored, because it is the largest, and the deepest positions in the array to be compared are $n-1$ and $n-2$.

The flowchart in Figure 4.2 defines the exchange sort. The data to be sorted are stored in the array X, and N is the number of data values present. NTOP indicates the last position in the array that must be compared; its value is decremented after each pass through the data array. The variable ISWAP is used as a flag indicating whether an interchange has been made. It is set to zero at the

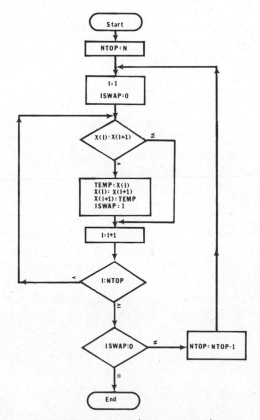

FIGURE 4.2 An exchange sort routine.

start of a pass and changed to 1 when a swap occurs. If a pass is completed without the flag having been "raised," the sort is finished.

Bubble sort. A slight modification of the simple exchange results in a more efficient procedure known as the bubble sort. In this algorithm, when an exchange is made, the direction of the scan through the data array is reversed so that the just located small value is bubbled up toward the top of the array until its proper location is found. Then the downward scan through the array continues from where it stopped. Apart from that modification, the bubble sort is identical to the exchange.

Shell sort. Another version of the exchange sort is the Shell sort (Boothroyd, 1963; Shell, 1959). The Shell sort provides a considerable improvement in efficiency over either the exchange or the bubble procedure. The critical element in the Shell sort is the comparison of items located some distance apart in the array, rather than just adjacent pairs. The procedure has the advantage of moving items closer to their final positions when they are interchanged. In the Shell sort, comparisons are made between elements located k positions apart in the array. Therefore, the comparison is always between x_i and x_{i+k}. In both the exchange and the bubble sorts, $k = 1$ for all passes through the array. In the Shell procedure, k is generally set initially at the largest power of 2 that is less than n; thus

$$2^k < n \leqslant 2^{k+1}$$

where n is the number of items in the array. Once k is selected, a pass is made through the data, generally using the bubble algorithm. After that pass, k is divided by 2 and the process repeats until, on the last cycle through the array, $k = 1$ and the procedure is an ordinary bubble sort.

The Shell algorithm is probably the most widely used and best known of the exchange sorts. A convenient version of it is presented as SUBROUTINE SHELL in Table 4.1.

All of the several varieties of exchange sorts described above have the advantage of being relatively easy to remember and code. They allow an array to be sorted "in place," with no additional storage required except for a temporary location used during an interchange. In addition, they function best when the number of items in the array is relatively small – generally less than about 20 elements. They are inefficient for large arrays, or when the data are on disk or tape.

Distributive Sorts

A second general variety of sort procedure is the distributive algorithm. There are several variations on the distributive theme but all divide the data initially into a few broad categories and then proceed to divide each subgroup into successively smaller and smaller segments until the data are sorted.

TABLE 4.1
A Shell Sort Subroutine

```
      SUBROUTINE SHELL(X,N)
C
C     SORTS THE N ELEMENTS IN THE ARRAY X INTO ASCENDING ORDER.
C
C     BASED ON THE ALGORITHM DESCRIBED IN SHELL, D. L. A HIGH
C     SPEED SORTING PROCEDURE. COMMUNICATIONS OF THE ACM,
C     1959, 2, 30-32.
C
      DIMENSION X(N)
      MID = N
    1 MID = MID/2
      IF(MID.LE.0) RETURN
      LIM = N-MID
      DO 2 J = 1,LIM
      IJ = J
    3 IM = IJ+MID
      IF(X(IM).GE.X(IJ)) GO TO 2
      SWAP = X(IJ)
      X(IJ) = X(IM)
      X(IM) = SWAP
      IJ = IJ-MID
      IF(IJ.GE.1) GO TO 3
    2 CONTINUE
      GO TO 1
      END
```

The sort begins with an estimate of the median of the data. The procedure used for the estimate is a major distinguishing feature of the several variants of the distributive algorithm. Once the estimate is computed, a first pass is made through the data, distributing the values into three groups: less than the estimated median, equal to the median, and greater than it. Each of the subsets is then individually submitted to the distributive sort, and so forth until the array has been partially sorted into several groups of 10–20 items each. Finally the subsets are individually sorted into proper order, generally with a bubble or Shell procedure.

Clearly, additional space is required for a distributive sort. Although the data generally remain in the array, a large collection of pointers must be maintained, indicating where the various subcategories begin and end. The complexity of the housekeeping makes the distributive sort considerably more complex to program. For a large array, however, a distributive sort is much more efficient. Booth and Chien (1974) present a good discussion and flowchart of one of the best known of the distributive sorts, the quicksort procedure. Details on other subvarieties can be found in Martin (1971) and Knuth (1973).

Sorting on List Structures

The simple linked list presents an ideal arrangement for maintaining a set of data in sorted order. The advantage is especially noticeable when the data must be kept sorted in the face of large numbers of insertions and deletions during the operation of the program.

In most cases, the best time to sort a list is when it is initially constructed. There are times, however, when that approach is not feasible and an existing linked list must be sorted. Knuth (1973, pp. 170–178) presents a procedure, known as the radix list sort, for just such a case. For our purposes here, we shall consider only the "sort while building" technique. Of course, it could be applied to an existing list too, simply by constructing a new list by taking elements one at a time from the existing list. Our procedure is called "sorting by insertion" and proceeds as follows.

The first datum value is placed in an array (call it LIST, for example) and two pointers (call them HEAD and TAIL) are set to indicate it. The HEAD pointer will always indicate the smallest value, and TAIL the largest.

Now a new item (INEW) is obtained to be inserted into the list. At this point there are three possibilities:

1. If INEW is less than LIST(HEAD), then INEW is inserted as the new head. It is stored at the first location on the free list, the HEAD pointer is set to it, and its pointer designates the previous HEAD.

2. If INEW is greater than LIST(TAIL), then it becomes the new tail. INEW is stored as designated by the free list, its pointer set to the end of list indicator,

the previous TAIL is made to point to INEW, and the availability pointer is adjusted.

3. If the new item is neither the new head nor the tail, then it must belong in the middle of the list. In order to find the proper location, a scan through the list is made. Starting with the pointer of LIST(HEAD), inspect the next item and so forth, until an entry larger than INEW is found. Then insert INEW preceding the just located item. Unless the list is doubly linked, take care to retain the location of the predecessor of each item to avoid having to trace through the list again to locate the proper predecessor for INEW.

When INEW has found its proper place in the list, the next value is obtained and the process repeats until all the values have been inserted.

If a great many searches of a sorted list are required, it may be advantageous to add a few additional steps to the insertion sort. In the discussion of searching ordered lists later in this chapter, we note what those modifications must accomplish.

An insertion sort is a highly efficient procedure when the items are to be maintained in order during frequent additions and deletions. It has the additional advantage that once an element is stored, it need never be moved, so there is no exchanging of data to be done. But, as usual, the price of advantage is some disadvantage. Clearly, a list structure requires more storage space than a simple array, unless, of course, the data values are so small that the value and pointer can be packed into the same location. A second disadvantage is the fact that a sequential search is often required to locate an item and, as we point out later, a sequential search is inefficient of computer time. Finally, the programming of a list structure is more complex than that for an ordinary array. However, in many cases in simulation programming, the ability to keep a list in order more than outweighs the disadvantages.

Wilde (1973) presents several useful algorithms for various list operations, including the insertion sort, as flowcharts.

Sorting in Trees

Tree structures are often used to store sorted data elements. When a tree is sorted, it is known as an "ordered tree." There is no reason, of course, that a tree must be ordered; SIMSAL's tree is not, and many simulation programs build unordered trees. Nevertheless, some tree operations, such as searching, are facilitated by having the data in order. In addition, ordering a tree is also an effective means of sorting, even if the data are not to remain in the tree except during the sort.

In an ordered binary tree, items less than a node are stored on its left-hand branch, and items greater than the node are stored on the right-hand branch.

Figure 4.3a shows an ordered tree containing a set of six alphameric items: ANT, CAT, COW, DOG, GOAT, and PIG. By following the left branch from any node, all of the preceding sorted items can be located. For example, the root node contains DOG, and all entries that precede DOG alphabetically are found on the lefthand branch. ANT, on the other hand, has no left-hand branch and it therefore precedes all of the items found on its right-hand branch. The same tree, stored as a set of arrays, is illustrated in Figure 4.3b.

Building an ordered tree.   In general, the sort by insertion routine is followed in constructing an ordered tree. The algorithm can be most easily described by the following outline. We shall assume that the arrays are as illustrated in Figure 4.3b and that available locations are stored on a free list, just as in a linked list.

1. Is the tree empty? If so, store the item in the first free location, set ROOT to point to it, and return for a new item.

2. If the tree is not empty, set a pointer (IPOINT) to the root.

3. Compare WORD(IPOINT) with the new item. If equal, then the new item is already in the tree. If the new item is less than WORD(IPOINT), go to Step 4; otherwise, go to Step 5.

4. We are now looking at the lefthand branch. Is the lefthand pointer of node IPOINT equal to −1? If not, set IPOINT to LBRNCH(IPOINT) and return to Step 3. Otherwise, insert the new item here at the end of this branch. Store the new item at the location given by the free list, adjust the free list pointer, and set LBRNCH(IPOINT) to the new location. Then get the next new item.

5. This is the righthand branch. Is the righthand pointer of node IPOINT equal to −1? If not, set IPOINT to RBRNCH(IPOINT) and return to Step 3. Otherwise, insert the new item at the location given by the free list, adjust the free list pointer, and set RBRNCH(IPOINT) to the new location. Return for the next item.

To illustrate the algorithm in action, let us construct the tree in Figure 4.3. Before the tree is built, the arrays are initialized; WORD and one of the pointers are set to zero, and the other pointer array (RBRNCH in this example) is used to link together a free list. This done, the first data value, DOG, is obtained. DOG is placed in Node 1, and the arrays appear as in Figure 4.4a.

The next item to arrive is ANT. Following the algorithm, IPOINT is set to the root of the tree. At Step 3, ANT is less than WORD(IPOINT − DOG − and Step 4 is taken next. The lefthand pointer of DOG indicates the end of the branch (−1) and ANT is placed at WORD(FREE), DOG's left pointer set, the free list updated, and ANT's right pointer assigned −1 because that node is no longer on the free list. Now the tree appears as in Figure 4.4b.

PIG comes next. Reaching Step 3, we find that PIG is greater than DOG and go to Step 5. This is the end of the righthand branch and we insert the new item

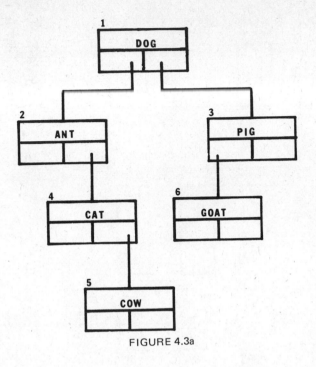

FIGURE 4.3a

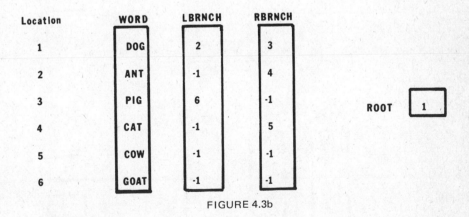

FIGURE 4.3b

FIGURE 4.3 (a) An ordered tree. (b) An ordered tree contained in three arrays.

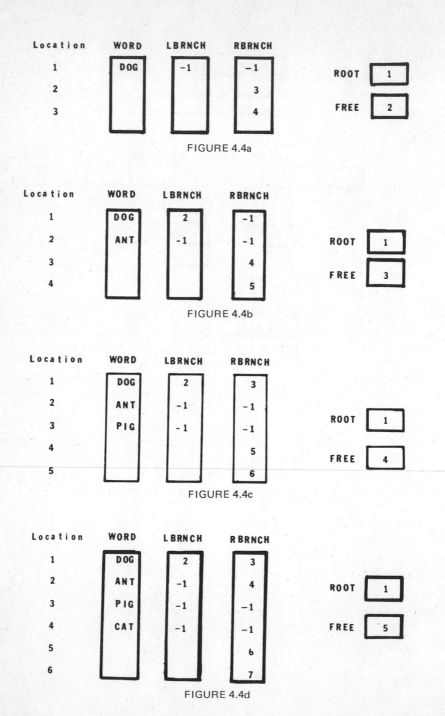

FIGURE 4.4 The tree arrays during insertion sorting. (a) the tree with the first item stored. (b) The tree after the second insertion. (c) A third item added. (d) After adding CAT as a fourth item.

as before, except that this time it is the right pointer of DOG that is changed. The resulting array is shown in Figure 4.4c.

CAT arrives next. At Step 3, CAT is less than DOG, and we go to Step 4 with IPOINT equal to 1. This time, however, the left pointer of IPOINT does not indicate the end of a branch. So we set IPOINT to LBRNCH(IPOINT) − 2 − and return to Step 3. Now IPOINT indicates ANT, and CAT is greater than ANT, so we branch to Step 5 where we find that the righthand branch of ANT is empty. CAT is now stored at Location 4, the pointers are adjusted properly, and we return for COW, resulting in the organization shown in Figure 4.4d. The process continues for COW and GOAT, with the final tree shown in Figure 4.3.

Deleting tree nodes. Adding a node to an ordered tree is a straightforward matter, as we have seen. The algorithm follows the branches until the correct terminal is located, and then new entry is inserted. Deleting an item is more complex, because the element to be removed may occur anywhere in the tree — the root node, a terminal node, or a branching node within the tree.

If the node to be deleted is a terminal, its removal is simple; the location is added to the free list, and the predecessor node has its pointer changed to indicate the end of the branch.

When a nonterminal node is to be removed, it must be replaced with another node, resulting in a partial reorganization of the tree. Any action taken must maintain the sorted order of the tree, and so picking the replacement node must be done carefully. Using as a replacement the node that immediately precedes or follows the removed node in the logical ordering of the tree will preserve the structure. A good procedure is to select as a replacement the highest-valued entry in the left subtree. This node is found by taking the left branch from the node to be deleted, and following its right branch to a terminal; that terminal thus becomes the immediate predecessor of the node to be removed.

For example, Figure 4.5a illustrates a tree with a node to be deleted. After the deletion, the tree appears as in Figure 4.5b. The algorithm is not complex but does involve keeping track of several pointers. If the node to be deleted, JOHN in this case, has a left branch it must be searched, following the right-hand pointers, until the terminal (GARY) is reached.

Once the replacement node is located, the following steps must take place:

1. The right and left pointers of the replacement node are set equal to those of the node being replaced. (JOHN's pointers are given to GARY.)

2. The deleted node's predecessor (MARY) has its left pointer changed to indicate the replacement.

3. The right pointer of the moved node's predecessor (EVE) is set to indicate the end of the branch.

4. The deleted node is added to the free list.

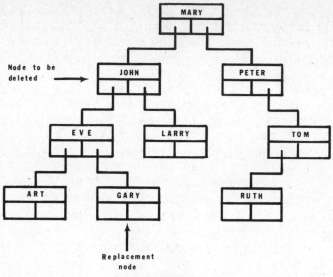

Node to be deleted →

Replacement node

FIGURE 4.5a

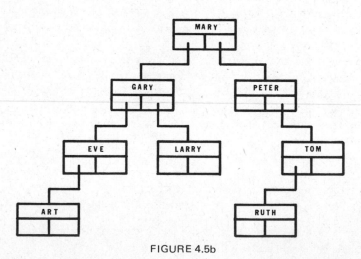

FIGURE 4.5b

FIGURE 4.5 Tree reorganization. (a) Tree before deletion. (b) The same tree after a deletion and reorganization.

If the node to be deleted has no left branch, it is removed by simply making its predecessor point to its successor. (Consider PETER, for example. To delete it, because it has no left branch, MARY's right pointer is merely set to the former value of PETER's right pointer, indicating TOM. PETER's node is then added to the free list.)

Given an ordered tree, the production of the items in sorted order is fairly straightforward; merely trace through the tree following a left branch when one is encountered. At the end of the left branch, the item at that terminal node is the next item in order. Then, the tree is "backed up" to the next node above, which is the next element in order. Then, if it has a right branch, it is followed, and so forth. The procedure is known as a "traverse" of the sorted tree and is considered more carefully later in this chapter.

Sorting with Keys and Pointers

The sort procedures discussed previously assume that the actual data items themselves are compared and/or interchanged. This need not necessarily be the case, as we have pointed out in Chapter 3. Suppose, for example, that the data for a simulation consist of records of students in a large university. Each record may contain a great deal of information needed by the program, such as student number, name, semester in school, grade point average (GPA), a code representing major field, and so forth. Suppose that it is necessary to maintain the records ordered by grade point average. In order to accomplish the sort, it is necessary only to compare and exchange GPAs; moving entire records only adds an unnecessary burden.

The problem can be handled by inspecting only the GPA part of the record in the sort. Then, instead of swapping entire records, only the record numbers need be moved, and they can serve as pointers to the full records. Table 4.2 illustrates a set of hypothetical student records. To sort the records, two arrays containing the record numbers (pointers) and the GPAs are formed (see Table 4.2b). The values to be sorted (GPA in this case) are called "keys." During the sort the keys are compared; when two keys are exchanged, the pointers are moved as well. After the sort, the key and pointer arrays appear as in Table 4.3. The full student records are never moved. In fact, it is not even necessary that the student records be maintained in main memory; they can reside on tape or disk.

The sorting of keys and the use of pointers are extremely useful techinques. The actual sorting procedure is best determined by efficiency considerations, but whether to sort the data itself or just keys is determined primarily by the size of the data elements that may be interchanged. If the data consist of only one or two computer words per item, and the data are easily maintained in core, then the sort is probably best done directly. If the data elements are long, however, such as strings of characters or student records as above, or if the data can be

TABLE 4.2
A Student Record File and Its Pointer and Key Arrays Prior to Sorting on the Keys

(a) The Student Record File

Record no.	Student no.	Name	Semester	GPA	Major
1	998312	College, Joe	7	1.87	03
2	156381	Sorority, Suzi	3	2.53	15
3	222593	Scholar, Sam	6	3.95	22
4	541336	Priss, Polly	5	3.06	19
5	112131	Lush, John	2	1.24	77
6	931227	Dragg, Doris	8	2.98	23

(b) Pointer and Key Arrays

Position	Pointer	Key
1	1	1.87
2	2	2.53
3	3	3.95
4	4	3.06
5	5	1.24
6	6	2.98

more conveniently stored externally, then a key sort, keeping the pointers in proper order, is the best solution.

SEARCHING

Another frequently encountered operation in programming, whether it be simulation, statistics, or data processing, is searching for a particular element in a data structure. The item being sought is called the target of the search. A search

TABLE 4.3
Pointer and Key Arrays for the Student Record File after
Sorting of the Keys

Position	Pointer	Key
1	5	1.24
2	1	1.87
3	2	2.53
4	6	2.98
5	4	3.06
6	3	3.95

is successful when the target is located. An unsuccessful search results when the item is not present in the data.

Searches are frequently programmed as subroutines or functions, although the coding may be written directly in the main routine. In either case, the search is invoked by passing to the routine the value of the target. When the search terminates, a value is returned to the main program; a successful search typically returns a subscript giving the location of the target. In the event of an unsuccessful search, the return is generally some unusual value, such as a negative subscript.

Our discussion of search algorithms centers on the various forms of data structure that have already been presented. First we present three techniques for searching in linear arrays, followed by the procedures applicable to two-dimensional arrays. Finally, searching trees and lists is outlined. Throughout, the illustrations assume that the data elements are value variables. The search can be for a specific key as well; as with sorting, all of the algorithms here are equally applicable to arrays of keys and pointers.

One-Dimensional Searches

Fortran's primitive, the one-dimensional array, lends itself to several search procedures. If the values are arranged randomly in the array, then a sequential search is employed. If the array has been sorted, however, two other kinds of search may be employed.

Sequential search. The simplest search consists of nothing more than stepping through an array sequentially, testing each value against the target. When a match is found, the procedure is terminated. If the entire array is scanned without a match, the search fails. Table 4.4 presents a simple sequential search subroutine.

The sequential search is the only procedure applicable to completely unordered data. If the data are arranged at random, the target can occur at any location in the array. On the average, it requires $n/2$ tests to locate an item in an n-item unordered array.

In contrast, if the data are sorted into sequential order or are at least partially ordered (as for example if a distributive sort has been done without the final bubble sort of the subgroups), then one of two other searches can be employed, both much more efficient than a sequential procedure.

Binary Search. If the data are fully sorted, a very efficient search procedure can be used. The algorithm begins by selecting the middle value in the array (call it MIDDL for now). If MIDDL is the target, the search is terminated. If not, then it is easy to determine whether we are too low in the array (the target is greater than MIDDL) or too high. In either case, we select one half of the array, pick the MIDDL of it, and repeat the test. The process continues by dividing the array in

TABLE 4.4
A Sequential Search Subroutine (SEQSER)

```
      SUBROUTINE SEQSER(X,N,WHAT,LOC)
C
C     THIS SUBROUTINE PERFORMS A SEQUENTIAL SEARCH THROUGH
C        THE REAL ARRAY X FOR THE FIRST OCCURANCE OF THE VALUE
C        WHAT.  THE LOCATION IS RETURNED AS LOC.
C        IF WHAT IS NOT FOUND IN THE ARRAY, LOC RETURNS
C        A NEGATIVE VALUE.
C
C     THERE ARE N ELEMENTS IN THE ARRAY X.
C
      DIMENSION X(N)
      DO 1 I = 1,N
      IF(X(I).EQ.WHAT) GO TO 10
    1 CONTINUE
      LOC = -1
      RETURN
   10 LOC = I
      RETURN
      END
```

half each time until the target is located or it can be concluded that it is not present. The continued halving of the array gives the binary search its name. A subroutine using the binary search is presented in Table 4.5.

To locate an item with a binary search requires an average of $\log_2 n$ comparisons for an n-element array. Because a sequential search requires an average of $n/2$ comparisons, the difference in efficiency is substantial. If, for example, the table contains 1,024 items, a sequential search requires an average of $1,024/2 = 512$ comparisons. To search the same size table with a binary algorithm takes only an average of $\log_2 1,024 = 10$ comparisons.

Probability search. A third search procedure is sometimes useful. Whether or not to apply it depends on three factors. First, the possible values in the array being searched must fall within a known range. Second, the distribution of actual values must be relatively uniform throughout the range. Third, the array must be at least partially sorted.

A probability search follows a logic that would be used for looking up a word in a dictionary. You don't start with AARDVARK and search through to ZYMURGY when looking for POLYNOMIAL (sequential search), nor do you first inspect LOUP, and then SANCTIFY, and so forth (binary search). Instead, you estimate how far through the dictionary the letter P occurs, insert a finger, and start looking sequentially.

The same general procedure is followed in the probability search. First, an estimate is made of how far into the array the target element is likely to occur by computing a subscript. Then, if the selected element is not right, it must be either above or below the target and a sequential search can be made. If the estimate is a good one, the sequential segment of the search is very short.

The key to the probability search is determining the most probable location. It can be computed as

$$\frac{\text{WHAT} * \text{N}}{\text{TOP}} + 1,$$

where WHAT is the target, N is the length of the array, and the possible values range uniformly from 1 to TOP. For example, the most likely location for the value 350 in a 200-item array of numbers between 1 and 500 is

$$\frac{350 * 200}{500} + 1 = 141$$

or 141/200s of the way through the 200-item array.

Table 4.6 presents a probability search subroutine. It would be instructive to invent an array of numbers and to "play computer" with this program, as well as the sequential and binary search routines, to gain a better understanding of the operation of the three procedures.

A slight modification of both the probability and binary searches makes them applicable to partially sorted arrays. In this case, the "most likely" location of the target will indicate only a general region of the array. Finding a value in the most probably location that is greater than the target need not indicate that a descending sequential search be made from that point. Instead, the entire subgroup of the array must be searched. If the pointers indicating the boundaries of the unsorted subgroups are still available from a previous incomplete distributive sort, the "most likely" computation can be used to determine which subgroup is to be searched sequentially.

In most cases when the array is in sorted order, the binary search is the most efficient. The probability search has an intuitive appeal when the data meet its requirements, but Knuth (1973) indicates that there appears to be no real difference between the two procedures in a number of simulation studies. The major reason for introducing the probability search here is that a version of it can be applied to a linked list, as we shall discuss later in this chapter.

On unordered data, a sequential search is the method of choice. However, the sequential procedure is so inefficient that it is often less time consuming to sort first and then use a binary procedure, especially if several items are to be located in the array before additional values are added.

Two-Dimensional Searching

Matrix searching is probably less common in programming than is scanning a single-dimensional array. Nevertheless, there are times when the conceptual model demands a matrix search.

TABLE 4.5

A Binary Search Subroutine (BINSER)

```
      SUBROUTINE BINSER(X,N,WHAT,LOC)

C
C     THIS SUBROUTINE PERFORMS A BINARY SEARCH OF THE REAL
C     ARRAY X FOR THE TARGET VALUE WHAT.  X MUST BE SORTED INTO
C     ASCENDING NUMERICAL ORDER.  THE LOCATION OF WHAT IS
C     RETURNED IN LOC.  IF THE TARGET IS NOT IN THE ARRAY,
C     LOC RETURNS A NEGATIVE VALUE.
C
C     THERE ARE N ELEMENTS IN X.

      DIMENSION X(N)
      IBOT = 1
      ITOP = N
   10 IF(IBOT.LE.ITOP) GO TO 20

C
C     IT'S NOT HERE
C
```

110

```
      LOC = -1
      RETURN
   20 MDN = (IBOT+ITOP)/2
      IF(X(MDN)-WHAT) 30,40,50
C
C     FOUND IT
C
   40 LOC = MDN
      RETURN
C
C     TARGET IS LARGER THAN X(MDN)
C
   30 IBOT = MDN+1
      GO TO 10
C
C     TARGET IS SMALLER THAN X(MDN)
C
   50 ITOP = MDN-1
      GO TO 10
      END
```

TABLE 4.6
A Probability Search Subroutine (PRBSER)

```
      SUBROUTINE PRBSER(X,N,WHAT,LOC,TOP)
C
C     PERFORMS A PROBABILITY SEARCH OF THE N ITEMS IN THE REAL
C     ARRAY X FOR THE TARGET VALUE WHAT.  THE VALUES IN X MUST BE
C     UNIFORMLY DISTRIBUTED IN THE INTERVAL 1-TOP, AND MUST
C     BE IN ASCENDING NUMERICAL ORDER.  THE LOCATION OF WHAT
C     IS RETURNED IN LOC.  IF THE TARGET IS NOT FOUND,
C     LOC RETURNS A NEGATIVE VALUE.
C
C     DIMENSION X(N)
C
C     ESTIMATE POSITION
C
      ITOP = TOP
      ITRY = (WHAT*N)/ITOP+1
      IF(ITRY.GT.N) ITRY = N
C
C     TRY IT
C
      IF(X(ITRY)-WHAT) 200,100,300
C
C     FOUND IT
C
  100 LOC = ITRY
      RETURN
```

```
C     TOO LOW---START SEQUENTIAL SEARCH UP
C
  200 ISTART = ITRY+1
      DO 201 ITRY = ISTART,N
      IF(X(ITRY)-WHAT) 201,100,202
  201 CONTINUE
C
C     NOT FOUND
C
  202 LOC = -1
      RETURN
C
C     TOO HIGH---START SEQUENTIAL SEARCH DOWN
C
  300 IWRONG = ITRY
      LAST = IWRONG-1
      DO 301 I = 1,LAST
      ITRY = IWRONG-I
      IF(X(ITRY)-WHAT) 202,100,301
  301 CONTINUE
      GO TO 202
      END
```

Matrices can be stored as Fortran arrays in the double-subscripted manner familiar to programmers. They can also be stored as linked lists when that storage mode is beneficial. The usual instance where list storage is appropriate is in the case of a "sparse" matrix — one that contains a large proportion of zero entries. In a sparse matrix, a considerable saving in storage space can often be achieved by using a list to hold only the nonzero values. Booth and Chien (1974, pp. 314–317) deal with the sparse matrices in detail and we discuss them briefly in Chapter 6. Our discussion here assumes that the full matrix stored in the standard Fortran fashion.

Sequential Searching. When the values of a matrix are arranged in a random order, and an individual value must be located, a version of the sequential search may be used. The procedure is a straightforward elaboration of the sequential scan of a one-dimensional array, except that the routine must deal with both rows and columns.

If the data in an array are ordered by columns — as in Table 4.7, for example — the search can be very efficient because a binary procedure can be used. Fortran almost universally stores its arrays by columns, so that in memory the array looks like:

$$X(1,1),\ X(2,1),\ X(3,1),\ \ldots,\ X(5,1),$$
$$X(1,2),\ X(2,2),\ \ldots,\ X(5,5)$$

Making the two-dimensional array equivalent to a one-dimensional array allows a binary or probability search to be used. Should the array be ordered by rows, the best procedure is to transpose it — interchange the rows and columns—and then use a binary or probability search on an equivalent array.

Once the search has located the item, finding the row (I) and column (J) subscripts can be accomplished by the statements:

```
J = INT(IZ/NR)+1
I = MØD(IZ,NR)
IF(I.GT.0) GO TO 1
J = J-1
I = NR
     1 CONTINUE
```

where NR is the number of rows in the array and IZ is the single subscript location of the target returned by the search.

Binary and probability searches. It will sometimes occur that a matrix is partially ordered as in Table 4.8. Here, the numbers generally increase from the top left to the lower right; each row is ordered, but the first entry in a row is not

TABLE 4.7
A Column-Ordered Array to Be Searched

		Column				
		1	2	3	4	5
	1	12	31	73	118	175
	2	17	40	85	119	203
Row	3	18	41	98	136	226
	4	23	49	106	189	319
	5	28	57	109	148	412

necessarily greater than the last value in the preceding row. Many statistical tables show this kind of ordering. In such a case, a modification of the probability or binary search procedures may be employed.

For example, to search Table 4.8 for the value 38, a binary or probability search of the largest row values (Column 4) might be carried out until a value larger than 38 is found (at Location 3,4), and then a forward and backward scan of the preceding elements in Row 3 and the first elements in Row 4 would locate the target.

Spatial searches. When the data in an array represent a spatial arrangement of the units in a model, as in CHEBO, a search in two dimensions around some selected starting point is often indicated. CHEBO's search is rudimentary — it merely visits all squares adjoining a piece. But a spatial search could be considerably more complex.

There are two ingredients to a spatial search — a starting point and a search pattern. The starting point can be obtained in many different ways. In CHEBO, each piece is used as the starting point for a search of all adjoining locations. In general, a starting point in a spatial search is determined by the conceptual model of the simulation. In the case of CHEBO, the search must simply represent a way of computing the value of each possible move; because a piece

TABLE 4.8
A Partially Ordered Array

		Column			
		1	2	3	4
	1	9	13	19	26
Row	2	17	21	28	33
	3	25	31	38	49
	4	41	53	68	77

normally can move but one space, the search area is small and its starting point defined by a piece.

The starting point is not a matter to be dismissed easily. Suppose that an array represented a map, and the simulation attempted to search for a vacant property to locate a new housing unit. Would randomly picking a starting row and column be satisfactory? Not likely; a procedure that attempts to find a space close to other similar spaces is probably far preferable.

The search pattern is also a matter of considerable choice. Given a starting point, the search could proceed outward in expanding squares around the starting point, or in an expanding square spiral beginning at the starting point. Even a random walk, with which square to visit next determined randomly, is a possibility.

Both the starting point and the search pattern have dramatic effects of the outcome of a spatial search, and therefore on the overall results of a simulation employing such a procedure. Because the spatial search is really a sequential search defined in two dimensions, there is no optimal procedure when the data contained in the array to be searched are essentially random. When there is some form of ordering imposed on the array, careful development of the procedures for determining the starting point and defining the search pattern may provide good results; no general algorithms exist.

Searching Linked Linear Lists

When the data are arranged in a linked linear list, one of two forms of search may be employed. Both are versions of two earlier search procedures — the sequential and probability searches. The decision as to which to select depends primarily on whether or not the data in the list are ordered.

Unordered lists. When a simple array is stored in an unordered form, only a sequential search can assure finding the target if it is present. An unordered list presents the same difficulty. The process begins by inspecting the element at the head of this list. If the head is not the target, then its pointer is followed to the next location, and so forth until either the target is found or the end of the list is encountered.

The sequential search is doubly inefficient in the list. Not only must each element be visited and tested, but the access to the storage locations cannot be controlled by a simple loop advancing the subscripts. To reach each successive location, the subscript must be retrieved from the pointer array and then used to locate the next item. The coding is only slightly more complex than for an array, but the efficiency of the search is worse. In addition, because the testing of data elements occurs haphazardly throughout the entire array rather than concentrating in one small local area of the array at a time, other kinds of computer inefficiencies can result as well. We discuss that problem in the context of paged memories in Chapter 6.

If minimizing computer time is important, a sequential search through a linked list should be avoided. Some improvement in efficiency may be possible by using a version of the probability search as discussed below, but only under certain conditions. In other cases, when the conceptual model demands a search of a list, then the inefficiency must simply be endured.

Ordered lists. When a linked list must be searched, an increase in efficiency over the sequential procedure is possible by using a version of the probability search. The list should be doubly linked, the values in it must meet the general requirements for a probability search (roughly evenly distributed over a known range), and it must be sorted. In addition, a special pointer array must be built during the sort as described below.

Suppose, for example, that a set of 10 numbers, chosen from the range 1–100, have been insertion sorted into the array LIST shown in Figure 4.6. The forward and backward pointers are in LINKF and LINKB, respectively. An additional array, called QTILE, is also shown. QTILE gives the first location in the linked list for the values larger than 25, 50, and 75. These three values divide the range of possible values into four segments. During the insertion sort, when a value greater than 25 is first stored, its location in LIST is stored as QTILE(1). As later values are entered the QTILE entries are updated until, when the sort is finished, each entry in QTILE points to the first location in LIST occupied by a value greater than or equal to the value represented by the QTILE entry.

To search LIST, the program must first scan through the QTILE array until the appropriate starting point is found and then enter LIST. From that point on, the search is sequential through the linked structure. For example, to locate the value 40 in LIST, a sequential scan through QTILE would select the value 25 as the largest number not exceeding the target. The pointer corresponding to 25 would then be taken as a starting point, and the search would proceed sequentially forward starting at LIST(5).

To make the search even more efficient, the back pointers can be used. In this case, a search could begin at the higher QTILE pointer if the target value was greater than one-half the distance between the QTILE values. For example, if the value sought is 40, the search should begin at LIST(8) because 40 is greater than 37.5, the midpoint between QTILE(1) and QTILE(2). The search would continue backward through the list as the starting location was above the target. Had the target been 31, in contrast, the search would have begun at the pointer for QTILE(1) and proceeded forward through the list.

Because the list is ordered, the search may be discontinued as unsuccessful whenever a list entry exceeds the target on a forward search, or is less than the target on a backward search. For example, in a search for the value 70, the process would begin at LIST(4), finding the value 87. Following the backward pointer, we go to LIST(1) and find 74. Its pointer indicates LIST(6), and we find 65. Because 65 is less than the target, we can safely conclude that 70 is not in the list.

location	LIST	LINKF	LINKB
1	74	4	6
2	18	5	7
3	40	9	5
4	87	10	1
5	31	3	2
6	65	1	8
7	9	2	-1
8	55	6	9
9	46	8	3
10	93	-1	4

QTILE

location	Value	Pointer
1	25	5
2	50	8
3	75	4

IHEAD 7

ITAIL 10

FIGURE 4.6   A doubly linked sorted list, with an auxilliary array, ready for probability searching.

A second example may help to clarify the search. Again assuming that the range of values in the list is 1–100, Figure 4.7 illustrates dividing the range into quartiles and suggests the course of action during the search. As before, a QTILE array has been constructed during the list sort, and the IHEAD and ITAIL pointers indicate the two ends of the list.

If the target is in the first quartile (1–25), then we can begin the search from either IHEAD and go forward, or from the QTILE(1) pointer and go backward. Best efficiency is obtained if we go forward from the beginning when the target is low (between 1 and 12.5) and backward if the target is higher (between 12.5 and 25). For example, to locate a target value of 8, the search should begin at IHEAD and proceed forward; to look for 19, the best procedure is to start at QTILE(1) and scan backward. The same logic can be generalized to the remaining quartiles of the data as indicated in the figure.

There is, of course, no logical reason why only quartiles should be used in this search procedure, but using only that few subdivisions of the range greatly

If the target is less than or equal to	12.5	25.0	37.5	50.0	67.5	75.0	87.5	100.0
Use this pointer	IHEAD	QTILE$_1$	QTILE$_1$	QTILE$_2$	QTILE$_2$	QTILE$_3$	QTILE$_3$	ITAIL
And go	Foreward	Backward	Foreward	Backward	Foreward	Backward	Foreward	Backward

FIGURE 4.7 The relationships between the QTILE and midpoint values, the QTILE pointers, and search direction.

speeds up the search. In a large array, with a wide range of possible values, it may be worthwhile to consider dividing the range of values as finely even as tenths.

Although this adaptation of the probability search to linked lists is somewhat complex, it can be programmed with comparatively little effort. That coding labor will be well rewarded in increased efficiency in simulation programs where a great deal of searching of sorted lists is required.

Tree Operations

The tree is the most complex of the data structures presented in this book. There are a number of operations that must often be performed on trees — searching is but one of them. We present first the search procedure used in SIMSAL, because it is the simplest of the searches.

Searching SIMSAL's tree. The SIMSAL tree has four items of information at each node, as discussed in Chapter 3. The first two entries are the "informational" items and consist of a letter from a syllable and the position (1, 2, or 3) in which the letter occurs. The remaining values are the left pointer ("correct") and the right pointer ("error"). In the case of a response terminal, the second entry is empty and the first data value contains a response instead of a letter.

The tree search begins at the root. The root is always a first-letter node, so the first letter of the stimulus syllable is compared with the first entry in the root node. If there is a match, the "correct" branch is taken to inspect the next letter. As long as matches continue, the lefthand, or "correct," branch is taken until the terminal is encountered.

When a mismatch occurs, the "error" pointer is followed, and the righthand branch taken. That branch is traced until a match is found and the scan shifts to the lefthand branch. If an entire "error" branch is followed without a match, the search ends up at an empty terminal, and SIMSAL makes a random guess at the response.

SIMSAL's tree search is located in the "RESPOND ENTRY" segment of the SUBJCT subroutine (see Appendix B). The search itself is accomplished in the statements reproduced below. This search differs from many in that the location of the target node is not returned; rather a special vector (IVECT) is set to indicate matching letter positions, and the branch is always followed to a terminal. Once an end node is found, the search returns the response value (or a random guess if the node is empty). The "target" syllable is stored in the STIM array and the search proceeds as follows.

```
     IPOINT = 1
```

This is a pointer to the next node to be visited. Setting it to 1 indicates that the search is to begin at TREE(1) which is always the root.

```
2003 IF(TREE(IPOINT,2)) 2002,2006,2002
```

This tests for a terminal node and marks the start of a scanning loop.

```
2002 ISB = TREE(IPOINT,2)
```

Sets a pointer to indicate position in the syllable occupied by the letter in node IPOINT.

```
     IF(STIM(ISB)-TREE(IPOINT,1)) 2004,2005,2004
```

The test of a stimulus letter (STIM(ISB)) against the letter in the node.

```
2004 IPOINT = TREE(IPOINT,4)

     GO TO 2003
```

This is the "error" branch — set the next-node pointer to the right branch and loop back to the start of the scan.

```
2005 ISB = TREE(IPOINT,2)

     IVECT(ISB) = 1

     IPOINT = TREE(IPOINT,3)

     GO TO 2003
```

The "correct" branch. Set ISB and the corresponding value in IVECT, set next-node pointer to the left branch, and loop back.

```
2006 IF(TREE(IPOINT,1)) 2007,2008,2007
```

We have reached the end of a branch — a terminal node has been trapped by statement 2003. Now we ask whether this is an empty node or whether there is a response stored.

```
2007 IGUESS = TREE(IPOINT,1)

     RETURN
```

It is not an empty node, so the program returns the stored response as IGUESS.

```
2008 IGUESS = IRAND(20)
     RETURN
```

Found an empty node — return a random guess in the interval 1—20.

SIMSAL's search is idiosyncratic to that program; the target is not located in a single node but is spread over as many as three, with the response occupying yet a fourth node. In addition, the scan of the tree always continues until a terminal is reached.

The usual tree search attempts to locate a target contained in a single node, and typically returns a storage location or a "not found" flag. But the SIMSAL example serves to introduce the general nature of tree operations; a search begins at the root and follows pointers to other nodes until the search terminates.

Searching an ordered binary tree. Searching a sorted binary tree is a special case of a binary search in an array. A test is performed on a node; if the node and the target agree, the search succeeds. If there is a mismatch, then the target is either greater or less in value than the node. In the first case, the right branch is followed to the next test; in the second, the left pointer is used. As an example, consider searching the tree in Figure 4.8 for the entry LARRY. Starting at the root, LARRY is less than MARY, and the left branch is taken to JOHN. However, LARRY is greater than JOHN and the right branch is followed, leading to the target.

Searching for an item not in the tree is also quite efficient. Consider the steps in looking for nonexistent KEVIN in Figure 4.8. KEVIN is less than the root, so a lefthand branch is taken to JOHN. KEVIN is larger than JOHN, and the right

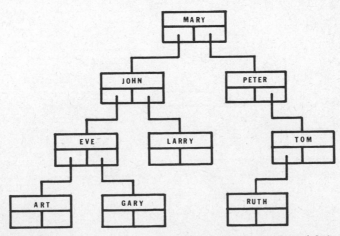

FIGURE 4.8 A sorted binary tree. (This is the same as Figure 4.5a.)

branch points to LARRY. KEVIN is less than LARRY, and the search follows the lefthand branch. However, there is no lefthand branch; therefore, KEVIN must not be in the tree for, if it were, LARRY would have a left branch.

The efficiency of the binary search procedure makes the ordered tree a very useful data structure in many situations. There are still the high costs involved in using trees at all, however — the additional storage and the tedious insertion and deletion procedures.

Traversing an ordered binary tree. Suppose that we wish to print the elements in Figure 4.8 in their sorted order. The sequence, of course, is implicit in the organization of the tree but retrieving it is not a straightforward matter. The procedure is known as traversal of the tree and consists of visiting each node in order and printing its contents. Of course, the information need not be printed but may be used in the program in some other way. The important point is that we wish to access the data elements in order.

The algorithm for a traverse starts at the root. If there is a left subtree, all items on it must be visited before returning to the root node. If the left branch indicates an additional subtree, then its left branch must be looked at first, and so forth. Figure 4.9 illustrates the order in which the nodes are visited in the traverse.

The traversal is best accomplished by using a stack to hold the locations of the nodes that must be visited later; the stack is built during the downward trace of a branch and popped on the way back up. For example, starting at the root, we note that there is a left branch. The location of the root is placed in a stack, and we turn our attention to the subtree headed by JOHN. But JOHN has a left

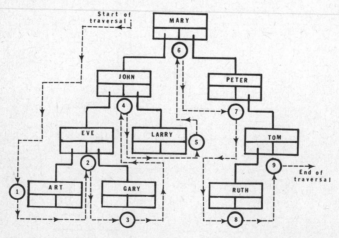

FIGURE 4.9   A traversal of an ordered binary tree. Circled numbers give the order in which the nodes are visited.

subtree, so JOHN's address is placed on the stack and we move on to EVE. Because EVE also has a left subtree, its location is added to the stack and we proceed to ART. Now there is no left subtree, and ART is reached.

With ART we find the end of a left-hand branch and print the node. Now the stack is popped and we obtain EVE, the next item. EVE has a right-hand subtree of items greater than it which must be visited before continuing back up the tree. GARY is printed next, and then the stack is popped again, leading to JOHN. JOHN has a right-hand subtree to be dealt with next, after which a final pop leads back to the root.

At this point, the entire left subtree of the root has been printed and the traverse proceeds down the right subtree, using the same rule — if there is a left-hand subtree, it is visited first, followed by the node, and then the right-hand subtree.

A flowchart of the traversal algorithm just discussed is presented in Figure 4.10. The tree in Figure 4.9 is shown as three arrays in Table 4.9. A trace of the traverse operation using the arrays in Table 4.9 is illustrated in Table 4.10. In

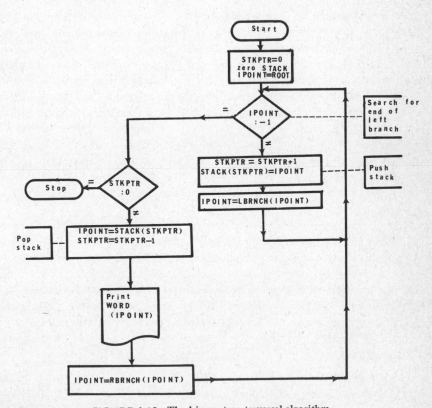

FIGURE 4.10 The binary tree traversal algorithm.

TABLE 4.9
An Ordered Tree Stored as Three Arrays, Ready for a
Traversal[a]

Location	WORD	LBRNCH	RBRNCH
1	MARY	2	3
2	JOHN	4	5
3	PETER	-1	6
4	EVE	7	8
5	LARRY	-1	-1
6	TOM	9	-1
7	ART	-1	-1
8	GARY	-1	-1
9	RUTH	-1	-1

[a]The root pointer has the value 1.

that table, the contents of the stack and the pointers IPOINT and STKPTR are shown at each step of the traversal. The first three initialization operations of starting the stack and setting IPOINT to ROOT are indicated as Step 0 in Table 4.10. Each of the succeeding steps in Table 4.10 represents the contents of the stack and pointers at the end of one circuit through a part of the flowchart in Figure 4.10. Following the righthand loop in the flowchart results in adding node locations to the stack. Reaching the end of a lefthand branch of the tree causes IPOINT to equal −1 and the left loop of the chart is followed. In this segment of the algorithm, two values of IPOINT are used. The first value shown is that obtained from the stack; it is used to indicate the data entry to be printed. Then a new value of IPOINT is obtained from the righthand pointer of the just printed node; the new value appears in Table 4.10 as the second IPOINT entry for a step.

It would be very instructive to follow through the traversal of the tree to see just how the values in Table 4.10 were derived and used.

The traversal of an ordered binary tree can be interpreted as the final stage in a rather complicated sort algorithm. It began earlier in the chapter with a discussion of insertion sorting to obtain the ordered binary tree. Retrieving the elements from the tree in the traverse completes the sort procedure. Complex, yes, but it does accomplish the desired aim of a sort. Certainly, if the task at hand is only to obtain a sorted set of data, other procedures are less cumbersome. But in some instances, the decision to use a tree is made on quite different grounds. The ability to traverse the tree to produce sorted data is often incidental.

Searching unordered binary trees. The search of an ordered binary tree is a relatively simple matter, and only a small segment of the tree need be inspected. However, if the tree is unordered, as is often the case, the search is more time consuming as it is essentially a sequential procedure. In order to make certain

TABLE 4.10
The Contents of the Stack and Pointers During a Traversal
of the Tree in Table 4.9[a]

Step	IPOINT	STACK	STKPTR	Entry printed
0	1	0	0	
1	1	0	0	
2	2	1	1	
3	4	1	2	
		2		
4	7	1	3	
		2		
		4		
5	−1	1	4	
		2		
		4		
		7		
6	7, −1	1	3	ART
		2		
		4		
7	4, 8	1	2	EVE
		2		
8	−1	1	3	
		2		
		8		
9	8, −1	1	2	GARY
		2		
10	2, 5	1	1	JOHN
11	−1	1	2	
		5		
12	5, −1	1	1	LARRY
13	1, 3	0	0	MARY
14	−1	3	1	
15	3, 6	0	0	PETER
16	9	6	1	
17	−1	6	2	
		9		
18	9, −1	6	1	RUTH
19	6, −1	0	0	TOM

[a]Each step represents a return to the IPOINT:−1 test in
Figure 4.10. When two values of IPOINT are shown, they are
changed during the step.

that a target element is not in a tree, each node must be tested — we cannot stop
after merely inspecting a subtree as with an ordered tree.

The search algorithm is identical to the traversal procedure in Figure 4.10,
with one minor modification. The print operation in the flowchart is replaced
with a test for equality between the node selected (WORD(IPOINT)) and the
target. If there is a match, the traversal ends, having successfully located the

target at node IPOINT. If the traversal ends at the STOP operation in the flowchart, however, then the search has failed.

*OTHER OPERATIONS ON DATA STRUCTURES

As data structures become increasingly intricate, more and more complex and esoteric operations are sometimes performed on them. In this section of the chapter, we offer brief overviews of three different sorts of procedures that are occasionally encountered. The intention here is not to present detailed algorithms but just to introduce some of the topics.

Occupying the first place is the operation with the intriguing name of "garbage collection." Garbage is anything that has outlived its usefulness and/or is a remnant of some process. Garbage accumulates in various data structures during some processing operations and from time to time must be accumulated and discarded. Several general algorithms have been devised for the management of garbage in computer storage and we introduce them briefly here.

Although garbage collection applies to nearly any data structure, two other kinds of processes occur almost exclusively in trees. Tree balancing refers, as you may suspect, to keeping a tree in balance, so that all of its branches are of nearly the same length. Certain tree operations, such as the traverse, can be greatly facilitated by maintaining another path through the tree, known as a thread, and we discuss the concept of threading later.

Garbage Collection

A number of sources discuss garbage collection (see, for example, Knuth, 1968; Harrison, 1973), and we shall deal with this rather advanced topic only very briefly. A programmer with serious storage problems should consult another source and give careful consideration to a language, such as LISP or ALGOL, that provides garbage collection facilities.

In the algorithms that we have discussed in this chapter, many have included a free list. When space is needed, it is taken from the free list. When an item is deleted, its location is added to the free list. Sometimes it is not possible to maintain the availability list in the manner discussed. As one example, the graph, a type of data structure that we have not presented, often causes problems. A graph is an elaboration of a tree. Our trees have had at least two branches leaving each node but only a single pointer to the node. A graph may have more than one. In this case, deleting a node is not accomplished by adjusting a single "entry" pointer. Removing one pointer may leave another pointer or pointers still indicating a node. To decide whether or not to add the node to the free list requires searching all storage locations to determine whether or not a pointer still remains. Generally it is more efficient to wait until the storage area becomes relatively full to search for available space, instead of adding nodes to the free list one at a time.

As a second example of the need for garbage collection, consider the case where there are a number of lists and/or trees, all sharing the same large array. Although we have always written our examples as if there was but a single data structure in an array, in actual practice a single very large array will often be used for storage, and a number of structures will reside there. When a data structure is no longer needed by the program, all of its locations must be returned to the free list; a garbage collection procedure usually handles that task.

When the free list is not maintained continually, for whatever the reason, occasionally the program requires additional space. When this happens, a garbage collector is invoked. It scans the storage area of the program and makes additions to the free list. Other functions are also sometimes performed, such as tree balancing and storage compacting, which we discuss below.

Two general procedures are used by garbage collectors. The first, generally called simply the garbage collection algorithm, scans the entire data area, usually sequentially. When a pointer is found to a node, that node is "flagged" in some way, perhaps by setting one of its pointers to a special value, or by making an entry in a special storage—use table. When the scan is completed, any location left unflagged can safely be added to the free list, along with any nodes that it points to.

In the second general procedure, the reference count algorithm, each node has a special counter associated with it. The counter may be either a part of the node itself or located in a separate table. Whenever a pointer is set to a node, the reference counter is incremented by 1. When a pointer is deleted, the node's counter is decremented. The garbage collector scans the reference counters. When a zero counter is found, the corresponding node is placed on the free list.

Most garbage collection routines also carry out a storage compacting operation. The aim of compacting is to move all occupied storage locations into one end of the storage area, concentrating the free list elements at the other end. The result is a data arrangement that is more compact; operations on it are generally confined to one end of the data array. On some systems, as is discussed in detail in Chapter 6, restricting operation to as small an area of memory as possible is a distinct advantage.

Balancing

A tree is said to be balanced if there are approximately the same number of left- and right-hand branches. Having a balanced tree leads to increased efficiency in the various tree operations. For example, in a traverse, having a tree in balance means that the stack to keep track of the upper nodes is roughly the same length when each branch is followed.

There are two general tree balancing procedures — top down and bottom up.

In the top-down algorithm, the process of rebuilding to achieve balance is begun at the root node. The root should be the item roughly in the middle of the items in the tree. In a tree of 15 elements, for example, the root should be the eighth in a sorted order. The second-level nodes, those just below the root, would be the fourth and twelfth elements.

A bottom-up procedure begins by forming a subtree of Elements 1, 2, and 3, and another of Items 5, 6, and 7. These two are linked together by a node containing Item 4. This procedure is repeated, resulting in a balanced tree structure.

Threaded Trees

If a traverse is to be performed many times, a slight modification to each node can make the process much more efficient. In a standard tree, space is provided to store the pointers to each successor. If, in addition, there is a pointer to the next node to be visited in a traverse, the tree is said to be threaded. To traverse a threaded tree, the algorithm need only follow the thread, usually called a "trace." In this tree, there is no need to employ a stack to store visited nodes. Indeed, the traversal will not even begin at the root but at a location specified by a pointer to the start of the trace. To traverse a threaded tree, a trace pointer is initially set to the start of the trace and the first threaded node is visited. Then the pointer is set to the trace value of the just visited node and the next node visited. The process continues until the last node has been visited. The algorithm is identical to sequentially processing a linked linear list. Table 4.11 illustrates a threaded tree; the tree is the same one traversed in Figure 4.9 and Table 4.9 with the addition of the trace array and the start of trace pointer.

TABLE 4.11
A Threaded Version of the Tree Shown in Figure 4.9 and
Table 4.9[a]

Location	WORD	LBRNCH	RBRNCH	TRACE
1	MARY	2	3	3
2	JOHN	4	5	5
3	PETER	−1	6	9
4	EVE	7	8	8
5	LARRY	−1	−1	1
6	TOM	9	−1	−1
7	ART	−1	−1	4
8	GARY	−1	−1	2
9	RUTH	−1	−1	6

[a]The trace path begins at node TRSTRT (7) and ends when the TRACE entry is −1.

Hash Tables

When data are maintained in a large table and individual items must occasionally be retrieved, an extremely efficient procedure for storage is available in what is known as a "hash table." In a hash table, data are originally stored at a location determined as a function of the data value itself. Typically, some part of the data is regarded as a key, and an arithmetic operation called "hashing" is performed on the key. The result of hashing is a location in the data table. When the item is to be retrieved, the key is again converted to an address and the entire item retrieved, with no search required.

We do not discuss hashing methods in detail here. They have relatively little application in simulation because they are not generally useful with tables that change frequently during the operation of the program; many data processing operations with large files often use a hash storage algorithm.

A very clear introduction to hash storage can be found in Maurer and Lewis (1975). Day (1972) also deals with hashing but without considering the various coding alternatives and their implications.

EXERCISES

4.1 Using the same list arrays that you developed for Exercises 3.4, 3.5, and 3.6, write a search function. The argument(s) should include the target item, and the function should return either the location of the target or an indication that it is not present.

4.2 Use the subroutines NUHEAD, NUTAIL, and NUMID from Exercises 3.4, 3.5, and 3.6 to write an insertion sort routine for a linked list. Your program should take input items, either numeric or alphabetic (single characters is probably easiest), and produce a linked list containing the data in proper numeric or alphabetic order.

4.3 Write subroutines, such as that in Table 4.1, for simple exchange and bubble sorts. Write a main program that has the same data sorted by each of the three sort subroutines – bubble, exchange, and Shell. If your computer has a time or clock function available, time the three sort routines.

4.4 Write a subroutine to search, using a modified binary procedure, a partially ordered array such as that shown in Table 4.8. Test your program with the data in Table 4.8 and with at least two other arrays of different sizes.

4.5 The urban development simulation might use a 50 × 50 array called MAP to store its basic data array. A vacant location (containing an alphabetic blank) indicates an unbuilt "lot" in the city; a "D" might indicate a single-family dwelling. Devise single-character codes for each of the remaining seven land uses suggested in the text. Now write a search subroutine that accepts as arguments one of the nine possible land-use codes (the target), and a starting location given as a row and column number. The subroutine should search, starting with the supplied row and column arguments, in expanding squares, until the target is located. The routine should return the row and column coordinates of the target or an error indication if the target is not present. (Hint: be careful that the expanding squares do not exceed the boundaries of the map.)

4.6 One approach to selecting a starting position for the urban growth simulation is to start the search at the row and column intersection that represents the center of the population. There are a number of ways of representing that location, but you may make use of auxilliary arrays that keep track of the number of each kind of property in each row and column. Then, assuming that the simulation has been attempting to build a dwelling, the program finds the row and column that contain the greatest number of dwellings; those row and column numbers then identify the starting point of the search. Develop the logic of this procedure and write two subroutines that implement parts of it. One subroutine should accept a 50 X 50 map as input and take a census of the numbers of each kind of property in each row and column. The second subroutine should accept a single character as an input argument (one of the land-use codes) and return the row and column coordinates giving the center of that kind of property.

*4.7 Write a program to produce an ordered binary tree. Accept as input single values and place each in the tree as in an insertion sort of a linked list. Store the tree in three separate arrays, one holding the data values, and the other two for the left and right pointers. Write a traverse subroutine to retrieve the sorted data from the tree.

*4.8 Write a program to search an unordered tree stored in three arrays as in Exercise 4.7.

*4.9 The probability search presented in Table 4.6 is designed for a rectangular distribution of values. Suppose that the distribution is not rectangular but normal. What modifications must be made? The problem is somewhat analogous to selecting a starting point in a spatial search; how is the starting value to be selected? If you can, write a probability search subroutine to deal with a normal distribution with known parameters. (Note: solving this problem requires a background in statistics.)

4.10 Modify the sort subroutines in Exercise 4.3 so that they operate in descending order.

SUGGESTED READINGS

The Suggested Readings in Chapter 3 are also appropriate for this chapter. In addition, the following offer some other sources.

Flores, I. *Computer sorting*. Englewood Cliffs, N. J.: Prentice-Hall, 1969. Not as encyclopedic as Knuth but offers a good coverage of the field.

Knuth, D. E. *The art of computer programming.* Vol. 3: *Sorting and searching.* Reading, Mass.: Addison-Wesley, 1973. This is but one of a masterful and authoritative series by the author. All of the techniques discussed in this chapter are presented here, and a wealth of other procedures as well. Although the discussion in all of Knuth's works is thorough and mathematical, they are so clearly written as to be highly readable by nearly any social or behavioral scientist.

Martin, W. A. Sorting. *Computing Surveys,* 1971, 3, 147–174. This is a concise and complete overview of a large number of sorting techniques, including procedures for disk and tape. Searching is discussed briefly.

5

Random Processes

Random processes are widely employed in simulation programming. For example, the conceptual model may specify a random order of processing as in CHEBO, or perhaps stimuli are to be selected from a normal distribution. A simulated subject may or may not respond in a particular situation, a stimulus may or may not exceed a critical threshold value, SIMSAL may or may not learn a syllable. Simulated trucks arrive in a toll plaza queue, are serviced, and move on. Demand for various products and services vary randomly following known supply—demand rules, and so on.

Random processes generally appear in simulations for reasons related to the level of analysis selected for the conceptual model. Rather than allow the model to become too detailed, matters frequently are simplified by an assumption of randomness. In a paired-associates learning task with humans, for example, whether a stimulus—response association is formed at any particular time is determined by a complex, and not fully understood, biochemical process in the brain. Partly because of ignorance, and partly for reasons of level of analysis, the establishment of stimulus—response bonds in SIMSAL is controlled by a probability. We consider SIMSAL's process later in this chapter in the discussion of Bernoulli events.

In a similar manner, the time between arrivals at a turnpike toll plaza, or at a supermarket check stand, is governed in the real world by a very large number of things. In most simulations of such phenomena, the level of analysis precludes a detailed representation of all factors. Instead, time intervals between arrivals are sampled from the exponential probability distribution because the exponential is known to describe the rate of arrivals in a queue. Its use therefore avoids a great deal of representational minutiae that otherwise force the model to a different level.

In most simulations, the random process consists of sampling from some known probability distribution. A number of the most commonly used distribution sampling algorithms are presented in this chapter, along with a discussion of their applicability.

All of the procedures are based on sampling from the unit rectangular distribution — a uniform distribution of numbers in the range 0–1. We begin our presentation of random processes with a discussion of algorithms for generating unit rectangular numbers. We then discuss simple transformations to expand the range of values from 0 to 1 to whatever is required.

After presenting rectangular generators, we address the very important topic of testing their adequacy. If a generator is producing values that do not meet the requirements of randomness, then no amount of "fudging" can correct the problem. Any additional use of the values, such as using them to develop samples from normal or exponential distributions, only compounds the problem.

Once we are assured that the unit rectangular generator is satisfactory, then it may be employed in controlling various processes in the program, and in algorithms for simulating a wide range of probability distributions. Discussion of those procedures occupies the bulk of this chapter.

GENERATING AND TESTING

Strictly speaking, computers do not generate random numbers. There is no "pick a number out of thin air" command in any machine's instruction set. Every computer operation is governed by a precisely stated procedure, and the output of any programmed "random" process is a strictly deterministic series of values. Starting the process at the same point will always result in the same sequence of numbers being produced. Computerized random number generation is therefore really a process of generating pseudorandom numbers, but we shall use the term "random" here for convenience.

The generation of random numbers is best conceived as a series of the form

$$x_i = f(x_{i-1}).$$

That is, any number is a function of the previous value. Clearly, if the same number appears again, then the entire sequence is going to repeat itself endlessly. This being the case, a great deal of care must be taken to provide a good starting point (x_0) for the generator. The procedure to be presented here requires that a starting value, or seed, be input. The seed can also be obtained in one of several other ways. In many computers, there is a system- or computer center-supplied function to provide a seed. Often the value is obtained by reading the system's real-time clock, usually selecting the least significant (fastest moving) digits. In the case of the generator provided here, the seed is assumed to be an input to the program. For most purposes, the initial value should itself be randomly selected by the user, and a different value given each time the program is executed.

In some cases, it is advantageous to start the program with the same seed. If, for example, we wished to run SIMSAL several times, perhaps varying one of the learning probabilities, it might be nice to have the same order of presentation of stimuli each time. This can be accomplished by providing the same seed but varying the learning parameter. The procedure is particularly advantageous in SIMSAL because the form of the memory tree is strongly influenced by the presentation order of the stimuli.

The ability to start the random sequence at the same point is also an advantage in program development. During the program testing period, there are enough other possibilities for error that randomness is undesirable. Starting a sequence at the same point throughout all debugging tests removes the effect of randomness by providing the same series of values on every program run. Attention can be directed to the real problems, therefore, and not those that may appear and then disappear as a function of the random sequence.

The random number algorithm must meet two general criteria, which we discuss in more detail later. First, the sequence of numbers must have a very long "period" before it repeats itself. Second, the resulting series must behave as if it is the result of a truly random process.

The first criterion, the periodicity of the series, lies within the province of computational mathematics. We will not discuss the rationale of our method here; to do so would take us too far afield. Instead, we present the most widely used of the generation algorithms, the multiplicative congruential procedure.

Before writing a new random number routine, the user should consult with his or her computing center about the existence of a generator. If one has been developed, there is probably no need to write one; most library generators are assembly coded and are more efficient than a Fortran procedure. However, unless the library generator is known to be good, it may be worthwhile to submit it to the several tests described below.

A Multiplicative Congruential Generator

The most successful pseudorandom number generator in current use is based on the congruence relationship in the mathematical theory of numbers. The use of congruence for generating pseudorandom sequences was first proposed by Lehmer (1951). Since then it has been studied extensively (see, e.g., Ahrens, Dieter, & Grube, 1970). The computational procedure is a simple one, requiring only a multiplication and a modulo operation. The basic function is

$$x_i = ax_{i-1} \text{ (modulo } 2^m),$$

where a is a constant, m is the word length of the computer in bits, and x_{i-1} is the previous number in the series.

The function in Table 5.1 gives a Fortran procedure for obtaining uniform random values in the interval 0–1. It is based on the program presented by Ahrens, Dieter, and Grube (1970). There are two entries to the routine. Using the RANDOM entry [as in the statement X=RANDOM(DUMMY)] will initialize

TABLE 5.1
A Uniform Random Number Generator Subroutine (RANDOM)

```
      FUNCTION RANDOM(XYZ)
C
C     GENERATES A SAMPLE FROM THE UNIFORM DISTRIBUTION
C        ON THE 0-1 INTERVAL.
C     BASED ON THE ALGORITHM PRESENTED IN AHRENS, J. H.,
C        DIETER, U., & GRUBE, A.  PSEUDO-RANDOM NUMBERS:
C        A NEW PROPOSAL FOR THE CHOICE OF MULTIPLICATORS.
C        COMPUTING, 1970, 6, 121-138.
C     USES THE MULTIPLICATIVE CONGRUENTIAL PROCEDURE.
C     THE RANDOM ENTRY INITIALIZES THE GENERATOR.
C        SUBSEQUENT REFERENCES TO RNDM(DUMMY) RETURN A SINGLE
C        RANDOM VALUE.
C
C     THIS ROUTINE REQUIRES A STARTING VALUE AS INPUT.
C        IT SHOULD BE A VALUE BETWEEN 0 AND 16383, PUNCHED
C        IN DOUBLE PRECISION FORMAT (D12.5).
C
C     THE PROGRAM COULD BE MODIFIED TO OBTAIN THE
C        STARTING VALUE FROM, PERHAPS, A CLOCK READING.
C
      REAL*8 R1,RF
C
C     READ STARTER VALUE
C
      READ(1,1) R1
    1 FORMAT(D12.5)
C
C     THE INITIAL VALUE (R1) CAN BE READ OR COMPUTED AS
C          (FOR EXAMPLE) A CLOCK READING.
      RANDOM = 0.
C
C     NOW SCALE THE INITIAL VALUE AND DEFINE THE MULTIPLIER.
C
      R1=R1/16384.0D0+1.0D0/16384.0D0/16384.0D0
      RF = 41475557.0D0
      RETURN
C
C     ENTRY TO DELIVER A RANDOM NUMBER.
C
      ENTRY RNDM(WXYZ)
      R1 = DMOD(R1*RF,1.0D0)
      RANDOM = R1
      RETURN
      END
```

the generator by reading a value for the start of the random sequence. That value should be a REAL*8 number in the range 0—16,383. RANDOM is to be used only once during the run of a program. Thereafter, using the RNDM entry [as in X=RNDM(DUMMY)] will result in a new value being returned in the variable X. The argument DUMMY is just that, a dummy variable. The function never pays any attention to it, and it is there only because Fortran requires a FUNCTION to have at least one argument.

This function is appropriate for any computer with a 32-bit word. Information about other word lengths and testing details for the generator can be found in Ahrens, Dieter, and Grube (1970). These two routines, RANDOM and RNDM, will appear throughout this chapter as sources for uniformly distributed random numbers required by other routines. They are also referenced throughout the example programs.

With a generation procedure available, we now consider the various tests that are applied to the output of a random number generator.

Testing Random Number Generators

The output of a generator must be a series of numbers meeting accepted requirements for randomness. Although the values must necessarily result from a deterministic process, if they meet the standards, they may be used as if they have resulted from an actual random process.

A great deal of attention has been paid to the meaning of randomness, and to tests applied to a series of numbers that are purported to be random. Knuth (1969) presents an elegant and exhaustive discussion of the problem. For our purposes here, however, we shall consider four important elements of randomness and refer the reader with a thirst for more detail to Knuth.

Of the several criteria that are applied to random numbers, the first — the periodicity of the series — is met by using a multiplicative congruential generator as discussed above. The remaining three canons concern the rectangularity of the distribution, the sequential independence of the numbers in the series, and a set of tests sensitive to runs and gaps. All three of the criteria are statistical. They suffer from the problems common to such procedures: one can never conclude with absolute certainty but can only make judgments as to the likelihood that the obtained values depart from what is expected of "truly random" numbers. In all cases, the statistical null hypothesis tested is that the distribution of values is "random."

Rectangularity. The statistical test for rectangularity is nothing more than a test of the hypothesis that the generator's output does not depart from a rectangular distribution and proceeds as follows.

Divide the range of the possible values into a set of equal intervals; 10 is a reasonable set. If the numbers are taken directly from the generator without scaling, the intervals would be

$$0.00-0.0999$$
$$0.10-0.1999$$
$$0.20-0.2999$$

.
.
.

Next, generate a relatively large number of random values, say 10,000. As each value is generated, find the interval into which it belongs by a search procedure and tally the frequency f_i in the interval.

When that is done, compute the "expected" number of values that should occur in each interval if the distribution were truly rectangular as:

$$E = \text{Expected frequency} = \frac{\text{Number of values generated}}{\text{Number of intervals}}.$$

For our example,

$$E = \text{Expected frequency} = \frac{10,000}{10} = 1,000.$$

Finally, compute the Pearson chi-square statistic as

$$\chi^2 = \sum_{i=1}^{n} \frac{(f_i - E)^2}{E},$$

where n is the number of intervals, and f_i is the obtained frequency in each interval.

The statistic χ^2 is distributed as approximately chi-square with $n - 1$ degrees of freedom. If the obtained value exceeds the critical value found in a standard table for df $= n - 1$ and the significance level desired, then the obtained values depart from rectangularity more than is expected by chance. In such a case, the random number generator may be suspect; but at least one additional test of rectangularity should be made on another set of values before it is discarded.

Sequential independence. A number of procedures might produce values which would meet the rectangularity criterion. Indeed, any computation generating the sequence 0, 1, 2, 3, 4, 5, 6, 7, 8, 9, 0, . . . will result in a very nice rectangular distribution!

Sequential dependencies in a generator, where a correlation exists between adjacent values, or between pairs removed from each other by some distance is a serious problem. True random numbers, of course, show no such serial relationship.

Two general procedures are used in testing sequential dependency. A test for adjacent pairs can be developed as an elaboration of the goodness of fit technique just used. This time, however, pairs of values x_i and x_{i+1} are tallied into a two-dimensional array. Figure 5.1 illustrates such a frequency table. In the table, the first member of a pair of random numbers is located in a row, and the second in a column. The occurrence of a pair such as .873991 and .225367 would be tallied into Row 9 (.80–.8999), Column 3 (.20–.2999). After a large number of random values is generated and tallied, the expected frequency per cell is computed as

$$E = \frac{\text{Number of values generated}}{\text{Number of cells}},$$

as before. Then the test statistic is computed as

$$\chi^2 = \sum_{i=1}^{R} \sum_{j=1}^{C} \frac{(f_{ij} - E)^2}{E},$$

where R and C are the number of rows and columns in the frequency table. The obtained value is then referred to a chi-square table with $(RC - 1)$ degrees of freedom.

When sequential dependencies for other than adjacent pairs are tested, a lagged product procedure is applied. A sequence of random numbers $x_1, x_2, \ldots, x_n$ on the 0–1 interval is generated. Then a lag is determined. The lag is the gap between numbers in the test. When the lag is one, the test is for adjacent pairs, two gives the covariance between alternate values, and so forth.

For a lag of k, the quantity

$$C_k = \frac{1}{n-k} \sum_{i=1}^{n-k} x_i x_{i+k}$$

gives the lagged product of the random numbers. Two alternative procedures can now be used to test the value C_k. Both are based on the fact the C_k is approximately normally distributed with $\mu_{C_k} = .25$ and

$$\sigma_{C_k} = \sqrt{13n - 19k}/12(n-k)$$

To test a single value, the obtained value C_k is standardized using the formula

$$z_C = \frac{C_k - .25}{\sigma_{C_k}}.$$

If the absolute value of z_C is greater than the chosen critical value for a normal distribution (1.96 at $\alpha = .05$ for example), then the hypothesis of sequential independence for a lag of k is rejected.

The second approach to testing the sequential independence for a lag of k is to generate a large number of sequences $x_1, \ldots, x_n$, compute C_k for each, and

Column (second number)

range	1 .00 – .099	2 .10 – .199	3 .20 – .299	. . .	10 .90 – 1.000
1 .00 – .099					
2 .10 .199					
3 .20 – .299					
. . .					
10 .90 – 1.00					

Row (first number)

FIGURE 5.1   A two dimensional frequency table for testing pair-wise independence.

determine whether the distribution of C_k follows the normal distribution by using a chi-square procedure.

Of course, to test for sequential dependencies in a generator, it will be necessary to repeat the lagged product procedure for a number of values of k. A generator producing satisfactory values for a lag of 3, for example, may show significant dependency for a lag of 4.

Runs and gaps. The final set of criteria deals with determining whether the random numbers tend to increase or decrease in a series (runs) and whether they are too closely packed or too spread out (gaps). These standards are generally met by random number generators that pass the preceding tests. Nevertheless, a thorough evaluation of a generator includes these procedures.

The test for runs and that for gaps are similar to the procedures used for rectangularity and for sequential independence in that both use a goodness of fit criterion. For the runs procedure, generate a series of n random values, x_1, $x_2, \ldots, x_n$. Now count the number of runs of length k, where $k \leqslant n - 1$; a run is defined as a series of values, where $x_i < x_{i+1}$ (ascending run) or $x_i > x_{i+1}$ (descending run) for k consecutive values. In defining runs, it is essential that a run of length k not be embedded in a run of $k + 1$; for example, the sequence .1543, .2377, .6582, .6689 counts only as an ascending run of $k = 4$ and not as three runs of 2, two runs of 3, and one run of 4.

A count is kept of the number of runs of each length in a sample from a generator. Those frequencies are then compared with the expected frequencies using a goodness to fit procedure. The expected frequency of a run up or down of length k in a series of n numbers is

$$\frac{2[(k^2 + 3k + 1)n - (k^3 + 3k^2 - k - 4)]}{(k + 3)!}$$

for $k < n - 1$, and $2/n!$ for $k = n - 1$. Thus, the expected number of runs of length $k = 2$ in a series of $n = 1000$ values is

$$\frac{2[(2^2 + 3 \times 2 + 1) \times 1000 - (2^3 + 3 \times 2^2 - 2 - 4)]}{(2 + 3)!} = 183.1.$$

A test for gaps is concerned with the number of digits intervening between two occurrences of the same digit in a series. This test is slightly different than the previous procedures in that it deals with single digits. To conduct the gaps test, obtain a series $d_1, d_2, \ldots, d_n$ of single digits from a random number generator. A gap of length k is defined as a series of k digits between the consecutive occurrences of the same digit. When the same digit appears twice in a row, the gap is of length zero.

For a random sequence of n digits, the number of gaps that is expected for any length of gap k is

$$(0.9)^k (0.1)n.$$

In a series of 1,000 values, for example, the expected number of gaps of length 1 is:

$$(0.9)^1 (0.1)1,000 = 90,$$

whereas the expected number of $k = 2$ gaps is:

$$(0.9)^2 (0.1)1,000 = 81$$

and that for $k = 3$,

$$(0.9)^3 (0.1)1,000 = 72.9.$$

To test a generator, then, we obtain a sequence of n values, count the number of gaps of length k for a series of values of k, and compare the obtained frequencies with those expected by chance using a goodness of fit test as before.

SIMULATING UNIVARIATE PROBABILITY DISTRIBUTIONS

A probability distribution function assigns a probability to each possible value, or range of values, in the value set of a variable. Selecting a value of the variable according to the probabilities defined by the distribution function is known as sampling from the probability distribution. Generating a random number between 0 and 1 is therefore equivalent to selecting a single value from a rectangular probability distribution on the unit interval. Likewise, obtaining an integer in the range 1–100 is comparable to sampling from the discrete rectangular distribution on the 1–100 interval. A rectangular distribution of values from a to b has a density function defined as:

$$f(x) = \begin{cases} \dfrac{1}{b-a} & \text{for } a \leqslant x \leqslant b \\ 0 & \text{otherwise} \end{cases}$$

and has a mean $\mu = (a + b)/2$ and a variance $\sigma^2 = (b - a)^2/12$.

If a rectangular distribution on the unit (0–1) interval is needed, the output of an acceptable generator can be used directly. Should an integer in the range 1–100 be needed, for example, the 0–1 value can be multiplied by 100, 1 added, and the integer part taken.

In general, to obtain a random value between 1 and N, the statement FUNCTION

```
IRAND(N) = INT(RNDM(DUMMY)*N+1)
```

accomplishes the task, where N is the upper limit of the possible values. This statement FUNCTION appears in SIMSAL.

A more general function can be written to scale values to any range

```
JRAND(IBOT,ITOP)
= INT(RNDM(DUMMY)*(ITOP-IBOT+1)+IBOT)
```

where IBOT and ITOP are the lower and upper limits of the desired range. Should a decimal value of a random number be needed, the function:

```
FRAND(IBOT,ITOP) = RNDM(DUMMY)*(ITOP-IBOT)+IBOT
```

delivers it.

The ability to simulate sampling from the rectangular or uniform distribution is important in simulation programming. But the range of probability distributions is large, and many of the phenomena of interest to behavioral scientists follow other forms of distribution. Intelligence, weight, height, life span of humans and light bulbs, and certain speed measures, for example, are normally distributed. Other important variables have different distributions: time between arrivals, reaction time, number of errors, and number of trials are but a few.

Variables, and their distributions, are sometimes grouped into two broad classes, continuous and discrete. A continuous variable is one that can assume any real number value; between any two values, another can conceivably occur. Number of trials to a criterion, or the number of errors, are two examples of discrete variables; a subject may make 10 errors, or 11, but not 10.5. Time measures, among other variables, are continuous. A response may require 15 sec, or 16, or 15.5, or even 15.25; indeed, any conceivable value lies within the value set of the variable.

Like variables, the procedures for simulating probability distributions can be grouped roughly into discrete and continuous. Examples of continuous distributions to be discussed in this chapter are the exponential and the normal. Among the discrete distributions to be presented are the binomial, the geometric, and the Poisson.

Many conceptually continuous variables appear to be discrete in practice. For example, time is continuous, but the clocks and timers used in research have only a certain degree of precision. Intelligence is a theoretically continuous variable but its measurement is by IQ test, and IQ tests yield only discrete values.

The discrete- versus continuous-variable problem is properly faced during the design of the simulation; it relates to the problem of measurement in behavioral science. When measurements are simulated, it should be done at a level of precision consistent with the practice in the field. A psychologist simulates IQ at a discrete level because that is what his or her tests can measure. An urban planner simulates buildings on a block, but not the precise placement, down to the inch, within a block. A political scientist often simulates percentages of votes, not individual voters.

In passing, we should note that simulating a continuous variable on a digital computer is itself an approximation. As we point out in detail in Chapter 6, a true continuous variable cannot be accurately represented on a computer because only a finite number of digits is available to represent any number.

So far, we have talked about only single variables the distribution of which is simulated. Of course, variables occur jointly too. People have an age and an IQ, are female and Republican, and so forth. In the final two sections of this chapter, we shall discuss some procedures for sampling from such joint distributions. For now, however, we limit ourselves to single variable, or univariate, probability distributions.

Bernoulli Events

The simplest probability distribution is that of a variable having but two possible values. The values may be a wide variety of things — heads and tails on a coin, perhaps, or sex, or success/failure. Such two-valued variables are generally called Bernoulli trials, after the Swiss mathematician Jakob Bernoulli (1654–1705). In general, one possible outcome of a Bernoulli trial is designated a "success" and the other a "failure." The probability of a success is designated p and that of a failure is $q = 1 - p$.

The generation of Bernoulli trials on a computer is simplicity itself. A number of the uniform 0–1 distribution is selected and compared with the probability of success p. If the obtained value is less than p, then a success has occurred; otherwise a failure is noted.

In order to determine whether a simulated subject is a male or female, for example, we can define "female" as a success with a probability of .50. If we generated a value of .322167, then our simulated subject would be a female.

The learning parameters in SIMSAL serve as probabilities in Bernoulli events. One of them is PADD, the probability of adding a node to the tree following an incorrect guess at the response. Learning is governed by the statement:

```
3001 IF(RNDM(DUMMY)-PADD) 3100,3002,3002
```

If the value obtained from RNDM is less than PADD, then a success has occurred and the program branches to statement 3100 where the node-building statements are executed. Conversely, if the value is greater than or equal to PADD, the trial has failed and the program proceeds to statement 3002 where similar tests are made on the change and overlearning parameters.

The Bernoulli distribution is a discrete variable and is closely related to several additional distributions, the geometric, the Poisson, and the binomial.

The Geometric Distribution

If a series of independent Bernoulli trials is performed, the number of failure trials before the first success follows a geometric distribution. The number of heads before the first tail, the number of women selected before the first man, the number of operations on a machine before the first breakdown, and the number of times SIMSAL forms a new node before it fails to do so are all geometric variables.

The geometric distribution is a probability function that assigns probabilities to the possible values of a variable x ($x = 0, 1, 2, \ldots$) and may be defined as

$$f(x) = pq^x,$$

where p is the probability of a success on any trial and $q = 1 - p$ is the probability of a failure. The distribution has the expected value $\mu = q/p$ and variance $\sigma^2 = q/p^2$.

The simulation of a value from the geometric distribution is not difficult, although two alternative procedures should be followed depending on the value of p. When p is close to either 0 or 1, the best approach for generating a geometric variable is the direct one; simply generate a series of Bernoulli events and count the number of trials before a success is noted. If $q = 1 - p$, generate a series u_i of uniform random numbers on the unit interval. Then, when $u_i > q$ for the first time, $i - 1$ is the value of the geometric variable. The short Fortran FUNCTION in Table 5.2 illustrates a procedure for generating a sample from the geometric distribution with probability of success p. The function reference RNDM(DUMMY) delivers a number on the unit interval.

The alternate procedure for sampling a geometric variable is also included in Table 5.2. It is the logarithmic algorithm

$$\left[i = \frac{\log u}{\log q} \right] ,$$

where i is the desired geometric value, u is a random number on the 0−1 interval, $q = 1 - p$, and [ ] indicates the integer part of the result. This procedure is hazardous when p is close to 0 or 1 because the precision of the ALOG function in Fortran is often quite poor near those two extremes; the counting approach is preferable.

TABLE 5.2

A Fortran Function for Sampling from a Geometric Distribution (GEO)

```
      INTEGER FUNCTION GEO(P)
C
C     GENERATES A SAMPLE FROM A GEOMETRIC DISTRIBUTION WITH
C        PROBABILITY PARAMETER P.
C     RETURN IS THE NUMBER OF FAILURES BEFORE THE FIRST SUCCESS.
C
      IF(P.LE..05.OR.P.GE..95) GO TO 1
C
C     SIMPLE METHOD FOR MODERATE VALUE OF P
C
      X = RNDM(DUMMY)
      GEO = INT(ALOG10(X)/ALOG10(1.0-P)+1.0)
      RETURN
C
C     DIRECT COUNTING METHOD FOR EXTREME VALUE OF P
C
    1 DO 2 I = 1,1000
      X = RNDM(DUMMY)
      IF(X.LT.P) GO TO 3
C
C     CONTINUE IF A FAILURE
C
    2 CONTINUE
C
C     NO SUCCESS IN 1000 TRIALS
C
      GEO = 10000
      RETURN
C
C     GET HERE ON FIRST SUCCESS
C
    3 GEO = I
      RETURN
      END
```

One operating characteristic of the GEO function in Table 5.2 should be noted. If the probability of failure is high (greater than .95), it is possible (but improbable) for the function to complete 1,000 trials without a success. In that case, the normal exit from the loop (DO 2 . . .) is made and a value of 10,000 is returned. That value could be either used as the geometric sample or used as a flag to take appropriate error action.

The Binomial Distribution

Like the geometric distribution, the binomial is based on a series of success–fail Bernoulli trials. In this case, however, a series of n Bernoulli trials is performed, and the number of successes is counted. The probability of each possible number of successes in n trials follows the binomial distribution.

A large number of variables follows the binomial. The number of male children in families of size n, the number of errors in n-unit T mazes, and the number of defective light bulbs in a group of n all have a binomial probability distribution.

When p and $q = 1 - p$ are the probabilities of success and failure, respectively, in a series of n Bernoulli trials, then the binomial variable may be defined as

$$f(x) = \binom{n}{x} p^x q^{n-x}$$

where $x = 0, 1, \ldots, n$ is the number of successes in n trials. The probability distribution has the expected value $\mu = np$ with a variance $\sigma^2 = npq$.

The procedure for sampling from the binomial also takes two alternative forms, this time depending on the value of n. If n is reasonably small – less than 20 or so – a direct approach may be followed. In this procedure, a series of n uniform random numbers is generated and a count is made of all those less than the probability of success p. The value of the count is then the value of the binomial variable.

For a larger value of n, the binomial can be approximated by the normal distribution. With a large n, the binomial is approximately normal with a mean of np and a variance of npq. A value can be obtained from a normal distribution, scaled to the appropriate mean and variance, and then rounded to an integer value, because the binomial is a discrete distribution. Table 5.3 presents a binomial sampling routine – the reference to RNORM produces a normal random value, as we discuss below.

The Poisson Distribution

A close relative of the binomial and geometric distributions is the Poisson, named for a nineteenth century French mathematician. This distribution most often appears when the variable being measured is the count of the number of occurrences (or successes, if you will) of some event within a certain time period

TABLE 5.3
A Function for Generating Samples from a Binomial Distribution(BIN)

```
      INTEGER FUNCTION BIN(N,P)
C
C     GENERATES A SAMPLE FROM A BINOMIAL DISTRIBUTION
C        WITH PARAMETERS N AND P.
C
C     A NORMAL DISTRIBUTION ROUTINE (RNORM) IS NEEDED
C
C
C     SELECT APPROPRIATE ALGORITHM
C
      IF(N.GT.25) GO TO 100
C
C     DIRECT COMPUTATION METHOD FOR SMALL N
C
      BIN = 0
      DO 1 I = 1,N
      IF(RNDM(DUMMY).LE.P) BIN = BIN+1
    1 CONTINUE
      RETURN
C
C     NORMAL APPROXIMATION METHOD FOR LARGE N
C
  100 X = RNORM(DUMMY)
      BMEAN = N*P
      BIN = INT(X*SQRT(BMEAN*(1.0-P))+BMEAN+.5)
      IF(BIN.LT.0 .OR. BIN.GT.N) GO TO 100
      RETURN
      END
```

or restricted small area. Typically, the probability of a success is very small, but there is a large number of time periods or possible areas. In physical science, several interesting phenomena, such as radioactive decay rates and distribution of bacteria on samples, follow the Poisson distribution. Other examples include the rate of misprints in books, the number of arrivals per unit time at toll booths or checkout lanes, numbers of accidents and insurance claims per unit of time, and so forth.

The Poisson is a discrete probability distribution, like the binomial. Indeed, the Poisson is identical to the binomial distribution with a very small p and a very large n. For a Poisson distribution,

$$f(x) = e^{-k} \left(k^x / x! \right),$$

where $x = 0, 1, 2, \ldots$. For the Poisson, $\mu = \sigma^2 = k$.

Because the Poisson is closely related to the binomial, it can be simulated by a binomial; however, the following procedure is easier.

To generate a Poisson value obtain a series of uniform random numbers on the 0–1 interval. Multiply them together until the product is less than e^{-k}, where k is the mean of the desired Poisson distribution. The required Poisson value is then n, the number of random numbers multiplied together, minus 1. If the first random number generated is less than e^{-k}, then the Poisson variable has the value 0.

The Exponential Distribution

When the variable is a measure of elapsed time, such as time between arrivals of automobiles at our hypothetical toll booth or between bar presses by a rat in a Skinner box, the probability distribution is usually exponential in form. This, our first instance of a continuous distribution, is very commonly employed in simulation programming.

The density function of the exponential is defined by

$$f(x) = \alpha e^{-\alpha x},$$

where $\alpha > 0$ and $x \geq 0$. In this continuous variable, $\mu = 1/\alpha$ and $\sigma^2 = 1/\alpha^2 = \mu^2$.

In an extensive survey of algorithms for sampling from exponential and normal distributions, Ahrens and Dieter (1972) conclude that the statement

```
X = -ALOG(RNDM(DUMMY))/ALPHA
```

where ALPHA represents the parameter α in the definition, is the most efficient procedure that can be coded in Fortran to generate an exponential variable X.

The Normal Distribution and Its Relatives

The normal is the most widely used continuous distribution in the social and behavioral sciences. This is true not only because a great many variables are normally distributed, but also because of its statistical applications. Nearly every student in an elementary statistics course knows that the sampling distribution of the mean is normal, given a sufficiently large sample size. What is perhaps not as well known, however, is the relationship between the normal distribution and the other commonly used statistical sampling distributions, such as chi-square, t, and F.

A normal distribution with a mean μ and a variance σ^2 has a density function defined by

$$f(x) = \frac{1}{\sigma\sqrt{2\pi}} \exp[-1/(2\sigma^2)(x - \mu)^2].$$

Generating normal variates. Two methods are suggested here for generating normal samples, a slow but easy to remember technique, and a highly efficient but complex algorithm.

The slow but simple approach makes use of the central limit theorem (CLT) from mathematical statistics. An often overlooked consequence of the CLT is its assertion that the sum of n independent samples from identical distributions, such as $x_1 + x_2 + \cdots + x_n$, is normally distributed with the mean equal to $n\mu_x$ and a variance of $n\sigma^2_x$ where σ^2_x is the variance of x. If, for example, the distribution of x is uniform on the $0-1$ interval, then a sum $y = x_1 + x_2 + \ldots + x_n$ of n such numbers is normally distributed with

$$\mu_y = .5n, \qquad \sigma^2_y = \frac{n}{12}$$

so that

$$z = \frac{y - .5n}{\sqrt{n/12}}$$

is standard normal with $\mu_z = 0$ and $\sigma_z^2 = 1$.

The CLT informs us that the larger the value of n, the better becomes the approximation to the normal distribution. For most purposes, a value of 12 is convenient and leads to a reasonable approximation. In this case, the denominator of the z equation will be:

$$\sqrt{12/12}$$

and thus vanishes, leaving the computation as:

$$z = y - .5(12) = y - 6,$$

an exceptionally easy formula to remember and program.

Despite its simplicity, the CLT generator is not the best one if more than a very few numbers are to be generated. It is very slow and it does not adequately sample the extreme tails of the normal distribution. An alternative is therefore preferable.

In their survey of normal distribution sampling algorithms, Ahrens and Dieter (1972) discuss several techniques and recommend one as being most efficient in Fortran. Other procedures are suggested when assembly coding is to be used. The Fortran method is a combination of three well-known approaches — a trapezoidal approximation to the normal curve, a procedure for dealing only with the tails of the distribution, and a technique known as an acceptance—rejection algorithm.

Table 5.4 presents a Fortran function RNORM based on their approach. The algorithm is taken directly from Ahrens and Dieter (1972, p. 879)* and coded in

---

*Copyright 1972, Association for Computing Machinery, Inc.

Fortran. The large number of constants in the routine result from numerical considerations in the solution of the various subalogrithms. In order to assure that all of the digits in the constants are represented, it may be necessary to use extended precision on some compilers.

The subroutine, as in the past, requires a generator RNDM for producing values from the uniform 0–1 distribution. The output of the subroutine is a single sample from a standard normal distribution with $\mu = 0$ and $\sigma^2 = 1.0$.

To convert a standard normal sample to one from a normal distribution of z' with a mean μ and a standard deviation σ, the simple transformation

$$z' = \sigma z + \mu,$$

where z is a standard normal variable can do the job nicely. To obtain a sample from the normal distribution of IQ scores, for example, the statement

```
IQ = 15.0*RNORM(XX)+100.0
```

result in an IQ that is sampled from the distribution of IQ scores – a mean μ of 100 and a standard deviation σ of 15.

Some statistical distributions. Many inferential statistical procedures are based on distributions closely related to the normal. Samples from three, chi square, F, and Student's t, may be generated as functions of the normal.

The chi-square distribution may be simulated as the sum of a series of squared normal scores. The relationship:

$$x = \sum_{i=1}^{m} z_i^2 ,$$

where each z_i is a standard normal variable, results in an x sampled from a chi-square distribution with m degrees of freedom. In Fortran, the statements:

```
S = 0.0
DO 1 I = 1,M
Z = RNORM(DUM)
S = S+Z*Z
1 CONTINUE
```

yield a value of S that is distributed as chi-square with M degrees of freedom.

In a similar fashion, the relationship between chi-square and Student's t is given by

$$t = \frac{z}{\sqrt{x/m}},$$

TABLE 5.4

A Normal Distribution Sampling Routine (RNORM)

```
C     FUNCTION RNORM(XXX)
C
C     GENERATES A SAMPLE FROM THE NORMAL DISTRIBUTION N(0,1).
C
C     ALGORITHM IS TAKEN FROM AHRENS AND DIETER, COMPUTER
C     METHODS FOR SAMPLING FROM THE EXPONENTIAL AND
C     NORMAL DISTRIBUTIONS, COMMUNICATIONS OF THE ACM, 15,
C     1972, 873-882.
C
C     USES A TRAPEZIODAL APPROXIMATION IN ABOUT 91.95% OF
C     THE CASES, A TAIL METHOD IN ABOUT 3.45% OF THE CASES,
C     AND AN ACCEPTANCE-REJECTION PROCEDURE FOR THE REST.
C
C     TRAPEZOIDAL PROCEDURE
C
      U = RNDM(DUMMY)
      UO = RNDM(DUMMY)
      IF(U.GE.0.919544405706926) GO TO 100
      RNORM = 2.403757656937 42*(UO+U*0.825339282536923)-2.1140280833374 2
      RETURN
C
C     TAIL PROCEDURE
C
100   IF(U.LT.0.96548713121385 8) GO TO 200
101   U1 = RNDM(DUMMY)
      Y = (4.46911473713927-2*ALOG(U1))**0.5
```

```
      U2=RNDM(DUMMY)
      IF(Y*U2-2.11402808333742) 300,300,101
C
C     ACCEPTANCE-REJECTION PROCEDURE
C
200   CONS = 0.39894228040401433
      IF(U.LT.0.94999070873302B) GO TO 250
201   U1 = RNDM(DUMMY)
      Y = 1.84039874739771+U1*0.27362935939706
      US = RNDM(DUMMY)
      TEST = CONS*EXP(-(Y**2)/2)-0.44329912582022+Y*0.20969405719548G
      IF(TEST-U2*0.04270258159079S) 201,300,300
250   IF(U.LT.0.92585233707704) GO TO 270
251   U1 = RNDM(DUMMY)
      Y = 0.28972957364U1*1.55066917379771
      U2 = RNDM(DUMMY)
      TEST = CONS*EXP(-(Y**2)/2)-0.44329912582022+Y*0.20969405719548G
      IF(TEST-U2*0.0159745226655238)251,300,300
270   U1 = RNDM(DUMMY)
271   Y = U1*0.28972957364
      U2 = RNDM(DUMMY)
      TEST = CONS*EXP(-(Y**2)/2)-0.38254455604251B
      IF(TEST-U2*0.0163977243589158) 271,300,300
C
C     PICK A SIGN RANDOMLY AND RETURN
C
300   RNORM = Y
      IF(UO.GE.0.5) RNORM = -RNORM
      RETURN
      END
```

where z is standard normal and x is chi square with m degrees of freedom. The value of t is distributed as Student's t with m degrees of freedom.

The F statistic may be expressed as the ratio of two independent chi-square variates:

$$F = \frac{x_n/n}{x_m/m}$$

where x_n and x_m are two chi-square variables with n and m degrees of freedom, respectively. The value of F follows the F distribution with n, m degrees of freedom.

SIMULATING MULTIVARIATE PROBABILITY DISTRIBUTIONS

When values are selected from the joint distribution of two or more variables, the procedure is known as multivariate sampling. Sampling from a normal distribution of two variables — a bivariate normal — such as the joint distribution of height and weight, age and IQ, age and income, or inventory size and unit price, is relatively straightforward. When a normal distribution of three or more variables jointly is needed, the algorithm is very complex and is presented only as a subroutine with little discussion. When the variables are not distributed as multivariate normal, their sampling can often be simulated by a contingency table. We discuss contingency procedures later.

The Bivariate Normal Distribution

In sampling from a bivariate normal distribution, the univariate distribution of each variable is normal, as is the joint distribution. In the following discussion, we deal with the variables x and y that are to be bivariate normal.

In the simplest case, both variables are in standard normal form; that is,

$$\mu_x = \mu_y = 0.0,$$

$$\sigma_x^2 = \sigma_y^2 = 1.0.$$

In this case, one value is generated directly as

$$x = z_1,$$

where x is the desired value and z_1 is the output of a standard normal generator, such as RNORM (Table 5.4).

The y value corresponding to x is obtained as a function of x, a second standard normal value (z_2), and the desired correlation between them

$$y = \rho z_1 + z_2\sqrt{1 - \rho^2},$$

where ρ is the correlation. The Fortran statements to produce an X,Y pair would therefore be:

```
RHO = (desired correlation)
Z1 = RNORM(XX)
Z2 = RNORM(XX)
X = Z1
Y = Z1*RHO+Z2*SQRT(1.0-RHO*RHO)
```

Usually we do not require standardized values of x and y but prefer that they be scaled to some more appropriate values. If the desired means and standard deviations are μ_x, μ_y, σ_x, and σ_y and the correlation is ρ, then the relationships are:

$$x = \sigma_x z_1 + \mu_x$$
$$y = \sigma_y \left(\rho z_1 + z_2 \sqrt{1 - \rho^2} \right) + \mu_y.$$

The series of Fortran statements below illustrates the process.

```
XMU = (desired mean for x)
YMU = (desired mean for y)
XSIG = (desired standard deviation for x)
YSIG = (desired standard deviation for y)
RHO = (desired correlation)
Z1 = RNORM(XXX)
Z2 = RNORM(XXX)
X = XSIG*Z1+XMU
Y = YSIG*(RHO*Z1+Z2*SQRT(1.0-RHO*RHO))+YMU
```

The General Multivariate Normal Distribution

The bivariate normal is a special case of the multivariate normal distribution of k variables when $k = 2$. Any sampling from a multidimensional normal distribution will result in a set of k values, representing a single observation. For example, suppose that a program required scores for a group of simulated subjects in a psychological research study. We might want three different intelligence tests, a college grade point average, and a test of verbal comprehension for each subject. All of the variables show some varying degree of correlation with each other. We wish an algorithm to generate sets of five scores, each set representing a single subject in the study, so that the correlations in the data represent those that theoretically obtain among the variables. This is the task of the general multivariate normal sampling procedure.

An essential ingredient in a multivariate normal sampling procedure is specifying the pattern of intercorrelations among the variables, just as RHO describes the correlation between two variables in the bivariate case. When there are a number of variables, there is a correlation between each pair of them, and the entire set of correlations is best represented by a matrix.

Two general approaches have been taken in developing a procedure to sample from a multivariate normal population with specified parameters. Neither results in data that exactly duplicate the population but both produce samples from the desired distribution. One approach may be described as a "reverse" factor analysis. It was presented by Wherry, Naylor, Wherry, and Fallis (1965). We will not discuss the technique here to avoid an extensive digression into the logic of factor analysis.

The second approach, which we do follow here, begins with the population matrix and develops samples from it. In a study of three algorithms using this technique, Barr and Slezak (1972) identified one that resulted in considerably faster execution for all sets of data studied. That procedure forms the basis for our algorithm. Another program based on the same algorithm is given by Sands (1973), and a related one is presented in Kaiser and Dickman (1962).

The multivariate normal routine consists of two major sections. The first takes an input correlation matrix and converts it into a variance/covariance matrix. The program presented here has the option of accepting a variance/covariance matrix directly, although most social and behavioral scientists find it much more comfortable to think in terms of correlations.

Once the variance/covariance matrix is available, it is factored into a lower triangular matrix so that

$$C = TT',$$

where C is the variance/covariance matrix and T is the triangular matrix. The factoring procedure follows a square root procedure described by Scheuer and Stoller (1962). A call to RANDOM completes the initialization phase of the routine. The program appears as the subroutine SETUP in Table 5.5

Once the generation routine has been initialized, a single sample of observations can be easily obtained. A vector of independent unit normal values is obtained (say, from RNORM), and those values are scaled by a function of the lower triangular matrix and the desired means. In the program presented in Table 5.5, this computation is carried out by the entry DATA.

Using the SETUP/DATA routine is a simple matter. The statement

```
CALL SETUP(N,IOK)
```

initializes the necessary matrices by obtaining the variance/covariance or correlation matrix. SETUP returns two variables to the calling program. The first, N, gives the number of variables in the input matrix. The second return, IOK, is an error indicator. Under most circumstances, SETUP will return a value of 1 for IOK, indicating that the routine has been initialized properly. A return of IOK = 0 informs the calling program that an error has occurred in SETUP and the routine has not initialized the matrix. An error return will occur in one of two instances. The first is a loss of precision in computing the triangular factor matrix, causing a diagonal element to become too small. If this happens regularly, the variables D, R, ROOT, and SUM in SETUP should be declared DOUBLE PRECISION.

The more common reason for an error return will be when the supplied matrix is singular, meaning that it has a determinant of zero. In this case, the triangular factoring cannot be completed. It is easy to invent singular matrices; because the routine is often supplied with a "made up" matrix, the singularity check is made by the subroutine.

Once SETUP has been called, a subsequent statement, such as

CALL DATA (VALUES)

can return a one-dimensional array of N scores in the vector VALUES.

SETUP and DATA can accommodate correlation matrices up to 30 X 30 in size as presented here. Should more variables be required, the DIMENSION statement can be modified easily. There is no limitation on the number of individual sets of scores that can be generated — each CALL DATA is independent of every other and returns a single vector of scores.

SOME OTHER RANDOM PROCESSES

A generator producing random numbers on the unit interval can be used for a number of purposes other than simulating probability distributions. This section presents two additional uses for random numbers, shuffling and array selection.

Shuffling

Shuffling an array is analogous to shuffling a deck of playing cards. The elements in the array — the cards — remain the same, but the order is changed. The array values may be used directly in further computation, or they may be pointers, such as SIMSAL's ORDER array. The shuffle is identical with a random permutation of the elements in an array. But because the term "shuffle" is almost universally used in the computing science literature instead of permutation, we will continue to use that term.

TABLE 5.5

A Multivariate Normal Distribution Sampling Routine (SETUP/DATA)

```
C     SUBROUTINE SETUP(N,IQK)
C
C     GENERAL MULTIVARIATE NORMAL SAMPLE GENERATOR.
C     BASED ON THE TRIANGULAR FACTORIZATION ALGORITHM GIVEN
C     BY SCHEUER, E. M., & STOLLER, D. S. ON THE
C     GENERATION OF NORMAL RANDOM VECTORS. TECHNOMETRICS,
C     1962, 4, 278-281.
C
C     REQUIRES INPUT AS FOLLOWS--
C     CARD 1, COLUMNS 1-2, NUMBER OF VARIABLES (MAX OF 30).
C     NEXT CARDS, ONE FOR EACH VARIABLE:
C        COLUMNS 1-5  DESIRED MEAN FOR THIS VARIABLE
C        COLUMNS 6-10 DESIRED STANDARD DEVIATION FOR THE VARIABLE
C        SUCCEEDING 5 COLUMN FIELDS, CORRELATIONS BETWEEN THIS
C           VARIABLE AND ALL OTHERS.  CONTINUE ON SUCCEEDING CARDS
C           AS NEEDED USING FORMAT 14F5.0 FOR EACH CARD.
C
C     PROGRAM WILL ALSO ACCEPT A VARIANCE/COVARIANCE MATRIX.
C     IN THIS CASE, STANDARD DEVIATIONS NEED NOT BE SUPPLIED
C     IN COLUMNS 6-10 OF THE FIRST CARD FOR A VARIABLE.
C
C     IF THE FIRST ENTRY IN THE INPUT MATRIX IS 1.0, THE
C     MATRIX IS ASSUMED TO CONTAIN CORRELATIONS. IF THE FIRST
C     ENTRY IS GREATER THAN 1.0, THE MATRIX IS ASSUMED TO BE
C     VARIANCES AND COVARIANCES.
```

```
C     THE ROUTINE RETURNS TWO VALUES TO THE CALLING
C     PROGRAM.  THE FIRST GIVES THE NUMBER OF
C     VARIABLES (N).  THE SECOND ARGUMENT RETURNS A
C     VALUE OF 1 IF THE RETURN IS NORMAL.  A RETURN
C     OF ZERO INDICATES A SINGULAR MATRIX WAS SUPPLIED,
C     OR IN SOME RARE CASES, AN ERROR HAS OCCURRED
C     LEADING TO A TOO-SMALL VALUE.  THE LATTER CASE
C     IS MOST LIKELY CAUSED BY A PROBLEM IN NUMERICAL
C     ACCURACY.
C
C     A RETURN OF ZERO INDICATES THAT THE ROUTINE HAS NOT
C     INITIALIZED THE MATRIX PROPERLY.
C
      DIMENSION D(30,30),R(30,30),SCORES(30),SD(30),XBAR(30),ZVECT(30)
C
C     SET UP INPUT DEVICE
C
      IN = 1
C
C     READ NUMBER OF VARIABLES
C
      READ(IN,10000) N
10000 FORMAT(I2)
```

(continued)

157

TABLE 5.5 (continued)

```
C     NOW READ MEANS, STANDARD DEVIATIONS, AND THE
C     VARIANCE/COVARIANCE OR CORRELATION MATRIX.
C
      DO 100 I = 1,N
      READ(IN,10001) XBAR(I),SD(I),(R(I,J),J = 1,N)
10001 FORMAT(14F5.0)
100   CONTINUE
C
C     CONVERT TO VARIANCE/COVARIANCE MATRIX IF NECESSARY
C
      IF(R(1,1).EQ.1.0) GO TO 150
C
C     WE HAVE A VARIANCE/COVARIANCE MATRIX.  COMPUTE SDS AND
C     STORE DUPLICATE MATRIX FOR DETERMINANT TEST.
C
      DO 101 I = 1,N
      SD(I) = SQRT(R(I,I))
      DO 101 J = 1,N
      D(I,J) = R(I,J)
101   CONTINUE
      GO TO 250
C
C     WE HAVE CORRELATIONS.  CONVERT TO VARIANCE/COVARIANCE MATRIX
C     AND STORE DUPLICATE MATRIX.
C
```

```
150   DO 200 I = 1,N
      DO 200 J = 1,N
      R(I,J) = R(I,J)*SD(I)*SD(J)
      R(J,I) = R(I,J)
      D(I,J) = R(I,J)
      D(J,I) = R(J,I)
200   CONTINUE

C     CHECK FOR SINGULARITY BY COMPUTING DETERMINANT.  PIVOTAL
C     CONDENSATION ALGORITHM USED.
C
C     IF THE DETERMINANT IS LESS THAN 0.0001, A ERROR RETURN
C     FOR SINGULARITY IS MADE.

250   NEXT = 2
      IWHAT = 1
252   DO 251 I = NEXT,N
      OVERD = D(I,IWHAT)/D(IWHAT,IWHAT)
      DO 251 J = NEXT,N
      D(I,J) = D(I,J)-D(IWHAT,J)*OVERD
251   CONTINUE
      IF(NEXT.GE.N) GO TO 260
      IWHAT = NEXT
      NEXT = NEXT+1
      GO TO 252
260   DET = 1.0
      DO 261 I = 1,N
```

(continued)

159

TABLE 5.5 (continued)

```
    261 DET = DET*D(I,I)
        IF(DET.LT.0.0001) GO TO 500
C
C
C       COMPUTE TRIANGULAR FACTORIZATION
C
    300 IF(R(1,1).LE.0.0) R(1,1) = 1.0
        ROOT = SQRT(R(1,1))
        DO 301 I = 1,N
        D(I,1) = R(I,1)/ROOT
        DO 301 J = 2,N
        D(I,J) = 0.0
    301 CONTINUE
        DO 310 I = 2,N
        SUM = 0.0
        KLIMT = I-1
        DO 311 K = 1,KLIMT
        SUM = SUM+D(I,K)*D(I,K)
    311 CONTINUE
        DIFF = R(I,I)-SUM
        IF(DIFF.LE.0.0) GO TO 500
        D(I,I) = SQRT(DIFF)
        DO 312 J = 2,I
        IF(J.EQ.I) GO TO 312
        SUM1 = 0.0
        KLIMT = J-1
```

```
      DO 313 K = 1,KLIMT
      SUM1 = SUM1+D(I,K)*D(J,K)
313   CONTINUE
      D(I,J) = (R(I,J)-SUM1)/D(J,J)
312   CONTINUE
310   CONTINUE
C
C     NOW CALL RANDOM AND QUIT
C
      XXX = RANDOM(DUMMY)
C
C     NORMAL RETURN
C
      IOK = 1
      RETURN
C
C     ERROR RETURN
C
500   IOK = 0
      RETURN
C
C     DATA ENTRY--RETURNS A VECTOR OF SCORES
C
```

(continued)

TABLE 5.5 (continued)

```
      ENTRY DATA(SCORES)
      DO 400 I = 1,N
      XX = RNORM(DUMMY)
      ZVECT(I) = XX
  400 CONTINUE

C
C     COMPUTE AND SCALE THE VALUES.
C

      DO 401 I = 1,N
      SCORES(I) = 0.0
      DO 402 J = 1,I
      SCORES(I) = SCORES(I)+D(I,J)*ZVECT(J)
  402 CONTINUE
      SCORES(I) = SCORES(I)+XBAR(I)
  401 CONTINUE
      RETURN
      END
```

The shuffle is simple to program. In essence, it involves randomly selecting two elements from an array, interchanging them, and repeating the process until the array is adequately jumbled. The process is illustrated in the following statements from SIMSAL. The array ORDER contains the numbers 1,2,3,..., NSYLAB which are to be used as pointers in the subsequent presentation of syllables to the subject. The random number function IRAND(J) delivers a rectangularly distributed random digit on the interval 1—J as discussed previously. The shuffle is performed by the statements

```
       DO 1201 J = 1,NSYLAB
       K = IRAND(NSYLAB-J)+J
       ITEMP = ORDER(K)
       ORDER(K) = ORDER(J)
  1201 ORDER(J) = ITEMP
```

The loop is performed NSYLAB times. Each time the value in ORDER(J) is interchanged with the value in a randomly selected position between 1 and J. The result is a thorough shuffling of the array. The entries in ORDER are used sequentially, from ORDER(1) through ORDER(NSYLAB), resulting in a random presentation of the syllables indicated by the pointers in ORDER.

Random Selection from Arrays

In SIMSAL, the entire ORDER array is shuffled at the start of each trial of the experiment because the logic of the program requires that the entire list — that is, all of ORDER — be presented on each trial. The same process might have been accomplished by an equally likely selection without replacement, as will be discussed below, but the shuffle was selected as more efficient in this instance.

In many instances, only a random subset from an array is desired. For example, in some kinds of learning experiments, a large number of stimulus—response pairs may be defined as the "vocabulary" of the experiment, but only a randomly picked subset is presented on any single trial. In such a case, it may be desirable to conceptually "reach into the hat" on each trial and pull out only a handful of items.

In many simulations, the occurrence of some event is controlled by a pointer selected from an array. We may wish, for example, to select a student from a set of students represented by pointers in an array. Picking a pointer indicates what array of student characteristics is to be the next one processed in a simulation of, perhaps, course selection. Likewise, in another context, selecting a pointer indicates what kind of machine is used next, what sort of vehicle is the next arrival at a service station, or what kind of freight is loaded into a railroad car.

There are two major considerations in programming an array selection. First, are the elements in the array equally likely or not? Second, is the selection to be conducted with or without replacement? (With replacement implies that when an item has been chosen it is returned to the "pool" and can be picked again. Without replacement means that once the element is used it cannot recur.) We consider first the equally likely algorithm, with and without replacement, and then turn to the procedures for unequal probabilities.

Equal probability selection.   For selection with replacement and equally likely alternatives, picking a single element is an easy matter. Generate a uniform random number in the interval 1–n, where n is the number of elements in the array. Use that random number as a pointer indicating the element selected.

In order to select without replacement, a procedure must be devised to eliminate any item already picked. One obvious solution is to maintain a list of those items already used and, whenever a new selection is made, check it against the list. However, that approach becomes very inefficient when the length of the already used list becomes long.

An alternate algorithm uses the simple expedient of removing an item from the array after it has been selected. To follow this procedure, generate a number k between 1 and n. As before, k points to the item selected. Once the item has been used, move the last item — the one in the nth position — into the space occupied by the just used element, and then decrease n by 1. The next time an element is picked, item k has been removed, and the length of the array has decreased.

Selecting without replacement destroys the data values in the array; when the kth has been used, it is overwritten by the nth. If it is ever necessary to repeat the sampling with the full set of values, the data must have been saved in another array and restored before the sampling can begin anew.

Unequal probability selection.   Suppose that we wished to select a vowel from the set [A, E, I, O, U] with probabilities approximating their frequency of use in the English language. In this case the choice cannot be equally likely but should follow roughly the probabilities:

Vowel (V)	Probability $P(V)$
A	.14
E	.43
I	.12
O	.20
U	.11

Two general approaches may be followed. First, we can fill an array with 100 letters, of which 14 are A, 43 are E, and so forth. Making a selection from the array by generating a number in the range 1–100, as in the equally likely case, will result in the desired probabilities.

This approach is fast, but it suffers from a major disadvantage. The array of only five vowels was expanded to 100 elements. The reason was that we wished to represent probabilities to two significant places. Had our probabilities been but single digits, such as:

Vehicle	Probability
Small car	.3
Large car	.3
Small truck	.2
Large truck	.1
Bus	.1

a 10-element array would suffice, with three each of small and large cars, two small trucks, and so forth.

Conversely, if probabilities are represented to three digits, the array must contain 1,000 locations; 10,000 locations for four digits, and so on. Clearly, when the desired precision of the probabilities is large, the efficiency of this method must be weighed against the space requirements. Often, the situation requires only one- or two-digit representation of probabilities so that the simple and effective procedure may be used.

The alternative approach for an unequal probability selection uses cumulative probabilities and a search procedure. To illustrate this algorithm, consider the following table:

Vowel (V)	P(V)	Cumulative probability CP(V)
A	.14	.14
E	.43	.57
I	.12	.69
O	.20	.89
U	.11	1.00

Here we have shown the probability of each vowel as well its cumulative probability — the probability of a vowel plus the probability of all those preceding it in the list. If we now generate a random number on the unit interval, a vowel can be selected according to the required probabilities. Simply search the CP(V) array to locate the first entry equal to or exceeding the generated number. The position of that value indicates the selected vowel. For example, if the generated value is .83, a search of CP(V) finds that .83 lies between .69 and

.89, indicating a selection of O as the vowel. A random value of .55 would lead to picking the letter E.

Any of the search procedures discussed in Chapter 4 may be employed; the binary is probably best. Note that a minor modification is required — we are not searching for a specific target but for the first value equalling or exceeding it.

Most often sampling from an array with unequal probabilities is with replacement. The array often represents an infinite population of possible events that may occur in the program; sampling from an infinite population is always with replacement. In some cases, the array may represent a small, finite population, and the sampling is without replacement. In that case, the array is established as in the first example, with the requisite number of each element. The sampling then proceeds as in the equally likely — without replacement — algorithm.

Simulating contingency tables. Not infrequently, a simulation requires a procedure for simulating a bivariate, but nonnormal, distribution. Suppose, for example, that the simulation deals with families. We may wish to sample from a population of families divided into those where the father is either present or absent, and simultaneously of some socioeconomic class. In the table below, the entries represent the probability with which each kind of family is to be sampled:

		Socioeconomic class		
		Low	Middle	High
Father	Present	.10	.20	.15
	Absent	.20	.20	.15

This table is known as a contingency table and is very common in many social science fields. It occurs most commonly in describing the results of statistical surveys; here it is regarded as a description of a hypothetical population from which samples are to be drawn.

Sampling from a contingency table of this form is easily accomplished by a minor modification to the unequal probability list selection procedure just described. Think of the array as it is stored in Fortran — by columns — and then replace the probabilities by cumulative probabilities. The result is the array CPROB shown in Table 5.6 where the first entry represents the probability of cell (1,1), CPROB(2) the probability of (1,1) + (2,1), and so forth. Now generating a random value on the 0–1 interval can lead to selecting a single location, and that location can be "decoded" as discussed in Chapter 4 to yield row and column values in the original array. For example, if a random value of .46 is obtained, a search of CPROB finds the third entry as the selected value. If

TABLE 5.6
A 2 X 3 Contingency Table Represented as a Fortran Array

Entry	Probability	CPROB
1	.10	.10
2	.20	.30
3	.20	.50
4	.20	.70
5	.15	.85
6	.15	1.00

the corresponding two-dimensional subscripts are found, the resulting simulated family is middle class with father present.

EXERCISES

5.1 Write a main calling program that initializes the random number routine by a reference to RANDOM and then uses RNDM to generate a series of N random values, where N is an input.

5.2 Conduct a test of the rectangularity of the values produced by the program you wrote in Exercise 5.1.

*5.3 Write a program that uses RANDOM/RNDM and BIN in Table 5.3 to generate samples from a binomial distribution with $n = 10$ and $p = .75$. Generate 1,000 values and find their frequency distribution. Use a goodness of fit procedure to compare the obtained distribution with that expected theoretically.

*5.4 Repeat Exercise 5.3 with some other distribution function of your choice.

5.5 Write a program to shuffle an array of 52 elements. Treat each value in the array as a card from a standard deck and have the program deal four hands of 13 cards each.

5.6 Write a program to simulate tossing a fair six-sided die.

5.7 Rewrite the program in Exercise 5.6 so that the die is unfair; let the "3" and "4" faces have the same probability as before (.1667), but arrange that "5" and "6" have probabilities of .20 each, with "1" and "2" each having a probability of .1333.

5.8 Exercise 4.6 suggested a means for selecting a starting point in a spatial search for the urban growth simulation using a "center of population" algorithm. A random starting point could also be used. Write a routine to select row and column values randomly to start the search.

5.9 Another procedure for defining a starting point in the urban growth model would be to think of the row and column entries as being obtained from a contingency table. The table would indicate that some areas were much more likely to be good candidates for starting a search than others (outlying areas, perhaps). Write a program to produce a row and column starting point for the search, where outlying areas (extreme ends of a row or column) are more likely to be picked, with the probability diminishing as the center of the "city" is approached.

SUGGESTED READINGS

Knuth, D. E. *The art of computer programming.* Vol. 2: *Semi-numerical algorithms.* Reading, Mass.: Addison-Wesley, 1969. Many of the algorithms in this chapter, and lots more, presented in Knuth's clear and concise style.

Lehman, R. S., & Bailey, D. E. *Digital computing: Fortran IV and its applications in behavioral science.* New York: Wiley, 1968. Although primarily a general introduction to computing and to Fortran in particular, Chapter 11 addresses some of the topics in this chapter.

Martin, F. F. *Computer modeling and simulation.* New York: Wiley, 1968. A general introduction to simulation, it gives a number of random process algorithms. Use with care, because several have been supplanted by better performing procedures. A number of quick, approximate, procedures for testing probability distribution generators are also described.

Naylor, T. H., Balintfy, D. S., Burdick, D. S., & Chu, K. *Computer simulation techniques.* New York: Wiley, 1966. Good coverage of much of the material in this book but largely directed toward the use of simulation in business. The coverage of random processes and testing procedures is especially recommended.

6
Coding: Accuracy and Efficiency

The efficiency of the program and its accuracy are important and interrelated topics. Surprisingly, however, all too little time is devoted to them in the computer training of most social and behavioral scientists. The aim of this chapter is to summarize some of the relevant computer science material, and thus, it is hoped, improve the programs written by social and behavioral scientists.

The discussion of accuracy leads us into numerical methods, usually a topic for courses in mathematics. We will not attempt to cover the field. What we shall do is to point out the sources of numerical difficulties in computation, explore some of their consequences, and offer a few suggestions for avoiding, minimizing, or at least recognizing the existence of inaccuracies.

In the best of all possible simulation worlds, there would be no concern with computer time or storage. But we do not live and work in the ideal world and there are real constraints on computer use. Simulations are usually written within a budget of money to buy computer resources. Even if we do not have actual dollar budgets, there are always limits placed on how much time we may expect on our computer.

There are also space limitations. No computer has limitless storage and sooner or later many simulation programmers become painfully aware of the computer memory available to them.

There is an intimate relationship between the topics in this chapter and the discussion of structured programming in Chapter 2. A structured program is easier to read, generally is less error prone, can often embody efficient and accurate procedures, and may even assist the compiler and operating system in minimizing computer time. Coupled with the advantages of structured programming cited earlier, it is little wonder that it is often called a revolution in programming.

SOME CONSIDERATIONS
IN COMPUTATIONAL MATHEMATICS

The topic of computational accuracy has been investigated extensively by mathematicians and computer scientists. Many social/behavioral scientists, not having been exposed to the results of those studies, continue using the computer under the assumption that the results are accurate, or at least accurate enough for their purposes.

Accuracy is not a matter to be taken lightly. A survey by Wampler (1970) shows that many of the common statistical programs used by social scientists are seriously in error. Not just small errors, but errors in several orders of magnitude. Some of the most widely used program packages cannot even produce a single accurate digit under some conditions!

Sources of Inaccuracy

At the root of computational inaccuracy is the nature of the computer and its method of representing numbers. (There are also errors caused by incorrect programming, wrong formulas, and so forth, but that is not the concern here.)

The computer does all of its computations on numbers. It is easy to assume that those numbers and the laws governing them are adequate representations of what a mathematician would call the "real number system." Fortran even reinforces the belief by calling one of its variable types REAL. The fact is that the laws followed by the computer representation of numbers is not a subset of the laws of the real number system of mathematics at all but differs in several very important ways.

The basic cause of computational difficulty is that a computer represents numbers in a finite-length computer word. No matter how many digits of precision a computer system may allow, there are many numbers, the fraction $1/3$ for example, that simply cannot be represented exactly on a binary computer. The result is a system of numbers known as "floating point" ('REAL' in Fortran!) whose arithmetical laws differ from those followed by the real numbers.

Part of the problem is that the real real number system is known as "dense" in mathematical parlance. This means that another value can always be found between any pair of values. Not so with floating point numbers where some intermediate values cannot be represented at all. To further compound the problem, the density of the floating point number system varies as a function of the magnitude of the values being considered. The representable values are very closely packed for values close to zero. But the gap between two adjacent floating point numbers may be huge when the values are very large.

To illustrate the density problem, suppose that we have a computer system that can represent numbers to six digits of accuracy. Now pick a very small number between 0 and 1, such as

$$.100000*10^{-38}.$$

With six digits of precision, the next larger value that can be represented on the computer is

$$.100001*10^{-38}.$$

The difference between the values is

$$.100000*10^{-43} = \underbrace{.00000 \cdots 0001}_{43 \text{ zeros}},$$

a very small difference between these two very small values.

Now consider the difference between two very large numbers, also written in six significant digits, such as

$$.100000*10^{+38},$$

and the next larger value that can be represented,

$$.100001*10^{+38}.$$

The difference between these two numbers is immense

$$.100000*10^{+33} = \underbrace{.10000 \cdots 000}_{32 \text{ zeros}}.$$

This huge number is the best we can do with only six digits of precision; the significant digits differ by only .000001, the closest that we can come. In each case, the denseness of the floating point number system is determined by the maximum number of significant digits, but the actual difference between pairs of values ranges from an extremely small number to something that is larger than the total number of grains of sand on all the beaches, lakes, and deserts in the world. The point is that with small numbers we can represent differences more precisely than we can with very large numbers. This uneven distribution of floating point numbers is a major disparity between them and real numbers.

But what does that have to do with social science? The numbers rarely ever get so large or so small in most of the everyday computations of a psychologist or sociologist. But they do! Consider, for example, a common formula for computing the variance.

$$\frac{N \sum X^2 - (\sum X)^2}{N(N-1)}$$

or a formula from the analysis of variance

$$\sum_i \sum_j \sum_k X_{ijk}^2 - \frac{1}{n} \sum_i \sum_j T_{ij}^2.$$

In each case, a difference between two numbers is to be computed, and the values may be very large or very small as a function of the particular set of data. The result of either subtraction may be catastrophic.

Catastrophic subtraction. The difference between two large floating point numbers is not well represented, a fact leading to a major source of inaccuracy in computing. When two nearly equal values are subtracted, the difference between them is in the least significant digits, and those are the very digits most poorly represented in the floating point system. Moreover, subtraction of potentially large values occurs frequently in statistics, as well as in other troublesome places.

For example, the formula

$$\sum_i \sum_j \sum_k X_{ijk}{}^2 - \frac{1}{n} \sum_i \sum_j T_{ij}{}^2$$

is from the analysis of variance, a widely used statistical procedure. This particular formula is for the "within groups" or "error" sum of squares. It is but one in statistics containing a subtraction and, because each of the terms to be subtracted consists of the summation of a number of squared values, the terms may be very large.

Assume that the exact values in the computation are

$$\sum_i \sum_j \sum_k X_{ijk}{}^2 = 2,316,512.5316 = .231651*10^7$$

on a six-digit computer and

$$\frac{1}{n} \sum_i \sum_j T_{ij}{}^2 = 2,316,506.1315 = .231651*10^7.$$

These are not unreasonably large, given the nature of analysis of variance computations. The exact difference between these values is 6.4001. Yet, if the computation were done on a computer with only six digits of precision, the result would be zero because each value, rounded to six significant digits, would be

$$.231651*10^7.$$

A zero in the error sum of squares will cause inaccuracy in every analysis of variance program. The difficulty may be unnoted or may cause a program termination, depending on the particular computer system. The error sum of squares is divided by a value known as its degrees of freedom. The result of that computation is zero in this case, because it always is permissible to divide zero by something.

The next step in the analysis of variance uses the previous result (zero in the example) as the divisor in a second division operation. It is at that point where the trouble will show itself. An attempt to divide by zero will generally cause an exit to the operating system of the computer. Among the various operating systems, one of three alternative courses of action is most likely to be taken, although some computers may do something else. First, and most properly, the program is terminated with a note that a division by zero has been attempted. Often, the error message says something about a "divide check" indicator.

Two other possibilities frequently occur in operating systems. In one case, a zero value is inserted for the result and the program resumes its operation. In the other, the largest possible value on the computer is supplied and the program continues. In either of these latter two solutions to the problem, the program simply continues. Often the error is not even noted by the computer, and the output looks normal to the casual observer.

The message to the programmer should be clear. Output must be inspected carefully. The presence of exact zeros, or of extremely large values, should be an alarm flag. Either may indicate the result of a division by zero where the operating system has not terminated the program but merely has supplied a value and continued.

Of all of the basic mathematical operations, subtraction is the most likely to produce serious errors because small differences cannot be represented when the magnitudes are large. A similar problem occurs, of course, in the addition of two quantities with opposite sign.

The programmer should be alert to the possibility of a catastrophic result whenever a subtraction is performed between values that may be nearly equal. In much of the programming undertaken by social and behavioral scientists, data processing and simulation alike, the actual values are determined by data. The programmer has little control over the data values when he or she develops the program and should consider the problem of subtraction when writing the program initially.

It is often possible to find an alternative computational procedure which results in smaller values entering the subtraction. For example, two formulas are generally recognized by elementary statistics students as alternative formulas for the variance of a sample:

$$s^2 = \frac{\Sigma X^2}{N} - \bar{X}^2 \quad [\text{Form 1}],$$
$$= \frac{\Sigma(X - \bar{X})^2}{N} \quad [\text{Form 2}].$$

Form 1 is preferred for hand computation, but Form 2 is much better for a computer because the values to be subtracted generally are not as large. Note, however, that to follow Form 2 requires that the mean be computed first and then subtracted from each value in the data. Form 2 is therefore somewhat wasteful of computer time, as we discuss shortly, but is less likely to cause computational error.

Roundoff errors. Most social scientists who are aware of computational error with floating point numbers attribute all inaccuracy to roundoff. It is often the culprit, but not always.

Roundoff occurs automatically in most computers when the result of a computation contains too many digits to be represented in the word size of the computer.

Rounding is often a progressive process — a small error introduced at each point in the sequence of operations is compounded by successive roundings.

Computer results are often assumed to be "close enough," but sometimes real trouble can ensue. For example, consider an operation common to many statistical formulas, summing such a group of numbers as

$$100,000 + .25 + .25 + .25 + .25.$$

The answer is 100,001, unless you happen to ask a computer whose maximum precision is six digits. In that case the answer is 100,000. Because the addition is performed sequentially, from left to right, after the first operation, the result (100,000.25) is rounded to the maximum precision of the computer, resulting in 100,000, which is added to .25, and so forth. Performing the operation in reverse order, as:

$$.25 + .25 + .25 + .25 + 100,000,$$

gives the correct result.

The solution to the problem can be generalized to a rule for summing a mixed set of very small and very large values: add the smallest numbers first. In that way the small values have a chance to sum to something large enough that they are not rounded out of existence when a large number is encountered.

The example also illustrates the failure of one of the major laws of arithmetic when applied to floating point numbers. The relationship

$$a + b + c = c + b + a$$

is known as the commutative law and applies to all real numbers. In the example, at least, it clearly does not apply to floating point values.

Another case of roundoff, combined with subtraction, leads to the possibility of a correct-looking but misleading answer. Again, suppose we are using a computer representing numbers to six digits and perform the following operation:

$$D = A*(B - C)$$

with the values of

$$A = .444444*10^6,$$

$$B = .123456*10^6,$$

$$C = .123455*10^6.$$

Because the precision is six digits, the last digit in each value could actually be the result of a roundoff; the true values represented by these floating point numbers are then

$$A = 444444.0 \pm .5,$$

$$B = 123456.0 \pm .5,$$

$$C = 123455.0 \pm .5.$$

When the computer makes the calculation, the value of D will be

$$D = .444444*10^6 *(.123456*10^6 - .123455*10^6) = .444444*10^6 = 444444.0,$$

apparently accurate to the full six decimal places. However, when we consider that each of the values entering into the computation could be in error by as much as .5 in the last position, we can see that other solutions are possible.

Take one case, where the result is the largest value of D. We give B its largest possible true value, and give C its smallest.

$$B = 123456.5 = \text{largest possible true value,}$$

$$C = 123454.5 = \text{smallest possible true value.}$$

Now the result of the computation is

$$D = 444444.0*(123456.5 - 123454.5) = 444444.0*2 = 888888.0,$$

twice as large as we had initially obtained.

In contrast, if we reverse the values of B and C, so that B now has its smallest possible value and C its largest,

$$B = 123455.5 = \text{smallest possible true value,}$$

$$C = 123455.5 = \text{largest possible true value,}$$

then

$$D = 444444.0*(123455.5 - 123455.5) = 444444.0*0 = 0.0.$$

So here is a situation where, as a result of rounding in the sixth decimal position, we have a result that looks correct but may be far from the true result obtained by computation without rounding.

Further exploration of this example reveals another arithmetic failure of floating point computation. A second important general relationship in the real numbers is

$$a(b + c) = ab + ac$$

which is known as the distributive law. To determine whether it applies to our floating point example, let us find the value of

$$E = A*B - A*C.$$

This expression is algebraically equivalent to $A*(B - C)$, at least for the real numbers. Using a six digit computer

$$A*B = .444444*10^6 *.123456*10^6 = .54869278464*10^{11}$$

will be rounded to

$$.548693*10^{11}$$

and

$$A*C = .444444*10^6 *.123455*10^6 = .54868834020*10^{11}$$

becomes

$$.548688*10^{11}.$$

The difference is

$$.548693*10^{11} - .548688*10^{11} = .500000*10^6 = 500,000.$$

This result differs by 55,556 from the original, illustrating that floating point numbers do not necessarily follow the distributive law either.

In this latter example, we did not even consider the problem of using extreme combinations of true values for A, B, and C; that, of course, would make the problem even worse.

The fuzzy zero. Another difficulty in using floating point numbers as an approximation of the real number system is in the zero. The problem can be illustrated by an example.

First, write the following innocent looking Fortran loop.

```
F = 1.0/3.0
S = 0.0
1 S = S+F

  .
  .
  .

IF(S-2.0) 1,2,1
2 CONTINUE
```

The loop should terminate when S equals 2, which should happen after six cycles. The problem is that the value of $\frac{1}{3}$ cannot be represented exactly, no matter how many significant digits the computer uses. The successive values of S are

$$0.0000000 \ldots$$
$$0.3333333 \ldots$$
$$0.6666666 \ldots$$
$$0.9999999 \ldots$$
$$1.3333333 \ldots$$
$$1.6666666 \ldots$$
$$1.9999999 \ldots$$
$$2.3333333 \ldots$$

so that S is never exactly equal to 2.0 and the loop is infinite. In the real numbers, of course, $6(^1/_3) = 2$ and the loop would terminate as expected. The solution to the problem is simple in this case; change the termination criterion to

$$IF(S-2.0) 1,2,2$$

The problem here is an example of a "fuzzy zero" introduced by the inexact representation of real numbers. Although a subtraction is involved in the example, the difficulty is not of the catastrophic variety. What we really meant was that the loop terminated when S had gotten as close to 2.0 as possible without going beyond it. That criterion is easy to express in Fortran, as we noted.

The solution of the fuzzy zero problem is not always so easy. In many kinds of problems, the decision to terminate some operation must be made on the basis of a fuzzy zero. For example, completing a factor analysis is usually on the basis of some value becoming very small. Mathematically, the analysis is continued to zero, but because the zero is fuzzy on a computer, the termination is most often on the basis of some small, arbitrary, value.

The general solution is to simply supply a small value, and if some critical term is less than it, a zero is assumed to have been reached. When that procedure is followed, the criterion value should be noted clearly in both the documentation and the program listing so that another user can change values if desired.

Series truncation.   Many mathematical operations result in an infinite series, such as

$$x - \frac{x^3}{3!} + \frac{x^5}{5!} + \frac{x^7}{7!} + \ldots,$$

which happens to be $\sin(x)$. An infinite series of this nature cannot be computed exactly. Typically, the series is summed for a fixed number of steps and then terminated or "truncated." A truncated series will always introduce error into the computation because the obtained result differs from the true value of the series for all but (at most) a few points.

Series are often used in the computation of various functions. As such, they are of primary concern to the writers of such Fortran supplied routines as SIN and COS. The user should be aware that using any function approximated by a truncated series may result in inaccuracy in his or her program. There is little that a social scientist can do about the problem apart from writing his or her own function, which should not be considered seriously.

Series problems crop up occasionally at various other points in social science computing. When they do, guidance can be obtained from a standard source such as Carnahan and Wilkes (1973), Hamming (1973), or Knuth (1968, 1969), or from a colleague in the mathematics department.

This brief survey of some of the arithmetic problems of computing has pointed out a few of the major problems. In general, the problems result from the use of a number system – the floating point system – that varies in several important ways from the real number system used by mathematicians and statisticians. First, floating point numbers are finite in range and are neither continuous nor uniformly dense. Second, floating point numbers are not evenly distributed throughout their range, making it impossible to represent differences between pairs of numbers with the same precision regardless of their value. Third, because only a finite number of digits is available, the problem of roundoff arises in several different kinds of situations. Finally, several of the laws of algebra do not necessarily apply in computation. In the next few pages, we offer some advice on programming to improve numerical accuracy.

Some Suggestions

The most important point to keep in mind about numerical accuracy is merely that there may be a problem with it. The major difficulties arise when the numbers become very small or very large so that significant digits are not adequately represented. In many instances, the values in the social and behavioral sciences computing are well within the range of reasonable safety, at least on most computer systems. Users of computers with 12- or 16-bit word lengths, of course, should become anxious about a possible loss of accuracy before a programmer on a 32-, 48-, or 60-bit word system. Clearly, any difficulty that can appear in a 12-bit computer can also show itself in a larger word length system, but it will do so less frequently.

We should also note that it is the relative difference in magnitude in values that causes the trouble. The value 3.778671 is small relative to 14276.0×10^{15} but is very large when compared to 0.77364×10^{-16}.

In order to minimize the chances of inaccuracy, several suggestions can be offered. These fall into four general categories: order, precision, grouping, and formula manipulation.

Order of computation.   As we noted in our discussion of the $a + b + c \neq c + b + a$ problem, it is best to add the smallest values first when computing a summation. The usual procedure for computing a mean, for example, simply adds up the numbers as they appear. When very large and very small values both occur in the data, the small ones may vanish. In many simulations, the data may be generated by the program as samples from some distribution and small values could well occur. When there is concern for the range of possible values, it may pay to scan the data for the presence of extremes. If small values are present, it is advisable to sort the data before summing, even though a sort results in a substantial increase in execution time. When there is a tradeoff between accuracy and efficiency, it is usually desirable to opt for accuracy.

Precision.   Nearly every recent version of Fortran allows the option of varying the length of the computer word – the so-called "variable precision" feature of the compiler. Increasing the number of bits, and therefore the number of significant digits, can cut down on the liklihood of roundoff error, but usually at the expense of efficiency. It takes considerably longer to compute with double-length words than with single, at least on most computers. Extended precision should be used sparingly and only applied to those variables where it is needed.

For example, in computing a mean of a set of values, it is probably unnecessary to have the data themselves stored in extended precision; the place where rounding takes place is in the summation and division. Declaring

DOUBLE PRECISION SUM,XBAR

obtains extra precision for two variables. The mean $X(1) \cdots X(N)$ now can be computed as

```
      DO 1 I = 1,N
    1 SUM = SUM+X(I)
      FN = N
      XBAR = SUM/FN
```

with $X(I)$ stored in standard precision. Note that in the statement SUM = SUM+X(I), and in the computation of XBAR, the expression involves a mixture of standard REAL variables and DOUBLE PRECISION variables. This combination may be rejected by some Fortran compilers. It is, however, permissible in American Standard Fortran as defined by the American National Standards Institute (1966). In any compiler meeting that standard, the result of such a mixed expression will be a double precision value.

We should also note that the technique of using extended precision for some crucial parts of a computation has been recommended by others. In particular, in his review of computational accuracy cited previously, Wampler (1970) calls for doing some parts of computations in double precision. Indeed, the most accurate of the programs he surveyed did just that.

Grouping. Another technique for increasing accuracy is the grouping of subexpressions. The aim here is to obtain subexpressions with values large enough to have an impact on the final value, where individual terms may not. For example, computing

$$100,000 + .25 + .25 + .25 + .25$$

with six-digit accuracy as before can be improved by grouping the expression as

$$100,000 + (.25 + .25 + .25 + .25),$$

causing the small values to be summed first. Then their combined value will have an impact on the final total.

Grouping can be applied to many series computations, such as the approximation of $\sin(x)$ discussed previously, as well. To discuss grouping as a general technique in series problems would take us even farther afield than we are already. The concerned programmer should consult one of the numerical analysis texts cited earlier or make an appointment with a competent mathematician.

Algebraic manipulation.   A final method for reducing computational error is the manipulation of formulas. One example of this approach was introduced in the discussion of catastrophic subtraction when we presented two formulas for variance.

In the case of the variance computation, selecting the appropriate computational formula was a matter is picking the best from among two well-known alternatives. Often the choices in a simulation program are not as clear, and a little work on the part of the programmer is indicated. For example, consider the formula

$$\sqrt{x+1} - \sqrt{x}$$

If the value of x becomes large, the result of a direct application of this formula often is meaningless because of catastrophic subtraction. Multiplying the formula by what an algebra teacher would call a "well-chosen 1," such as

$$\frac{\sqrt{x+1} + \sqrt{x}}{\sqrt{x+1} + \sqrt{x}},$$

results in

$$\sqrt{x+1} - \sqrt{x} = \sqrt{x+1} - \sqrt{x} \left[\frac{\sqrt{x+1} + \sqrt{x}}{\sqrt{x+1} + \sqrt{x}} \right]$$

$$= \frac{1}{\sqrt{x+1} + \sqrt{x}}.$$

Because no subtraction is involved, the latter form is preferable.

The process just completed, multiplying the fraction by a "well-chosen 1," is called "rationalizing" the numerator and is a component of the mathematical method of computing limits. For the reader with a difficult formula who does not have sufficient calculus background to attempt this kind of solution, several of the Suggested Readings at the end of this chapter may provide assistance.

COMPUTING EFFICIENCY

The previous section presented some considerations in accuracy. Now we direct our attention to another problem — making the program do its work efficiently, using a minimum of computer time and resources.

The best time to optimize a program is when it is first written. Most simulation programs are "one-shot" affairs, typically run only a few times after the initial debugging. In such a case, going back through a running program to save a few seconds in execution is usually not worth the trouble. If the program is to be executed many times, for example a system routine, standard statistical or data processing package, or something similar, improving even a running program becomes time well spent. Saving as much as a second or two in a common routine can result in substantial benefit if the program is run often.

Computer time and computer storage are finite resources. They are not without constraint, whatever you may have been led to believe. Many academic computing centers encourage use as if there were no tomorrow, at least for students. If you are in such a fortunate situation, you may think that this section does not apply to you. But being a good citizen of the computing community requires that you attend to using no more of a finite resource than you must.

If your computer use is being charged to a research account, you are only too aware of the constraint of your budget, and it is certainly to your best interest to minimize both time and space.

The following pages suggest several techniques for minimizing the amount of the computer used. In general, attention is directed to time and storage separately. Nearly all computer centers charge for, or at least keep tract of, computation time. Most recent systems also record and charge for storage as well. Sometimes, procedures for minimizing computation time also reduce storage. In other cases, a decrease in time is accompanied by an increase in storage. When there is a tradeoff, we point it out.

In discussing procedures for optimizing time, we will often note another side effect — a decrease in the "readability" of the program. By readability we mean the clarity with which the Fortran source statements describe the process represented by the program. The goal in producing a readable program is to have the program nearly self-documenting — virtually everything needed to understand the program is present in the listing. Readability is influenced by several factors, including the presence of abundant comments and a clear structure in the source program. In addition, the program statements themselves should be readily understandable.

The goal of readability sometimes conflicts with an attempt to make a program more efficient, or indeed more accurate. We saw an example in the preceding section. It is not immediately obvious to the mathematical novice that the expression

$$\sqrt{x+1} - \sqrt{x}$$

is equivalent to

$$\frac{1}{\sqrt{x+1} + \sqrt{x}}.$$

The latter is the best form for computational accuracy, but the former is easier to understand. The use of the computational form thus leads to a decrease in readability while increasing accuracy. In the same way, many of the procedures for increasing speed decrease readability. In this particular example, as in most cases, the readability can be restored by inserting a few comments to explain the situation.

In general, when there is a tradeoff between readability and efficiency, we note it too. Programming preference and style can then dictate whether to use the readable but inefficient procedure, or the efficient form with accompanying comments.

Choice of compiler. Most large computer centers offer a choice of at least two different Fortran processors, "debugging" and "optimizing" compilers. The two have different aims, produce different outputs, and are useful at different times. Choosing the right compiler at the right time can greatly facilitate optimizing a program.

A debugging compiler is designed to operate quickly and produce detailed error messages. It will produce an operable but inefficient object program. Often called a "quick and dirty" compiler, it is extremely useful in the first stages of program debugging to find relatively simple errors. Debugging compilers, of which the University of Waterloo's WATFOR and WATFIV are the best known, were originally designed to process a large number of relatively simple programs, such as class assignments, and do so very quickly. Beginning programmers use considerably more computer time in compiling and debugging than in the actual running of the completed code. The compiler therefore operates very fast and produces exhaustive and informative messages, with little concern for the efficiency of the resulting object program because it is probably executed only once.

An optimizing compiler, in contrast, has as its goal the production of a highly efficient object program, at the expense of a much longer compilation time. A good optimizing compiler can do a great deal to reduce the running time of the program. To discuss compilers in detail would take us far beyond the scope of this book. We can point out some things that they can and cannot do, however, and some things that the programmer should do to aid an optimizing compiler.

The point should be clear. Use a debugging compiler initially, perhaps even through the first full test run. After that, invest the time needed for an optimizing compiler to produce a good "clean" object program for logic tests and production runs.

A word of caution. There are generally some important differences between debugging and optimizing compilers even on the same computer system. For example, a debugging compiler may not allow arrays of greater than three dimensions, DATA statements, logical variables, EQUIVALENCE, and perhaps other kinds of expressions essential in writing the program. It may be necessary to make some substantial changes in the program before it can be submitted to the optimizing compiler, thus introducing the possibility of new errors. Nevertheless, a debugging compiler is highly recommended at first, if one is available.

Minimizing Computer Time

The resource of most concern to programmers is usually time. Every run of a program results in an elapse of time on the computer, and often time represents money. Reducing the running time of a program is not difficult, given a little understanding of the operation of compilers and a few simple rules and guidelines. Nearly all of the procedures can be incorporated at the initial writing of the program and will, if done consistently and carefully, result in considerable saving of time.

There are two cardinal rules for optimizing programs. They are so manifestly simple as to appear almost gratuitous, but following them is not always as obvious as it seems:

1. Never recompute any expression or subexpression.
2. Use the fastest form available.

These two rules are the basis of nearly all of the procedures suggested below. Let us look at them first in their pure forms and then see how they are applied in a variety of other situations.

In order to use the fastest computational form, we must recognize that the elementary computer operations differ considerably in speed of execution. The fastest operations are addition and subtraction, followed by multiplication and division. All four are faster than exponentiation, which is usually accomplished by a subprogram; the others are usually machine instructions.

An implication of the fast form rule is that the expression

$$d = \sqrt{a^2 + b^2}$$

in CHEBO is coded in Fortran as

```
DIST = SQRT(A*A+B*B)
```

instead of

```
DIST = SQRT(A**2+B**2)
```

An example of not repeating a computation can be seen in the simple loop:

```
  DO 1 I = 1,100
1 X(I) = A/B+Y(I)
```

As written, the subexpression A/B is computed 100 times, which is exactly 99 times too many. It never changes in value and can be removed from the loop as below, thus increasing the efficiency considerably.

```
  AOVERB = A/B
  DO 1 I = 1,100
1 X(I) = AOVERB+Y(I)
```

Fortran's built in functions are often costly, and whenever possible minimizing their use is beneficial. For example, the expression

$$SUM = COS(X)*A+COS(X)*B+COS(X)*C$$

can be written more efficiently as

$$COSX = COS(X)$$
$$SUM = COSX*A+COSX*B+COSX*C$$

or, by applying a little elementary algebra, we can make use of the principle of faster forms and replace three costly multiplications with but one,

$$SUM = COS(X)*(A+B+C)$$

assuming that the values are not to be so large as to cause a failure of the distributive law of arithmetic. Note that in this case no advantage is gained by computing COS(X) separately as it is only done once.

The two general principles for minimizing computer time can be extended to general algorithms as well. When a faster procedure is available, use it if at all possible. Don't use a bubble sort for more than a very few items, use a Shell sort instead. Don't search sequentially if you can possibly employ a binary or probability search.

Having introduced the two most important rules for optimizing a program, we turn now to a consideration of their use in several kinds of Fortran operations. In the process of this discussion, we also introduce a few other principles applicable in more limited situations.

Arithmetic Operations

The preceding examples presented several ways of optimizing arithmetic expressions. Avoid repetitive computations, pick faster forms, and sometimes rearrange the computational formula to allow a faster form to replace a slower.

In addition to the illustrated operations, a few other tricks of the trade are available to an experienced programmer. For example, on many Fortran systems, multiplication is faster than division, so that it is advantageous to replace a division with a multiplication by a reciprocal. For example,

$$XR = 1.0/X$$
$$SUM = A*XR+B*XR+C*XR$$

is often better than

$$SUM = A/X+B/X+C/X$$

The careful use of integer arithmetic can often produce considerable savings. In nearly every computer system, integer arithmetic is much faster than that for floating point numbers. (A notable exception is the Control Data 6000 series computers. They first convert integer values to floating, perform the operation, and then truncate the answer.) To take advantage of the speed of integer operations, use integer variables and entirely integer expressions when possible. If a group of values can never have a decimal part, it is a waste of time (and sometimes storage) to treat them as floating point numbers. But remember that the largest number that can be stored as an integer is always a great deal less than the maximum for floating point numbers.

However, careless use of integers can lead to inefficiencies. With but one exception, mixed mode expressions — those involving a combination of floating point and integer values — should be avoided. Some compilers will perform any entirely integer subexpression in integer arithmetic — others convert it to floating point, and conversion is time consuming. For example, in the expression

$$BAD = A*B+C/I+J/K$$

the subexpression J/K might be computed as entirely integer, resulting in a truncation of any fractional part. In any compiler, there will have to be several time wasting conversions from integer to floating point.

The exception to the mixed mode rule occurs in exponentiation. Exponentiation is not a basic machine operation, and the compiler must supply a prewritten set of code. Most compilers have at least four routines, covering such cases as integer to an integer power, integer to a floating point power, and so forth. Of these, the procedures for an integer power are by far the fastest. An integer exponent therefore should be used, even if the remainder of the expression is floating point. For example, write

$$XPOWER = (X+Y)**10$$

and not

$$XPOWER = (X+Y)**10.0$$

When reasonable, of course, use repeated multiplication instead of exponentiation. But don't go to extremes:

$$XPOWER = (X+Y)*(X+Y)*(X+Y)* \ldots 10 \text{ times}$$

or even

$$XPLUSY = X+Y$$

$$XPOWER = XPLUSY*XPLUSY*XPLUSY* \ldots 10 \text{ times}$$

are carrying a good thing too far. In most compilers, an exponentiation costs as much as four or five multiplications; for any power greater than 4 or 5, use exponentiation instead of repeated multiplication.

Another technique for optimizing arithmetic computations involves specifying constants. Do a little arithmetic, save the compiler both time and space, and get a more efficient program as well. There is always a temptation to write an expression, such as

$$SLOW = Y*1056.0*95.0+Z$$

and let the computer do the arithmetic. An optimizing compiler may make the expression into

$$FASTER = Y*100320.0+Z$$

but the programmer can do it just as well and save a little compilation time.

There are cases where the rule to compute constants manually should not be followed. Consider the constant X = 2./3., for example. In this case it is better to write

$$X = 2.0/3.0$$

than it is to write either

$$X = .667$$

or even

$$X = .6666666667$$

The reason is that, because the constant cannot be expressed exactly in floating point, it is far preferable to let the computer carry out the computation to as many significant digits as possible instead of having the limitation defined by the programmer.

Even a good optimizing compiler will have difficulty making the best of such an expression as

$$A = 4.0$$
$$B = 2.0$$
$$X = Y**(A/B)$$

when the programmer can just as easily write

$$X = Y*Y$$

with the same result. This example illustrates two common shortcomings of optimizing compilers; sometimes they do not combine several lines of code, and they nearly always use the time-consuming floating point exponentiation routine in such an instance.

In arithmetic statements, it is best to keep in mind another difficulty with most compilers, even the optimizing ones. Although a good compiler removes repeated subexpressions, it must first be able to recognize them. Most optimizing compilers cannot determine, for example, that

$$X*5.0$$
$$X*5.$$
$$5.0*X$$

are the same subexpressions. Thus,

$$TRUBLE = (A+X*5.)*(B+X*5.0)$$

cannot be optimized by the compiler, whereas

$$LSTRBL - (A+X*5.)*(B+X*5.)$$

can be. Of course, the programmer can help the compiler by writing

$$X5 = X*5.0$$

$$BETTER = (A+X5)*(B+X5)$$

A great deal of computer time can be saved by careful attention to arithmetic expressions. This is particularly true, of course, when the computation is inside a loop to be executed many times.

Control Statements

Little direct advice can be offered for optimizing such control expressions as the IF and GO TO, as their efficiency varies across compilers. The arithmetic IF, with its three branches, is an efficient statement in most Fortrans. Whether it is preferable to a logical IF on a particular system can be determined by experiment. Write a simple program that performs the two equivalent tests

$$IF(X-10.)\ 1,1,2$$

and

$$IF(X.GT.10.)\ GO\ TO\ 2$$
$$1\ ...$$

a large number of times and check the time for each form. Use the fastest throughout your programming.

The principle of not computing the same expression twice can easily be overlooked in constructing IF statements. For example, the test might be made on

$$IF(X*100.3-68.95)\ 1,2,3$$

with one of the consequences being

$$1\ PROD = X*100.3$$

This case of double computation can be improved by writing

$$PROD = X*100.3$$
$$IF\ (PROD-68.95)\ 1,2,3$$

A logical IF statement can often be improved when the test expression contains several parts. Many compilers generate machine code that terminates the evaluation of a logical expression as soon as possible. In a logical connected with .AND. operators, a compiler can generate code that terminates when the first false subexpression is found. With .OR. connectives, evaluation can be terminated whenever a true subexpression is found, because the entire expression must be true if any part of it is true. With the .AND., all subexpressions must be true for the expression to be true, but a false can be assigned when any part is false.

To obtain the best execution from an optimized program then, the proper order of expressions in a logical is essential. When the connectives are .AND., place the most likely to fail subexpression first, followed by the next most likely, and so on. This allows the program to terminate the logical test when the first false is found. Conversely, when constructing expressions using the .OR., place the most likely to be true subexpression first. For example, the logical

```
IF(A.LE.100.0 .AND. X.EQ.100.0) GO TO 500
```

is best if A.LE.100.0 is the most likely to be false. Because the expression is scanned from left to right, its evaluation can be terminated if A.LE.100; the test of X.EQ.100 need not even be performed because the entire expression is false if A.LE.100 is false.

Current programming practice, with the increasing emphasis on the elements of structured programming, diminishes the importance of the branching control statements. As we have noted, in Fortran it is impossible to avoid GO TOs entirely, and some attention therefore should be paid to making them efficient.

Loops and Subscripts

Loops and subscripts are among the most powerful tools a programmer has at his or her disposal. They make it possible to write very general programs, expressing iterative computations easily. The loop is such an able worker that its overhead is often disregarded. Initiating and terminating a loop are relatively costly operations. In addition, although a subscript is an indispensible device in writing general program statements, finding the value of a subscript and locating the data value it indicates are also costly of time.

Fortunately, several procedures are available to aid in minimizing the costs of loops and subscripts, while preserving and even enhancing their benefits. Some are almost self-evident and are used by most reasonably competent programmers. For example, never use several loops over the same range when one will do the job. In writing a mean program for two variables, X and Y, the code

```
      SUMX = 0.0
      SUMY = 0.0
      DO 1 I = 1,N
      SUMX = SUMX+X(I)
      SUMY = SUMY+Y(I)
    1 CONTINUE
```

is much better than

```
        SUMX = 0.0
        DO 1 I = 1,N
        SUMX = SUMX+X(I)
      1 CONTINUE
        SUMY = 0.0
        DO 2 I = 1,N
        SUMY = SUMY+Y(I)
      2 CONTINUE
```

The first example initiates a loop once and terminates it N times, whereas the second opens twice and closes 2N times. There are several other techniques that may also be incorporated in this simple and often-written example; they deal with subscript computations, and we consider them shortly.

Loops and subscripts are sometimes unnecessary. A little thought when programming can save computer time later. For example, when the range of the subscripts that are to be incremented by a loop is relatively small, eliminate the loop. To find the product of the first three elements of an array, we might write

```
        PROD = 1.0
        DO 1000 I = 1,3
   1000 PROD = PROD*ARRAY(I)
```

We can avoid the loop entirely by writing

```
   PROD = ARRAY(1)*ARRAY(2)*ARRAY(3)
```

Likewise consider the following simple program from a beginning programmer.

```
        DIMENSION X(100)
        READ(5,100) N
    100 FORMAT(I3)
        DO 1 I = 1,N
      1 READ(5,101) X(I)
    101 FORMAT(F5.0)
        SUM = 0.0
        DO 2 I = 1,N
      2 SUM = SUM+X(I)
        XBAR = SUM/N
        WRITE(6,102) XBAR
    102 FORMAT(' MEAN = ',F10.3)
        STOP
        END
```

The last example contains several inefficiencies, including poor use of I/O as we will discuss later. For now, however, note two things about the loops: first, the loops could be combined so that reading and summing is accomplished in one loop; second, there is no reason why X must be subscripted at all. Once an X value is read and summed, it is no longer needed; yet the program reserves space for up to 100 values, stores and retrieves each of them, and then discards the whole array when the program ends. The procedure can be written in a shorter and more efficient manner as follows.

```
      READ(5,100) N
100   FORMAT (I3)
      SUM = 0.0
      DO 1 I = 1,N
      READ(5,101) X
101   FORMAT(F5.0)
      SUM = SUM+X
  1   CONTINUE
      FN = N
      XBAR = SUM/FN
      WRITE(6,102) XBAR
102   FORMAT(' MEAN = ',F10.3)
      STOP
      END
```

The point of this example is to illustrate that subscripted variables and loops may be used needlessly; before writing either, consider whether or not they are really essential.

There is a simple and often overlooked trick that may cut down the number of iterations of a loop. For example, writing:

```
      SUM = 0.0
      DO 500 I = 1,1500,3
500   SUM = SUM+X(I)+X(I+1)+X(I+2)
```

reduces the number of loop operations, and thus loop terminations, by two-thirds. Some care must be exercised in this approach. When exactly 1,500 elements are in X, the coding works very well. If there are fewer than 1,500, the array should be initially set to zeros in all locations, else some unintended value be added to SUM as the subscript goes beyond the last occupied location. For example, if only the first 1498 locations of X contain legitimate values, then the final execution of the loop adds the values of X(1498), X(1499), and X(1500). If locations 1499 and 1500 contain "garbage," SUM is in error, and the error may vary from one execution of the program to the next — an extremely difficult problem to locate in debugging.

The technique just illustrated of reducing the loop iterations by increasing the looping increment is valuable on some compilers but not all. Depending on the particular compiler, it may take longer. As simple experimental timing program, such as that suggested for the logical and arithmetic IF statements, will reveal the difference clearly. Also note that this example is particularly likely to be treated differently by debugging and optimizing compilers, so that a timing test on one may show different results with the other.

Computing the location of an array element indicated by a subscript can take considerable time. When a subscripted value is used more than once in a adjacent block of coding, as for example in a loop, it is often desirable to set a single variable to the subscripted value and use that equivalent variable throughout. Thus we may write the summing operations for a segment of an analysis of variance routine as follows.

```
        SUM = 0.0
        SUM2 = 0.0
        DO 1 I = 1,N
        XI = X(I)
        SUM = SUM+XI
        SUM2 = SUM2+XI*XI
    1 CONTINUE
```

This approach results in only a single subscript evaluation. If we combine this with the previous example reducing the number of loop iterations, we can rewrite the summing loop with considerably more efficiency.

```
        SUM = 0.0
        SUM2 = 0.0
        X(N+1) = 0.0
        DO 1 I = 1,N,2
        X1 = X(I)
        X2 = X(I+1)
        SUM = SUM+X1+X2
        SUM2 = SUM2+X1*X1+X2*X2
    1 CONTINUE
```

This final code is about as efficient a procedure as we can write for the summing operations, assuming that X needs to be subscripted at all, and that the incrementing procedure is beneficial. Note that the (N + 1)th location of X is set to zero, avoiding the problem just discussed.

This example brings us to a possible tradeoff between efficiency and accuracy. The summation in the example assumes that the variance of X is to be computed using the formula:

$$\frac{\Sigma X^2}{n} - \bar{X}^2 .$$

We noted earlier than this form opened the possibility of an accuracy problem, and that the form

$$\frac{\Sigma(X - \bar{X})^2}{n}$$

might be better. In this case, we would write a mean and standard deviation program segment as follows.

```
      SUM = 0.0
      X(N+1) = 0.0
      DO 1 I = 1,N,2
      SUM = SUM+X(I)+X(I+1)
    1 CONTINUE
      FN = N
      XBAR = SUM/FN
      SUM2 = 0.0
      DO 2 I = 1,N,2
      XDEV1 = X(I)-XBAR
      XDEV2 = X(I+1)-XBAR
      SUM2 = SUM2+XDEV1*XDEV1+XDEV2*XDEV2
    2 CONTINUE
      SDX = SQRT(SUM2/FN)
```

In this version of the routine, we have used two loops, with a consequent increase in running time, to employ the most accurate computational formula for the variance.

The use of expressions that require evaluation of subscripts can be time consuming. Most compilers can do a reasonable job of optimizing the computation of a subscript if it is written in an appropriate form. The following forms can be optimized by most compilers.

$$v$$

$$c$$

$$v + c$$

$$c * v$$

$$c_1 * v + c_2$$

where v is a variable and c_1 and c_2 are constants. All of the following subscript expressions therefore can be optimized by a good compiler.

```
X(I), X(58), X(I+7), ALPHA(3*J), BETA(10*K+3) ,
```

whereas these may not be suitable for optimization

```
ALPHA(J*3), X(7+I), BETA(3+10*K), BETA(3+K*10) ,
```

although they are algebraically permissable. Older programmers will recognize that these recommended subscript forms are the only ones allowed by some early Fortran compilers.

Because any expression written separately can be optimized by a good compiler, it follows that any subscript computation should be done outside of the expression where the value is needed to reference an array location. For example, in CHEBO we find the statements

```
JPX = (J+NDISP)*4-2
```

```
1002 NHEAD(JPX) = ANUM(J)
```

This subscript computation may not even be allowed by some compilers. Even if it is, independent computation is best.

In some instances, separate computation of a subscript is necessary to avoid a subscript that is itself subscripted. Subscripted subscripts are generally forbidden by Fortran compilers, although they are allowed in some other languages. A subscripted subscript frequently appears in some data structures, where pointers and data are both stored in arrays. In SIMSAL, for example, the statements

```
2002 ISB = TREE(IPOINT,2)
```

```
IF(STIM(ISB) ...
```

appear in the tree scanning segment of SUBJCT, avoiding the use of a sub-scripted subscript. In fact, this avoids a doubly subscripted subscript, because IPOINT itself is set by the statement:

```
IPOINT = TREE(IPOINT,3)
```

A very common operation with subscripted variables is setting all locations to a constant. If multidimensional arrays are to be initialized, looping inefficiencies can result. For example, the statements

```
DO 1 I = 1,10
    DO 1 J = 1,12
    DO 1 K = 1,15
1 BIG(I,J,K) = 0.0
```

initialize the 10×12×15 array BIG. This executes the zeroing statement 1,800 times, at a cost of 131 loop openings and 1,930 loop closures. The excessive cost can be greatly reduced by using an equivalent one-dimensional array, as for example

```
DIMENSION BIG(10,12,15),EQBIG(1800)
EQUIVALENCE (BIG(1,1,1),EQBIG(1))
    .
    .
    .
DO 1 I = 1,1800,2
EQBIG(I) = 0.0
EQBIG(I+1) = 0.0
1 CONTINUE
```

This example combined an equivalent array with a larger increment on the single loop, resulting in a loop iterating only 900 times, with one loop opening and 900 closings. The result is a more efficient program because the number of openings and closings, and the total number of iterations, has decreased.

The use of an equivalent array speeds array initialization but decreases readability. In the example, the three-dimensional array was presumably used because it had meaning in the program. Even with the similar variable name assigned to the equivalent array, however, it would be easy to lose track of the fact that it really was the three-dimensional array being initialized. Often, then, the multidimensional array is initialized directly, simply because it facilitates reading the source code.

Nested loops occur frequently in both complex and simple programs. Consider, for example, the following statements from the initialization routine in CHEBO.

```
DO 1005 I = 1,4
    DO 1005 J = 1,53
1005 A(J,I) = KBB
```

The statements set the 53 × 4 array A to a constant KBB. The arithmetic statement

$$A(J,I) = KBB$$

is executed 212 times and the outer loop (I - 1,4) is initiated once while the inner loop (J = 1,53) is initiated four times, once for each iteration on the outer loop. There is therefore a total of five loop initiations. An alternate form of the nested loops might be

```
DO 1005 I = 1,53
DO 1005 J = 1,4
1005 A(I,J) = KBB
```

clearly accomplishing the same end. This time, however, the outer loop is initiated once, whereas the inner is opened 53 times, for a total of 54 loop initiations. The former example is much more efficient; it saves the cost of 49 loop initiations.

When nested loops are written, the outermost should be the one that iterates the smallest number of times. The most active loop — the one that goes around the most times — should be buried most deeply in the nest. The rule generalizes to nests of any depth; for example,

```
DO 100 I = 1,20
DO 200 J = 1,30
DO 300 K = 1,60
```

is far better than

```
DO 300 K = 1,60
DO 200 J = 1,30
DO 100 I = 1,20
```

Special attention should be paid to the computations within a loop; any improvement there is multiplied by the number of loop executions. When optimizing the arithmetic statements in a program, first pay attention to the innermost nested loops, then work on the statements in the next most frequently executed loop, and so forth.

The procedures presented here for efficient use of loops and subscripts have expanded our rules for optimizing. The basic two still apply — never recompute and use faster forms — but a few additional points have been introduced specifically for loops and subscripts. We will continue to introduce a few additional concepts as we discuss ways to improve input and output.

Input and Output

One obvious way to make output more efficient is to do less of it. The ease of writing output statements, especially those inside loops, make it very easy for a programmer to walk away from his or her computer with very large quantities of output. Most of that paper is soon discarded or used as scratch paper, because there is usually no need to see a great deal of output from a program, at least not on every run.

One solution to the paper problem is to have several types or levels of output, controlled by an input value. In SIMSAL, one of the parameters to the subject is named PRINT, and it controls the amount of output of the program. When PRINT=2, a great deal of paper is generated. The program prints each syllable, the guessed response, and the memory tree. Because that output occurs after each presentation of each stimulus syllable on each trial, and the tree may grow to 50 or more lines, a carton of output can result. Most of the time, the tree is not needed after each syllable; but in order to see it grow over trials, the option is present. The second level of PRINT (1) traces syllables and guesses but yields only the final tree. The lowest level of output (PRINT=0) shows only the final protocol sheet that is kept in a real experiment.

Doing as much input and output in a single operation as possible is a good way to reduce computer time. For example, the first three statements below accomplish roughly the same thing as the fourth, but the single statement is far more efficient.

```
READ(5,100) A
READ(5,101) B
READ(5,102) C

READ(5,103) A,B,C
```

The reason for the difference in efficiency is that each READ (or WRITE) sets up a call to a compiler-supplied routine to do the actual input or output, and each call transmits all of the values on the list. In the examples we have three calls to transmit three values, or a single call to transmit all three.

The general rule here is that, when possible, transmit as much information between the computer and an I/O device in each operation as possible. Unless changed by the presence of a solidus (/) in the FORMAT statement, each READ or WRITE transmits one physical record of information. The physical record is most easily conceived as a card but can just as well be a line of print, or a record written on magnetic tape or disk. The suggestion here is to fill each record as full as possible; you can read 80 columns of a card, so use as many as feasible.

It is very easy, and often justifiable, to make exceptions to the rule. Jamming too many values into a printed line makes the output difficult to understand. In the same way, trying to use all 80 columns on an input card may result in errors because a full card is difficult to check visually. So we offer a modifying clause to the rule: fill an I/O record as full as practical while still maintaining an aesthetically pleasing and useful physical record. The tradeoff is not easy in many instances, but the judicious use of the solidus in FORMATs can certainly help.

In order to gain the benefit of fewer calls to the system routines, the list in an I/O statement should be as long as possible, but all of the values need not appear on a single output line. Consider the following statements from the SIMSAL experimenter which print a summary of the input parameters.

```
      WRITE(IOUT,10002) ID,NSUBS,MXTRL,NLIST
10002 FORMAT('1THIS IS SIMSAL EXPERIMENTER RUNNING ',17A4///
     *  ' NSUBS = ',I4/' MAX TRIALS ON ORIGINAL LEARNING (OL) ='
     *  ' MAX TRIALS ON INTERPOLATED LEARNING (IL) =',I3/
     *  ' MAX TRIALS ON RELEARNING (RL) =',I3/
     *  ' NLIST ='I3)
```

The list calls for four items, of which two are arrays (ID and MXTRL), and the values are printed on the total of six output lines. The statement is efficient; a number of values are transmitted with a single call to the system output routine, but the FORMAT statement specifies a number of different lines, making the output much easier to read.

There is another efficiency illustrated in the previous example. The transmission of an entire array was specified by merely using the array name. The list used the form:

```
      WRITE (   ) ID
```

and not

```
      WRITE (   ) (ID(I),I=1,17)
```

The latter form, often called the "implied DO," is typically more time consuming. It requires that the compiler set up an index variable (I), increment it, and test for termination (is I greater than 17?). The simple form allows the compiler to produce code to begin at the starting location of the array and continue to the end. Because the compiler "knows" the size of the array, it can establish the necessary code much more efficiently than with an implied DO.

There are two important qualifications for the use of the array name instead of the implied DO. First, it can only be used to transmit the entire array in the form that it is stored. With a one-dimensional array there is usually little problem. In a two-dimensional array, however, the values will be transmitted "columnwise" as X(1,1), X(2,1), . . . , X(1,2), X(2,2), ... If that is not an acceptable sequence, then an implied or direct DO must be used.

The second qualification involves the impact on the readability of the source program. To fully understand the previous example, the reader must remember, or look in the declaration statements to find out, that both ID and MXTRL are arrays. With a variable named ID, probably a string of alphameric identifying information, there is little problem, but MXTRL is less obvious.

Although the use of the array name is generally faster than the implied DO, this is not universally true. Some experimentation with your compiler is indicated again.

Another technique that may save time on some computers is to intersperse arithmetic and output. Some modern computers allow I/O and computation to take place simultaneously and independently. In these systems, there is a considerable advantage to be gained from doing some computing, then calling for output, more computing, then more output, and so forth. Contrast this with the more usual procedure of waiting until the end of the program to do all of the output. When a program is written in the latter way, with WRITE statements one after the other, the system must complete one output operation before it can do anything else, because the next command is for more output. However, if a WRITE is followed by a block of computational code, the output can be overlapped.

Before we turn the topic to minimizing storage requirements of a program, we should mention one additional procedure for optimizing I/O. Although in general we are concerned only with data stored in main memory or core, simulations and large data processing programs often require temporary external storage. When a very large array must be stored, it is often convenient to use some external medium, such as magnetic tape or disk. In most systems, the programmer has his or her choice of formatted or unformatted I/O to external devices. If the material is written on a tape, for example, to be printed later or to serve as input to an entirely different program, the formatted output procedure is best as it may be written as card or line images. This procedure is not only easier for the programmer to conceptualize, because he or she is familiar with cards, but makes interprogram compatibility far simpler.

In contrast, if the data are being stored temporarily to be reread by the same program, the use of unformatted I/O is preferable. The compiler uses a different system routine; binary or core-image data are written out, and the record size and other essential information is determined optimally by the compiler. The transfer rate is a great deal faster because no conversion from binary to BCD (binary coded decimal) or other external representation is needed.

Minimizing Storage Requirements

Programmers don't worry about space until they run out of it. When that unhappy event occurs, after much weeping and moaning, the typical solution is to scale down the size of some major arrays. Often that is a good approach, if it does not do grave injustice to the nature of the simulation and its ability to reflect the underlying model adequately.

Procedures for reducing or otherwise living with memory shortage fall into two rough categories — more and less drastic.

Moderate Techniques

Among the less extreme are procedures for shortening a program that "almost fits." Here we find suggestions to compress character strings, define arithmetic constants, and use shorter computer words.

In Fortran, FORMAT statements are stored as literals in a special area of the object program. Any shortening of FORMAT statements can cut down the size of that area and perhaps make the program fit. The simplest way to shorten FORMATs is to reduce the length of the literal or Hollerith constants. These are strings of characters appearing as labels on output to aid in interpreting the results of the program. Overly verbose output explanations are often unnecessary, and cutting them back decreases the size of the object program. In this context, also remember that

$$\text{FORMAT('}\qquad\qquad\text{X ='},\text{F3.0)}$$

and

$$\text{FORMAT(15X,'X=',F3.0)}$$

accomplish exactly the same thing but the latter requires less storage in the compiled program.

Initializing constants correctly can save a surprising amount of space in an object program. Instead of

$$\text{X = (5.0/2.0)*A+B**(1./2.)}$$

write out the constants as

$$\text{X = 2.5*A+SQRT(B)}$$

Although it may seem that this merely shortens running time, it saves space as well. In the first expression the compiler must store the values of three constants (5.0, 2.0, and 1.0) as well as the code necessary to make the computations. In the latter, only a single constant (2.5) need be saved, and the code for evaluating the entire expression is shorter.

Similarly, the DATA statement can pare down an object program. Using the statements

$$\text{ACONS = 58.93}$$
$$\text{BCONS = -1.05}$$
$$\text{CCONS = .0032}$$

will store the three numeric constants; reserve three different locations to receive the values of ACONS, BCONS, and CCONS; plus generate the code to make the assignments when the program is executed. The entire process can be shortened, as far as both space and time are concerned, by writing

$$\text{DATA ACONS,BCONS,CCONS/58.93,-1.05,.0032/}$$

The DATA statement reserves space for the three values, places the values there, and does it during compilation. We have saved the three locations for the constants, plus the object code to transfer them to ACONS, BCONS, and CCONS, not to mention the execution time for the three replacement operations.

Most compilers allow variable precision. If the values to be stored in an array are relatively small, there is often no need to use an entire computer word for each. The use of REAL*2 or INTEGER*2 declarations can accomplish a considerable savings. The packing techniques discussed in Chapter 3 can also be employed.

More Extreme Measures

The more drastic techniques for saving space include reducing array size by decreasing dimensions and using other storage techniques, equivalencing variables, and perhaps employing system overlay and chaining facilities.

The simplest technique to save on large amounts of space is reducing array dimensions. Often this means a general scaling down of the program, perhaps accumulating data on fewer simulated events during each program run, eliminating some "nice" but not essential features of the program, or perhaps not reserving space for the "worst case."

In the latter instance, it may be necessary to test on an array overflow and terminate the particular run. In SIMSAL, for example, a large array is reserved for the tree. Its size is approximately the worst case value. It would be possible to reduce the size of the tree because all of the locations are rarely if ever used. To do so, a test must be inserted for the value of the variable I1 in SUBJCT. If I1 were ever to advance beyond the largest number of rows in the tree, the processing could be terminated with an indication that the tree had overflowed.

If a great deal of storage is occupied by a large array, and if many of its locations contain zeros, then space may be saved by changing the manner of array storage. An array with a large number of zero entries is known as a sparse array, and a number of algorithms have been developed for making their storage more compact.

Suppose that an array of 100,000 locations is required by the logic of the program, but no more than 1,000 of the values are ever anything other than zero. This sparse vector can be stored in two 1,000-element vectors, at a saving of 98,000 locations. The nonzero values are stored in one array, and their corresponding subscripts in the nonexistent 100,000-element vector in the other. To compute with the arrays, a search of the subscript vector is made. If a subscript entry is located, then the corresponding value is taken from the value vector. If the subscript is not found, then the corresponding value must be zero.

When a two-dimensional or a higher order array is sparse, then the algorithm is somewhat more complex. The storage can be accomplished by using a form of a linked list with some added pointers. To store a two-dimensional array, for example, each value is stored in a node that contains the value itself, the row and column subscripts from the hypothetical matrix, and two pointers. One pointer designates the next nonzero datum in the same column, and the other the next nonzero row element. Access to any row or column of the array is gained through a set of row and column entry pointers.

Booth and Chien (1974) describe the process in more detail. Sparse array algorithms appear occasionally in the *Communications of the ACM* as well. The reader with a storage problem involving sparse arrays is referred there for additional details.

In some programs, memory may be shared by using the EQUIVALENCE statement. Although often useful, EQUIVALENCE is no all-purpose cureall. Its use for space conservation is limited to the case where two blocks of memory are not needed at the same time. If a large array is needed early in the program and some other arrays later, the EQUIVALENCE statement can help. In many programs, however, data are needed throughout and significant space cannot be saved by equivalencing.

A particularly valuable use of the EQUIVALENCE statement is the case of the symmetric matrix. A symmetric matrix is one in which the upper and lower triangles are mirror images; in other words, the transpose of the matrix is the same as the matrix itself. In this case, only the upper or lower triangle need be stored. The EQUIVALENCE statement can be used to refer to the same storage; however, care must be exercised so that one half-matrix is referred to only by subscripts giving the upper portion, whereas the other is referenced only by lower-half subscripts.

The EQUIVALENCE procedure is especially valuable when the diagonal of the matrix can be shared — as in correlation matrices in which the diagonal consists entirely of 1.0 values. When symmetric matrices with different diagonals are stored, a single matrix can still be used. Suppose that matrices **X** and **Y** are both 20 X 20, and symmetric. If a program array is declared by

$$\text{DIMENSION XY(20,21)}$$

it can hold both arrays, with their diagonal elements. **X** can be stored in the lower triangular part of XY, for example. Then **Y** can be stored in the upper triangle but offset one column, so that referencing an element in **X** is by an expression involving the lower triangle directly; as for example XY(4,2). To refer to the corresponding entry in **Y**, the expression would be XY(2,5).

Overlaying and chaining. When all of the previous storage reduction techniques have been tried without sufficient savings, only two procedures remain short of a complete redesign of the program — overlaying and chaining.

The essence of the overlay procedure can only be sketched here, because the specific details differ drastically between operating systems. System reference manuals are often unclear and help from computer center personnel is often essential in using overlays.

An overlay procedure defines several sections for the program and its data. Some sections remain resident the entire time a program is operating. Other segments of the program, called overlays, are brought into the main memory from an auxilliary device (such as a disk) when they are needed. As an overlay is loaded, it replaces or overlays a region of core used by a previous segment.

An analogy can be drawn with a main program with subroutines, although the parallel is not really exact. Initially, the main program, some COMMON storage, and a small set of subroutines with their associated storage are loaded into core and execution is begun. At some point, the main program calls for a subroutine that is not present. Then the overlay processor of the operating system takes control. It interrupts the program and brings the next overlay segment into core, locating it in the space previously occupied by the subroutines and their data. Control is then returned to the main program, which resumes operation with the new set of subroutines. During the whole process, the main program and the COMMON storage — often called the "root segment" — were unchanged.

The use of overlays can expand the storage available in a computer system virtually without limit. The only major requirement is that the program and its data be amenable to subdividing into mutually exclusive segments.

There is, of course, a penalty associated with overlays. Processing time increases, sometimes dramatically so, because it now includes not only the execution of the main program itself, but all of the additional time required to load and unload the overlay processor when it is needed, plus the time taken to load each segment. A less tangible but just as real cost is the added burden placed on the programmer. Often he or she must seek out help and advice on using overlays on his or her computer, must segment the program, and is likely to make numerous errors in the course of controlling the overlay process itself. In short, using overlays is not to be undertaken lightly. But if there is no alternative, an overlay scheme can be the answer.

If overlays are not available on the computer, or if they are inappropriate for some other reason (for example, if no one knows how to use them), another choice is available — chaining.

Chaining is an extension of overlaying in one sense — it involves doing the task in parts, one followed by another. The primary difference is that in chaining no segment of memory remains intact from one link of the chain to the next. Any shared data are stored externally and read by the next element in the chain. The first part of the program is run, and it leaves some key results on a storage device. The next program in the chain is then executed, taking as its input the output from the previous job.

The chain may be operated manually or be under computer control, depending on the system facilities available. In the simplest manual case, the first program is executed, producing a set of output on cards. The next part of the chain is then run, with the cards as input, and so forth. If the cards must physically come back to the programmer to be resubmitted as a new job, the complete operation of a chain can take up to several days.

If chaining is available as a part of the operating system, each element on the chain may be able to call the next link as if it were a subroutine. Many systems have a special subroutine, often named LINK or CHAIN, to cause the next segment to be loaded and executed. This facility operates much like an overlay, except that the entire memory is replaced. It is the programmer's responsibility to see that any data needed by the next part of the chain are safely stored on an intermediate device before the current link terminates.

Some recent computer systems perform a kind of automatic overlaying called "paging." Because a paged memory has some special characteristics that must be considered by a programmer, we should devote a few words to these computers.

Virtual memory systems. In some computers, the memory is organized into small units, called "pages." Any single program may occupy one or more pages. The pages are like overlay segments, except that their management is under the control of the operating system and not the user. Associated with a paged memory is a large high-speed auxilliary storage device, often a magnetic drum. When a program is loaded, all of its pages may be placed in core, or some may be in core and some on the drum. The loaded program begins operating on the first core page. Then, when all of that page has been executed, the executive system automatically finds the next one. If the required page is not resident in core at the moment, it must be found on the drum. The program is interrupted until the required page is loaded, often replacing another page that may be written onto the drum until it too is needed again. The process of moving pages into and out of main memory is generally referred to as "swapping."

A paged main memory system offers several advantages to the programmer. The greatest benefit lies in the apparent memory available. A program does not have to be bound by the physical size of the main memory; if a program is too large, it is simply broken into pages, some of which are stored on the drum until needed. A paged memory system can allow a programmer to act as if he or she had a very large memory available. Indeed, an apparent memory size of a million or more computer words is not uncommon in paged computers. The large memory is illusory because there is only a relatively small physical core memory; but it is supplemented by an immense storage capacity for pages. This illusory storage is generally called a "virtual" memory to distinguish it from the actual physical memory. The management of the paging process is entirely automatic, or "transparent" to the programmer; he or she simply writes as if a million words of core were available.

If a virtual memory sounds like the answer to the core-bound programmer's dream, in a sense it is. Of course, there is a price to pay for the very large memory. Just as overlays incur the costs of loading a new segment into core, so swapping is expensive. A programmer on a swapping system who does not pay attention to the pecularities of his or her memory is risking greatly increased running times, and thus usually costs, because of the excessively large amounts of time that may be spent in swapping. When a program is being swapped, it is doing no useful work, but the clock keeps running. In addition, many virtual memory systems charge not only for total elapsed time but also for the number of pages used and the number of swaps required.

The key to efficient use of a virtual memory system lies in what is called the "locality" of a program. By locality we mean the tendency for a program to operate in one, or at least very few pages for some time before calling for a swap. Keeping in mind that both a program and its data are paged, we may direct our attention to the problem of maintaining locality in the program and data separately.

Fortran stores its arrays in a known order; keeping that order in mind can help a great deal in maintaining data locality. Fortran arrays are typically allocated to storage locations in the order mentioned in DIMENSION or type statements. For example, the first part of SIMSAL's declarations are

```
INTEGER QUE(3),ORDER(20),PCOL(40,21), ...
```

resulting in storage being allocated as shown in Figure 6.1.

In order to maximize locality in the data, variables and arrays that are used at the same time should be stored close together. For example, if QUE were used only at the beginning of SIMSAL, and ORDER only at the end, then the illustrated arrangement might not be best. Keeping arrays together maximizes the liklihood of their being stored on the same page. Then, when one is needed and swapped into core, the chances are good that other data to be needed soon will be loaded as well.

Of particular importance in paged systems is the way a large array is accessed. Suppose, for example, that we are working on a virtual memory computer whose page size is 1,024 words. The entire program, data and all, will be broken down into pages of 1,024 words. Suppose further that we have an array TERBLE defined by

$$DIMENSION \ TERBLE(1024,10)$$

Because Fortran arrays are stored by columns, each column of TERBLE occupies a full page of memory. Now let us initialize the array to zero.

```
DO 1 I = 1,1024
DO 1 J = 1,10
1 TERBLE(I,J) = 0.0
```

The two loops will zero one element on each page and then require a new page to access the next element. The operation is illustrated in Figure 6.2. Reversing

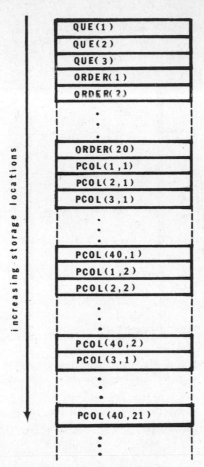

FIGURE 6.1   Part of the memory arrangement in SIMSAL.

the order of the loops, as

$$DO\ 1\ J\ =\ 1,10$$
$$DO\ 1\ I\ =\ 1,1024$$
$$1\ TERBLE(I,J)\ =\ 0.0$$

allows 1,024 elements on the first page to be zeroed, and then the next page called, and so forth. The first ordering crossed a page boundary to reach each element, opening the possibility of 10,240 swaps, whereas the second procedure could cause only 10 swaps. Of course, 10,240 swaps are very unlikely to occur, but the more chances there are to swap, the more the run time may expand.

In this particular example, the best ordering of the loops follows the general rule for optimizing loops given earlier — bury the most frequent loop the

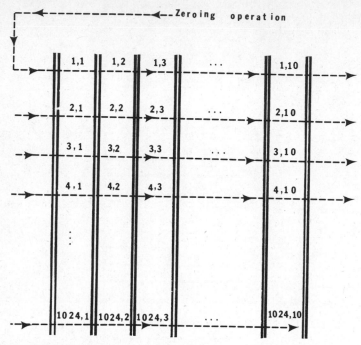

FIGURE 6.2 Zeroing a large array in a paged memory. Whenever the route of the zeroing operation crosses a page boundary, a paging interrupt may be generated.

deepest. That need not always be the case, however. Suppose that the dimensions of TERBLE were reversed to 10 X 1,024. If we were to follow the usual rule for nested loops, we would write

```
DO 1 I = 1,10
DO 1 J = 1,1024
1 TERBLE(I,J) = 0.0
```

and the zeroing would proceed as illustrated in Figure 6.3; only the first 103 elements on Row 1 can be zeroed before a new page is required. Reversing the order of the loops to

```
DO 1 J = 1,1024
DO 1 I = 1,10
1 TERBLE(I,J) = 0.0
```

will result in zeroing an entire page before the next page is required; a considerable improvement. Here, we violate the rule for nested loops because we are working on a paged computer. Previously we ordered the nested loops to

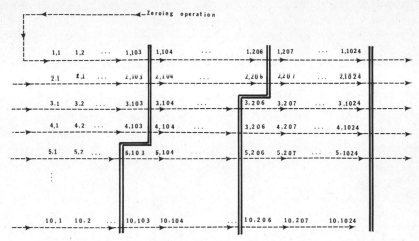

FIGURE 6.3   Another example of zeroing a large array in a paged memory.

minimize loop openings and closings; now we order them differently to mini-mize swaps. Whenever a tradeoff between loop initiations and swaps is indicated, minimize swapping as it costs a great deal more.

The procedures for maintaining data locality occasionally run counter to other programming practices, as we have just noted. Fortunately, the techniques for maintaining program locality are those which also represent good programming practice in nonpaged systems. For maximum program locality, we must have control remain in a small region of the program for as long as possible and then progress smoothly to the next section of the program. This suggests that programs should do a great deal of their work inside relatively small loops. A small loop stands a better chance of being located entirely on a single page; and as long as we execute on a single page, we need not swap.

Another implication for programming here is that we should avoid jumps (with GO TOs, IFs, and so forth) to relatively distant parts of the program. Any jump is likely to be to a different page, thus requiring a swap.

Programs structured into a number of discrete subroutines or functions can also aid in locality. Calling a subroutine is likely to cause a swap, but if the subroutine is on a single page, the result is better than jumping around in a single large program. In addition, the subroutines and functions should appear in the source code in the order that they are likely to be called during execution. Most executive systems load object programs in the sequence that the source code was processed. Thus routines that are likely to be needed at close to the same time may be allocated to the same page, and calling the first may result in the second being loaded as well.

If the programming practices suggested for maintaining program locality sound familiar, they should; they are the same as the recommendations of structured programming. Indeed, much of the importance of structured programming stems from the development of large paged computer systems.

A LAST COMMENT ON ACCURACY
AND EFFICIENCY

This chapter has led us through two major topics that are somewhat foreign to most social and behavioral scientists. Numerical accuracy is traditionally the province of mathematics. Efficient programming, if taught at all, usually appears in a computer science department, as does an elementary discussion of computer architecture.

Throughout the discussion, the effort has been directed toward illustrating that writing a good computer program, whether for a simulation or for something else, is not a haphazard process. Such seemingly trivial matters as the order of computation, the choice of formula, and the method of writing loops can have profound effects on both efficiency and accuracy.

Accuracy, efficiency, and the discipline of coding a program have received a great deal of attention by computer scientists. By presenting an introduction to this material in this book, it is hoped that it can reach a fast-growing group of computer programmers and users — the social and behavioral scientists.

EXERCISES

6.1 Write a program that computes s^2 for a sample using the two algebriacally equivalent formulas

$$s^2 = \Sigma \frac{X^2}{N} - \bar{X}^2 = \Sigma \frac{(X - \bar{X})^2}{N}.$$

Test your program with 10 different sets of data containing both very large and very small values. You may wish to use one or more of the probability distribution sampling routines in Chapter 5 to generate the data. Compare the results of the two computational formulas.

6.2 Recompile the program in Exercise 6.1 in extended precision. Use the same sets of data and compare the results again.

6.3 The logic of a program requires two large matrices, **A** and **B**, to be stored. Both are symmetric 30 × 30 matrices, but their diagonals have different values. When the program starts, **A** is to be set to values of 1.0 and **B** to −1.0. Following the suggestion made earlier, write the necessary declaration and initializing statements. (Hint: store both **A** and **B** in the same matrix AB, but do not use an EQUIVALENCE statement.)

6.4 Two symmetric 40 X 40 matrices, **C** and **D**, are stored in the same way as **A** and **B** in Exercise 6.3. Write the program segment to replace each element of **C** with an element of **C** plus the corresponding element of **D**. In other words, you want to equivalent of $c_{ij} = c_{ij} + d_{ij}$.

6.5 Among the several timing tests suggested in this chapter was one to determine the difference in execution time for the two forms of the IF statement. Write a program to make equivalent IF tests a large number of times, using both the arithmetic and logical IF. Time both forms of the test and determine which is fastest on your computer.

6.6 Repeat Exercise 6.5 for the implied DO as compared with the simple array name on both input and output.

6.7 Write a timing test routine to investigate how your compiler handles

$$DO \ 1 \ I \ = \ 1,1000$$

as compared with

$$DO \ 1 \ I \ = \ 1,1000,2$$

6.8 Following the same logic of timing tests, find out whether multiply and divide are equally fast on your computer and, if not, decide which is faster.

6.9 Repeat Exercises 6.5 through 6.8 using both debugging and optimizing compilers, if they are available on your computer system. What do the results imply?

*6.10 If you have a paged memory computer system, find out the page size. Now determine how large an array can fit on a single page. (That's not as easy as it sounds.) Pay attention to the differences in how your computer stores real and integer variables.

6.11 Pick any old program that you have written. Rewrite it to minimize computer time. Compare the running times of the two programs.

6.12 The urban growth simulation requires as input at least the following: a list of the characters to be used to identify the various land uses, the population that can be accomodated in each land-use type, an annual growth rate, a set of priorities for building new areas, a set of corresponding priorities for destroying old land to build new, and a starting map configuration. Write the necessary declarations, efficient input statements to obtain the initial values, and then print (again, efficiently) the obtained information as a general header for the program. You may consider having a special subroutine to take a census (a count of various land uses and population) and to print the map.

SUGGESTED READINGS

Andree, R. V., Andree, J. P., & Andree, D. D. *Computer programming: Techniques, analysis, and mathematics.* Englewood Cliffs, N. J.: Prentice-Hall, 1973. This is an excellent and clearly written introduction to Fortran programming, with many additional topics included as well. Especially recommended are Chapter 6, on numerical methods and Chapter 9, which presents a great many hints, suggestions, and a discussion of what makes a good computing problem.

Booth, T. L., & Chien, Y. T. *Computing: Fundamentals and applications.* Santa Barbara, Calif.: Hamilton, 1974. This good general text can be cited again here as it was in Chapters 3 and 4. This time, note especially their good coverage of computational costs, optimization and error.

Carnahan, B., & Wilkes, J. O. *Digital computing and numerical methods (With FORTRAN-IV, WATFOR, and WATFIV Programming).* New York: Wiley, 1973. This will certainly be difficult reading for most social scientists. However, the coverage is thorough and the examples profuse.

Dahl, O. J., Dijkstra, E. W., & Hoare, C. A. R. *Structured programming.* New York: Academic Press, 1972. Probably the definitive work on the subject, written by the developers of many of the techniques. Not an easy book, by any means, but well worth the effort.

Kernighan, B. W., & Plauger, P. J. Programming style: Examples and counterexamples. *Computing Surveys,* 1974, 6, 303–319. An excellent and easily read paper. Gives many examples of good and bad style, programs that appear to be structured and are not, and vice versa. While looking at this fine paper, don't overlook the rest of the entire issue devoted to programming, and including the papers by Knuth and Yohe noted below.

Kernighan, B. W., & Plauger, P. J. *The elements of programming style.* New York: McGraw-Hill, 1974. Highly recommended for anyone who seriously wants to become a good programmer.

Knuth, D. E. Structured programming with go to statements. *Computing Surveys,* 1974, 6, 261–302. A moderately difficult paper in which an outstanding authority in programming discusses structured programming and argues for the use of the GO TO statement in some instances. Contains a good history of structured programming and many hints on programming in general.

Pennington, R. H. *Introductory computer methods and numerical analysis.* New York: Macmillan, 1965. This book contains a good discussion of error in computation and a number of Fortran examples.

Van Tassel, D. *Program style, design, efficiency, debugging, and testing.* Englewood Cliffs, N. J.: Prentice-Hall, 1974. Informally written and easy to read, it provides a reasonably good coverage of the topics.

Yohe, J. M. An overview of programming practices. *Computing Surveys,* 1974, 6, 221–247. This paper covers the entirety of programming, from problem analysis through coding and debugging, to maintenance. Highly recommended reading; even the most experienced programmer can benefit from the many hints and suggested practices.

7
Debugging and Documentation

The preceding several chapters have dealt with the detail of programming and coding a simulation in Fortran. In this chapter we deal with two additional topics essential to the full process of programming – debugging and documentation. The final step of testing and validation is addressed in Chapter 8.

Documentation is a user- or programmer-oriented description of the program, its logic, its algorithms, and its input and output. Its goal is to explain, clarify, and illustrate the inner workings of the program and its underlying model. There are two general parts to the documentation, a written report whose nature varies according to its audience, and the program listing. Both are essential to a complete documentation of the program. A program is incomplete until the documentation is prepared, and, of course, the program operating properly.

DEBUGGING

Anyone who has ever written a program knows that it rarely runs correctly the first time it is tried. The novice programmer is usually disheartened by the appearance of those annoying programming bugs. The more experienced programmer expects there to be errors and, indeed, often enjoys the challange offered by locating and exterminating them.

Rare indeed is the program that is completely bugfree. Even the most thoroughly tested routines can be forced to fail when given appropriate input. However, we are not concerned with such perverse cases here. Our interest is with the more conventional bug – the error in logic, the syntactic error, the program that does not terminate, the subscript that runs amuck and destroys the program itself, and the various forms of output bug.

One of the best aids in writing programs with a minimum of bugs is the strict adherence to the tenants of structured programming discussed in Chapter 2.

Avoiding GO TO and other branching statements as much as possible has two benefits in debugging. First, developing an algorithm with a minimum of branching requires a great deal of thought, and as a result the routine is likely to be both more concise and better understood. Second, a program following the top to bottom logic resulting from minimal branching is much easier to trace through in debugging.

The use of structured programming's small modules is also a good debugging aid. It is much easier to locate an error in a small block of coding than in a large one because a single page of code is much more comprehensible. In addition, the use of a subroutine structure tends to keep bugs confined to a small area of the program; there is less tendency for a bug to affect a distant area of the program.

Locating Bugs

A good debugging compiler is an invaluable aid in locating a great number of minor but annoying mistakes. The compiler messages generally help the programmer locate missing commas, unbalanced parentheses, and arithmetic errors that result in a syntactically incorrect statement.

Even the best compiler cannot guard against all kinds of blunders. For example, the following statements will be accepted by any compiler, but may result in an error.

```
DIMENSION BIG(50)
        .
        .
        .
ISUB = I*10+3
BIG(ISUB) = 0.
```

Any value of I greater than 4, or any negative value of I, will result in zeroing a location outside of the bounds of the array BIG. Depending on where BIG is stored, the result may be zeroing some unintended data value or even a part of the program itself.

Some compilers will generate code to trap an attempt to access an element beyond the declared bounds of an array, but many do not. Some compilers will also note that a subscript value is undefined if there is no route through the program that can result in assigning a value to the subscript variable.

Examples of errors that even the best compiler cannot locate include omitting a part of a program, using an incorrect formula, arrays that are too small, or branching the wrong direction on an IF (the author's personal favorite).

Locating an error, as we have mentioned, is greatly facilitated by having the program structured into small segments. Adding to this the ability to trace the operation of the program will make localizing even easier. Tracing is simply printing a message occasionally during operation. Many programs are organized so that some output is done early, followed by computing, often in a sequence of subroutines, and finally more output. If something has gone astray during the computation phase, locating the error may be very difficult. Inserting output statements before and after a subroutine call or loop is a good method of tracing a program. For example, during the debugging of CHEBO, the search of squares surrounding a piece on the board was apparently malfunctioning, and it was not clear that the function computing the value of each position was being entered properly. In order to isolate the problem, several trace statements were added to the program. In CHEBO, the subroutine SEARCH accepts a piece number (I) as an argument and searches a square area around the piece, computing the value of each possible move by referencing the function VALUE. Just before the reference to VALUE, the following statements were used for the trace:

```
      WRITE(NPR,20000) I,ISUB2,JSUB2
20000 FORMAT(' FOR PIECE ',I2,' LOOKING AT SQUARE ',2I3)
```

Then the reference to VALUE occurred as

```
      TEMP = VALUE(ISUB2,JSUB2,NTO,NTX)
```

where ISUB2 and JSUB2 give the row and column subscripts of the cell in question. These statements produced output that indicated that the search around each piece was operating properly and eliminated SEARCH as a possible source of error.

In VALUE, the following statements were added just before the RETURN:

```
      WRITE(NPR,20000) ISUB,JSUB,VALUE
20000 FORMAT(' THE VALUE OF LOCATION ',2I3,' IS ',F6.3)
```

These statements produced output demonstrating that the arguments indicating the tested position (ISUB and JSUB in VALUE) were being communicated to the function properly, but that the computation of the value itself was incorrect. Once the problem was located and corrected, the tracing statements were removed from the program.

Sometimes it is advantageous to leave some tracing in the program permanently as an output option. The PRINT variable in SIMSAL's SUBJCT subroutine originated during debugging as a means of controlling the amount of output, and remains there to allow selective printing during operation.

Tracing statements are placed at critical points in the program. Before and after subroutine calls are good points, as are just before and after major loops. Avoid putting a trace inside a loop unless it is clear that the trouble is there. Often printing the sequential values of the loop's index variable is helpful.

Marking any debugging inserts with a special code in Columns 73–80, asterisks, for example, is a useful technique. With those codes present, it makes it very easy to locate and remove the statements when they are no longer needed.

Printing a statement such as

NORMAL PROGRAM TERMINATION

just before the STOP and END statements is often helpful; it is easy to overlook the possibility of an error at the end of an otherwise apparently good run.

Locating logical errors is more difficult than finding syntax mistakes. A thorough job of developing the conceptual model and a careful translation into the program will go a long way. Time spent in "playing computer," or desktop debugging is also essential. Select some simple data and go through the operation of the program by hand, with both the flowchart and the listing. Either flowchart or code may be a satisfactory check on logic, but using both helps in locating errors introduced in translating from one to the other.

In desktop debugging, pay particular attention to not only the logic of the program, but to the items where the compiler cannot detect an error. Also carefully check array sizes and loop indices, data and format types, precision of variables, and whether variables have been properly initialized. Failure to set a location to zero and then adding something to it is a common and difficult to locate bug, as is an unexpected truncation resulting from an integer computation.

Attend to all of the output from a compiler. Compiler messages are often grouped into "fatal" and "nonfatal" errors or warnings. A nonfatal warning should be an immediate indication that something may be wrong, but not so wrong as to prevent compilation. Warnings often turn into serious difficulties when the program is executed; they generally deal with mixed mode computations, problems in COMMON storage, or perhaps questionable equivalencing.

A great deal of other information is presented by a compiler, and a good programmer uses it. For example, a load map is often available as a compiler option. It shows the storage location of each variable, constant, FORMAT statement, and subroutine in the program. Scanning through the map is a good practice. For one thing, you may find spelling errors that can otherwise slip past. For example, suppose the load map for CHEBO showed a variable named BROAD. After some familiarity with the program, we could recognize that BROAD is not a variable in the program but could be an easy keypunching transposition of BOARD, a correct variable. The presence of an extraneous variable name in the load map should be an immediate cue to locate a possible misspelling in the source program.

When the error cannot be located precisely but is suspected to involve a variable or index, investigate the kinds of dumps available from your system. A dump is a printing of all or part of memory, along with certain critical registers. Most computers offer a postmortem dump, which occurs after a program failure. The dump may be automatic, or you may have to enter a special code on a job control record to obtain it.

Often a postmortem dump is not what is needed, and some systems allow a dump and continue operation. Obtaining a dump sometimes can be accomplished with a call to a special system subroutine. For example, the statement

$$IF(I.GT.100) \quad CALL \quad PDUMP(3)$$

might call on a system dump routine when a critical value became too large. PDUMP is a real subroutine on some computer systems; its argument gives the format of the dump selected from among several choices (for example, all variables in hexadecimal notation, index registers in floating notation). A special routine, such as PDUMP, is exceptionally useful in purging some difficult bugs, especially I/O problems where the standard Fortran routines cannot be relied on to transmit values properly.

During compilation, some computer systems allow an option for inserting special pauses called "breakpoints" into the object program at specific locations. Later the program can be executed, using a special debugging supervisor, with pauses at the breakpoints to allow the programmer to display the contents of various registers and memory locations. In a time-sharing system, the programmer can interact with his or her operating program under the debugging supervisor and can literally step the program from one machine language instruction to the next. This special debugging aid is usually found on only the most sophisticated of the time-sharing systems (or on minicomputers) and is of real use mainly to the programmer who is familiar with assembly language.

DOCUMENTATION

Even the best program is worthless if no one can understand and use it. Documentation is an essential part of the program itself, and no program is complete, no matter how well it operates, until it is written.

Just as with writing an efficient program, there is a best time to write at least the first draft of the documentation. Just as with efficiency, moreover, that time is when the program is being written. The working documentation may consist of nothing more than a collection of rough flowcharts and half-finished pieces of code. But it is essential that notes and documentation be kept throughout the entire project. That done, producing the final documentation is much less troublesome and is likely to be better and more accurate as well.

Program documentation is written for two, or sometimes three, distinct audiences. The first audience is the programmer himself. It is essential that the details of the program and its underlying model be written down, specifying the nature of the program, its model, its algorithms, its limitations, and its uses. Without documentation, the program may be of little use as a research simulation. After the program has been written, even its designer and programmer are not likely to remember all of its features.

During program development, some form of documentation is necessary as many details in the complex task of simulation programming slip out of memory very fast. Among other suggestions, Brown (1974) urges programmers to

". . . document everything, continually assuming we are going to have an attack of amnesia next week" (p. 219).

A second audience for documentation is another researcher interested in the program and its model. Often, the most important kind of documentation for this audience is the detailed specification of the conceptual model as described in Chapter 2. Sometimes another scholar will want to obtain the simulation program to study its inner workings and perhaps add his own modifications. For her or him, the documentation must be very complete and detailed.

A third sort of audience is rarely encountered in simulation programming (with the exception of some educational simulations); the reader with no desire or need to understand the inner detail of the program. For this audience, a document called a "user's manual" is often prepared. Not a technical description of the program, the user's manual is an indispensible tool for large programs to be operated by many diverse users, as for example most large data processing programs.

In this chapter, we are concerned primarily with the first two audiences. Simulations are generally operated by their programmers, or by those who are intimately familiar with computer use. For them, there is little need of a user's manual hiding most of the technical detail. An excellent example of the third kind of documentation — the user's manual — is Rajecki (1972).

Documentation probably is best presented in two forms, within the program itself and as a separate document. A carefully written program, with adequate comments and clear structure — in short, a readable program — is the best documentation available. We will consider shortly the content and organization of a program listing necessary to make it a key part of the documentation.

A written document to accompany the program listing accomplishes several things that a listing in general cannot. It includes, for example, an extended discussion of the rationale and underlying model of the program, which becomes cumbersome in a listing. Flowcharts and illustrative input and output are also more conveniently placed in a separate document.

Written Documentation

The written documentation is like a research report describing the simulation. Indeed, many of the written reports of simulation projects are primarily documentation, together with descriptions of some of the results of operating the program. There are four parts of the written documentation of a simulation program; a fifth is included if the documentation is a research report: rationale, assumptions and algorithms, flowcharts, annotated input and output, and research results.

Rationale. This section of the documentation presents such items as the background of the model, including a discussion of the theoretical work underlying it and previous related efforts, the aims of the project, its theoretical and practical impact, and a general description of the process being simulated. The most important element is a thorough presentation of the conceptual model of the simulation, as discussed in Chapter 2. The conceptual model, including the units, properties, processes, and so forth, are spelled out carefully so that the reader can understand precisely what is being represented, and how.

Assumptions and algorithms. As we pointed out earlier, the translation from conceptual model to Fortran program inevitably involves making a number of assumptions. The kinds of phenomena covered by the program, the ranges of its variables, restrictions placed on the inputs (such as the three letter syllables in SIMSAL), and so forth, all reflect assumptions and restrictions to be discussed. In addition, the algorithms are spelled out in detail. If the field in which social interaction is to take place is simulated by something like a checkerboard, a discussion of the pros and cons of that representation is included, along with the techniques for evaluating a position on the board, deciding whether to move and where, and so forth. In short, this is the section that introduces some of the technicalities of the program and its representation of the conceptual model.

The first two sections of the documentation spell out very carefully the underlying theoretical logic of the simulation and show how that logic is represented in the computer program. The result here is a communication between the simulation developer and the reader. The reader must be convinced both that the theory is sound and that it is correctly represented by the operating program.

Frijda (1967) discusses the communication between reader and writer in detail. He also makes two important suggestions to be kept in mind during both the development of the model and simulation, and in writing the documentation. First, the structure of the program should represent the structure of the theory. By this he means that the program, and the documentation, should in general separate the theory-relevant portions of the program from those sections that are primarily technical or housekeeping.

Frijda's second suggestion is a comment on the inadequacy of many published reports of simulations. As he says, "... the statement of the theoretically important program segments should contain all details about auxiliary operations and other conditions (such as memory storage registers or counters) which influence or codetermine the operation of the main routine" [p. 612]. The reason for this suggestion is that the language chosen for the simulation has two impacts on the way in which the program is written. In the first place, the language is at a high level — it is not in assembly code, and a number of important operations are obscured by the language itself.

More importantly, however, the nature of the language imposes very real constraints on how the model is expressed. Fortran, as we have noted, forces all data to be stored in variables and arrays, and the algorithms developed to implement the model are therefore different than if the program were written in LISP, for example, which treats the list as its basic data. The same process may be represented in any language, but its particular expression is largely deter-mined by the rules of the language. Moreover, it is important that the relation-ship between the processes of the model, and the model's realization in a specific programming language, be clear.

Flowcharts.   A flowchart is perhaps the most economical means of describing the sequencing of the simulated process, as we have pointed out in Chapter 2. The flowchart is a valuable part of the documentation because it can show how the stimulated process progresses from one phase to the next in a very concise way. A flowchart should be at a reasonably high level; every little operation need not be shown. Figure 2.3, illustrating the major subprocess in CHEBO, is about the right level of detail.

Annotated input and output.   For anyone who wishes to operate the simula-tion program her- or himself, a sample of the input and output is essential. The specimens must be annotated, showing the exact locations and meanings of all input values, and explanatory comments on the output. Even if a reader does not plan to implement and operate the program her- or himself, a sample of the input and output is valuable to understanding the program and its operation. Indeed, many programs represent their processes in a spatial manner (CHEBO, for example), so that to really appreciate the simulation, the output must be seen.

Research results.   When a simulation program is operated, it is often as a test of its model, or an exploration of various phenomena by means of the simula-tion. In this section of the documentation, the writer summarizes the studies conducted with the simulation. The results often appear as a formal research report, as Hintzman (1968) has described his experiments with SAL. The process of attempting to validate the simulation as we discuss in Chapter 8 usually provides the results described here.

The Program Listing

The program listing completes the package begun with the written documenta-tion. Material essential for understanding the simulation not presented in the written text appears in the listing. For example, the documentation for SIMSAL indicates that the memory is to be represented by a tree; the listing shows the actual tree operations. CHEBO operationalizes the distance model of the theory that was described in the text. In a sense, the written documentation and the listing serve as the conceptual statement of the model and as its operating realization. In order to appreciate the entire simulation project, both elements must be presented.

The exact statements in the Fortran program reflect the verbally described conceptual model. Following Frijda's suggestions, the program listing should be organized so that the theory-relevant material stands out from the housekeeping. All of the material in the listing should be readable and clearly organized. Certainly, having the program well structured and clearly organized helps here as it does in debugging.

Source code organization. Like a book, a program can be viewed in several ways. The individual program statement is much like a sentence; it is short and expresses a single idea. A statement, and a sentence, should be clear and concise, easily understandable by itself.

Sentences are grouped into paragraphs, each generally devoted to a single topic. Likewise, program statements are often grouped, with those having to do with a single algorithm or small process located together. Paragraphs are grouped into chapters or sections of chapters; these form the subroutines and functions in a program. Books are not thrown together aimlessly, and neither are programs. First things must come first and then must progress in a systematic order, reflecting the underlying process or model. In viewing the organization of the programs, we should attend to the flow of the action in the process, as well as to the clarity with which each individual statement and segment is formed.

An important element of the program is the comment statement. Comments are used for two major purposes — to mark the boundaries between groups of statements (paragraphs, if you will) and to describe on a general level what is accomplished in each segment of the program. The extensive use of good comments can greatly improve the readability of the program. We emphasize "good" comments because not all comments are. A comment, such as

```
C    SET I TO I+1
```

does not add anything to what can be seen in the program. However, if we describe what is happening, such as

```
C    INCREMENT POINTER I TO NEXT LOCATION
```

then the comment is valuable.

Program listings should be organized with the main program first, followed by all of the subprograms. The ordering of the subprograms follows the order in which the routines are most often called; the order should parallel that of the flowchart as well.

Communication in scientific writing is facilitated by the use of a standardized report format (the American Psychological Association's publication manual, 1974, is one example and generally has been followed in this book). In the same way, communicating a simulation is greatly enhanced if the listing of the main program and all subprograms is done clearly and in a consistent format. In the remainder of this chapter, we discuss the individual elements of the program listing — statements, comments, and so forth — and offer guidelines for communicating each clearly.

Statement format. Writing readable and clear Fortran code is facilitated if each statement follows a consistent rule. The rules listed below are those that have been used in preparing all of the code illustrated in this book. You may quibble with any or all of the suggestions offered; nevertheless, it is certainly true that having a rule for each statement, and following it faithfully, results in a more readable program.

1. *Comments.* Each comment is preceded and followed by a blank comment line. The text of each comment line is begun in Column 7, except that additional indenting is used for long comments.

2. *Continuation of statements.* A continuation line is marked by an asterisk (*) in Column 6. The continuation itself begins in Column 10 unless the continued material is a literal string in a FORMAT or DATA statement. In writing continuation statements, words or variable names are never divided but are written entirely on the same line.

3. *Statement numbers.* Major subsections of code are designated by statement numbers beginning with 1000, 2000, and so forth. Subsections are numbered by 100s. FORMAT statements are given five-digit numbers, beginning with 10000 and continuing sequentially throughout the program. Within subsections, statements are assigned increasing numbers according to the order in which a statement is mentioned, and not by linear position in the listing. Statement numbers are packed right in Columns 1–5.

4. *Declaration statements.* Declarations are written with a single space after the key word, with no space in the body of the declaration. Within the listing, the order of the declarations is

```
Type statements (e.g., INTEGER)
DIMENSION
COMMON
EQUIVALENCE
DATA
```

In most cases, variables are listed alphabetically in a statement.

5. *FORMAT statements.* FORMAT statements are written with no embedded spaces except in literal strings. The form 'string of characters' is used for literals instead of an H specification. All format specifications are separated with either a comma (,) or a solidus (/). A comma is always used after a string terminating apostrophe (') unless the next character is a solidus (/). Only the characters +, 0, 1, and blank are used for carriage control.

6. *Arithmetic statements.* A single space is used on each side of the replacement symbol (=) and no space appears in the expression itself.

7. *Input/output statements.* READ and WRITE statements are written with no embedded spaces except for a single space following the right parenthesis

enclosing the device and format designations and spaces on each side of the = in an implied DO.

8. *Control statements.* GO TO statements are written with no embedded blanks except for a single space after the words GO and TO. A DO statement has single spaces after the word DO, after the statement number, and surrounding the = symbol. No space appears in the initial, terminal, and increment values. All DO loops end with a CONTINUE, except for loops in which there is but a single statement. IF statements are written without embedded blanks except for a single space following the closing parenthesis of the test condition. In a logical IF, the .TRUE. consequence follows the rule for its statement.

9. *Logical statements.* Logical statements and expressions follow the rules for arithmetic and logical IF statements, except that any connective operators (.AND., .OR., or .NOT.) are surrounded by single spaces.

10. *Subprograms.* CALL, SUBROUTINE, and FUNCTION statements are written with no embedded spaces except for a single space following the key word (CALL, SUBROUTINE, or FUNCTION). An arithmetic statement function has no embedded spaces except for those surrounding the replacement operator (=). An arithmetic statement function is placed in the listing immediately following the declarations. Any system-specific routines are clearly designated by comments so that they can be easily located and replaced. Subprograms are ordered in the program listing according to the sequence in which they are most often to be called.

A topic near and dear to some programmers is not addressed by these suggestions — the indenting of statements. A frequent suggestion is to indent all of the statement in the body of the loop. The argument is that if all statements in a loop are indented, for example, three spaces, the range of the loop becomes visually clear.

Indenting has not been used in our examples for two reasons. First, because all of the example simulations have sets of loops nested several levels deep, indenting each loop would cause the innermost statement to be set so far to the right that a great many continuations would be required. Second, the range of most loops in the examples is always specified by comments. Indeed, there are comments located throughout the loops, and the visual impact of the indenting would be considerably lessened by their presence.

Front matter. A publisher calls everything that appears before the beginning of the text "front matter." In a book, front matter includes at least the title page, the table of contents, and the preface. In a program the front matter is written as comments and should contain the following material.

1. *A brief description of the program or subroutine.* In the main program, this would involve a very much abbreviated summary of the conceptual model. In its shortest form, it may be merely a descriptive title for the program.

2. *References, if any.* If the program is based on a published theory, the reference should appear here. A sort subroutine might contain a reference to Shell's (1959) paper or to some other source of the algorithm.

3. *A description of the input.* It is often convenient to include not only what is to go in what column of what data card, but also the name, limits, meaning, and format of each variable read. The listing of SIMSAL in Appendix B provides an example of a clear input specification.

4. *A description of the output.* This section may be very brief if the output is entirely self-explanatory. If the program produces error messages, a description of them should be included here, along with suggestions as to the cause of each possible error stop.

5. *Programmer identification.* The programmer's name should appear in the listing, as well as the date. If several versions of the program have been written, a version number should be presented along with the date.

6. *Known idiosyncracies.* Any departures from the standard Fortran language should be carefully noted, as well as any system-dependent features of the program. For example, the random number function in the examples is system specific and is so noted. If there are any known or suspected bugs remaining in the program, note them here to save a great deal of trouble for someone else. For example, a comment such as

```
C         FOR SOME REASON, THE PROGRAM BLOWS UP IF
C         SUPPLIED WITH A VALUE OF I EQUAL TO 42.
```

could prove very helpful to a user who innocently supplied such a value.

Segment comments. Major subsections of each routine should be clearly separated by descriptive comments. The four sections of the SUBJCT subroutine of SIMSAL in Appendix B provide a good example of segment comments. If the program is written in a strict structured programming style, there are no segments because only subroutines and functions are present.

Other comments. In general, it is almost impossible to have too many comments in a program listing. They are used to help the reader follow the flow of the program. Any obscure coding should be explained in comments and the ends of major loops and processes noted.

Form of Documentation

The form in which the documentation is presented varies with its audience. In some cases, a notebook on the researcher's desk will suffice. If the simulation is to be published, the overall format of the documentation is dictated by the journal or publisher. Usually only the written material is published; with few exceptions, program listings are not. Most publications carry a footnote to the effect that a listing can be obtained from the author.

Whatever the final outcome of the project, from publication to a dusty back shelf, documentation is essential; remember the possibility of an amnesia attack! It's inevitable. And it's also fortunate for a programmer's sanity that many of the details are forgotten in a short time. However, it is just those tiny details that are so exasperatingly important when trying to reconstruct the logic of a program later.

EXERCISES

7.1 Produce the complete documentation for the Shell sort subroutine presented in Table 4.1.

7.2 Complete the coding for the urban development simulation, supply it with some data, and apply the debugging techniques discussed in this chapter.

7.3 Write the documentation for the urban growth simulation.

SUGGESTED READINGS

Andree, R. V., Andree, J. P., & Andree, D. D. *Computer programming: Techniques, analysis, and mathematics.* Englewood Cliffs, N. J.: Prentice-Hall, 1973. Although debugging and documentation scarcely appear in the index, the entire thrust of this exceptional book is toward writing efficient, errorfree, and readable programs. It deserves careful study.

Fosdick, L. D. The production of better mathematical software. *Communications of the ACM*, 1972, 15, 611–617. A good summary of many good programming and debugging practices.

Rustin, R. (Ed.) *Debugging techniques in large systems.* Englewood Cliffs, N. J.: Prentice-Hall, 1971. Devoted mainly to very large systems, many valuable techniques and hints are presented.

Van Tassel, D. *Program style, design, efficiency, debugging, and testing.* Englewood Cliffs, N. J.: Prentice-Hall, 1974. This book devotes an entire chapter to debugging and offers lots of suggestions and helpful hints. Unfortunately, documentation is not dealt with in as thorough a manner.

Yohe, J. M. An overview of programming practices. *Computing surveys*, 1974, 6, 221–246. This paper contains a good section on debugging as well as a short summary of the essentials of documentation.

8
Validation

Validating a simulation implies the adequacy of the underlying model, particularly with regard to the stated aims of the simulation project. Certainly, if the aim of the simulation is to project how an electorate is going to vote in a presidential campaign, the results must be weighed against the final vote. In our earlier discussion, however, we indicated that there were at least two general approaches to election prediction — simulating individual voters and a regression model based on precinct sampling. If two such different simulations produce identical, and accurate, predictions, then a simple output analysis is not sufficient to decide which is the more valid program; that decision hinges on the purpose of the simulation. If a simple prediction is needed, either program suffices. If the purpose of the project is to understand the ways in which individual voter attitudes determine the final vote, however, then the individual voter model is preferred.

Validation may be easily confused with verification or testing. The latter topic refers to the testing of the program *qua* program, with no regard to its content and representation; it is a debugging matter. The important question in verification is "does this program operate correctly?" and not "does this program adequately represent its model and produce output that resembles the real world?" In other words, looking at the program simply as a program, are the results correct, or are there design or coding errors which make the results appear improper? In SIMSAL, for example, we expect to see the program cycle through a number of trials on a list of syllables, making a response after each syllable, building a tree, and so on until a criterion is reached and the program terminates. Such an analysis is verification. When the question becomes one of whether the program forms clusters, as human memory apparently does, or whether the number of trials needed to learn a list varies with the intralist similarity, we are investigating validity; the focus has changed to the relationship between program performance and human behavior.

Figure 8.1 helps illustrate the areas to which attention must be directed in validation. The figure is derived from Figure 1.1 — which summarized the parallels between real and simulated phenomena — but with a few additions.

At the top of Figure 8.1 is the conceptualization of a natural phenomenon as presented in Chapter 1, and the parallel diagram for the simulation is at the bottom. The two diagrams are joined by the major intervening stages in the development of the simulation, the theory and the conceptual model. The two are separate in the figure, as would be the case when the simulation is developed on the basis of an existing theory. When the simulation program itself is viewed as the theory then theory and model become one and the same.

One obvious area of study in validation is the comparison of the two outputs. Certainly, for a simulation to be valid, its output should be highly similar to that of the real system, given comparable inputs. The study of output similarities is conducted by employing what are known as "indistinguishability tests," and we shall devote considerable time to them later. The use of the indistinguishability procedure is adequate to establish the validity of the simulation. But it does not make any evaluation of the adequacy of the theory itself, or of the validity of the simulation program as a representation of the theory. An indistinguishability test will establish either a simulation or a synthesis as valid or invalid. It cannot draw a distinction between them, and so indistinguishability alone cannot inform us that the model can really advance scientific understanding. In order to

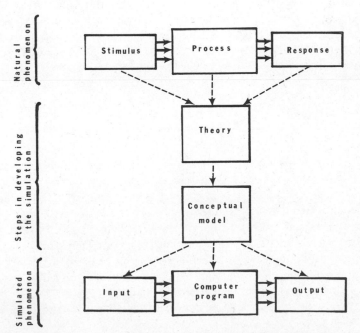

FIGURE 8.1   A conceptualization of the overall process of simulation.

make those kinds of inferences, attention must be paid to the vertical dimension in Figure 8.1.

The theory underlying, or embodied in, a simulation is expected to fulfill the requirements of scientific theory. This aspect of validity is often overlooked in the rush to demonstrate indistinguishability but is critical. Particularly when the program is in fact regarded as a theory, it must conform to the criteria expected of any theoretical statement in science.

In addition, the derivation of the simulation program from the theory, and indeed the theory's own development from observation about the phenomenon, must be properly accomplished. If the theory is inadequately represented by the program, or if the theory is insufficient in its account of the world, then the simulation cannot be regarded as a valid test of a theory, regardless of how well the output may agree with the facts.

This third consideration refers to the validation of the model as a representation of the theory. If the simulation results agree with real data (indistinguishability), and if the theory can stand on its own merits, and if the simulation program is an adequate representation of the theory, then the simulation can be a valuable contribution to scientific understanding. If the theory is satisfactory, however, as is the representation in the program, and the results do not agree, then we have an indication that the theory is erroneous. This occurrence would prompt a revision of the theory and model, and thus a subsequent better understanding of nature. Both of these outcomes result in scientific progress.

However, if the results of the program agree with real data but the program is not a valid representation of the theory, then we have achieved a synthesis, although no better theoretical understanding. Therefore, it is extremely important to attend to the theoretical validity of the model. We turn our attention to two separate aspects of it first and then consider the indistinguishability procedures.

CRITERIA OF THEORY

The first of three general problems of validity concerns the adequacy of the theory embodied in the simulation program. This topic is of particular concern when the simulation is not derived from an existing theory; that is, when the simulation program itself is regarded as the theory. Scholars of the artificial intelligence persuasion (see, for example, Simon & Feigenbaum, 1964) maintain that their programs are theories. They do not evolve from an existing theoretical corpus but attempt to meet an input—output indistinguishability test with no regard to representing the underlying process. Traditionally, validation of this class of simulation has relied solely on indistinguishability tests. If the program—theories are to be taken seriously, however, they must meet the criteria of theory developed in the philosophy of science.

We shall not attempt here to present a detailed discussion of the numerous criteria developed in the philosophy of science. Our presentation focuses on five central areas of criteria for theory and only summarizes the important requirements. The interested reader is referred to a major work such as Popper (1959) for additional discussion

Generality. When two theories deal with the same phenomenon, the one with the wider applicability to a range of problems is preferred. For example, the General Problem Solver (GPS) (Newell & Simon, 1963) would be chosen over the geometry theorem prover of Gelernter and his associates (Gelernter, 1963). Although both programs deal with proofs of various symbolic propositions, GPS has a wider range. Likewise, the recent exposition of verbal learning theory by Anderson and Bower (1973) is preferred over Hintzman's SAL or our own SIMSAL as it deals with a much broader range of learning phenomena.

Falsifiability. Closely related to precision of a theory is the ability of the theory to be proved incorrect. A theory must generate testable predictions; it must be subject to falsification. A theory so vague or self-contradictory that it cannot be subjected to a critical test is worthless as a scientific statement. Of course, theories abound that do not meet the criterion of falsifiability but have an impact nonetheless. A notable example is Freud's classical psychoanalytic theory of personality. Without scientific value because it cannot be definitively proved or disproved, psychoanalysis has had considerable impact nevertheless.

Not only do we expect a good theory to be testable, but we also prefer a theory that generates a large number of predictions. Indeed, the mark of a good theory or model is its ability to generate new hypotheses, thus leading to even better understanding through further investigations. If a simulation or theory can generate new thinking and lines of research, it is scientifically worthwhile, even if it is ultimately replaced by another formulation.

Accuracy. A theory must agree with the known facts. If it makes incorrect predictions or does not account for critical elements of the phenomenon, a theory does not generally enjoy a long scientific life. As a theory of learning, SIMSAL does not accommodate all of the facts. However, it does predict many of the known results of learning studies. The extent of agreement is often important in assessing a theory, and we point out below that SIMSAL is a useful theoretical formulation for some purposes but that it is not the final answer in learning theory.

The accuracy requirement of theory implies, of course, that if a simulation program is based on the theory, then the output must be an accurate representation of real results. In other words, accuracy implies an indistinguishability test.

Simplicity. Other things being equal, the simpler of two theories will be selected. A simple theory makes a minimum of assumptions, postulates fewer hypothetical constructs, and flows through a less complex logical argument than does a complex theory. As theories, both of our examples are relatively simple. They make minimal demands on logic and do not postulate complicated assumptions or hypothetical operations. Indeed, computer simulation requires that any assumed intervening operations be made very explicit and can often help in understanding and simplifying the inner logic of an otherwise intricate theoretical formulation.

VALIDITY OF THE THEORETICAL REPRESENTATION

The theory must be sound, but that alone is insufficient in evaluating a simulation. In order that we may regard the results of the simulation as having any bearing on the theory, and hence on the understanding of nature implied by it, the model must be a faithful representation of the theory.

As is the case in evaluating a scientific theory, no absolute yardsticks can be provided for quantifying the degree of fit between the theory and the model, and between the model and the program. By and large, the final assessment is the responsibility of the reader of a simulation report. However, the simulation writer her- or himself bears a considerable responsibility; he or she must be satisfied that the program does in fact represent the theory and must convince his or her reader as well.

The only opportunity that the writer has to expound on the logical linking of theory and simulation is in the documentation. The section of the documentation describing rationale and algorithms must set forth the following elements of the theory and program clearly and explicitly so that the final judge, the reader, can decide on the adequacy of the program as an expression of the theory.

1. The theory must be stated clearly and concisely. Any simplifications or modifications made in the original theoretical formulation must be specified. If some elements of the theory have been omitted, careful note of and rationale for that action must be made.

2. The domain of phenomena to which the theory, as represented by the program, is to apply must be stated so that the reader may judge whether the original theory has been restricted too severely to be of general use.

3. The parallelism between the program's processes and the activities of the real system should be given special attention. If, for example, a temporal sequence of events is being simulated, that sequence should be present in the program and identified explicitly. In the real world, activities typically proceed in a parallel fashion; the program cannot operate in that way. The logic by which parallel events were converted into a set of sequential operations should be explained.

4. The similarities and differences in the input and output of the real and simulated process should be discussed, along with a thorough discussion of the internal representation of the units of the system and their properties.

5. Particularly when the theory is developed essentially in the conceptual model of the program, a careful justification of the processes and postulates must be presented. For example, in the presentation of CHEBO, Sakoda (1971) showed the development of the checkerboard formulation as an outgrowth of two previous theoretical approaches and justified the processes and functions in that broader context.

In short, the point here is the same one made in Chapter 7, and by Frijda (1967) and by Abelson (1968) among others — the documentation of the program must include the logic and rationale of the program. It is the only place where the reader may judge the fidelity with which a theory is represented by the simulation program. This is a crucial step in the logic and is lacking or sorely incomplete in many simulation reports. Without it, there is no way to know whether the simulation is really a model of the process that can advance our theoretical understanding or whether we have nothing but a possibly interesting synthesis.

INDISTINGUISHABILITY TESTS

The adequacy of the theory as a scientific statement and the faithfulness of the simulation to its theoretic origins are two important elements of validation illustrated in Figure 8.1. They refer to the relationships within the theory construction operation and to the vertical relationships in the process, respectively. Even if the theory is logically sound and is represented satisfactorily in the simulation program, however, the simulation must produce results that are comparable with the real-world process being simulated. The output similarity of the real and simulated processes is really the criterion used to assess the accuracy of the theory's prediction. That accuracy is determined by an indistinguishability test.

In essence, an indistinguishability procedure asks the question: "Can the results of the computer simulation be identified as different from 'the real thing'?" If the answer is in the negative, then the simulation has passed the indistinguishability test. A great deal of attention has been given to developing procedures for deciding whether the result of a simulation is sufficiently similar to real data to justify placing some confidence in the program and model. These procedures fall into two general groups — Turing-type tests and known results techniques.

The Turing Test

The most famous of the indistinguishability procedures was formulated by Turing (1950) in an attempt to provide an answer to the question of whether or not a computer can think. Turing's original statement of the test was as a form of party game, which goes as follows. A man and a woman are hidden from view and are questioned by an interrogator using written (or typewritten, or teletype) messages. The interrogator asks questions of both the man and the woman in an attempt to establish which is male and which is female. The man and woman may give any responses, including deceptions and misleading cues. At some point, the interrogator is allowed to guess which is which.

Turing then proposes that one of the hidden participants be replaced by a computer. (It is unclear whether the interrogator is even informed that the switch may be made.) We then ask whether the interrogator is correct as often in identifying the computer as he or she has been in picking the person it replaced. If so, then the computer may be said to be thinking.

A frequent misunderstanding of the Turing procedure is the requirement that the identification rate be the same whether the human or the computer is being questioned. The confusion was clarified by Abelson (1968) in his proposal for an Extended Turing Test.

The Extended Turing Test

Abelson's extension of the Turing test requires a series of guesses at the identity of the subject (man, woman, computer) by the interrogator. In a baseline series, the man and woman are paired and the correct identification rate is established. After that series, the computer is substituted for one of the participants and the correct guess rate is determined again.

Over a long series of guesses by the interrogator, if the guess rates for the two pairs (for example, man—woman, man—computer) do not differ significantly, and both differ significantly from chance (50% correct), then the computer may be said to successfully simulate intelligent behavior.

Abelson also dealt with another difficulty in Turing's original procedure in that he specifies a dimension along which a discrimination is to be made. Turing alluded to the problem briefly but did not deal with it systematically. In Turing's party game, the dimension to be judged is masculinity—femininity, not physical strength, or length of hair, or any other possible attribute. Abelson makes the requirement of dimension of judgment explicit.

The Turing procedure, and Abelson's extension of it, may be applied to a large number of simulated situations and judgmental dimensions. In addition, there are many components of the party game that are not essential in indistinguishability tests. There is no reason, for example, why the back and forth questioning need proceed in real time. Indeed, there is no compelling reason why questioning must be a part of the test situation at all. A judge (or interrogator) can be presented with pairs of output samples and asked to determine which is the output of a computer and which is from some real process. Of course, to use the Abelson extension of the test, one half of the pairs should be real—real and the other half real—computer.

The Abelson extension of the Turing test has the advantage that it is widely applicable and is quantifiable. Certain constraints are implied, of course. Output to be inspected by a judge or set of judges should be comparable. It would be nonsense to present the computer output as it came from the program, while real output was typed transcript, annual reports to stockholders, or some other form providing extraneous cues.

The Abelson extension was employed by Colby (1973; Colby, Hilf, Weber, & Kraemer, 1972) in an impressive demonstration of his model of paranoid behavior. Colby had eight psychistrists interview two patients through a teletype; unknown to any of them, one of the patients was real and the other was a simulated paranoiac. The transcripts of the interviews were submitted to 33 additional psychiatrists for ratings on the dimension of degree of paranoia. The ratings of the total group of 41 physicians indicated that the paranoid simulation was indistinguishable from the real paranoid patient. Altogether, a most impressive demonstration.

Colby's work, incidentally, is in a strict synthesis mold. He makes no attempt to base his model of paranoia on any existing psychological or psychiatric theory. His goal is to develop a program incorporating the delusional system of a real patient and to do it in such a way that it can pass an input/output indistinguishability test. (An interesting elementary introduction to Colby's model can be found in Loehlin, 1968; for a more detailed treatment, see Colby & Gilbert, 1964.)

The Turing test and its extension are the most widely used and recognized of the indistinguishability procedures. Other approaches exist and we consider a few of them now under the general heading of "matching to known results" techniques. None of these additional indistinguishability procedures, however, has the wide general applicability or the simple elegance of the Turing test.

Matching to Known Results

A carefully conducted Turing procedure, with its implied attempt to deceive a judge or rater, is often more cumbersome than necessary. In most simulation areas, there is a body of empirical data about the phenomenon, and the task of validating the simulation is that of assessing the degree of fit between the simulated and real data. Such a procedure is often erroneously called a Turing test but is really something different.

In the studies with SIMSAL, for example, there is no need to present real and simulated data in a series of pairs and test for discriminability, as the Turing procedure would require. Indeed, all that is really necessary is to establish a series of experimental runs of the program, simulating the various standard learning tasks that SIMSAL should be able to accomodate. The results of human performance in these situations are available and all we need do is gather the SIMSAL data and determine whether or not it agrees.

Depending on the nature of the simulation and real phenomenon, a number of different kinds of procedures may be employed in evaluating a match, ranging from simple inspection to somewhat more sophisticated techniques. In many instances, as with SIMSAL, formal statistical tests of fit are not necessary. In inspecting the results presented later in this chapter, the fit or lack of it is obvious even to an untrained reader. Such informal "testing" of fit is very common in simulation. In many simulations, the program is a model of a process in great detail, and perhaps the best testing procedure is a side by side comparison of protocol output. This procedure has been employed extensively in the studies of problem solving by Newell and Simon and their associates (see, for example, Newell & Simon, 1972; Simon & Hayes, 1976). Both Abelson (1968) and Frijda (1967) refer to this sort of "matching by inspection" technique as well.

A few other techniques have been developed for matching as well; yet, surprisingly, in this technically sophisticated area, precise statistical techniques are not often used. Abelson (1968) notes the possibility of tabulating response matches between person and simulation in protocol comparison and points out that there is no real criterion for a "good" number of matches. In some instances, it is possible to test against a count of possible random matches (see, for example, Hunt, Marin, & Stone, 1966), but in practice this technique has rarely been employed.

Reitman (1965) addresses another possibility — that of the processing sequences exhibited by the program and the real process. This technique is applicable in instances where the process goes through readily identifiable stages or subprocesses. By noting what subprocess follows which other in both the simulation and actual data, and by counting frequencies of occurrence, a series of contingency tables can be developed. If the simulation and real process do not differ in the pattern of sequential moves, then the simulation may be judged successful.

Abelson (1968) offers an additional technique in matching — a sort of cross-sectional approach. Many simulations involve large numbers of simulated individual units, such as individual persons, groups of voters, aggregates of cells of a particular type, and so forth. During the course of both the real and simulated process, it is possible to obtain various measures on the units. Attitude change after each interaction, membrane permeability, number of social interactions per unit time, and number of words learned by trial three, are but a few examples. In this case, it should not be difficult to design an appropriate statistical procedure to investigate the similarity between real and simulated phenomena.

As noted, the statistical sophistication displayed by simulation researchers is strangely lacking. In part the deficiency can be attributed to a preoccuptation with the tasks involved in writing the simulation, but in part as well to a failure to perceive the need for statistical treatment of simulation results. Abelson

(1968) has recognized the problems and has made an attempt to develop some new techniques; the extended Turing procedure is one example. In addition, he introduces the notion of the panel simulation, which is applicable in some social situations. But apart from a few scattered efforts, the statistical treatment of simulation results remains underdeveloped. Much of the treatment of results appears unsophisticated and almost cursory; often it seems that validation, although recognized as important, is treated in a highly subjective or informal fashion. Whereas this is often an incorrect assessment of the situation, a great deal more effort can be devoted to handling simulation data.

"COMPREHENSIVE" VALIDATION

We have identified three major areas with which validation must be concerned. The theory that underlies, or is embedded in, the simulation must meet the general standards expected of scientific theory. The translation from theory to operating model must be accurate so that the model is a valid representation of the theory. Finally, the results of the simulation must agree with data gathered from the real situation. This last requirement reflects the demand of predictive accuracy in a scientific theory.

Simulation reports typically stress one or another of these three aspects of validation, usually with little in the way of formal criteria in view. Validation is usually in a more all-encompassing or global sense than has been implied so far. Indeed, in the broad view of the progress of science, perhaps such approaches are really the most important. What is really crucial in a scientific theory, and the theory involved in a simulation is no exception, is that it advance our understanding and generate new and testable hypotheses. No matter how good the fit between simulated and real data, no matter how faithful the translation from theory to model, if no overall progress in understanding and exploration of new areas is realized, then simulation is largely a meaningless exercise in computer programming.

In many cases, the point by point validation of a simulation may be less than perfect, yet the overall result is positive. Hintzman's SAL, the parent of our SIMSAL, is lacking in both generality and accuracy as a scientific theory. However, it has served well in advancing theoretical understanding in the area of verbal learning. SAL illustrated that many phenomena in learning could be accounted for by a relatively simple discrimination process. Discrimination processes had become somewhat disfavored in learning theory, and Hintzman's work served to bring them back into focus. Thus, on an overall level, the work with SAL was highly successful, even though the theory was less than optimal and the indistinguishability tests unsophisticated.

VALIDATION OF THE EXAMPLE SIMULATIONS

In this section, we consider our example simulations in light of the preceding discussion of validity. For each program, we note the purpose of the simulation, sketch the underlying theoretical model and its translation into the program, and discuss the output of the program itself.

CHEBO

As described by its author (Sakoda, 1971): "The checkerboard model provides a concrete means of portraying social interaction as an ongoing process among members of groups" (p. 119). The simulation is a simplification and abstraction of a number of possible real situations. Sakoda intends to show by example that psychological concepts (individual attitudes in this case) can be fruitfully applied in a sociological situation (the action of the entire group). There is no attempt to represent the entirety of social interaction, but only to allow the manipulation of a few variables.

CHEBO is derived from two primary theoretical bases; field theory (Lewin, 1951), which describes a social field where interaction can occur, and social attitude theory (e.g., see Volkart, 1951), which ascribes the attraction between members of social groups to their mutual attitudes. In the program, the social field is made up of rows and columns, as on a checkerboard, so that the location of each individual in each group can be determined precisely. It may be noted in passing that some field research has used the locations of individuals, for example at a cocktail party, by reference to a row and column grid defined by floor tiles.

In the model, each of the two groups possesses two attitudes, toward members of their own group and toward members of the other group. Of course this is a simplification; people have a great many more attitudes, and additionally may not feel the same toward all members of their own or even the other group.

Attraction in the social field is governed by attitudes. Individuals tend to approach others to whom they have a positive attitude and retreat from those to whom they have a negative attitude. In most theories, attitudes may vary in value or intensity, as well as in sign, and both of those elements are represented in the simulation. A neutral attitude is usually represented theoretically by zero, as it is in the program. Neither of the two background formulations attempts to relate movement or attraction to attitude in a precise way; Sakoda found it necessary to develop the explicit formula presented in Chapter 2. Here was a clear instance of a simulation forcing clarification in a theory; the exact means by which attitudes might cause movement was unspecified, and the simulation writer filled the gap. A number of possible formulas could have been proposed; the one selected was viewed as best because it both was easy to understand and accomplished the desired aims.

The overall theory underlying CHEBO is a very broad conceptualization of the nature of attitudes as influences on human social behavior. It is perhaps significant that Sakoda does not base his model on a single theoretical statement; there is none. The model in this case is a sort of minitheory in and of itself. It is designed specifically for an artificial situation in which there are only two groups of actors, each possessing but two attitudes. There is, of course, no exactly comparable real-world situation. What we have here is a simplification, for purposes of modeling and simulation, into an elementary form where the effects of some of the theoretical consequences can be explored. To some extent, the result is an ideal illustration of a computer model. The theoretical structure is broad but its implications are relatively clear — positive attitudes attract and negative repel. The consequences are simplified — movement toward or away — where in a real situation social attraction is much more difficult to determine precisely. In humans, social attraction may be measured by physical approach, of course, but also by such differing behaviors as group memberships, contributions, frequencies of correspondence between individuals, or measures that can be obtained only by detailed examination ("how much do you feel attracted to individual X"), and so forth.

In inspecting output from CHEBO, we cannot rely on an indistinguishability procedure; there are no appropriate comparison data from so simple a situation. We can, however, describe what may be expected from the theory given a particular pattern of input attitudes and determine whether the model's output agrees. In this chapter, we present two different sets of CHEBO results. Additional data are given in Appendix A.

The first output, shown in Figure 8.2, results from input attitudes giving each group a neutral attitude toward itself and a slightly negative attituce toward the other group. In this output, the members of the two groups are represented by open and closed circles. Each cycle in the program represents an opportunity for each individual on the checkerboard to move one space in any direction (unless a space is occupied or off the board) if there is value in doing so. The value of each possible move is computed as described in Chapter 2 and the move made. In this example, there is no positive attraction among any of the pieces and so the greatest benefit will be derived from retreating from members of the opposite group. Because the attitude toward other members of the group is neutral, the position of same-group members has no influence.

On the basis of a theoretical analysis we expect to find members of the two groups moving apart, and that is just what the output shows. Note that there is no tendency for members of the same group to come together, at least not until a boundary is encountered. Look particularly at the group of four solid circles in roughly the center at Cycle O (the random starting position). If there is positive intragroup attraction, these four should move together because they start close together and nearby pieces have a greater impact than do distant ones. What happens instead, however, is that they retain their same configuration for two

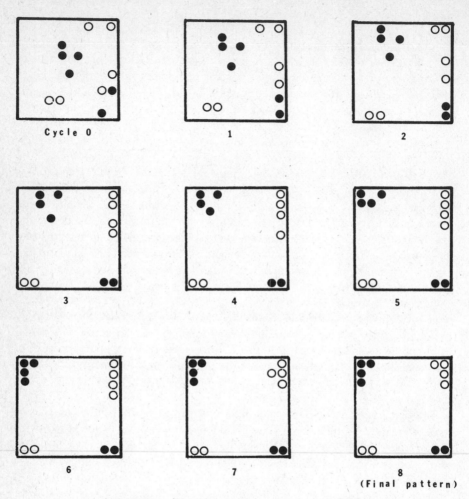

FIGURE 8.2 'Mutual suspicion' output from CHEBO.

cycles; they are moving away from the open circles that are simultaneously congregating at the lower left and upper right. Only when the entire configuration cannot move further because of the boundary do the groups become more compact.

Sakoda has named this pattern of movement — away from the opposite group and being forced together with ones peers — mutual suspicion. A real-world parallel is not difficult to construct. It is not unusual for coalitions of mutually neutral individuals to form based on their mutual dislike of some other group.

Two versions of a second variety of CHEBO output are shown in Figure 8.3a and b. Sakoda has dubbed these patterns "social workers and lost souls." In Figure 8.3a the social workers (open circles) have a positive attitude both toward

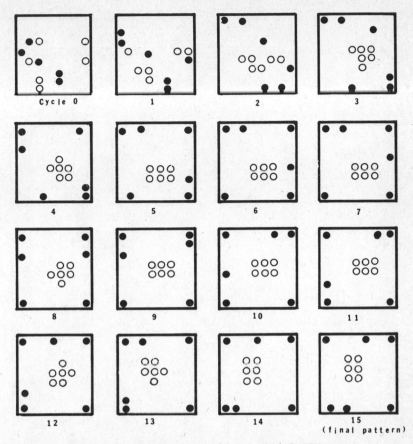

FIGURE 8.3   (a) 'Social workers and lost souls' CHEBO output.

each other and toward the lost souls (solid). The solid circles, in contrast, have negative attitudes toward both groups. The result is a clustering of the social workers in the center of the board caused by their mutual attraction; the lost souls, repelled by everyone, disperse around the periphery.

In the second version of the "social workers" example, the attitude pattern remains the same, except that the social workers (open) are given a neutral attitude toward each other. A marked difference is noted in the output. This time, in Figure 8.3b, the social workers do not cluster in the center but move toward the lost souls, which are in turn moving away toward the borders of the social field.

In Figure 8.3a, the social workers cluster into a relatively stable rectangular pattern quickly but change their orientation slightly. The change is occasioned by continued movement by the lost souls on the periphery of the board.

What are we to conclude about CHEBO on the basis of this inspection of two

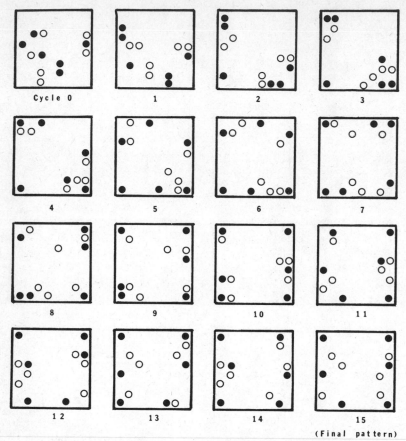

FIGURE 8.3   (b) 'Social workers and lost souls' CHEBO output.

sets of results? As far as the output is concerned, it does agree with what can be expected given the patterns of attitudes. In other words, it "fits" with what we expect.

As a model expressing a theory, moreover, CHEBO seems quite satisfactory. It is not an expression of a complete theory of human interaction but it is not intended to be. It does clarify an existing theoretical approach and simplify it into a specific, if artificial, situation; and that is one of the most important things that we expect of a simulation.

Does CHEBO suggest interesting hypotheses to pursue? Indeed it does. As noted earlier, CHEBO contains a counter that terminates the program after a preset number of cycles if a stable configuration (where no moves are made) has not been reached. The reason that the termination criterion was inserted was that it was discovered that some patterns of input attitudes resulted in output patterns that never became stable. One of these, called pursuit by Sakoda, is easily constructed by giving both groups neutral attitudes toward members of their own groups but giving one group a positive attitude to the other, whereas the other group has a negative intergroup attitude. Such a pattern of attitudes results in one group being constantly attracted to the other, which is in turn constantly being repelled from the first.

The simulation thus suggests that there should be some attitude patterns that are unstable in the sense that a final pattern, or even a standoff, is never reached. Are there real situations resembling the pursuit situation, and do they show the predicted attitudes? As but one example (and it's fun to think of them) consider preadolescent boys and girls. Girls typically show interest in the opposite sex first, and there is often a stage when girls attempt to attract boys in any number of ways. Meanwhile, the boys actively avoid the girls. Also (if you remember) the attitudes of the two groups tend to be as predicted by the model.

A related CHEBO observation leads to another prediction. In Figures 8.2 and 8.3, we note that a final configuration is reached much more quickly (in fewer cycles) in the mutual suspicion case than in the social workers example. The prediction here is a refinement of the simple stable—unstable observation made previously. Here we predict that two-group interaction situations differ in the length of time (or number of interactions, if that is a convenient measure) that is required to establish some measure of stability. We shall leave it as an exercise for the reader to think of examples and check on the predicted attitudes.

SIMSAL

Of the example simulations, SIMSAL is in some ways the most complex and elegant and has the most serious purpose. In his presentation of the original SAL, Hintzman (1968) placed the program into a context of several competing theories of paired-associates learning. The purpose was not to present SAL as a final theory of the phenomenon, but do demonstrate that simple discrimination among stimuli was more in conformity with the research results than was thought at the time. Although CHEBO is meant primarily as a demonstration, SIMSAL is intended as a theoretical expression, and one hoped to have an impact on future theory development in its area. For that reason, then, the validation criteria applied to SAL (and to SIMSAL as well) should be more thorough and careful than has been required for CHEBO.

SIMSAL deals with a well-defined range of phenomena. The requirements of a theory of paired—associates learning are clear — the theory must account for the research data. The validation procedure, therefore, can be of the known results variety; there is no need to employ a Turing procedure with its implicit attempt to deceive a judge.

The subject in a paired-associates experiment is confronted with a simple task — over a series of trials, he or she is to learn to produce the correct response for each stimulus item. The program has the same job — over a set of presentations of the list, it must "learn" to distinguish among the stimuli and associate a correct response with each. In the program, the stimulus discrimination and response storage is accomplished in a memory tree, or discrimination net, to use Hintzman's phrase. Just how the process is accomplished in humans is not understood in detail but is thought to involve similar processes.

The program's tree is a sequence of nodes, each containing a single letter from a syllable. As a stimulus is processed, a search is made through the tree, testing the syllable against the contents of nodes. When a match occurs, the stored response is made. If there is a mismatch, a new node may be formed to incorporate the differences between the new syllable and a previously learned one.

Hintzman presents three versions of SAL. New features were added to the original program (SAL-I) in order to account for additional data and phenomena. The SIMSAL program is parallel only to SAL-I and SAL-II. (The modification to produce SAL-III is not difficult but complicates the program more than desired for this book.)

Hintzman's paper is a theoretical presentation and extended validation. The known results procedure presented the program with a standard verbal learning experiment, generated several simulated subjects, and compared the results with those obtained from real subjects. The analysis of degree of fit was largely qualitative for several reasons, largely centering on the inability of SAL to operate in the wide range of different stimulus environments encountered in the human learning literature.

Hintzman presents 10 different experiments with SAL-I and SAL-II. From them and some related observations, a total of 12 conclusions about the adequacy of SAL were drawn; eight were in agreement with the human learning literature.

A thorough presentation of all of Hintzman's results would require a more extended discussion of human paired-associates learning than is appropriate in this volume. The interested reader is referred to the original paper. Instead, we present three studies conducted with SIMSAL as partial validation. In them, the two programs agree well.

The first SIMSAL study concerned intralist similarity, or the degree of "confusability" among items on the list — a major variable in many human learning studies. For testing SIMSAL's performance, the three lists of syllables and responses shown in Table 8.1 were presented to a series of 20 SIMSAL subjects in each condition. For all subjects, the learning parameters were PADD = .40, PCHNG = .50, and POVLRN = 0.0.

A simple measure of learning difficulty is the number of trials to criterion; for SIMSAL, the mean trials are as follows (Hintzman's results with SAL are given in parentheses): low similarity, 5.00 (4.60); medium similarity, 7.40 (5.50); high similarity, 7.20 (6.75). SIMSAL's results do not agree precisely with those obtained from SAL. Nevertheless, they do show that high-similarity lists in

TABLE 8.1
Stimuli and Responses for the Intralist Similarity Experiment

Condition					
High similarity		Medium similarity		Low similarity	
Stim.	Resp.	Stim.	Resp.	Stim.	Resp.
ACE	1	AEI	1	AIQ	1
ACF	2	AFJ	2	BJR	2
ADE	3	BGK	3	CKS	3
ADF	4	BHL	4	DLT	4
BCE	5	CEI	5	EMU	5
BCF	6	CFJ	6	FNV	6
BDE	7	DGK	7	GOW	7
BDF	8	DHL	8	HPX	8

general require more trials for mastery than do low-similarity lists. Both SAL and SIMSAL produce data that are comparable to those resulting from humans; see, for example, Restle (1964).

A notable failure of both SAL and SIMSAL is in the effect of list length. Hintzman's study on list length was repeated with SIMSAL, with the same general results. In typical human research, the longer a list of syllables, the more trials required for learning. SAL and SIMSAL were presented with two lists of words of medium intralist similarity; one list contained eight syllables and the other 16. The results were as follows (again, Hintzman's results are in parentheses): with eight items, the mean errors per syllable—response pair was 3.26 (1.59); for 16 items, mean errors per pair was 3.36 (1.55). Here again, the point is not that SAL and SIMSAL do not agree precisely but that neither simulation shows any major difference because of list length.

Hintzman's SAL-I makes use of two input parameters, as discussed previously. The variable PADD governs the probability of SIMSAL's forming a new mode following an incorrect response. PCHNG controls changing a stored response following an error if a new node has not been formed. The third parameter, POVLRN, distinguishes SAL-I from SAL-II. If it is zero, the program operates as SAL-I. When POVLRN is assigned a value between O and PADD, the program operates as SAL-II. SAL-II allows the program to learn more than is necessary for correct discrimination of syllables by forming a new node, with probability POVLRN, following a correct response. Such additional learning is called over-learning, and SAL-II is known as the overlearning model. Hintzman reports three studies with SAL-II; we shall report on a single SIMSAL experiment replicating one of them.

In a typical study with SAL-II, two lists of syllables are presented. The first list is learned to some criterion, then the second list is learned, and finally the first list is relearned. Typically, the learning of the second list interferes with memory as shown by less than perfect recall of the first list, a phenomenon known as retroactive interference. One of the several factors that influence retroactive interference is the degree of interlist similarity — the similarity between the first and second lists. Table 8.2 illustrates the lists presented to SIMSAL in this experiment. Ten simulated subjects learned each pair of lists with the parameter values (the same as those used by Hintzman) of PADD = .40, PCHNG = .50, and POVLRN = .20. The results, which agree precisely with Hintzman's, are presented in Figure 8.4.

Finally, we should note one important deficiency common to both SAL and SIMSAL. Once a stimulus letter is entered into the tree, it remains there throughout the computer run of that simulated subject. The response entry in a terminal node may change, but never the letter itself. In addition, once the tree is built and the subject has learned a list, the tree remains fixed — if there is a second list as in the last example, the tree is elaborated but not basically changed. In other words, the simulation program never forgets a syllable once it is learned. This characteristic of the program is a clear weakness and source of an important discrepancy between the simulations and real data.

In light of the successes and failures of SAL and SIMSAL, what are we to say about the overall validity of SAL and SIMSAL? Hintzman's goal was to demonstrate that a large variety of paired-associates learning phenomena could be accommodated by a simple discrimination network model. At the time, much theorizing in human learning had moved away from a study of discrimination learning, and Hintzman's results had a considerable impact and brought discrimination learning back into a current focus. Certainly, SAL cannot account for all

TABLE 8.2

Stimuli and Responses for an Interlist and Retroactive
Interference Experiment

List 1		High similaritiy		Medium similarity		Low similarity	
Stim.	Resp.	Stim.	Resp.	Stim.	Resp.	Stim.	Resp.
AEI	11	AEB	1	ABC	1	ZCD	1
AFJ	12	AFC	2	ADE	2	EGH	2
BGK	13	BGD	3	BFG	3	IJL	3
BHL	14	BHE	4	BHI	4	MNO	4
CEI	15	CEF	5	CJK	5	PQR	5
CFJ	16	CFG	6	CLM	6	STU	6
DGK	17	DGH	7	DNO	7	VWX	7
DHL	18	DHI	8	DPQ	8	YZA	8
DIK	19	DIJ	9	DRS	9	BCE	9

List 2 condition spans the High, Medium, and Low similarity columns.

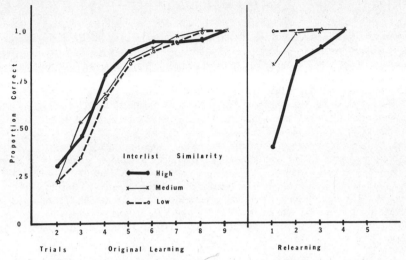

FIGURE 8.4   Retroactive interference in a two-list SIMSAL experiment.

paired-associates phenomena; but Hintzman never intended that it should. The extent of agreement that he found was surprising and certainly indicated that the model was valid for its stated purpose.

Our program, SIMSAL, seems to be an adequate parallel to SAL-I and SAL-II, at least insofar as the studies reported here illustrate. A few additional informal studies with SIMSAL, so incomplete as to not warrant reporting here, support that conclusion as well. We may thus conclude that SIMSAL is as valid as SAL for its purposes. Keeping in mind that the simulations presented in this book have the additional purpose of providing illustrative material, we may also conclude that SIMSAL is valid as a demonstration of a learning and tree building program as well.

EXERCISES

8.1 Think of at least one additional social situation where an element of pursuit is present. Do the attitudes there agree with CHEBO's predictions?

8.2 Think of two different social situations where the rate of achieving stability differs. What attitudes are involved, and what does CHEBO predict?

8.3 Present the urban growth simulation with historical data from a known city and allow it to develop. How do the results compare with the actual present city map?

8.4 Is Exercise 8.3 an indistinguishability test? Why or why not? What is implied in an indistinguishability procedure, and how may one be conducted with the urban simulation?

SUGGESTED READINGS

Abelson, R. P. Simulation of social behavior. In G. Lindzey & E. Aronson (Eds.), *The handbook of social psychology.* Vol. 2: *Research methods.* (2nd ed.) Reading, Mass.: Addison-Wesley, 1968. Contains a careful discussion of validation, including the extended Turing test and its rationale.

Colby, K. M. Simulations of belief systems. In R. C. Shank & K. M. Colby (Eds.), *Computer models of thought and language.* San Francisco: Freeman, 1973. A very interesting presentation of Colby's model of paranoia, along with a discussion of validation and an account of an outstanding validation experiment.

Frijda, N. H. The problems of computer simulation. *Behavioral Science,* 1967, **12,** 59–67. [Also in Dutton, J. M., & Starbuck, W. H. (Eds.), *Computer simulation of human behavior.* New York: Wiley, 1971.] A very valuable paper in many respects, particularly so to this chapter for the emphasis on relating theory to program. Well worth reading.

Turing, A. M. Computing machinery and intelligence. *Mind,* 1950, **59,** 433–460. [Also in Feigenbaum, E. A., & Feldman, J. (Eds.), *Computers and thought.* New York: McGraw-Hill, 1963.] This classic paper is often cited and seldom read. It should be required reading by anyone concerned with the validation problem.

9

CODA

The task of bringing matters to an orderly conclusion invariably is relegated to the final chapter. In this chapter are threads of several recurring themes, along with some new material, that is hoped to bring the discussion of previous chapters into a final focus.

One of the discussions that has recurred occasionally in earlier chapters is the nature of computer programming, and we address that issue first. After that, two topics that have not had systematic treatment so far, namely other languages and suggestions for additional study, are discussed. Finally, we return to an issue that has appeared in the early pages of the book, and again more recently in Chapter 8 – the real nature and benefit of simulation.

PROGRAMMING AS ART AND TECHNOLOGY

Instructing a digital computer to carry out a series of operations – that is, programming – is a complex and multifaceted business. On the one hand, there is the problem of clearly defining the task that the computer is to carry out. On the other hand is the problem of actually writing the computer instructions to accomplish the goal. The latter is often easier than the former, and especially so in the case of writing a simulation program.

To some extent, professional programmers, at least those in a very large programming operation, have their task simplified in two ways. The most obvious simplification is that the problem to be solved is typically easier to specify than is the conceptual model of a simulation. The requirement is to produce a system that inverts a matrix, or keeps track of an inventory, or schedules production, or handles airline reservations. Although the design of such programs may be complex, at least general guidelines can be established initially specifying what the completed project is to accomplish. This is not usually so with simulations.

The second simplification is a division of labor between programming and coding. This distinction is clear in the software industry but not in the experience of most social and behavioral scientists. In industry, programming refers to the definition of the overall process, development of the algorithms, and specification of the input, output, and operating sequence. Coding is the actual writing of computer instructions to implement the program. In most social and behavioral science computing, programming and coding are accomplished by the same individual, or in large projects, by the same group.

There is a message in the industrial model that may well be important in simulation programming and in writing programs for other tasks that scientists assign to the computer as well. Careful analysis must precede actual program coding. The use of two separate terms, programming and coding, to designate the two activities serves to keep the distinction clear. Better programs result from careful definition of the program's task. Our emphasis on the goals of the simulation project, and on the careful development of the conceptual model, has had as its aim the separation of the tasks. Thorough understanding of the inputs and outputs, the processes and their sequencing, and the logic underlying the project has been stressed in Chapter 2. We return to that same point here, this time to note that it is an element of good programming practice, as are documentation, readability, and good structure.

A computer simulation is, in many ways, similar to a project undertaken by commercial programming firms. It involves a program, often a large one, that is to accomplish some specific purpose. As a programming project per se, simulation programming is not different from commercial programming and can benefit from the same conceptual division of labor. But a simulation has a different purpose, and it is here that simulation programming differs from commercial.

The purpose of simulation is not simply to write an operating program, even a highly efficient and accurate one. The goal is to express, explore, test, and better understand a theory. The use of the analogy to industrial programming is to suggest that we can learn something about the programming process, not that the purposes are identical — they are not. The industrial model of programming stresses the separation of program design and coding, putting an emphasis on the proper design of the entire system. The message for simulation is to develop the conceptual model with care and, as much as possible, to not let the mechanics of coding interfere with the scientific goals of the project.

Programming bugs and the other mechanical elements of simulation must be kept in perspective. They are extremely important, of course, but are only incidental; and that is really the most important message to be conveyed about programming. The computer is a seductive research tool. It is so easy to become enamored of it that the importance of the scientific endeavor becomes secondary. Computing can be undertaken for its own sake, for amusement, and for enjoyment (see, for example, any issue of *Creative Computing*). But when the computer is used in simulation, those elements must be given lesser importance.

Despite the previous comments, however, good computer programming can be considered an art. Any artform requires a medium — the computer and its language in this case — and combines the technical with the creative. The art in the case of programming is more like that of the engineer who realizes the concepts of the scientists in concrete form. A pleasing bridge design, incorporating the technical understanding of the function required with the detailed knowledge of the strengths and weaknesses of the materials employed, is an artistic creation. Likewise, a computer simulation, expressing the elements of a scientific theory in terms of the computer, is a creative effort that may also be called artistic. The medium is very different than most works considered as art, the aims are quite dissimilar, and almost certainly the intended audience is more limited. Nevertheless, the art and the creativity are present, and very real to the scientist and programmer. It is not without good reason, then, that Knuth (1968, 1969, 1970) has entitled his definitive collection of algorithms *The Art of Computer Programming*.

OTHER LANGUAGES

All of the coding in this book has been in Fortran. Fortran has not been used because it is necessarily the best language for simulation, but because it is likely to be the language of the audience of the book. At the outset, it was assumed that the typical reader of this book would have some, perhaps minimal, experience in programming. Because the first language learned is usually Fortran or another closely related algebraic language, this second-level book has been written for that kind of background.

A great many simulations are written in Fortran or a similar language such as BASIC, ALGOL, or PASCAL. The general availability of these languages, together with the wide understanding of them in the behavioral sciences, makes them a logical choice.

A large number of other languages have been developed for various purposes. In this section we consider a few of them briefly. In general, they are not as widely available as Fortran and typically are not the first language learned by a novice programmer. However, they are extremely powerful and very important in advanced simulation.

Apart from the general purpose algorithmic languages, the languages most widely used in simulation programming fall into roughly three groups. Each group has its group of devoted followers and tends to be used primarily for one or more general types of simulations.

"Simulation" Languages

A large class of languages has appeared seemingly devoted to nothing but simulation, and the uninformed may assume that all simulations are programmed in one of them. As we have noted, such is not the case; a good simulation can be written in Fortran, BASIC, COBOL, or indeed any language.

The special simulation languages can be divided into two subgroups, discrete- and continuous-event languages. Discrete-event languages are widely employed in business and operations research simulations. The processes involved are often finite activities, such as a manufacturing step, a transaction, or something similar. The discrete events are controlled by a timing routine causing the events to occur at their appointed times. The most common discrete-event languages include SIMSCRIPT (Markowitz, Hansner, & Karr, 1964) and GPSS (IBM, 1967b).

Continuous-event languages are often employed in econometric models and in various other situations where elements (commodities, money, population, etc.) are subject to continuous modification over time. Indeed, these languages are in some ways themselves simulations of analog computation, where actual voltage levels vary continuously to represent physical quantity. One of the most widely known of this subclass of language is DYNAMO (Forrester, 1961; Pugh, 1963), although CSMP often has a strong following at IBM-dominated installations (see IBM, 1967a).

List Processing Languages

A great many simulations are written in a list processing language. In these, the basic data organization is not an array but a list. As all of the necessary housekeeping chores for maintaining lists are accomplished automatically by the compiler, programming of complex models is greatly simplified.

Among the earliest list processing languages was IPL-V (Newell, 1964). Currently, LISP (McCarthy, 1963) and its several dialects (such as MLISP at Stanford) is by far the most popular of the list processors. Bobrow and Raphael (1964, 1974) offer careful comparisons of several list languages.

List processors are found in many areas of simulation. The most notable are in artificial intelligence, where LISP or one of its relatives is the language of choice; in social process simulation (see Abelson, 1968); and in cognitive and learning psychology.

LISP's data structure is a singly linked list the elements of which may be either single items (called atoms) or the names of other lists. The basic operations in LISP include several elementary functions, including a procedure for selecting the first element on a list, joining lists, and testing the equality of two list elements. There are also the expected kinds of control functions such as a conditional expression, a transfer, and a function return. A very powerful feature of the language is the ability to define functions, including recursive ones. (A recursive function is one that calls itself, as discussed in Chapter 3.)

Anyone seriously considering writing a simulation program involving lists or trees may do well to investigate LISP. At first glance, LISP programs will look very peculiar to the programmer familiar with Fortran or BASIC. In fact, it is sometimes recommended that LISP be learned first, when it appears to be significantly easier than as a second language. A good introduction to the language can be found in Friedman (1974). For readers of this book, it may be awkward initially, but it is often the best language for coding a complex simulation.

String Languages

A small group of programming languages uses a string of characters as its basic data form. Anyone who has attempted any large-scale processing of alphabetic data in Fortran can appreciate a language that handles all of the necessary character packing and unpacking automatically and includes a pattern match procedure as its basic function. These features are offered by SNOBOL, by far the most widely used string processor (see Griswold, Poage, & Polonsky, 1971).

SNOBOL is ideally suited for manipulating any material in which a string of characters must be represented. It is widely used for processing literary works in content and stylistic analysis (for an excellent survey of the entire field, see Sedelow, 1970). However, SNOBOL is not limited to the humanities. Any algorithm that requires searching for and matching patterns, without a great deal of arithmetic, is suitable for SNOBOL coding. The language is used widely in simulations of various perceptual processes, such as pattern recognition. Indeed, Uhr (1973) bases an entire text on pattern recognition, learning, and thought on a series of example programs written in a SNOBOL-like language called EASy-1. (In fact, the EASy-1 compiler is written in SNOBOL and translates EASy-1 code into SNOBOL!)

The statement format of SNOBOL includes a pattern matching operation and allows a conditional transfer upon success (the pattern was located) or failure. The pattern to be matched may be a simple string of characters, or a more broadly defined element called simply a "pattern." The generalized pattern is made up of concatenations or functions of previous strings, or any combinations of them. For example, a pattern defined as SPAN('ABCD') will match any string of characters made up of only the letters ABCD in any order.

Choosing a Language

Selecting a programming language for a simulation project is influenced by two major factors — the nature of the program and local tradition.

If a programming language is not available locally, the decision may be simple.

If LISP is not implemented on the computer at hand, there is little point in learning the language and writing in it. Even if a LISP processor is available, it would be wise for the novice to look for experienced users. If the language has no local following, attempting to pick it up alone can be extremely frustrating. Experienced advice is important, not only in learning to code but also in making the compiler operate. Such languages as SIMSCRIPT, LISP, or SNOBOL are not often supplied by a computer manufacturer as a part of the "standard" system software package and have usually been imported from some other installation, generally making their operation more difficult.

If a language is available and easily usable, then the choice is dictated by the nature of the program to be written. The advice here is nearly the same as that offered by Abelson (1968): if the data are almost entirely arrays, use one of the algebraic languages. Use LISP or another list language when the data are lists and consider a special simulation language, such as SIMSCRIPT, if the nature of the simulated processes seems appropriate. Finally, "in cases of serious doubt about the appropriateness of the above-mentioned languages . . . carefully investigate other possibilities such as SNOBOL-IV, or agitate and/or wait for the development of a better language" (Abelson, 1968, p. 302).

SOME SUGGESTIONS FOR ADDITIONAL STUDY

As you approach the end of this discussion on simulation and modeling, you, the reader, may have concluded that you know more about simulation and modeling than you wanted to know and may not pursue the subject any further. That may be a perfectly justifiable conclusion; but be forewarned that if you are a student in any of the social or behavioral sciences and plan to continue in that discipline, simulation is going to be with you for many years to come and may be hard to avoid.

Likewise, you may wish to read further into the various kinds of simulations that have been developed to date. A good place to start for that purpose would be with some of the Suggested Readings at the end of Chapter 1.

In order to follow the current developments in the literature of a discipline, you will need a sharp eye and the ability to peruse the content listings of large numbers of journals. Reports of simulations appear in a bewildering array of books, journals, and technical reports. Among the key sources might be *Behavioral Science* and *Simulation and Games*. Both are broad-based professional publications; at least one paper of interest to almost anyone can be found in every issue. Within any discipline there is at least one journal devoted to primarily quantitative developments. Certainly *The Journal of Mathematical Psychology, Political Methodology,* and *The Journal of Mathematical Sociology* are examples, and there are many others.

Perhaps your interests are more technical in nature. In that case, you may want to investigate course offerings in mathematics or computer science. Learning an additional programming language is a good next step, as is becoming affiliated with a professional organization, such as The Association for Computing Machinery (ACM). The ACM is the major professional society for computer scientists and publishes several journals. Two of the ACM publications are worthy of regular attention by anyone seriously interested in computing: *The Communications of the ACM* and *Computing Surveys*. The ACM supports local and student chapters throughout the country; find out if there is one nearby and attend its meetings. If there is no local chapter then work to have one formed.

The ACM also sponsors a number of special interest groups (SIGs) made up of individuals interested in particular areas. Membership in a SIG is not limited to ACM members but is open to anyone interested. Of particular relevance to social and behavioral scientists would be: SIGART (artificial intelligence), SIGBIO (biomedical computing), SIGCAS (computers and society), SIGCUE (computer uses in education), SIGGRAPH (computer graphics), and SIGSOC (social and behavioral science), among others. The ACM Central Office[1] can supply a complete listing of all SIGs and the names and addresses of their chairmen.

Getting acquainted with some computer scientists is an excellent way to learn more about computing. Visit a local college or university and meet the faculty "computer freak" in some department related to your interests, or go to an ACM meeting and talk with people. In this new and rapidly developing field of computer modeling and simulation, news of current developments often travels most quickly through the informal channel of friendship. Try to get into that channel.

SIMULATION AND SCIENCE

Science and technology have, over history, exhibited an interesting synergistic relationship. Science supplies a foundation on which a new technology is based. That technology, in turn, provides an analogy and often a new tool for further advancement of basic science. The development of the telephone, for example, yielded at least two different theoretical conceptions for basic science to apply in new theorizing. The telephone switchboard served for many years as an analogy for the human nervous system. Many theoretical models of neural conduction were based on the analogy to the wires and switching circuits of the telephone system.

In like manner, the development of the telephone and related communications technology gave impetus to the mathematical formulation of information the-

[1] 1133 Avenue of the Americas, New York, N.Y. 10036.

ory, which in turn had a major impact in the scientific theories in many disciplines.

Like the telephone, the computer is a product of technology building on the basic findings of science. It is not surprising to find the computer, the most complex technological invention to date, filling a major role in the redirection of scientific thought in many disciplines, serving in some ways as modern telephone analogy.

At the level of discrete binary processes, the parallel has not been successful. At a higher level, however, regarding human behavior as a series of individually understandable subprocesses, the computer has had a revolutionary impact on scientific theorizing. Models of human behavior now use the terminology of the computer — there are processing functions, comparisons, inputs and outputs. Theories identify and describe behavioral sequences in terms of separate processing algorithms, predefined functions, and individual elementary operations, just as with programs.

The computer brings something to science that it had not had in any of its earlier conceptual tools, however — the ability to use the new technology not just as an analogy but also as a device to express and investigate theories. This is the real power of the computer simulation. It allows a theory to be expressed, tested, refined, and retested on the same device that may be serving as an analogy.

The computer is a most useful analogy for the social and behavioral scientist. Behavioral phenomena are complex, involve multiple separate subprocesses, and develop over time. The social sciences are primarily concerned with behavior, and behavior must occur over some span of time. In some cases, the time unit may be very small, as in the functioning of individual neural units. In other cases, the time period is longer, covering minutes, days, or even longer intervals in the case of such phenomena as cultural change.

The computer, when carrying out the processes embedded in a program, also operates over time; thus the computer can serve not only as a process analog but as a parallel to the dynamic nature of behavior as well.

What is unique in the computer is not its ability to serve as an analog, even a dynamic analog. What the computer offers to the scientist is the ability to write a series of instructions that embody a theory about a process, and then have the instructions carried out by the computer. The computer therefore serves both as analog and as the medium in which the theory, or a derivation of it, may be expressed. The computer offers the scientist the ability to express a theory and observe it in operation, so that the consequences of the theoretical formulation can be readily explored. In addition, the theory itself is expressed in clear and unambiguous terms; it must be, or the computer cannot operate.

The availability of the computer as a theoretical tool for the scientist is destined to have a profound impact on theories of behavior. It is the theories that give science its strength, and it is the computer that is revolutionizing theory construction.

SUGGESTED READINGS

Baer, R. M. *The digital villain.* Reading, Mass.: Addison-Wesley, 1972. This is an interesting, light reading book. Despite some editing errors and other inaccuracies, it deserves a place on a bookshelf. It deals with the history of computing, talks some about simulation, and presents a fair amount of material on the computer in literature.

Bobrow, D. G., & Raphael, B. A comparison of list-processing computer languages. *Communications of the ACM,* 1964, 7, 231–240. A point by point comparison of four important languages for list processing and symbol manipulation – COMIT, IPL, LISP, and SLIP. It is not a tutorial but does introduce a new programmer to several widely used languages.

Bobrow, D. G., & Raphael, B. New programming languages for artificial intelligence research. *Computing Surveys,* 1974, 6, 155–174. A survey of more recent developments in programming languages developed specifically for artificial intelligence. Requires familiarity with LISP-like languages to be fully comprehensible, but a novice can derive some benefit.

Computing Reviews. This ACM publication is the major publication outlet for reviews and abstracts of the world's computing literature. Over 100 publications have their contents abstracted here. It is well worth a regular review by any serious computer user or programmer.

Gotlieb, C. C., & Borodin, A. *Social issues in computing.* New York: Academic Press, 1973. This book is one of several recent contributions with a sociology of computing focus. Little about simulation here, but it (or another book with a similar title) should be required reading for any social scientist.

Sammet, J. E. *Programming languages: History and fundamentals.* Englewood Cliffs, N. J.: Prentice-Hall, 1969. A monumental work. This book is a thorough and systematic survey of all programming languages developed at the time. Lists the history and essentials of each. A good source for anyone wanting to learn something about a language.

Uhr, L. *Pattern recognition, learning, and thought.* Englewood Cliffs, N. J.: Prentice-Hall, 1973. This interesting book illustrates the fusion of artificial intelligence with psychology. A great many psychological topics are presented, with illustrative simulation programs written in a close relative of SNOBOL.

Weizenbaum, J. *Computer power and human reason.* San Francisco: Freeman, 1976. An eloquent plea to consider the proper use of computers and simulation, this book appears again in this list as it did in Chapter 1. Perhaps the most powerful statement yet on the promises and pitfalls of computing, it should be of great interest to the readers of this book.

APPENDIX A
CHEBO:
The Checkerboard Model
of Social Interaction

This appendix presents the checkerboard model of social interaction developed by Sakoda (1971). The overall conceptual model has been presented in Chapters 1 and 2, and the complete flowchart of the program is in Figure 2.2. A detailed flowchart of the "move all pieces" routine appears in Figure 2.4.

A complete listing of the program appears in Table A.2. The program was written in ANSI Fortran by William J. Sakoda and modified slightly by myself. The modifications consisted mainly of editing to the specifications used in this book, changes in routine names, and removal of materials specific to the IBM 1130 on which it was originally run. This version of the program was compiled and executed on the Univac 70/46 computer system at Franklin and Marshall College.

The CHEBO program consists of a main program, five subroutines, and three functions. In addition, a RANDOM/RNDM function, such as that presented in Table 5.1, is required. The only known departure from ANSI Fortran is the presence of the PROGRAM statement on the first line of the main program.

CHEBO has been discussed in detail throughout the book. As an aid to the reader in locating the various components of that discussion, Table A.1 presents an index for CHEBO; another index appears for SIMSAL, and all of the entries are in the overall index as well.

Two examples of CHEBO input are presented in Table A.3. In the first, a single card is required; this input resulted in the output in Table A.4.

An option allows CHEBO to be supplied with a pattern representing the initial configuration of the pieces on the board. In this instance, the input consists of three cards. The first card gives the same information as the previous example, whereas the next two give the starting positions of the squares and crosses, respectively. This set of cards is illustrated in the lower records in Table A.3. No output is illustrated from this input; it is the social workers example presented in Figure 8.3.

TABLE A.1
Index to the Presentation of CHEBO

```
PROGRAM CHEBO

    THE CHECKERBOARD MODEL OF SOCIAL INTERACTION.
    BY JAMES M. SAKODA, DEPARTMENT OF SOCIOLOGY,
    BROWN UNIVERSITY.  PROGRAMMER, WILLIAM J. SAKODA.

    FOR A DISCUSSION READ JAMES M. SAKODA, "THE CHECKERBOARD
    MODEL OF SOCIAL INTERACTION," JOURNAL OF MATHEMATICAL
    SOCIOLOGY, 1, 1971, 119-132.

    CAPABILITY FOR DIFFERENCE IN SPEED OF MOVEMENT ADDED
    TO PUBLISHED VERSION.

    MINOR MODIFICATIONS BY R. S. LEHMAN, NOVEMBER, 1974.

CONTENTS OF FIRST PARAMETER CARD --

    COL  01        NFLAG - NON-ZERO IF STARTING POSITIONS ARE TO BE
                           INPUT
    COLS 02 - 05    NMAX - MAXIMUM NUMBER OF CYCLES
    COLS 06 - 07    NBRD - SIZE OF THE BOARD (12 MAXIMUM)
    COLS 08 - 09    NPCO - NUMBER OF SQUARES
    COLS 10 - 11    NPCX - NUMBER OF CROSSES
    COL  12        NPOWR - 0 = EQUAL POWER. 1  =  CROSSES CAN
                           JUMP ONE SPACE.
```

256

```
C     COL   13        INCR  - NON-ZERO IF INCREMENTAL MOVES ARE TO BE
C                             PRINTED
C     COL   14        ISUPR - 0 = SUPPRESS ALL PRINTING UNTIL FINAL
C                             CONFIGURATION. 1 = PRINT BOARD ONLY
C                             AT EACH CYCLE. 2 = PRINT BOARD AND
C                             CENTROID STATISTICS AT EACH CYCLE.
C     COLS  15  -  16    OO  -  ATTITUDE OF SQUARES TOWARD THEMSELVES
C     COLS  17  -  18    OX  -  ATTITUDE OF SQUARES TO CROSSES
C     COLS  19  -  20    XX  -  ATTITUDE OF CROSSES TO THEMSELVES
C     COLS  21  -  22    XO  -  ATTITUDE OF CROSSES TO SQUARES
C     COLS  23  -  24    NEXP -  DISTANCE WEIGHT
C     COLS  25  -  26    NSTOP - 0 = CONTINUE ALL RUNS.
C                             1, 2, ETC. = END THE RUN IF NO MOVES
C                             OCCUR FOR THAT MANY CYCLES.
C     COLS  27  -  66    NTITL - TITLE (40 CHARACTERS)
C
C     SEE BELOW FOR THE CONTENTS OF THE SECOND AND THIRD PARAMETER CARDS
C          (USED ONLY IF NFLAG IS NON-ZERO).
C
C     THE VARIABLES USED IN THIS PROGRAM ARE DEFINED AS FOLLOWS --
C     A       -OUTPUT ARRAY. A IS FILLED WITH SIX LINES OF
C                     OUTPUT AT A TIME.
C     INCR    -SET NON-ZERO IF INDIVIDUAL MOVES ARE TO BE LISTED.
C     ISUPR   -SET NON-ZERO IF THE BOARD DISPLAYS ARE TO BE
C                     SUPPRESSED.
C     NBRD    -SIZE OF THE BOARD USED. THE BOARD IS ASSUMED
C                     TO BE SQUARE.
```

(continued)

257

```
C
C   NPCO        -THE NUMBER OF SQUARES USED.
C   NPCX        -THE NUMBER OF CROSSES USED.
C   XX          -THE ATTITUDE OF THE CROSSES TOWARD THEMSELVES.
C   XO          -THE ATTITUDE OF THE CROSSES TOWARD THE SQUARES.
C   OO          -THE ATTITUDE OF THE SQUARES TOWARD THEMSELVES.
C   OX          -THE ATTITUDE OF THE SQUARES TOWARD THE CROSSES.
C   NPR         -DATA SET REFERENCE NUMBER OF THE PRINCIPAL OUTPUT
C                DEVICE.
C   NRD         -DATA SET REFERENCE NUMBER OF THE INPUT DEVICE.
C   NCNT        -CYCLE COUNTER.
C   NEXP        -DISTANCE WEIGHT FACTOR.
C   NEXPD (REAL)  = 1/NEXP
C   NTB         -TOP AND BOTTOM MARGIN FOR THE OUTPUT ARRAY.
C   NHEAD       -TOP LINE OF THE OUTPUT ARRAY (CONTAINS COORDINATE
C                NUMBERS).
C   NDISP       -DISPLACEMENT FACTOR. THIS IS USED TO KEEP THE
C                OUTPUT DISPLAY CENTERED.
C   NTITL       -HOLDS THE TITLE (A2 FORMAT).
C   NFLAG       -SET NON-ZERO IF THE STARTING POSITIONS ARE TO BE
C                TAKEN FROM CARD.
C   NMAX        -MAXIMUM NUMBER OF CYCLES (MAY BE OVER-RIDDEN).
C   NSTOP       -IF NO MOVES OCCUR DURING A CYCLE NSTOP TIMES, END
C                THAT RUN. USUALLY SET TO 3 SINCE CHANGE IN ORDER
C                OF MOVE MAY ALLOW A MOVE EVEN AFTER A NO MOVE CYCLE
C   NPOWR    0 = EQUAL POWER. 1 = UNEQUAL POWER WITH CROSSES
C                GIVEN THE ABILITY TO JUMP OVER ONE SQUARE. IT
C                WILL HAVE GREATER SPEED OF MOVEMENT.
C
C   THE VARIOUS PIECES ARE REPRESENTED BY ENTRIES ON THE ARRAYS MAP AND
```

258

```
C   BOARD.  BOARD IS A 12X12 ARRAY, THUS HAVING ONE ENTRY FOR EACH
C   POSSIBLE LOCATION ON THE BOARD.  A BOARD ENTRY IS ZERO IF THE POSI-
C   TION IS UNOCCUPIED, -1 IF OCCUPIED BY A SQUARE, AND +1 IF OCCUPIED
C   BY A CROSS.  MAP CONTAINS THE COORDINATES OF THE RESPECTIVE PIECES
C   ON BOARD.
C   IN THE EXPRESSION MAP(I,J,K),
C                    I = THE PIECE NUMBER,
C                    J = 1 FOR A HORIZONTAL COORDINATE, 2 FOR A VERTICAL
C                        COORDINATE,
C                    K = 1 FOR A SQUARE, 2 FOR A CROSS.
C   THUS, MAP(I,1,1) CONTAINS THE HORIZONTAL COORDINATE OF THE ITH
C   SQUARE.  ALL MANIPULATION OF THE PIECES IF PERFORMED BY CHANGING THE
C   MAP AND BOARD ENTRIES.
C
C **********************************************************************
C *                                                                    *
C *                                                                    *
C *   NOTE ON MACHINE-SPECIFIC ROUTINES                                *
C *                                                                    *
C *   THE RANDOM NUMBER GENERATOR IS GIVEN A RANDOM STARTING           *
C *   POINT BY THE STATEMENT                                           *
C *         CALL RANDOM                                                *
C *   THEREAFTER, USING THE FUNCTION RNDM AS                           *
C *         XRAND = RNDM(DUMMY)                                        *
C *   WHERE DUMMY IS ANY VARIABLE, RESULTS IN A VALUE OF XRAND         *
C *   SAMPLED FROM A RECTANGULAR DISTRIBUTION ON THE 0-1               *
C *   INTERVAL.  CALLS TO RANDOM AND RNDM OCCUR IN THE MAIN PROGRAM    *
C *   AND IN THE FUNCTION JRAND.  THEY MUST BE CHANGED TO MEET         *
C *   LOCAL REQUIREMENTS OR REPLACED BY A USER-SUPPLIED ROUTINE.       *
C **********************************************************************
```

(continued)

259

TABLE A.2 (continued)

```
      INTEGER A(53,6),XX,XO,OO,OX,BOARD(12,12)
      REAL NEXPD
      COMMON A,NBRD,NPC(2),XX,XO,OO,OX,BOARD,MAP(12,2,2),NPR,NRD
      COMMON NCNT,NEXP,NEXPD,NTB(52),NHEAD(48),NDISP,NTITL(20),NFLAG
      COMMON NMAX,INCR,ISUPR,NSTOP,NOMOV,KK,KKCUM,NPOWR
      EQUIVALENCE (NPC(1),NPCO),(NPC(2),NPCX)
    1 FORMAT(I1,I4,3I2,3I1,6I2,20A2)
    2 FORMAT(I2(1X,2I2))
C
C     SET I/O DEVICES
C
      NRD = 1
      NPR = 2
C
C     READ IN PROGRAM PARAMETERS
C
 1000 READ(NRD,1,END=4000)NFLAG,NMAX,NBRD,NPCO,NPCX,NPOWR,INCR,ISUPR,OO,
     *    OX,XX,XO,NEXP,NSTOP,NTITL
C
C     STOP THE JOB WHEN A BLANK CARD IS ENCOUNTERED.
C
      IF(NMAX) 1001,1001,1002
 1001 STOP
C
C     INITIALIZE
C
```

260

```
1002 KKCUM = 0
     NOMOV = 0
C
C    SET COUNT INDICATOR
C
     NCNT = 0
C
C    CALCULATE DISPLACEMENT FACTOR.
C
     NDISP = (12-NBRD)/2
C
C    CHECK TEMPORARY FLAG ON
C
     IF(NFLAG) 1003,1003,1004
C
C    FLAG IS ON -- READ IN STARTING POSITION FROM CARDS.
C    THIS REQUIRES 2 ADDITIONAL DATA CARDS.  THE FIRST SPECIFIES THE
C    COORDINATES FOR ALL THE SQUARES.  THE FORMAT IS 1X,2I2 AND THE DATA
C    WILL OCCUPY THE FIRST 60 COLUMNS.  THE ORDER OF THE DATA IS
C    HORIZONTAL COORDINATE 1, VERTICAL COORDINATE 1, HORIZONTAL
C    COORDINATE 2, VERTICAL COORDINATE 2, ETC.  IF IF FEWER THAN 12
C    PIECES ARE USED, THE REMAINING SPACES MAY BE LEFT BLANK.
C    THE SECOND CARD SPECIFIES THE SAME PARAMETERS FOR THE CROSSES.
C
1004 READ(NRD,2)((MAP(I,J,1),J=1,2),I=1,12),((MAP(I,J,2),J=1,2),I=1,12)
C
C    CALL SUBROUTINE TO PRINT STATUS INFORMATION
C
```

(continued)

```
1003 CALL STATUS(1)
C
C        CALL INTIALIZATION ROUTINE
C
         CALL INITL
C
C        CALL OUTPUT ROUTINE
C
         CALL OUTPUT
C
C        CALL MODIFICATION ROUTINE.
C
2000     CALL MOVE
C
C        IF KKCUM IS 0 INCREASE NOMOV
C
         IF(KKCUM) 2001,2001,2002
2001     NOMOV = NOMOV+1
         GO TO 2003
2002     KKCUM = 0
         NOMOV = 0
2003 IF(NOMOV-NSTOP) 2004,2005,2005
2005 WRITE(NPR,3) NOMOV
   3 FORMAT(/36X,' RUN TERMINATED DUE TO',I3,' CYCLES WITH NO MOVES')
         GO TO 3000
2004 CONTINUE
```

```
C     CHECK FOR MAX REACHED.
C
      IF(NCNT-NMAX) 2006,3000,3000
C
C     TERMINATION NOT SPECIFIED.  INCREMENT COUNTER AND CONTINUE.
C
 2006 NCNT = NCNT+1
C
C     CHECK FOR SUPPRESSION OF DISPLAY.
C
      IF(ISUPR) 2000,2000,2007
C
C     BOARD NOT SUPPRESSED -- PRINT IT.
C
 2007 CALL OUTPUT
      IF(ISUPR-1) 2000,2000,2008
C
C     STATUS NOT SUPPRESSED -- PRINT IT.
C
 2008 CALL STATUS(2)
C
C     CONTINUE CYCLE.
C
      GO TO 2000
C
C     PRINT BOARD, SUMMARY INFORMATION, AND BEGIN NEXT PATTERN.
C
```

(continued)

```
3000 NCNT = NCNT+1
     CALL OUTPUT
     CALL STATUS(2)
     GO TO 1000
4000 STOP
     END

     SUBROUTINE STATUS(ISTSP)

C    THIS SUBROUTINE HANDLES THE CALCULATION AND OUTPUTTING OF STATUS
C    INFORMATION FOR THE PROGRAM.  IF THE ARGUMENT IS EQUAL TO 1, THE
C    SUBROUTINE PRINTS ATTITUDES OF THE TWO GROUPS AS INITIALIZATION
C    INFORMATION.  WITH AN ARGUMENT OF 2, THE PROGRAM CALCULATES AND
C    PRINTS OUT SUMMARY INFORMATION.
C
     INTEGER A(53,6),XX,XO,OO,OX,BOARD(12,12)
     REAL NEXPD
     DIMENSION FDISP(2),FSUM(2,2)
     COMMON A,NBRD,NPC(2),XX,XO,OO,OX,BOARD,MAP(12,2,2),NPR,NRD
     COMMON NCNT,NEXP,NEXPD,NTB(52),NHEAD(48),NDISP,NTITL(20),NFLAG
     COMMON NMAX,INCR,ISUPR,NSTOP,NOMOV,KK,KKCUM,NPOWR
     EQUIVALENCE (NPC(1),NPCO),(NPC(2),NPCX)
```

C

```
1 FORMAT('1',53X,20A2//41X,'THE CHECKERBOARD MODEL OF SOCIAL INTERAC
*TION'///)
2 FORMAT(/40X,I2,' SQUARES AND ',I2,' CROSSES ON A ',I2,' X ',I2,
* ' BOARD'/)
3 FORMAT(42X,'SUMMARY INFORMATION AFTER ',I3,' CYCLE(S)'///)
4 FORMAT(45X,'**********************************'///)
5 FORMAT(51X,'STATUS INFORMATION'///)
6 FORMAT(45X,'*',8X,'*',8X,'*',8X,'*')
7 FORMAT('+',37X,'TOWARD')
8 FORMAT(45X,'*          SQUARE  *   CROSS  *')
10 FORMAT(54X,'ATTITUDES OF'/)
11 FORMAT(45X,'* OWN   *',I5,3X,'*',I5,3X,'*')
12 FORMAT(45X,'* OTHER *',I5,3X,'*',I5,3X,'*')
13 FORMAT(//55X,'CENTROIDS'/)
14 FORMAT(//38X,'DISTANCE BETWEEN CENTROIDS = ',F8.4///)
15 FORMAT(45X,'* X *',F7.4,' *',F7.4,' *')
16 FORMAT(45X,'* Y *',F7.4,' *',F7.4,' *')
17 FORMAT(1H1,/54X,'DISPERSION'/)
19 FORMAT(50X,'**********************************')
20 FORMAT(50X,'*                *')
21 FORMAT(50X,'*   SQUARE  *   CROSS  *')
22 FORMAT(50X,'*',F7.4,' *',F7.4,' *')
23 FORMAT(47X,'THE DISTANCE WEIGHT IS ',I3)
24 FORMAT(///62X,'NMAX IS ',I3)
25 FORMAT(//55X,'SPEED FACTOR IS ',I2,//19X,' 0 = EQUAL, 1 = C
*ROSS HAS GREATER SPEED THAN SQUARE.')
```

(continued)

```
C
C     PRINT STATUS INFORMATION
C
      WRITE(NPR,1) NTITL
      WRITE(NPR,2) NPCO,NPCX,NBRD,NBRD
C
      IF ISTSP IS 1, INITIALIZE, IF 2, SUMMARIZE
C
      GO TO (200,201),ISTSP
C
  201 CONTINUE
      WRITE(NPR,3)NCNT
      GO TO 202
C
C     PRINT INITIALIZATION INFORMATION
C
  200 CONTINUE
      WRITE(NPR,5)
C
C     DISPLAY ATTITUDES
C
  202 WRITE(NPR,10)
      WRITE(NPR,4)
      WRITE(NPR,6)
      WRITE(NPR,8)
```

```
      WRITE(NPR,6)
      WRITE(NPR,4)
      WRITE(NPR,6)
      WRITE(NPR,11) DO,XX
      WRITE(NPR,6)
      WRITE(NPR,4)
      WRITE(NPR,7)
      WRITE(NPR,6)
      WRITE(NPR,12) OX,XO
      WRITE(NPR,6)
      WRITE(NPR,4)
      GO TO (300,301),ISTSP
  300 CONTINUE
      WRITE(NPR,24) NMAX
      WRITE(NPR,23) NEXP
      WRITE(NPR,25) NPOWR
      RETURN
  301 CONTINUE
C
C     CALCULATE SUMMARY STATUS
C     GET MEAN X AND Y COORDINATES FOR EACH GROUP
C     ZERO OUT ARRAY
C
      DO 1100 I = 1,2
      DO 1100 J = 1,2
 1100 FSUM(I,J) = 0.
```

(continued)

```
C
C    FIND CENTROIDS
C
     DO 1101 I = 1,12
     DO 1101 J = 1,2
     DO 1101 K = 1,2
     IF(I-NPC(K)) 1102,1102,1101
1102 FSUM(J,K) = FSUM(J,K)+FLOAT(MAP(I,J,K))/FLOAT(NPC(K))
1101 CONTINUE
C
C    PRINT CENTROID CALCULATION
C
     WRITE(NPR,13)
     WRITE(NPR,4)
     WRITE(NPR,6)
     WRITE(NPR,8)
     WRITE(NPR,6)
     WRITE(NPR,4)
     WRITE(NPR,6)
     WRITE(NPR,15)  FSUM(1,1),FSUM(1,2)
     WRITE(NPR,6)
     WRITE(NPR,4)
     WRITE(NPR,6)
     WRITE(NPR,16)  FSUM(2,1),FSUM(2,2)
```

```
      WRITE(NPR,6)
      WRITE(NPR,4)
C
C     GET DISTANCE BETWEEN CENTROIDS
C
      AA = FSUM(1,1)-FSUM(1,2)
      B = FSUM(2,1)-FSUM(2,2)
      DIST = SQRT(AA*AA+B*B)
      WRITE(NPR,14) DIST
C
C     GET DISPERSION
C
      FDISP(1) = 0.
      FDISP(2) = 0.
      DO 1150 I = 1,12
      DO 1150 J = 1,2
      DO 1150 K = 1,2
      IF(I-NPC(K)) 1151,1151,1150
 1151 AA = FSUM(J,K)-MAP(I,J,K)
      FDISP(K) = AA*AA/NPC(K)+FDISP(K)
 1150 CONTINUE
C
C     GET SQUARE ROOT
C
      FDISP(1) = SQRT(FDISP(1))
      FDISP(2) = SQRT(FDISP(2))
```

(continued)

269

```
C
C     PRINT DISPERSION CALCULATION
C
      WRITE(NPR,17)
      WRITE(NPR,19)
      WRITE(NPR,20)
      WRITE(NPR,21)
      WRITE(NPR,20)
      WRITE(NPR,19)
      WRITE(NPR,20)
      WRITE(NPR,22) FDISP(1),FDISP(2)
      WRITE(NPR,20)
      WRITE(NPR,19)
      RETURN
      END


      SUBROUTINE INITL
C
C     INITIALIZE PROGRAM PARAMETERS AND SET UP BOARD AND MAP
C
      INTEGER A(53,6),XX,XO,OO,OX,BOARD,MAP(12,2,2),NPR,NRD
      REAL NEXPD
      COMMON A,NBRD,NPC(2),XX,XO,OO,OX,BOARD,MAP(12,2,2),NPR,NRD
      COMMON NCNT,NEXP,NEXPD,NTB(52),NHEAD(48),NDISP,NTITL(20),NFLAG
      COMMON NMAX,INCR,ISUPR,NSTOP,NOMOV,KK,KKCUM,NPOWR
```

```
      EQUIVALENCE (NPC(1),NPCO),(NPC(2),NPCX)
      DATA KAA,KBA,KAB,KBB/'**','*',' ',' '/
      DATA ANUM/'01','02','03','04','05','06','07','08','09','10',
     *          '11','12'/
C
C     PAGE HEADER AND MARGINS ARE DISPLACED ACCORDING TO NDISP
C     SET NEXPD
C
      NEXPD = 1./NEXP
C
C     BUILD PAGE HEAD
C     CLEAR LINE
C
      DO 1001 J = 1,48
      NHEAD(J) = KBB
      DO 1002 J = 1,NBRD
      JPX = (J+NDISP)*4-2
      NHEAD(JPX) = ANUM(J)
 1002 CONTINUE
C
C     PAGE HEAD COMPLETE
C     BUILD TOP AND BOTTOM MARGIN
C     CLEAR ARRAY
C
```

(continued)

271

```
      DO 1003 I = 1,52
1003 NTB(I) = KBB
      NTB(4*NDISP+1) = KBA
      IGT1 = NDISP*4+2
      IGT2 = (NDISP+NBRD)*4+2
      DO 1004 I = IGT1,IGT2
1004 NTB(I) = KAA
      NTB(IGT2+1) = KAB
C
C     MARGIN COMPLETE
C     SET VERTICAL MARGINS FOR OUTPUT ROUTINE
C     CLEAR OUTPUT ARRAY
C
      DO 1005 I = 1,4
      DO 1005 J = 1,53
1005 A(J,I) = KBB
      IGT1 = (NDISP*4)+2
      IGT2 = (NBRD+NDISP)*4+4
      DO 1006 I = 1,4
      A(IGT1,I) = KBA
1006 A(IGT2,I) = KAB
C
C     VERTICAL MARGINS COMPLETE
C     ZERO OUT BOARD
C
```

```
      DO 1007 I = 1,12
      DO 1007 J = 1,12
1007  BOARD(I,J) = 0

C     BEGIN PLACING MEN ON BOARD
C     CHECK NFLAG. IF IT IS ON, PARAMETERS FOR PLACING THE MEN
C        HAVE ALREADY BEEN READ IN.
C
      IF(NFLAG) 2000,2000,3000
C
C     PLACE THE MEN ON THE BOARD AT RANDOM
C
C     ZERO OUT MAP
C
2000  DO 2001 J = 1,2
      DO 2001 K = 1,2
      DO 2001 I = 1,12
2001  MAP(I,J,K) = 0
C
C     PLACE SQUARES
C
2003  DO 2002 I = 1,NPCO
      ISUB = JRAND(NBRD)
      JSUB = JRAND(NBRD)
C
C     IF NOT VACANT, BACK UP
C
```

(continued)

```
      IF(BOARD(ISUB,JSUB)) 2003,2004,2003
C
C     POSITION IS VACANT -- SET MAP AND BOARD INDICATORS
C
2004  MAP(I,1,1) = ISUB
      MAP(I,2,1) = JSUB
      BOARD(ISUB,JSUB) = 1
2002  CONTINUE
C
C     REPEAT PROCEDURE FOR CROSSES
C
      DO 2005 I = 1,NPCX
2006  ISUB = JRAND(NBRD)
      JSUB = JRAND(NBRD)
      IF(BOARD(ISUB,JSUB)) 2006,2007,2006
2007  MAP(I,1,2) = ISUB
      MAP(I,2,2) = JSUB
      BOARD(ISUB,JSUB) = -1
2005  CONTINUE
C
C     RANDOM PLACING OF MEN ON BOARD IS COMPLETE -- RETURN TO CALLER
C
      RETURN
```

```
C       THIS PHASE OF THE ROUTINE IS USED IF THE PIECES ARE TO BE PRE-SET
C           ON THE BOARD.
C
3000 DO 3001 I = 1,NPCO
        ISUB = MAP(I,1,1)
        JSUB = MAP(I,2,1)
        BOARD(ISUB,JSUB) = 1
3001 CONTINUE
        DO 3002 I = 1,NPCX
        ISUB = MAP(I,1,2)
        JSUB = MAP(I,2,2)
        BOARD(ISUB,JSUB) = -1
3002 CONTINUE
C
C       BOARD POSITIONS HAVE BEEN SET  --  RETURN TO CALLER
C
        RETURN
        END

        SUBROUTINE OUTPUT
C
        INTEGER A(53,6),XX,XO,OO,OX,BOARD(12,12),ANUM(12)
        REAL NEXPD
        COMMON A,NBRD,NPC(2),XX,XO,OO,OX,BOARD,MAP(12,2,2),NPR,NRD
        COMMON NCNT,NEXP,NEXPD,NTB(52),NHEAD(48),NDISP,NTITL(20),NFLAG
```

(continued)

275

```
      COMMON NMAX,INCR,ISUPR,NSTOP,NOMOV,KK,KKCUM,NPOWR
      EQUIVALENCE (NPC(1),NPC0),(NPC(2),NPCX)
      DATA ANUM,IBLANK/'01','02','03','04','05','06','07','08','09','10'
     *  ,'11','12',' '/
C
C     THE LOGICAL LINES OF THE CHECKERBOARD ARE PRINTED ONE AT A TIME,
C     REQUIRING A BUFFER OF 6 PHYSICAL LINES (EACH PIECE OCCUPIES 6
C     PHYSICAL LINES).  AS EACH LOGICAL LINE IS PRINTED, MAP IS SCANNED
C     TO PICK OUT ALL ENTRIES ON THAT LINE.  THESE ARE PLACED IN THE
C     BUFFER, THE LINE NUMBER IS ADDED, AND THE BUFFER IS PRINTED.  THIS
C     PROCEDURE CONTINUES UNTIL NBRD LINES OF OUTPUT HAVE BEEN PROCESSED.
C     THE DISPLACEMENT FACTOR (NDISP) IS USED TO CENTER THE PATTERN TOP
C     AND BOTTOM AND LEFT AND RIGHT.  THE PATTERN IS DISPLACED THE PROPER
C     NUMBER OF SPACES, THUS KEEPING IT CENTERED REGARDLESS OF SIZE.
C
    1 FORMAT(1H1,10X,'CYCLE  ',I3,4X,20A2,3X,'(',4(I2,','),I2,')')
    2 FORMAT(5X,53A2)
    3 FORMAT(7X,52A2)
    4 FORMAT(//)
    5 FORMAT(/11X,48A2)
C
C     SPACE TO NEW PAGE AND PRINT HEADING
C
      WRITE(NPR,1) NCNT,NTITL,OO,OX,XX,XO,NEXP
```

```
C     TURN ON FIRST LINE INDICATOR
C
      NTAG = 0
C
C     SKIP PROPER NUMBER OF LINES
C
      IF(NDISP) 1000,1000,1001
1001  DO 1002 NNNN = 1,NDISP
1002  WRITE(NPR,4)
1000  CONTINUE
C
C     PRINT PAGE HEAD
C
      WRITE(NPR,5) NHEAD
C
C     PRINT TOP MARGIN
C
      WRITE(NPR,3) NTB
C
C     MAIN OUTPUT ROUTINE
C
      DO 2000 I = 1,NBRD
C
C     CLEAR OUTPUT BUFFER
C
```

(continued)

```
      IGT1 = 4*NDISP+4
      IGT2 = IGT1+4*NBRD-1
      DO 2001 M = 1,6
      DO 2001 N = IGT1,IGT2
 2001 A(N,M) = IBLANK
C
C     SPACE ONCE IF THIS IS THE FIRST LINE
C
      IF(NTAG) 2002,2003,2002
 2003 WRITE(NPR,2) (A(N,1),N = 1,53)
C
C     SET FIRST LINE INDICATOR OFF
C
      NTAG = 1
 2002 CONTINUE
C
C     PLACE LINE NUMBER IN PROPER PLACE
C
      ISUB = 4*NDISP+1
      A(ISUB,2) = ANUM(I)
C
C     CHECK EACH PIECE ON MAP TO DETERMINE IF IT BELONGS IN THIS
C     LINE OF THE BUFFER
C
      DO 2004 J = 1,12
```

```
C
C     CHECK CROSS AND SQUARE PIECES
C
      DO 2004 K = 1,2
      IF(NPC(K)-J) 2004,2005,2005
 2005 IF(MAP(J,2,K)-I) 2004,2006,2004
C
C     FILL OUTPUT BUFFER WITH PROPER ENTRY
C
 2006 CALL INSERT(K-1,MAP(J,1,K)+NDISP,1,J)
 2004 CONTINUE
C
C     PRINT OUTPUT ARRAY
C
C     IN THE FOLLOWING LOOP, 4 GIVES 6 LINES PER INCH ON PRINTOUT.
C
      DO 2000 M = 1,4
 2000 WRITE(NPR,2) (A(N,M),N = 1,53)
C
C     PRINT BOTTOM MARGIN
C
      WRITE(NPR,3) NTB
      RETURN
      END
```

(continued)

```
      SUBROUTINE INSERT(ISXY,I1,J1,NUM)

C     THIS ROUTINE PLACES THE SYMBOL SPECIFIED IN THE PROPER LOCATION IN
C     THE OUTPUT BUFFER.  THE ARGUMENTS ARE --
C           ISXY -- = 0 FOR SQUARE, = 1 FOR CROSS
C           I1   -- SPECIFIES THE HORIZONTAL COORDINATE ON THE
C                   OUTPUT BUFFER.  WITH THE SMALL BUFFER USED
C                   BY THIS VERSION OF THE PROGRAM, THIS
C                   ARGUMENT IS ALWAYS 1.
C           J1   -- VERTICAL COORDINATE.
C           NUM  -- THE NUMBER OF THE PIECE.
C
      INTEGER A(53,6),XX,XO,OO,OX,BOARD(12,12),ANUM(12)
      REAL NEXPD
      COMMON A,NBRD,NPC(2),XX,XO,OO,OX,BOARD,MAP(12,2,2),NPR,NRD
      COMMON NCNT,NEXP,NEXPD,NTB(52),NHEAD(48),NDISP,NTITL(20),NFLAG
      COMMON NMAX,INCR,ISUPR,NSTOP,NOMOV,KK,KKCUM,NPOWR
      EQUIVALENCE (NPC(1),NPCO),(NPC(2),NPCX)
      DATA KAA,KBA,KAB,KBB/'**',' ','*',' ',' '/
      DATA ANUM/'01','02','03','04','05','06','07','08','09','10','11',
     *    '12'/

C     ICHAR IS CHARACTER REPRESENTATION FOR THE NUMBER SPECIFIED
C
      ICHAR = ANUM(NUM)
      I2 = 4*(I1-1)+4
      J2 = 6*(J1-1)+1
```

```
C
C      CLEAR AREA TO BE FILLED BY BLOCK
C
       J2P5 = J2+5
       I2P2 = I2+2
       DO 100 J = J2,J2P5
       DO 100 I = I2,I2P2
100    A(I,J) = KBB
       A(I2+1,J2+1) = ICHAR
C
C      BRANCH ON 0 OR X CHARACTER
C
       IF(ISXY) 200,200,300
C
C      FORM 0
C
200    DO 201 I = 1,3
       I3 = I2+I-1
       A(I3,J2) = KAA
       A(I3,J2+2) = KAA
201    CONTINUE
       A(I2,J2+1) = KAB
       A(I2+2,J2+1) = KBA
       RETURN
C
C      FORM X
C
```

(continued)

```
300 A(I2+1,J2)   = KAA
    A(I2,J2+1)   = KAA
    A(I2+1,J2+2) = KAA
    A(I2+2,J2+1) = KAA
    RETURN
    END

    SUBROUTINE MOVE

C   THIS SUBROUTINE CALCULATES THE OPTIMAL MOVE FOR EACH PIECE ON MAP
C   AND MOVES THE MAP AND BOARD ENTRIES ACCORDINGLY.
C   THIS ROUTINE SEARCHES AN AREA OF +-1 AROUND ALL PIECES. IF A
C   BETTER POSITION IS NOT FOUND, AN AREA OF +-2 IS SEARCHED.
C   BETTER POSITIONS FOUND ON EITHER OF THE SEARCHES ARE ENTERED ON MAP
C   AND BOARD.

    INTEGER A(53,6),XX,XO,OO,OX,BOARD(12,12)
    REAL NEXPD
    DIMENSION ISEQ(12,2)
    DIMENSION NO(2),NX(2)
    DIMENSION ANAME(3,2)
    COMMON A,NBRD,NPC(2),XX,XO,OO,OX,BOARD,MAP(12,2,2),NPR,NRD
    COMMON NCNT,NEXP,NEXPD,NTB(52),NHEAD(48),NDISP,NTITL(20),NFLAG
    COMMON NMAX,INCR,ISUPR,NSTOP,NOMOV,KK,KKCUM,NPOWR
```

282

```
      EQUIVALENCE (NPC(1),NPCO),(NPC(2),NPCX)
      DATA ANAME/'SQ ','UA ','RE ','CR ','OS ','S  '/

C
C     OPTIMAL MOVES ARE MADE AT RANDOM FOR X AND O PIECES
C
    1 FORMAT(/36X,I2,4X,3A2,1X,I2,9X,I2,4X,I2,8X,I2,4X,I2)
    2 FORMAT('1',35X,20A2/)
    3 FORMAT(38X,I2,' SQUARES AND ',I2,' CROSSES ON A ',I2,' X ',I2,
     *  ' BOARD'//)
    4 FORMAT(45X,'INDIVIDUAL MOVES FOR CYCLE ',I3///)
    5 FORMAT(35X,'MOVE   PIECE   FROM VERT HORZ TO  VERT HORZ'//)

C
C     RE-ORDER ATTITUDES IN NO, NX ARRAYS TO ALLOW SUBSCRIPTED
C         OPERATION.
C
      NO(1) = OO
      NO(2) = XO
      NX(1) = OX
      NX(2) = XX

C
C     CHECK TO SEE IF EACH MOVE REQUESTED.
C
      IGO = 1
      IF(INCR.GT.O) IGO = 2

C
C     INITIALIZE ISEQ ARRAY.
C
```

(continued)

```
      DO 100 J = 1,2
      DO 100 I = 1,12
100   ISEQ(I,J) = I

C     INITIALIZE MOVE COUNTER (NMOVE) AND PRINT HEADING SWITCH (IPAGE).
C

      NMOVE = 0
      IPAGE = 0

C     BEGIN MOVING PIECES.
C

      DO 1000 J = 1,12
      DO 1000 INDX2 = 1,2

C     SELECT PIECE FOR MOVE
C
      IGT1 = NPC(INDX2)-J+1

C     IS VALUE FOR IGT1 LEGAL (GREATER THAN ZERO).
C
      IF(IGT1) 1000,1000,1001

C     GET RANDOM PIECE.
C
```

```
1001  IGT2 = JRAND(IGT1)
      I = ISEQ(IGT2,INDX2)
C
C     SHUFFLE RANDOM ARRAY.
C
      ISEQ(IGT2,INDX2) = ISEQ(IGT1,INDX2)
C
C     GET BOARD SUBSCRIPT VALUES FOR PIECE CHOSEN.
C
      ISUB = MAP(I,1,INDX2)
      JSUB = MAP(I,2,INDX2)
C
C     GET BEST MOVE FROM SEARCH ROUTINE.
C
      KK = SEARCH(NO(INDX2),NX(INDX2),1,INDX2,I)
C
C     TEST FLAG
C
      IF(KK) 1002,1003,1002
C
C     THIS PHASE IS ENTERED IF THE PIECE WAS NOT MOVED.
C     SEARCH A LARGER AREA.
C     SKIP SEARCH OF LARGER AREA IF NPOWR = 1 AND PIECE IS A CROSS.
C
1003  IF(INDX2-2) 1004,1005,1005
1005  IF(NPOWR) 1004,1004,1006
1004  KK = SEARCH(NO(INDX2),NX(INDX2),2,INDX2,I)
```

(continued)

```
C
C     IF AT LEAST ONE MOVE IS MADE DURING THE CYCLE, SET KKCUM = 1
C
      IF (KK) 1006,1006,1002
1002  KKCUM = 1
1006  CONTINUE
      GO TO(1000,2000),IGO
C
C     PRINT EACH MOVE.   CHECK IPAGE TO SEE IF HEADING MUST BE PRINTED.
C
2000  IF(IPAGE)2002,2001,2002
C
C     PRINT HEADING.
C
2001  IPAGE = 1
      WRITE(NPR,2)   NTITL
      WRITE(NPR,3)   NPCO,NPCX,NBRD,NBRD
      WRITE(NPR,4)   NCNT
      WRITE(NPR,5)
2002  NMOVE = NMOVE+1
      ISUB2 = MAP(I,1,INDX2)
      JSUB2 = MAP(I,2,INDX2)
      WRITE(NPR,1) NMOVE,(ANAME(INDEX,INDX2),INDEX = 1,3),I,JSUB,ISUB,
     *    JSUB,ISUB2
1000  CONTINUE
      RETURN
      END
```

```
      FUNCTION JRAND(LMAX)
C
C     RANDOM NUMBER GENERATOR.  RETURNS A RANDOM NUMBER BETWEEN 1 AND THE
C     VALUE OF THE ARGUMENT.
C
C *** SEE NOTE ON MACHINE SPECIFIC ROUTINES IN THE MAIN PROGRAM
C
      JRAND = INT(RNDM(DUMY)*LMAX+1)
      RETURN
      END

      FUNCTION SEARCH(NTO,NTX,NSIZE,MAPI,I)
C     THIS FUNCTION SEARCHES AN AREA OF +- NSIZE AROUND THE PIECE
C     SPECIFIED.  IF ANY OF THE SEARCHED POSITIONS IS BETTER THAN THE
C     PRESENT ONE, THE PIECE IS MOVED AND THE FUNCTION RETURNS A 1.  IF
C     THE PRESENT POSITION IS THE BEST, THE PIECE IS NOT MOVED AND THE
C     FUNCTION RETURNS A 0.
C     ARGUMENTS ARE --
C           NTO   --   ATTITUDE PREVAILING TOWARDS 0
C           NTX   --   ATTITUDE TOWARD X
C           NSIZE --   THE SIZE OF THE AREA· TO BE SEARCHED
C                      AROUND THE SPECIFIED PIECE.  NSIZE = 1
C                      SPECIFIES A SEARCH OF +-1 SQUARE, OR
C                      9 POSTIONS.
C           MAPI  --   = 1 FOR A SQUARE,  = 2 FOR A CROSS.
C           I     --   THE MAP NUMBER OF THE PIECE IN QUESTION,
```

(continued)

287

TABLE A.2 (continued)

```
      INTEGER A(53,6),XX,XO,OO,OX,BOARD(12,12)
      REAL NEXPD
      DIMENSION IBEST(2)
      COMMON A,NBRD,NPC(2),XX,XO,OO,OX,BOARD,MAP(12,2,2),NPR,NRD
      COMMON NCNT,NEXP,NEXPD,NTB(52),NHEAD(48),NDISP,NTITL(20),NFLAG
      COMMON NMAX,INCR,ISUPR,NSTOP,NOMOV,KK,KKCUM,NPOWR
      EQUIVALENCE (NPC(1),NPCO),(NPC(2),NPCX)
C
      ISUB = MAP(I,1,MAPI)
      JSUB = MAP(I,2,MAPI)
C
C     GET VALUE OF POSITION
C
      BEST = VALUE(ISUB,JSUB,NTO,NTX)
      IBEST(1) = ISUB
      IBEST(2) = JSUB
C
C     ZERO OUT PRESENT BOARD POSITION
C
      BOARD(ISUB,JSUB) = 0
C
C     IFLAG IS POSITIVE IF THE BEST MOVE IS NOT THE ORIGINAL
C
C     RESET IFLAG
```

```
      IFLAG = 0
C
C     WHEN NPOWR = 1, LET NSIZE = 1 AND 2 BOTH FOR CROSSES ONLY.
C
      KSIZE = NSIZE
      NONN = 1
      IF(NPOWR) 1000,1000,1001
 1001 IF(MAPI-2)1000,1002,1002
 1002 NONN = 2
 1000 CONTINUE
      DO 2000 ISIZE = 1,NONN
      JDO1 = KSIZE*2+1
      JDO2 = KSIZE+1
      DO 2100 K = 1,JDO1
      ISUB2 = ISUB-JDO2+K
C
C     TEST FOR LEGAL VALUES
C     IS NUMBER NEGATIVE OR ZERO
C
      IF(ISUB2) 2100,2100,2101
C
C     IS NUMBER TOO LARGE
C
 2101 IF(ISUB2-NBRD) 2102,2102,2100
 2102 DO 2110 L = 1,JDO1
      JSUB2 = JSUB-JDO2+L
```

```
C
C      CHECK FOR LEGAL VALUES--IS VALUE ZERO OR NEGATIVE
C
       IF(JSUB2) 2110,2110,2103
C      IS VALUE TOO LARGE
C
2103   IF(JSUB2-NBRD) 2104,2104,2110
C
C      IS SPACE OCCUPIED
C
2104   IF(BOARD(ISUB2,JSUB2)) 2110,2105,2110
C
C      VALUE IS LEGAL -- MAKE CALCULATION
C
2105   MAP(I,1,MAPI) = ISUB2
       MAP(I,2,MAPI) = JSUB2
       TEMP = VALUE(ISUB2,JSUB2,NTO,NTX)
C
C      COMPARE WITH OLDER VALUE
C
       IF(TEMP-BEST) 2110,2110,2106
2106   BEST = TEMP
       IBEST(1) = ISUB2
       IBEST(2) = JSUB2
       IFLAG = 1
```

```
      2110 CONTINUE
      2100 CONTINUE
           KSIZE = KSIZE+1
      2000 CONTINUE
C
C          PLACE BEST MOVE ON MAP
C
           MAP(I,1,MAPI) = IBEST(1)
           MAP(I,2,MAPI) = IBEST(2)
C
C          SET BOARD INDICATOR
C
           IGT1 = IBEST(1)
           IGT2 = IBEST(2)
           BOARD(IGT1,IGT2) = MAPI*2-3
           SEARCH = IFLAG
           RETURN
           END

      FUNCTION VALUE(ISUB,JSUB,NTO,NTX)
C
C          CALCULATES THE VALUE OF THE POSITION SPECIFIED FOR
C          THE PIECE SPECIFIED. THE VALUE IS RETURNED BY THE FUNCTION.
C          THE MAP ENTRIES FOR THE PIECE BEING TESTED MUST BE SET TO THE VALUE
C          OF THE HORIZONTAL AND VERTICAL SUBSCRIPTS SENT INTO THIS ROUTINE.
```

(continued)

291

TABLE A.2 (*continued*)

```
C     IF THIS IS DONE, THE ROUTINE IN EFFECT IGNORES THE PIECE BEING
C     TESTED.  WHEN THE DISTANCE IS CALCULATED, A ZERO RESULTS AND THE
C     POSITION IS NOT SUMMED.
C     THE ARGUMENTS ARE --
C                ISUB    --    HORIZONTAL COORDINATE OF THE POSITION
C                              BEING TESTED
C                JSUB    --    VERTICAL COORDINATE OF THE POSITION BEING
C                              TESTED.
C                NTO     --    ATTITUDE PREVAILING TOWARD SQUARES
C                NTX     --    ATTITUDE TOWARD CROSSES.
C
      INTEGER A(53,6),XX,XO,OO,OX,BOARD(12,12)
      REAL NEXPD
      COMMON A,NBRD,NPC(2),XX,XO,OO,OX,BOARD,MAP(12,2,2),NPR,NRD
      COMMON NCNT,NEXP,NEXPD,NTB(52),NHEAD(48),NDISP,NTITL(20),NFLAG
      COMMON NMAX,INCR,ISUPR,NSTOP,NOMOV,KK,KKCUM,NPOWR
      EQUIVALENCE (NPC(1),NPCO),(NPC(2),NPCX)
C
      TEMP = 0.
      IF(NTX) 1000,2000,1000
1000  DO 1001 ISUB3 = 1,NPCX
C
C     GET SUM OF SQUARES
C
```

```fortran
      NDIFH = ISUB-MAP(ISUB3,1,2)
      NDIFV = JSUB-MAP(ISUB3,2,2)
      ITEMP = ((NDIFV*NDIFV)+(NDIFH*NDIFH))
      IF(ITEMP) 1002,1001,1002
 1002 TEMP = TEMP+NTX/(FLOAT(ITEMP))**NEXPD
 1001 CONTINUE
C
C     BY ATTITUDE TOWARD SELF
C
 2000 IF(NTO) 2001,3000,2001
 2001 DO 2002 ISUB3 = 1,NPCO
      NDIFH = ISUB-MAP(ISUB3,1,1)
      NDIFV = JSUB-MAP(ISUB3,2,1)
      ITEMP = ((NDIFH*NDIFH)+(NDIFV*NDIFV))
      IF(ITEMP) 2003,2002,2003
 2003 TEMP = TEMP+NTO/(FLOAT(ITEMP))**NEXPD
 2002 CONTINUE
 3000 VALUE = TEMP
      RETURN
      END
```

TABLE A.3
Example CHEBO Input

```
0   10 8 6 6001-1 1-1 1 4 3BOY-GIRL, A    8 X 8


1   20 8 6 60010101-1-1 4 3SOCIAL WORKERS AND LOST SOULS
    3 3   3 8   5 2   5 8   7 3   8 3
    3 2   4 1   4 8   5 2   6 5   7 5
```

TABLE A.4
Example CHEBO Output

BOY-GIRL, A   8 X 8

THE CHECKERBOARD MODEL OF SOCIAL INTERACTION

6 SQUARES AND 6 CROSSES ON A 8 X 8 BOARD

STATUS INFORMATION

ATTITUDES OF

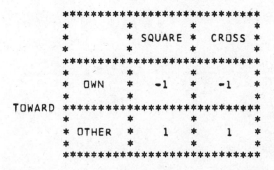

NMAX IS   10

THE DISTANCE WEIGHT IS   4

SPEED FACTOR IS 0

0 = EQUAL, 1 = CROSS HAS GREATER SPEED THAN SQUARE.

(continued)

TABLE A.4 (continued)

CYCLE 0   BOY-GIRL, A   8 X 8   (-1, 1,-1, 1, 4)

CYCLE   1   BOY-GIRL, A   8 X 8   (-1, 1,-1, 1, 4)

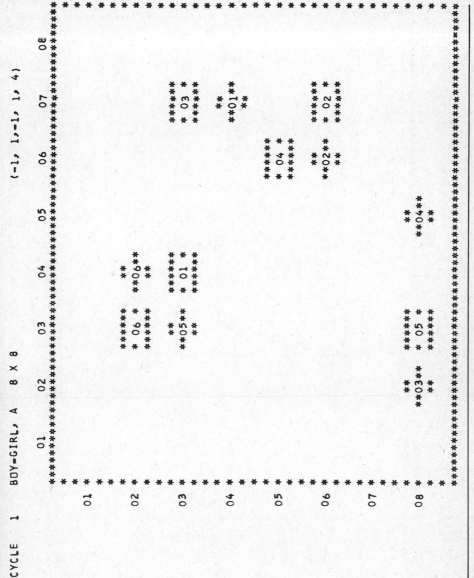

(continued)

TABLE A.4 (continued)

CYCLE 2 BOY-GIRL, A 8 X 8 (-1, 1,-1, 1, 4)

```
        01    02    03    04    05    06    07    08

  01  ***********************************************
      *                                             *
  02  *          ******    **                       *
      *          * 06 *   **06**                    *
      *          ******    **                       *
  03  *          **       ******                    *
      *         **05**    * 01 *                    *
      *          **       ******                    *
  04  *                                 **      ******
      *                              **01**    * 03 *
      *                                 **      ******
  05  *                          ******                *
      *                          * 04 *                *
      *                          ******                *
  06  *                            **                  *
      *                         **02**                 *
      *                            **                  *
  07  *                          ******                *
      *                          * 02 *                *
      *                          ******                *
  08  *  **       ******    **                         *
      *  **03**   * 05 *   **04**                       *
      *  **       ******    **                          *
      ***********************************************
```

CYCLE 3   BOY-GIRL, A   8 X 8   (-1, 1,-1, 1, 4)

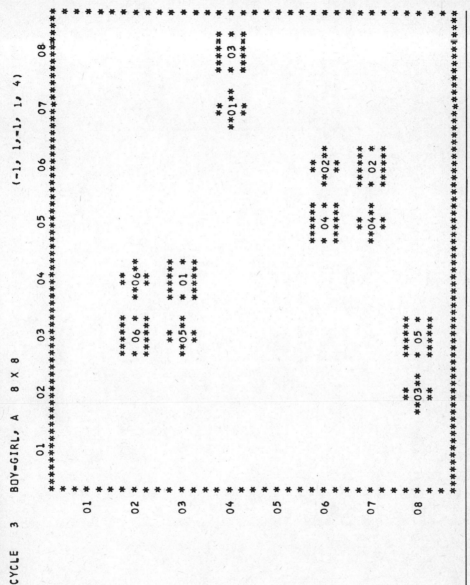

(continued)

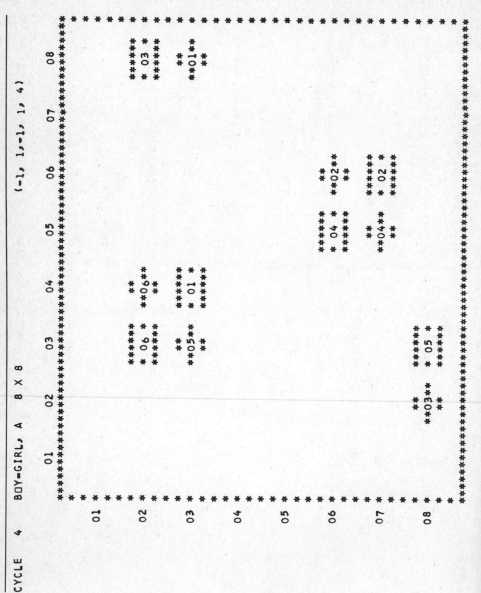

TABLE A.4 (continued)

CYCLE   4   BOY-GIRL, A   8 X 8   (-1, 1,-1, 1, 4)

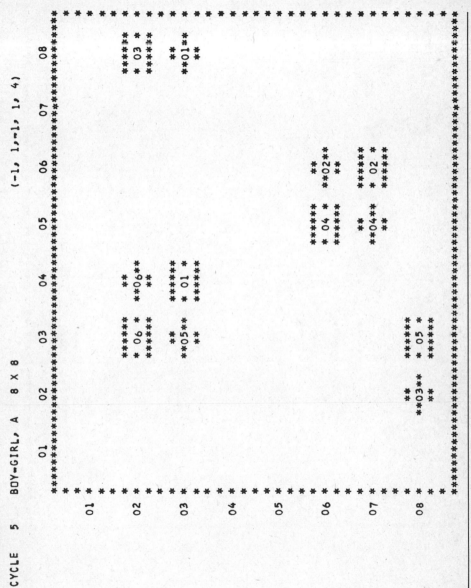

CYCLE 5   BOY-GIRL, A   8 X 8   (-1, 1,-1, 1, 4)

(continued)

301

TABLE A.4 (continued)

CYCLE 6 BOY-GIRL, A 8 X 8 (-1, 1, -1, 1, 4)

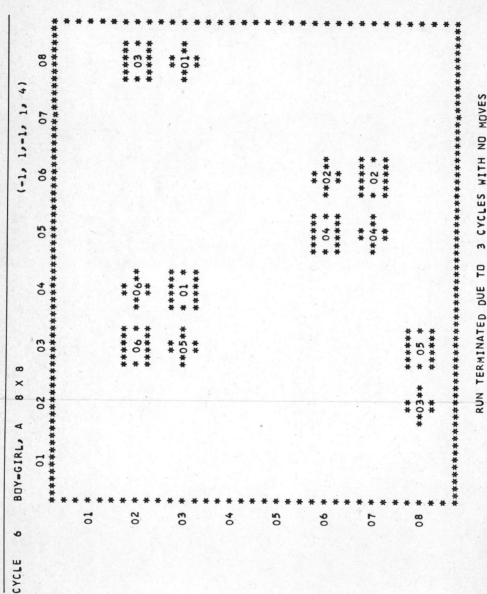

RUN TERMINATED DUE TO 3 CYCLES WITH NO MOVES

302

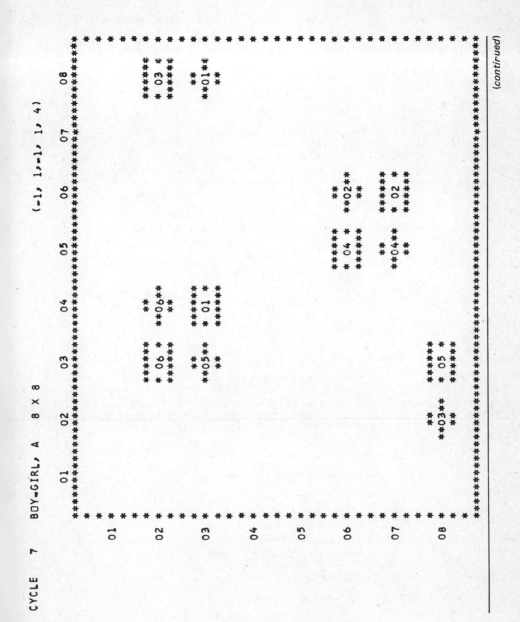

CYCLE 7 BOY-GIRL, A 8 X 8 (-1, 1,-1, 1, 4)

(continued)

BOY—GIRL, A   8 X 8

THE CHECKERBOARD MODEL OF SOCIAL INTERACTION

6 SQUARES AND 6 CROSSES ON A 8 X 8 BOARD

SUMMARY INFORMATION AFTER   7 CYCLE(S)

ATTITUDES OF

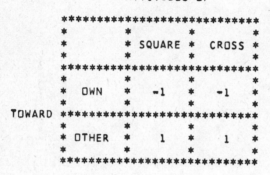

```
***************************
*         *         *         *
*         * SQUARE * CROSS *
*         *         *         *
***************************
*         *         *         *
* OWN     *   -1    *   -1    *
*         *         *         *
TOWARD ***************************
*         *         *         *
* OTHER   *    1    *    1    *
*         *         *         *
***************************
```

CENTROIDS

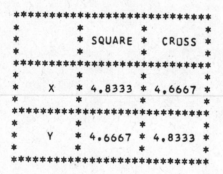

```
***************************
*         *         *         *
*         * SQUARE * CROSS *
*         *         *         *
***************************
*         *         *         *
*    X    * 4.8333 * 4.6667 *
*         *         *         *
***************************
*         *         *         *
*    Y    * 4.6667 * 4.8333 *
*         *         *         *
***************************
```

DISTANCE BETWEEN CENTROIDS =   0.2357

DISPERSION

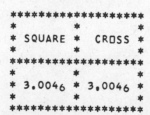

```
*********************
*         *         *
* SQUARE * CROSS *
*         *         *
*********************
*         *         *
* 3.0046 * 3.0046 *
*         *         *
*********************
```

APPENDIX B

SIMSAL:
A Simple Stimulus
and Association Learner

This appendix presents the SIMSAL model of human paired-associates learning. The model and program are based on the SAL-I and SAL-II programs of Hintzman (1968). The conceptual model of the program is presented in Chapter 2 and the flowchart appears in Figure 2.4.

The complete program listing, as operated on the Univac 70/46 computer at Franklin and Marshall College, appears in Table B.2. The program consists of a main program (the experimenter) and a single subroutine (the subject). A random number function (RANDOM/RNDM) is also required.

Table B.1 indexes the detailed presentation of SIMSAL throughout the book. The only known departure from ANSI standard Fortran is, as in CHEBO, the PROGRAM statement. However, the tree output algorithm in the SUBJCT subroutine is somewhat obscure and needs a few words of explanation. The tree array, named TREE, contains a mixture of alphabetic characters — stimuli — and integer values that serve as pointers and responses. In order to print the tree array easily, it is converted to an entirely literal array and an A4 format specification is employed. On the Univac 70/46, an integer value of zero prints as a blank when an A format is used, but other integers must be converted to their literal equivalents. In the internal representation of the computer, all alphabetic characters have integer values of greater than 120, and it is therefore a simple matter to determine which TREE locations must be converted to literals. An array called D is established in a DATA statement and holds the alphameric characters corresponding to the integer values 1–120, the only values that can occur in TREE. When an integer is to be converted to a literal, its value serves as a pointer into D, and the appropriate character string can be selected. The array TREE is unchanged in the process; a second array (PTREE) is used for printing purposes only and holds the completely literal equivalent of the mixed literal and integer TREE.

Tables B.3 and B.4 contain an illustrative set of input and output for a single subject in the intralist similarity experiment described in Chapter 8.

TABLE B.1
Index to the Presentation of SIMSAL

```
C      PROGRAM SIMSAL
C
C      MAIN ROUTINE (EXPERIMENTER)
C
C      BASED ON THE PROGRAMS SAL1 AND SAL2, DESCRIBED IN
C      D. L. HINTZMAN, EXPLORATIONS WITH A DISCRIMINATION NET
C      MODEL FOR PAIRED-ASSOCIATE LEARNING. JOURNAL OF
C      MATHEMATICAL PSYCHOLOGY, 1968, 5, 123-161.
C
C      INPUT DESCRIPTION
C
C      COLUMNS CONTENT                                    FORMAT
C      FIRST CARD
C      1-2     NO. SYLLABLES IN LIST 1 (MAX=20)           I2
C      3-4     NO. SYLLABLES IN LIST 2 (MAX=20)           I2
C      5-6     MAX TRIALS ON OL (MAX=40)                  I2
C      7-8     MAX TRIALS ON IL (MAX=40)                  I2
C      9-10    MAX TRIALS ON RL (MAX=40)                  I2
C      NOTE-IF MAX.LT.40 ON ANY OF THESE, FORCED OVERLEARNING
C             WILL BE USED IN THAT PHASE OF THE EXPERIMENT.
C      11-12   NUMBER OF SUBJECTS (MAX=99)                I2
C      13-80   ID FOR THIS RUN                            17A4
C      NEXT NSYLB1+NSYLB2 CARDS
C      1-3     SYLLABLE                                   3A1
```

(continued)

307

```
C    4-5      RESPONSE DIGITS                                    I2
C    LAST CARD (PARAMETERS FOR SUBJECT)
C    1-3      PADD (PROB OF ADDING TO TREE)                      F3.3
C    4-6      PCHNG (PROB OF CHANGING ENTRY)                     F3.3
C    7-9      POVLRN (OVERLEARNING PARAM)                        F3.3
C    10       TRACE CONTROL =0 FOR NO TRACE                      I1
C                           =1 FOR SIMPLE TRACE
C                           =2 FOR TRACE WITH TREE
C
C    INTEGER QUE(3),ORDER(20),PCOL(40,21),D(20),RESP(40),PLUS,PRINT
C    DIMENSION LIST(40,3),ID(17),MXTRL(3)
C
C    THE FOLLOWING STORAGE ALLOCATION GETS AROUND A BUG IN THE
C    70/46 FORTRAN COMPILER.
C
C    COMMON /BUGBLK/PCOL
C
C    DATA IBLANK,D,PLUS/' ','1','2','3','4','5','6','7','8','9','10',
C   *'11','12','13','14','15','16','17','18','19','20','+'/
C
C    PCOL IS A PROTOCOL SUMMARY:
C    ROWS = TRIALS
C    COLUMNS 1-20 = SYLLABLES
C    COLUMN 21 = NO. ERRORS ON THIS TRIAL
```

```
C     DEFINE A FUNCTION WHICH RETURNS A RANDOM NUMBER IN RANGE 1-ARG
C
      IRAND(N) = INT(RNDM(DUMMY)*N)+1
C
C     *************************************************************
C     ******                                                 ******
C     ****** NOTE ON A SYSTEM-SPECIFIC ROUTINE               ******
C     ******                                                 ******
C     ****** CALL RANDOM INITIALIZES A RANDOM NUMBER GENERATOR ******
C     ******    TO A RANDOM STARTING POINT                   ******
C     ****** SUBSEQUENT CALLS TO THE FUNCTION RNDM(DUMMY)     ******
C     ******    PRODUCE RANDOM NUMBERS IN THE RANGE 0-1       ******
C     ******                                                 ******
C     *************************************************************
C
C     SET I/O UNITS
C
      IN = 1
      IOUT = 2
C
C     INITIALIZE RANDOM NUMBER GENERATOR
C
      CALL RANDOM
```

(continued)

309

```
C
C    READ AND COMPUTE CONTROL PARAMETERS
C
   3 READ(IN,10000,END=2000) NSYLB1,NSYLB2,MXTRL,NSUBS,ID
10000 FORMAT(6I2,17A4)
      NSYLAB = NSYLB1+NSYLB2
      NLIST = 1
      IF(NSYLB2.GT.0) NLIST = 2
      LIST2 = NSYLB1+1
C
C    READ LIST OF SYLLABLES
C
      DO 100 I = 1,NSYLAB
  100 READ(IN,10001) (LIST(I,J),J=1,3),RESP(I)
10001 FORMAT (3A1,I2)
C
C    PRINT MESSAGE
C
      WRITE(IOUT,10002) ID,NSUBS,MXTRL,NLIST
10002 FORMAT('1THIS IS SIMSAL EXPERIMENTER RUNNING ',17A4//
     *     ' NSUBS = ',I4/' MAX TRIALS ON ORIGINAL LEARNING (OL) =',I3/
     **    ' MAX TRIALS ON INTERPOLATED LEARNING (IL) =',I3/
     **    ' MAX TRIALS ON RELEARNING (RL) =',I3/
     **    ' NLIST =',I3)
      IF(MXTRL(1).LT.40 .OR. MXTRL(2).LT.40 .OR. MXTRL(3).LT.40)
     *     WRITE(IOUT,10003)
```

```
10003  FORMAT('0AN OVERLEARNING PROCEDURE IS IN EFFECT.')
       WRITE(IOUT,10004)
10004  FORMAT('0LIST OF ITEMS')
       IF(NLIST.EQ.2) WRITE(IOUT,10005) LIST2
10005  FORMAT('+',16X,'(LIST 2 BEGINS AT ITEM ',I3,'.)')
       WRITE(IOUT,10006) (I,(LIST(I,J),J=1,3),RESP(I),I=1,NSYLAB)
10006  FORMAT(' NUMBER ITEM      RESPONSE'//(I4,5X,3A1,4X,I5))
       WRITE(IOUT,10007)
10007  FORMAT('1')
C
C      START LOOP FOR SUBJECTS
C
       DO 1000 ISUB = 1,NSUBS
C
C      NOW INITIALIZE THE SUBJECT
C
       DO 1101 I = 1,3
1101   QUE(I) = IBLANK
       ICORR = 0
       IGUESS = 0
       ISW = 1
       CALL SUBJCT(QUE,ICORR,IGUESS,ISW,ISUB,PRINT)
C
C      SET UP FOR LIST 1
C
```

(continued)

311

```
      NSYLAB = NSYLB1
      IEXPER = 1
      IJUMP = 0
      LISTNO = 1
      MAXTRL = MXTRL(1)
      IWROTE = 0
C
C     CLEAR THE PROTOCOL ARRAY AND PRINT LIST NOTATION
C
 1102 DO 1103 J = 1,21
      DO 1103 I = 1,40
 1103 PCOL(I,J) = 0
      IF(PRINT.NE.0) WRITE(IOUT,10008) LISTNO
10008 FORMAT(' *** LIST ',I2,' ***')
      IF(PRINT.NE.0 .AND. MAXTRL.LT.40) WRITE(IOUT,10009) MAXTRL
10009 FORMAT(' ',25X,'(OVERLEARNING RULES FORCE ',I3,' TRIALS.)')
C
C     SET UP INITIAL ORDER ARRAY
C
      DO 1104 I = 1,20
 1104 ORDER(I) = I
C
C     START TRIALS LOOP
C
      DO 1200 NTRIAL = 1,MAXTRL
```

```
      IF(PRINT.NE.0) WRITE(IOUT,10010) NTRIAL
10010 FORMAT (//'0TRIAL ',I3,' BEGINNING   ')
C
C     FIRST PERMUTE THE ORDER LIST BY SHUFFLING
C
      DO 1201 J = 1,NSYLAB
      K = IRAND(NSYLAB-J)+J
      ITEMP = ORDER(K)
      ORDER(K) = ORDER(J)
      ORDER(J) = ITEMP
1201  CONTINUE
C
C     NOW SET UP TO RUN THIS SERIES
C
      NCORCT = 0
      DO 1202 J = 1,NSYLAB
      ITEMP = ORDER(J)+IJUMP
      ICORR=RESP(ITEMP)
C
C     ICORR IS THE CORRECT RESPONSE
C     ITEMP IS THE STIMULUS NUMBER
C     NOW FILL THE STIMULUS ARRAY   (QUE)
C
      DO 1203 K = 1,3
1203  QUE(K) = LIST(ITEMP,K)
```

(continued)

```
C
C      CALL THE SUBJECT, WHO DOES NOT HAVE ACCESS TO ICORR
C
       IDUM = 0
       ISW = 2
       CALL SUBJCT(QUE,IDUM,IGUESS,ISW,ISUB,PRINT)
C
C      LOOK AT SUBJECTS GUESS
C
       ITMP2 = ITEMP-IJUMP
       IF(IGUESS-ICORR) 1206,1204,1206
C
C      CORRECT RESPONSE
C
1204   NCORCT = NCORCT+1
       PCOL(NTRIAL,ITMP2) = PLUS
       IF(PRINT) 1208,1208,1205
1205   WRITE(IOUT,10011) QUE,ICORR
10011  FORMAT('0CORRECT,THE RESPONSE FOR  ',3A1,' IS ',I4)
       GO TO 1208
C
C      INCORRECT RESPONSE
C
1206   PCOL(NTRIAL,ITMP2) = D(IGUESS)
       IF(PRINT) 1208,1208,1207
1207   WRITE (IOUT,10012) QUE,ICORR,IGUESS
```

```
10012 FORMAT('0WRONG. THE RESPONSE FOR ',3A1,' IS',I4,', GUESS WAS ',I4)
C
C     GIVE FEEDBACK
C
1208  ISW = 3
      CALL SUBJCT (QUE,ICORR,IGUESS,ISW,ISUB,PRINT)
C
C     END OF TRIAL
C
1202  CONTINUE
C
C     CHECK FOR CRITERION
C
      PCOL(NTRIAL,21) = NSYLAB-NCORCT
      IF(NCORCT.LT.NSYLAB) GO TO 1200
      IF(IWROTE.NE.0 .AND. MAXTRL.LT.40) GO TO 1200
      IF(PRINT.GE.1) WRITE(IOUT,10013) NTRIAL
10013 FORMAT (///'0CRITERION REACHED ON TRIAL    ',I3/////)
      IF(MAXTRL.EQ.40) GO TO 1300
      IWROTE = 1
      WRITE(IOUT,10014)
10014 FORMAT('0OVERLEARNING PROCEEDS.'////)
      GO TO 1200
C
C     END OF SERIES OF TRIALS
C
```

(continued)

315

```
1200 CONTINUE
     NTRIAL = MAXTRL
     IF(MAXTRL.LT.40) GO TO 1300
     WRITE(IOUT,10015) MAXTRL
10015 FORMAT(////'OCRITERION NOT REACHED AFTER  ',I4,' TRIALS' /////)
1300 ISW = 4
     IF(PRINT.NE.0) CALL SUBJCT (QUE,ICORR,IGUESS,ISW,ISUB,PRINT)

C
C    PRINT PROTOCOL IN ONE OF TWO FORMATS DEPENDING UPON NUMBER OF
C    SYLLABLES.  IF LESS THAN TEN, COLUMNS=SYLLABLES, IF MORE THAN
C    TEN, COLUMNS=TRIALS.
C
     IFIRST = IJUMP+1
     ILAST = IJUMP+NSYLAB
     IF(NSYLAB.GT.10) GO TO 1302
     WRITE(IOUT,10016) ISUB,LISTNO,(RESP(I),(LIST(I,J),J=1,3),I=IFIRST,
    *   ILAST)
10016 FORMAT('1',30X,'PROTOCOL FOR SUBJECT ',I3,' ON LIST ',I2/
    *   '0',40X,'PAIR'/10X,10(I2,1X,3A1,4X))
     WRITE(IOUT,10017)
10017 FORMAT('+',112X,'ERRORS')
     DO 1301 I = 1,NTRIAL
     WRITE(IOUT,10018)I,(PCOL(I,J),J=1,NSYLAB)
10018 FORMAT('0',3X,I2,4X,10(4X,A2,4X))
1301 WRITE(IOUT,10019)PCOL(I,21)
10019 FORMAT('+',115X,I2)
```

```
      GO TO 1400
1302  WRITE(IOUT,10020) ISUB,LISTNO,(I,I=1,NTRIAL)
10020 FORMAT('1',30X,'PROTOCOL FOR SUBJECT ',I3,' ON LIST ',I2/'0',40X,
     *  'TRIAL'/'0PAIR',3X,40I3)
      DO 1303 I=IFIRST,ILAST
1303  WRITE(IOUT,10021) RESP(I),(LIST(I,J),J=1,3),(PCOL(JJ,I),JJ=1,
     *  NTRIAL)
10021 FORMAT('0',I2,1X,3A1,1X,40(1X,A2))
      WRITE(IOUT,10022) (PCOL(I,21),I=1,NTRIAL)
10022 FORMAT('0ERRORS ',40I3)
C
C     HANDLE MULTIPLE LIST EXPERIMENTS
C
1400  IF(NLIST.EQ.1) GO TO 1000
C
C     BRANCH TO SET UP APPROPRIATE EXPERIMENT
C
      GO TO (1500,1600,1000),IEXPER
C
C     SET UP FOR LIST 2
C
1500  NSYLAB = NSYLB2
      IEXPER = 2
      IJUMP = NSYLB1
      LISTNO = 2
      MAXTRL = MXTRL(2)
```

(continued)

```
      IWROTE = 0
      GO TO 1102
C
C     SET UP LIST 1 AGAIN
C
1600  NSYLAB = NSYLB1
      IEXPER = 3
      IJUMP = 0
      LISTNO = 1
      MAXTRL = MXTRL(3)
      IWROTE = 0
      GO TO 1102
C
C     END OF LOOP FOR NUMBER OF SUBJECTS
C
1000  CONTINUE
C
C     NOW GO BACK TO SEE IF THERE'S ANOTHER SET OF SUBJECTS TO BE RUN
C
      GO TO 3
C
C     END OF PROGRAM
C
2000  STOP
      END
```

```fortran
      SUBROUTINE SUBJCT(STIM,ICORR,IGUESS,ISW,ISUB,PRINT)
      INTEGER TREE(120,4),STIM(3),PRINT,D(120),PTREE(120,4)
      DIMENSION IVECT(3)
      DATA D/'1','2','3','4','5','6','7','8','9','10',
     *      '11','12','13','14','15','16','17','18','19','20',
     *      '21','22','23','24','25','26','27','28','29','30',
     *      '31','32','33','34','35','36','37','38','39','40',
     *      '41','42','43','44','45','46','47','48','49','50',
     *      '51','52','53','54','55','56','57','58','59','60',
     *      '61','62','63','64','65','66','67','68','69','70',
     *      '71','72','73','74','75','76','77','78','79','80',
     *      '81','82','83','84','85','86','87','88','89','90',
     *      '91','92','93','94','95','96','97','98','99','100',
     *      '101','102','103','104','105','106','107','108','109','110',
     *      '111','112','113','114','115','116','117','118','119','120'/
C
C     THE FOLLOWING GETS AROUND THAT COMPILER BUG FOR SUBJCT
C
      COMMON /BUG2/ TREE,PTREE
C
C
C     DESCRIPTION OF SUBJECT ARRAYS AND VARIABLES
C
C     BASIC MEMORY ARRAY IS CALLED TREE (120,4)
C     EACH ROW IS A NODE OF THE TREE
```

(continued)

TWO POINTERS ARE TO ENTER TREE:
  I1 IS THE LAST LINE USED--THE LOCATION TO START A NEW ENTRY.
  IPOINT IS AN ENTRY POINT. INITIALLY IN A SEARCH IT IS
    SET TO 1, THEREAFTER IT INDICATES THE START OF EACH
    SUCCEEDING NEW WORD. AT THE END OF THE SEARCH, IT MARKS THE
    LINE OF A NON-MATCHING LETTER.

A TEMPORARY ARRAY IVECT(3) IS USED IN BOTH THE SEARCH AND
LEARNING ROUTINES. IT IS ZEROED INITIALLY, AND AT THE END OF
THE SEARCH CONTAINS ONES AT EACH LOCATION WHERE A MATCH WAS FOUND
BETWEEN THE STIMULUS AND A SYLLABLE IN MEMORY.

TREE ENTRIES (NODES) ARE AS FOLLOWS:
  COL. 1 - A STIMULUS LETTER OR A RESPONSE NUMBER.
  COL. 2 - WHAT POSITION IS THIS LETTER IN THE SYLLABLE. IF ZERO,
    THIS IS THE LAST SYLLABLE IN THE ENTRY, AND COLUMN ONE OF
    THIS ROW IS THE RESPONSE.
  COL. 3 - POINTER TO THE NEXT LETTER IN SYLLABLE. ON THE LAST LETTER
    OF A SYLLABLE, THIS INDICATES THE ROW OF THE RESPONSE.
    THIS POINTER ALSO CALLED THE "CORRECT" BRANCH.
  COL. 4 - POINTER TO ANOTHER POSSIBLE LETTER AT THIS POSITION,
    OR TO AN EMPTY NODE. CALLED THE "ERROR" BRANCH.

DEFINE RANDOM NUMBER FUNCTION

```
      IRAND(N) = INT(RNDM(DUMMY)*N+1)
C
C ***** SEE NOTE IN MAIN ROUTINE REGARDING SYSTEM-SPECIFIC ROUTINES
C
C
C
C
C
C
C     BRANCH ON SWITCH
C
      GO TO (1000,2000,3000,4000),ISW
C
C     INITIALIZING ENTRY POINT
C
1000  DO 1001 J = 1,4
      DO 1001 I = 1,120
1001  TREE(I,J) = 0
      IN = 1
      IOUT = 2
      I1 = 1
      IPOINT = 1
      IF(ISUB.GT.1) RETURN
      READ (IN,10000) PADD,PCHNGE,POVLRN,PRINT
10000 FORMAT (3F3.3,I1)
C
C     PADD IS THE PROBABILITY OF ADDING TO THE TREE
```

(continued)

TABLE B.2 (continued)

```
C     PCHNGE IS THE PROBABILITY OF CHANGING A RESPONSE
C     POVLRN IS THE OVERLEARNING PARAMETER
C        = 0 FOR SAL1 VERSION
C        = BETWEEN 0 AND PADD FOR SAL2
C
C     PRINT IS A SWITCH
C        0 = NO TRACING (ONLY PROTOCOL OUTPUT)
C        1 = TRACE EACH TRIAL
C        2 = FULL TRACE WITH TREE ON EACH SYLLABLE
C
C     PRINT MESSAGE
C
1005  WRITE(IOUT,10001)ISUB, PADD,PCHNGE,POVLRN
10001 FORMAT(//////' ****THIS IS SIMSAL SUBJECT  NO. ',I2,
     *       //' PADD = ',F6.4,'  (HINTZMAN''S A)',
     *       //' PCHNGE = ',F6.4,'  (HINTZMAN''S B)',
     *       //' POVLRN = ',F6.4,'  (HINTZMAN''S C)')
      IF(PRINT-1) 1004,1002,1003
1002  WRITE(IOUT,10002)
10002 FORMAT(///' I WILL NOT PRINT THE MEMORY TREE UNTIL AFTER CRITERION
     1.'/'1')
      RETURN
1003  WRITE(IOUT,10003)
10003 FORMAT(///' I WILL PRINT THE MEMORY TREE AFTER EACH ITEM.'/'1')
      RETURN
```

```
      WRITE(IOUT,10004)
10004 FORMAT(///' PROTOCOL OUTPUT ONLY.'/'1')
      RETURN
C
C     RESPOND ENTRY
C
C     FIRST ZERO THE MATCH-POINTER ARRAY
C
2000  DO 2001 I = 1,3
2001  IVECT(I) = 0
C
C     NOW SCAN THE TREE FOR MATCH
C
      IPOINT = 1
2003  IF(TREE(IPOINT,2)) 2002,2006,2002
2002  ISB = TREE(IPOINT,2)
      IF(STIM(ISB)-TREE(IPOINT,1)) 2004,2005,2004
2004  IPOINT = TREE(IPOINT,4)
      GO TO 2003
2005  ISB = TREE(IPOINT,2)
      IVECT(ISB) = 1
      IPOINT = TREE(IPOINT,3)
      GO TO 2003
```

(continued)

```
C
C   CLOSEST MATCH FOUND---MAKE A GUESS AND RETURN
C
C   IF NO ENTRY IN TREE, MAKE A RANDOM GUESS
C
2006 IF(TREE(IPOINT,1)) 2007,2008,2007
C
C   TRY WHAT WORKED BEFORE
C
2007 IGUESS = TREE(IPOINT,1)
     RETURN
C
C   RANDOM GUESS
C
2008 IGUESS = IRAND(20)
     RETURN
C
C   LEARN ENTRY
C
C   IF ANSWER CORRECT CHECK ON OVERLEARNING PARAMETER
3000 IF(ICORR-IGUESS) 3001,3050,3001
C
C   IF ANSWER WRONG, ADD TO TREE WITH PROBABILITY PADD
C
3001 IF(RNDM(DUMMY)-PADD) 3100,3002,3002
```

```
C    IF WE DON'T BUILD A TREE, CHANGE RESPONSE WITH PROBABILITY PCHNGE
C
3002 IF(RNDM(DUMMY)-PCHNGE) 3200,3200,3003
3003 TREE(IPOINT,1) = ICORR
     GO TO 3200
3050 IF(RNDM(DUMMY)-POVLRN) 3100,3100,3200
C
C    TREE BUILDING SEGMENT
C
C
C    FIRST CHECK MATCH-POINTER ARRAY FOR FIRST NON-MATCHING LETTER
C
3100 DO 3101 IZ = 1,3
     IF(IVECT(IZ)) 3101,3105,3101
3101 CONTINUE
     GO TO 3003
C
C    ADD NEW ENTRIES TO TREE
C
3105 TREE(IPOINT,2)   = IZ
     TREE(IPOINT,1)   = STIM(IZ)
     TREE(IPOINT,3)   = I1+1
     TREE(IPOINT,4)   = I1+2
     TREE(I1+1,1)     = ICORR
     TREE(I1+2,1)     = 0
     I1 = I1+2
```

(continued)

```
C     CHECK FOR PRINTING
C
C
3200  IF(PRINT-1) 3201,3201,4000
3201  RETURN
C
C     WRITE ENTRY
C
C     FIRST COPY TREE INTO ITS LITERAL EQUIVALENT PTREE
C
4000  DO 4001 I=1,I1
      DO 4001 J=1,4
      PTREE(I,J)=TREE(I,J)
      IF(ABS(TREE(I,J)).GT.120) GO TO 4001
      ITEMP=TREE(I,J)
      PTREE(I,J)=D(ITEMP)
4001  CONTINUE
      DO 4002 I=1,I1
4002  WRITE(IOUT,10005) I,(PTREE(I,J),J=1,4)
10005 FORMAT(I5,3X,4A4)
      WRITE(IOUT,10006) I1,IPOINT,STIM,IVECT,IZ
10006 FORMAT('0I1= ',I5,'  IPOINT= ',I7,' STIM = '3A1/' IVECT = '3I2/
     *      ' IZ = 'I3)
      RETURN
      END
```

TABLE B.3
Example SIMSAL Input

```
 800404040 1STUDY 1, MEDIUM SIMILARITY
AEI  1
AFJ  2
BGK  3
BHL  4
CEI  5
CFJ  6
DGK  7
DHL  8
4005000000
```

TABLE B.4
Example SIMSAL Output

THIS IS SIMSAL EXPERIMENTER RUNNING STUDY 1, MEDIUM SIMILARITY

NSUBS =   1
MAX TRIALS ON ORIGINAL LEARNING (OL) = 40
MAX TRIALS ON INTERPOLATED LEARNING (IL) = 40
MAX TRIALS ON RELEARNING (RL) = 40
NLIST = 1

LIST OF ITEMS
NUMBER ITEM   RESPONSE

   1   AEI   1
   2   AFJ   2
   3   BGK   3
   4   BHL   4
   5   CEI   5
   6   CFJ   6
   7   DGK   7
   8   DHL   8

****THIS IS SIMSAL SUBJECT   NO.   1

PADD = 0.4000 (HINTZMAN'S A)
PCHNGE = 0.5000 (HINTZMAN'S B)
POVLRN = 0.0000 (HINTZMAN'S C)

PROTOCOL OUTPUT ONLY.

(continued)

TABLE B.4 (continued)

PROTOCOL FOR SUBJECT 1 ON LIST 1

	1 AEI	2 AFJ	3 BGK	PAIR 4 BHL	5 CEI	6 CFJ	7 DGK	8 DHL	ERRORS
1	5	1	4	18	16	+	2	7	7
2	2	1	+	6	6	5	20	+	6
3	2	+	+	+	6	+	+	+	2
4	6	1	+	+	6	+	+	+	3
5	17	+	+	+	+	11	+	+	2
6	+	+	+	+	+	+	+	+	0

329

APPENDIX C

CITY:
A Simulation of Urban Growth
Based on a Fixed Set of Priorities

Each set of chapter exercises has included one or more problems relating to a simulation of urban growth and development. The exercises are designed to encourage the development of a simulation program through their completion. This appendix presents one simulation that may result from that series of problems. The program and model presented here are an extension and elaboration of the program CITY described by Vandeportaele and Garside (1972).

CITY is intended primarily as a classroom and student demonstration program. The authors state two primary objectives that have guided the development of the program. The first is to "... actually produce the results of establishing priorities on city growth, rather than ... mere discussion of theory relating to such growth patterns" (p. 8). A second goal of the program is to offer the opportunity to study its algorithm "... in order to open the classroom experience to building new models to test other growth theories" (p. 8).

The conceptual model for CITY does not derive from any previous theoretical bases with respect to urban growth. Very specifically, the authors have made no attempt to represent any of the classical theories of growth, such as the concentric zone, sector, or polynuclear models. These theories are mentioned primarily to suggest ways in which students studying the simulation may consider modifying the program.

It is easy to describe CITY's basic processes. The program simulates four ten-year intervals of urban growth. At the start of a ten-year cycle, there is a certain population and an established city map showing various land uses. The population of the region increases by some percentage of its initial value during each cycle. The increased population is assigned to housing areas and new housing is constructed. In addition, new supporting facilities, such as businesses, factories, and parks, are built to accommodate the increased population. All of the new requirements, both housing and support, are reflected in increased occupation of the land of the city. A map showing the changed land uses is printed each 10 years to document the growth of the urban area over time.

The Conceptual Model

The most elementary units in the simulation are the individual lots on which "buildings" may be placed. The lots are stored in a 50 × 50 array representing the map of the city. Each lot in the map array contains one of nine different alphameric characters indicating the use of that piece of property.

In addition to the map containing the units, several other arrays contain properties that control the overall process of urban development. Priorities for building and destroying space are stored in two arrays. One array, named PRIORT, contains the order in which the needs of the growing city are to be met. If the first entry in PRIORT is a 3, then the third land use (high-rise dwelling unit) is to be satisfied first; that done, the second land use given in PRIORT is filled, and so forth. Another priority array is named DESPRI. It gives the order in which properties are destroyed in order to meet higher priority needs.

An array named RATE holds the number of people that can be served by each of the kinds of property. In the case of a residential lot, the entry here gives the number of people who can live in each class of dwelling; for support facilities, the entry gives the number of people who can be served by a particular support property. For example, the first value in RATE gives the number of people housed in a single dwelling unit − if its value is 25, then 25 people can reside in a single dwelling lot. The fifth value in RATE gives the service rate for business units. If its value was 100, for example, then whenever the population increased by 100 a new business unit would have to be constructed.

Map summary arrays are of two different kinds, in addition to a variable (TOTPOP) giving the total population count. One pair of arrays, ROTOT and COTOT, hold the total number of each kind of property for each row and column in the map. A second array, named POPCNT, stores the mean row and column numbers for each kind of property. One or the other of these two sets of arrays is used by the algorithm that locates space for building new units.

Inputs. The program requires considerable input. The initial map must be supplied, along with the various service rates and priorities as discussed above. The exact nature of the input is described in the program listing (Table C.2) and illustrated in Table C.3.

The user must exercise considerable caution in preparing the input for CITY. An "interesting" starting map can be provided, but it is critical that the total number of each kind of unit, combined with the provided service rates, result in the input starting population. For example, if the residential service rates are 25, 50, 300, and 40 for dwellings, apartments, high-rise units, and ghettos, respectively, then the total of number of units of each kind multiplied by their service rates must total the starting population as provided to the program. If they do not, disaster may result. For example, in one series of debugging runs of CITY, the author provided a total population greater than could be accounted for by the housing on the map. To his great consternation, the first cycle of the program showed a large number of units being destroyed.

Processes.   A number of separate subprocesses can be identified in the course of urban growth. There is a demographic subprocess, which consists of census taking and map printing. Computing an expected new population for the city during the next simulated time period is a separate process, and it can be logically followed by determining the requirements that the new populace is going to place on the city. Once the needs are defined, the priority for meeting them is established. Then another subprocess can locate a building lot where a new facility is to be constructed, and it can be built there. In some cases, a property may have to be demolished before a new one can be built; both building and destroying are separate subprocesses.

In the CITY program, each of these subprocesses has been written as a subroutine. They are discussed in more detail in a discussion of the program's algorithms; the sequencing of the processes is implied in the preceding discussion and is illustrated in Figure C.1.

Consequences.   The most graphic method of portraying the growth of a city is by a detailed map. The map is the major output of CITY and is the primary consequence of the program. Along with the map, the various summary arrays are printed as well.

Assumptions

Because the program was intended as an educational demonstration, the assumptions were more unrealistic than would be the case if the goals of the effort were more lofty. The most important simplifying assumption is that the priorities and other input data remain constant throughout the entire simulated time period. Because the program models a 40-year cycle of city growth, this assumption is clearly unrealistic.

A more subtle assumption is embodied in the program. A property cannot be built unless another like it is already present. This proved to be a handicap in one series of validation runs where an actual city was simulated. Beginning 40 years before the present, an initial map was provided. At the historic time, high-rise apartments did not exist. Nevertheless, it was necessary to supply one, simply so that more could be built as the population demanded.

A seeming constraint on the program is that the map may be only 50 × 50, thus containing 2,500 lots. The reason that this is not a real restriction is that a "lot" can be conceived as an individual city lot, an entire block, or even a square

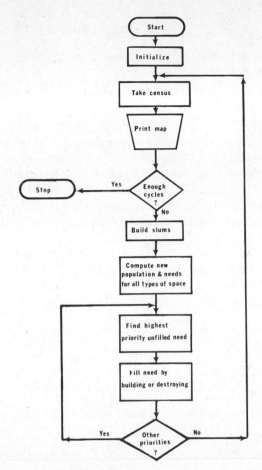

FIGURE C.1   Flowchart for CITY's conceptual model.

mile. The difference is seen in service rates but nowhere else. If, for example, a dwelling unit can accommodate 40 individuals, it seems likely then for a "lot" on the map to correspond to a city block. If a dwelling houses four people, in contrast, the map unit is best interpreted as a single lot; an ability to house 350 leads to an interpretation based on a much larger area.

A few other relatively minor restrictions are also imposed. For example, there must be exactly seven land uses (dwellings, apartments, high rises, ghettos, businesses, factories, and recreational). All of the arrays assume exactly seven; rewriting to add another land use (agricultural, for example) would be tedious but not difficult. Finally, a fixed percentage of the dwelling areas is converted to ghettos during each cycle of the program. The percentage can vary, but not as an input parameter. Changing the percentage or eliminating the automatic conversion would entail some minor reprogramming.

Algorithms

Each subprocess is represented by a separate subroutine. Each routine operates on one or more of the major arrays discussed in more detail below.

The main program. The main routine accomplishes two major purposes. First, it initializes all of the important arrays used in the program. Some of the initialization is a matter of input – the priority, service rate, percentage of housing, and map arrays are filled in this manner. Other arrays, particularly the row and column totals (ROTOT and COTOT) and the population centers (POPCNT), are computed here. They are updated by other routines, primarily by CENSUS.

Among the several housekeeping functions performed in the main routine, a general heading is printed, and processing terminates after the appropriate number of cycles.

The other purpose of the main program is to call on the subroutines in the proper order so that the process proceeds as required.

CENSUS. This subroutine accomplishes primarily what its name implies. Major summary arrays and variables are updated for use by other subprocesses.

DISPLA. This routine does all of the output from the program except for the overall heading. The most important array printed is the map but the total population in each housing area, the count of each kind of property, and the population centers are also printed.

SLMBLD. When called, this routine converts 2% of the housing area into slum property. It calls on the routines LOCATE and BUILD to do its major work.

EXPT. This subroutine computes a new population figure and then determines how many of each kind of property unit are required to service that population. It returns an array named EXPECT containing the total number of each kind of property needed to serve the increased population.

NEEDS. Here the requirements set by EXPT are compared with the property of each type already present. The difference between on hand and required is returned in an array named NEED. Note that the need may be positive, meaning that there is more population than can be accommodated by existing property, or negative, indicating a surplus. A negative need usually results in properties being destroyed (converted to vacant space).

PLANER. This simpleminded urban planner functionally pops a stack containing the order in which needs are to be met. It merely returns the next requirement to be satisfied.

LOCATE. This routine returns a map location, as row and column coordinates, where a new building is to be placed. LOCATE is called with several arguments, only one of which is important for the present discussion. That argument, called JJJ, gives the target character as a pointer into an array CHAR; if JJJ is 1, CHAR(JJJ) contains the symbol 'D,' and so forth. The basic test in LOCATE

$$IF(MAP(I,J).EQ.CHAR(JJJ))...$$

occurs several times in the subroutine. The procedure by which values are assigned to the subscripts I and J for MAP define the search algorithm. The test is made for a particular location, the subscripts are adjusted, and then the test is repeated. The starting values of I and J, along with the rules by which they are modified, define the spatial search in CITY.

The two key elements, a starting point and a search pattern, are dictated by the conceptual model. CITY's search begins at one of two points, selected according to one of two slightly different theoretical approaches to the development of a city. In the original version of CITY, a starting point was picked by determining the row and column containing the greatest concentration of the target property. For example, if LOCATE is called to find a place for a dwelling unit, two additional arrays — ROTOT giving row totals for houses, and COTOT giving the same information for columns — are consulted to find the largest row and column entries for houses. In the listing of LOCATE, this procedure is called the modal algorithm.

For this book, a second algorithm was devised for selecting a starting point. An array called POPCNT holds the population centers for several kinds of building areas. Whenever a new building is added to the map, POPCNT is updated. The values in POPCNT are in effect weighted mean row and column numbers for housing units (a combination of dwellings, apartments, high rises, and ghettos), businesses, factories, or recreation areas. The result is a center of gravity definition of the starting point. The location selected for a house tends to be in the geographic center of all housing units; in a modal search, by contrast, outlying areas are sometimes picked to start the search. We illustrate in Tables C.4 and C.5 how the selection of the starting point influences the growth of the city; for now we comment that the center of gravity selection makes for a more compact city. At any rate, the selection of the starting point is not an arbitrary decision; it is closely related to the underlying theoretical model.

The second element in the spatial search is the algorithm for expanding outward from the selected starting point. Any of several procedures can be devised — up and down the column to the left, then the next column to the left, and so forth until the target is found or the left side of the array exhausted, then shift to the right, etc.

The search algorithm in CITY defines concentric squares expanding outward from the starting point. The procedure is illustrated in Figure C.2. The starting point is marked X and the search expands outward from that point, visiting the adjoining cells in the order indicated. In the event that the target character is not

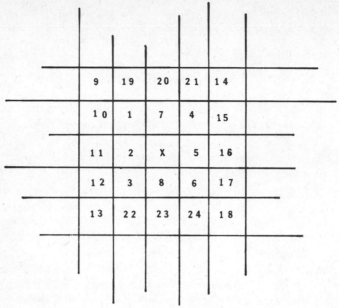

FIGURE C.2   The order of cells visited by CITY's search routine.

located in the first "square," then next-larger square is selected, and so forth until a match is made or the array exhausted. In the latter case, LOCATE returns an error indication.

DESTRY.   This subroutine converts a filled lot into an empty one. It stores the blank character in a map location and decrements the row and column totals.

PRIO.   This subroutine returns the top value in the destruction priority array, as long as there is any of that property to be used.

BUILD.   This subroutine is the converse of DESTRY. It places a character on the map and increments the total arrays, thereby building a new property.

The relationships among all of the subroutines in CITY is shown in Figure C.3. This figure is a flowchart of the program, whereas Figure C.1 summarizes the conceptual model.

The storage allocation for CITY is particularly interesting, because it illustrates the use of labeled COMMON blocks as discussed in Chapter 2. All of the subroutine communication in CITY is accomplished through the use of either arguments or two labeled COMMON blocks.

Table C.1 presents the storage arrangement for CITY as it was developed during the modification of the program for this book. CITY's subroutines are listed as columns in the table. The rows show the major arrays and variables of the program, and an "X" in the table indicates that a variable is needed by a

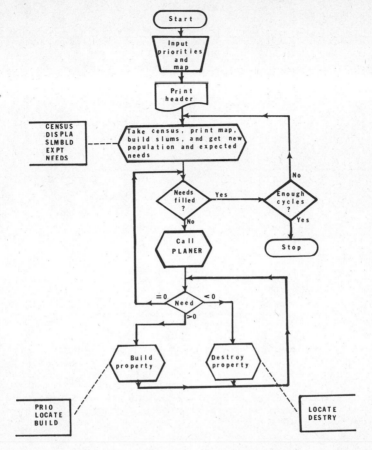

FIGURE C.3   Flowchart of the CITY program.

particular subroutine. From this table, it was determined that the arrays MAP, ROTOT, COTOT, and POPCNT are needed by LOCATE, BUILD, DISPLA, CENSUS, and DESTRY but not by others. These arrays are stored in a COMMON block named SPACE, and access is given to the main program and the required subroutines. Another block, named TALLY, contains a group of arrays and variables required by a different set of subroutines. A number of other variables, as shown in the table, are communicated by arguments. They could have been placed in blank COMMON but were needed by either very few or nearly all subroutines and so the argument list was selected. In general, if only one or two subroutines require a particular variable, the communication is best accomplished by an argument list.

The complete listing of CITY is presented in Table C.2. Of the three complete programs presented in this book, CITY most nearly represents a structured program. Except for the LOCATE routine, all of the component subprograms

TABLE C.1

COMMON and Argument Communications for CITY

Variable	Main program	CENSUS	DISPLA	SLMBLD	EXPT	NEEDS	PLANER	LOCATE	DESTRY	PRIO	BUILD	Type[a]	Size[b]	Communication[c]
COTOT	X	X	X					X	X		X	I	50,9	SPACE
MAP	X	X	X					X	X		X	I	50,50	SPACE
POPCNT	X	X	X					X	X		X	I	5,2	SPACE
ROTOT	X	X	X					X	X		X	I	50,9	SPACE
B	X	X	X									I		TALLY
F	X	X	X									I		TALLY
HSDPOP	X	X	X									I		TALLY
PERCEN	X	X	X									I	4	TALLY
R	X	X	X									R	9	TALLY
SLMPOP	X	X	X									I		TALLY
CHAR	X		X	X				X	X		X	I	9	Arg
COUNT	X	X	X	X		X			X	X	X	I	9	Arg
DESPRI	X									X		I	8	Arg
EXPECT	X				X	X						I	7	Arg
GRATE	X				X	X						R		Arg
NEED	X					X						I	7	Arg
PERHSE	X				X							R	4	Arg
PRIORT	X						X					I	7	Arg
RATE	X	X			X							I	7	Arg
TOTHSD	X	X										I		Arg
TOTPOP	X	X	X		X							I		Arg

[a]Integer (I) or real (R).
[b]Dimensions of a subscripted variable. No entry indicates single variable.
[c]How communicated—block name or argument.

TABLE C.2

Listing of CITY, the Urban Growth Model

```
C     PROGRAM CITY
C
C     URBAN GROWTH AND DEVELOPMENT MODEL
C
C     BASED ON PROGRAM CITY BY D. VANDERPORTAELE AND D. B.
C       GARSIDE, ILLINOIS INSTITUTE OF TECHNOLOGY.
C       RELEASED THROUGH NORTH CAROLINA EDUCATIONAL COMPUTING SERVICE,
C       DOCUMENT #CEG-SOC-04, 1972.
C
C     INPUT DESCRIPTION
C
C     CARD 1
C     COLS.     CONTENT                              NAME         FORMAT
C       1       0=NO TRACE, 1=TRACE                  ITRACE       I1
C       2       1=MODAL ROW & COLUMN FOR SEARCH      ISW          I1
C               2=MEAN ROW & COLUMN FOR SEARCH
C      3-78     RUN TITLE                            TITLE(19)    19A4
C     CARD 2
C      1-9      CHARACTER VECTOR--GIVES GRAPHICS     CHAR(9)      9A:
C               FOR HOUSE, APARTMENT, HIRISE
C               GHETTO, BUSINESS,FACTORY,
C               RECREATION, BOUNDARY, AND
C               VACANT SPACE IN THE ORDER.
```

(continued)

TABLE C.2 (continued)

```
C   CARDS 3-52
C     1-50     MAP OF INITIAL CITY              CITY(50,50)  50A1
C   CARD 53
C     1-35     SERVICE RATES--# PEOPLE          RATE(7)      7I5
C              SERVED BY EACH TYPE OF AREA (HOUSE-
C              RECREATION)
C    36-41     POPULATION GROWTH RATE           GRATE        F6.2
C    42-51     INITIAL POPULATION               TOTPOP       I10
C   CARD 54
C     1-14     BUILDING PRIORITIES FOR          PRIORT       7I2
C              HOUSE-RECREATION
C    15-30     DESTROY PRIORITIES FOR           DESPRI       8I2
C              HOUSE-RECREATION,VACANT SPACE
C   CARD 55
C     1-24     PERCENTAGE OF POPULATION         PERHSE(4)    4F6.2
C              TO BE HOUSED IN HOUSE, APARTMENT,
C              HIRISE, AND GHETTO
C
C   OTHER IMPORTANT ARRAYS
C
C     ROTOT(50,9)   TOTALS FOR EACH TYPE OF SPACE BY ROW
C     COTOT(50,9)   TOTALS FOR EACH TYPE OF SPACE BY COLUMN
C     POPCNT(5,2)   POPULATION CENTERS--SEE SUBROUTINE CENSUS
```

```fortran
      INTEGER MAP(50,50),ROTOT(50,9),COTOT(50,9),HSDPOP(4),CHAR(9),
     * RATE(7),PRIORT(7),COUNT(7),EXPECT(7),NEED(7),DESPRI(8),SLMPOP,
     * B,F,R,TOTHSD,TOTPOP,TITLE(19),POPCNT(5,2)
      DIMENSION PERCEN(9),PERHSE(4),LABEL(10)
      COMMON /SPACE/MAP,ROTOT,COTOT,POPCNT
     *       /TALLY/PERCEN,HSDPOP,SLMPOP,B,F,R
      DATA LABEL(1),LABEL(2)/'MODE','MEAN'/
C
C     SET I/O DEVICES AND INITIALIZE RANDOM NUMBERS
C
      NP = 6
      NR = 5
      CALL RANDOM
C
C     READ CHARACTER ARRAY AND MAP
C
 1000 READ(NR,10000,END=4000) ITRACE,ISW,TITLE
10000 FORMAT(2I1,19A4)
      IF(ISW.GT.O .AND. ISW.LE.4) GO TO 1001
      WRITE(NP,10001) ISW
10001 FORMAT(' ISW OUT OF RANGE',I4,' SET TO 1.')
      ISW = 1
 1001 READ(NR,10002) CHAR
10002 FORMAT(9A1)
      READ(NR,10003) ((MAP(J,I),J=1,50),I=1,50)
10003 FORMAT(50A1)
```

(continued)

341

TABLE C.2 (continued)

```
C
C     READ PARAMETERS FOR THIS RUN
C
      READ(NR,10004) (RATE(I),I=1,7),GRATE,TOTPOP
10004 FORMAT(7I5,F6.2,I10)
      READ(NR,10005) (PRIORT(I),I=1,7),(DESPRI(I),I=1,8)
10005 FORMAT(15I2)
      READ(NR,10006) PERHSE
10006 FORMAT(4F6.2)
C
C     PRINT INITIAL PARAMETERS FOR THIS RUN
C
      WRITE (NP,10007) CHAR,RATE,PERHSE
10007 FORMAT ('IMAP LEGEND --'/
     *        '0 CATEGORIES',T16,'HOUSE APARTMENT HIRISE GHETTO BUS
     *INESS FACTORY RECREATION BOUNDARY VACANT LOT'/
     *        ' SYMBOLS',T18,A1,T27,A1,T36,A1,T44,A1,T53,A1,T63,A1,
     *T73,A1,T84,A1,T95,A1/
     *        ' RATES',T16,I5,T25,I5,T34,I5,T42,I5,T51,I5,T61,I5,T71,
     *I5,/
     *        ' PERCENT',T15,F6.2,T24,F6.2,T33,F6.2,T41,F6.2)
      WRITE(NP,10008)
10008 FORMAT('OPRIORITIES --'/' ORDER  BUILD  DESTROY')
      DO 1002 I = 1,7
      ISUB = PRIORT(I)
      ISUB2 = DESPRI(I)
```

```
1002  WRITE(NP,10009) I,PRIORT(I),CHAR(ISUB),DESPRI(I),CHAR(ISUB2)
10009 FORMAT(5X,I1,5X,I1,1X,A1,5X,I1,1X,A1)
      ISUB = DESPRI(8)
      WRITE(NP,10010) DESPRI(8),CHAR(ISUB)
10010 FORMAT(5X,'8',13X,I1,1X,A1)
      WRITE(NP,10011) TOTPOP,GRATE,LABEL(ISW)
10011 FORMAT('OCURRENT POPULATION ',I10,2X,'GROWTH RATE ',F6.2,' PERCENT
     *,PER YEAR'/' THE ',A4,' WILL BE USED TO DETERMINE THE STARTING POI
     *NT FOR LOCATE')
C
C     SET CYCLES COUNTER
C
      ISTOP = 0
C
C     CLEAR AND INITIALIZE COUNTERS AND ROW AND COLUMN TOTALS
C
      DO 2000 I = 1,9
      COUNT(I) = 0
      DO 2000 J = 1,50
      ROTOT(J,I) = 0
2000  COTOT(J,I) = 0
      DO 2001 I = 1,50
      DO 2002 J = 1,50
      DO 2003 K = 1,9
      IF(MAP(J,I).NE.CHAR(K)) GO TO 2003
      COUNT(K) = COUNT(K)+1
```

(continued)

343

TABLE C.2 (continued)

```
      ROTOT(I,K) = ROTOT(I,K)+1
      COTOT(J,K) = COTOT(J,K)+1
      GO TO 2002
 2003 CONTINUE
 2002 CONTINUE
 2001 CONTINUE
C
C     START PROCESSING CYCLE
C
 3000 ISTOP = ISTOP+1
      CALL CENSUS(COUNT,RATE,TOTPOP,TOTHSD)
      CALL DISPLA(TOTPOP,CHAR,COUNT)
      IYEAR = (ISTOP-1)*10
      WRITE(NP,10012) IYEAR,TITLE
10012 FORMAT(//' YEAR ',I3,' FOR ',19A4)
      IF(ISTOP-5) 3001,1000,1000
 3001 CALL SLMBLD(COUNT,CHAR,ISW)
      CALL EXPT(TOTPOP,RATE,EXPECT,PERHSE,GRATE)
      CALL NEEDS(NEED,EXPECT,COUNT)
 3002 CALL PLANER(III,PRIORT,K9)
      IF(ITRACE.LE.0) GO TO 3003
      WRITE(NP,10013) ISTOP
10013 FORMAT(' AT CYCLE ',I2/' EXPECT    NEED    COUNT')
      DO 3004 IDUM = 1,7
```

```
3004    WRITE(NP,10014) EXPECT(IDUM),NEED(IDUM),COUNT(IDUM)
10014   FORMAT(3I7)
        WRITE(NP,10015) COUNT(8),COUNT(9)
10015   FORMAT(2(14X,I7/))
3003    GO TO (3000,3005),K9
3005    IF(NEED(III)) 3006,3002,3008
3006    CALL LOCATE(III,III,J,I,CHAR,K90,ISW)
        GO TO (3011,3007),K90
3007    CALL DESTRY(J,I,III,COUNT,CHAR)
        NEED(III) = NEED(III)+1
        GO TO 3005
3008    CALL PRIO(JJJ,III,DESPRI,COUNT,L50)
        GO TO (3011,3009),L50
3009    CALL LOCATE(III,JJJ,J,I,CHAR,K50,ISW)
        GO TO (3011,3010),K50
3010    CALL BUILD(J,I,JJJ,III,COUNT,CHAR)
        NEED(III) = NEED(III)-1
        GO TO 3005
3011    WRITE(NP,10016) III
10016   FORMAT('0ATTEMPT TO LOCATE SPACE FOR TYPE',I2,' HAS FAILED')
        GO TO 3002
4000    STOP
        END
```

(continued)

345

TABLE C.2 *(continued)*

```
      SUBROUTINE CENSUS(COUNT,RATE,TOTPOP,TOTHSD)
C
C     THIS ROUTINE FINDS ALL POPULATION COUNTS AND POPULATION CENTERS
C
      INTEGER MAP(50,50),ROTOT(50,9),COTOT(50,9),HSDPOP(4),COUNT(1),
     *  RATE(1),SLMPOP,B,F,R,TOTPOP,TOTHSD,POPCNT(5,2)
      DIMENSION PERCEN(9)
      COMMON /SPACE/MAP,ROTOT,COTOT,POPCNT
     *       /TALLY/PERCEN,HSDPOP,SLMPOP,B,F,R
C
C     FIND POPULATION IN ALL TYPES OF HOUSING
C
      TOTHSD = 0
      DO 1000 I = 1,4
      HSDPOP(I) = COUNT(I)*RATE(I)
      TOTHSD = TOTHSD+HSDPOP(I)
1000  CONTINUE
      SLMPOP = TOTPOP-TOTHSD
      DO 1001 I = 1,9
1001  PERCEN(I) = COUNT(I)/25.0
C
C     NOW FIND POPULATION SERVED BY BUSINESS, FACTORY, AND RECREATION
C
      B = COUNT(5)*RATE(5)
      F = COUNT(6)*RATE(6)
```

```
      R = COUNT(7)*RATE(7)

C
C     NOW FIND POPULATION CENTERS AND STORE IN POPCNT
C
C     POPCNT IS 5X2---COLUMNS 1 AND 2 GIVE COLUMN AND ROW
C        COORDINATES FOR CENTERS OF EACH TYPE OF POPULATION
C        (ARITHMETIC MEAN ROW AND COLUMN, WEIGHTED BY
C        POPULATION).
C     ROWS GIVE TYPES OF POPULATIONS AS:
C        1 RESIDENTIAL (DWELLING, APARTMENT, HIRISE, GHETTO)
C        2 BUSINESS
C        3 FACTORY
C        4 RECREATION
C        5 COMMERCIAL (BUSINESS AND FACTORY)
C
      DO 1002 I = 1,5
      POPCNT(I,1) = 0
      POPCNT(I,2) = 0
 1002 CONTINUE
      DO 1003 I = 1,50
      DO 1004 J = 1,4
      POPCNT(1,1) = POPCNT(1,1)+RATE(J)*COTOT(I,J)*I
      POPCNT(1,2) = POPCNT(1,2)+RATE(J)*ROTOT(I,J)*I
 1004 CONTINUE
      POPCNT(2,1) = POPCNT(2,1)+COTOT(I,5)*I
      POPCNT(2,2) = POPCNT(2,2)+ROTOT(I,5)*I
```

(continued)

347

TABLE C.2 (continued)

```
      POPCNT(5,1)  =  POPCNT(5,1)+POPCNT(2,1)
      POPCNT(5,2)  =  POPCNT(5,2)+POPCNT(2,2)
      POPCNT(3,1)  =  POPCNT(3,1)+COTOT(I,6)*I
      POPCNT(3,2)  =  POPCNT(3,2)+ROTOT(I,6)*I
      POPCNT(5,1)  =  POPCNT(5,1)+POPCNT(3,1)
      POPCNT(5,2)  =  POPCNT(5,2)+POPCNT(3,2)
      POPCNT(4,1)  =  POPCNT(4,1)+COTOT(I,7)*I
      POPCNT(4,2)  =  POPCNT(4,2)+ROTOT(I,7)*I
 1003 CONTINUE
      POPCNT(1,1)  =  POPCNT(1,1)/TOTPOP
      POPCNT(1,2)  =  POPCNT(1,2)/TOTPOP
      DO 1005 I = 2,4
      DO 1005 J = 1,2
 1005 POPCNT(I,J)  =  POPCNT(I,J)/COUNT(I+3)
      POPCNT(5,1)  =  (POPCNT(2,1)+POPCNT(3,1))/2
      POPCNT(5,2)  =  (POPCNT(2,2)+POPCNT(3,2))/2
      RETURN
      END

      SUBROUTINE DISPLA(TOTPOP,CHAR,COUNT)
C
C     PRINTS MAP AND POPULATION STATISTICS
C
      INTEGER MAP(50,50),ROTOT(50,9),COTOT(50,9),TOTPOP,CHAR(1),
```

```
*     COUNT(1),HSDPOP(4),SLMPOP,B,F,R,POPCNT(5,2)
      DIMENSION PERCEN(9)
      COMMON /SPACE/MAP,ROTOT,COTOT,POPCNT
*            /TALLY/PERCEN,HSDPOP,SLMPOP,B,F,R
      NP = 6
      WRITE(NP,10000)
      WRITE(NP,10001)    ((MAP(J,I),J=1,50),CHAR(I),COUNT(I),
     *   PERCEN(I),I=1,9)
      WRITE(NP,10002)    ((MAP(J,I),J=1,50),I=10,15)
      WRITE(NP,10003)
      WRITE(NP,10004)    ((MAP(J,I),J=1,50),CHAR(I-15),HSDPOP(I-15),
     *   I=16,19)
      WRITE(NP,10002)    ((MAP(J,I),J=1,50),I=20,30)
      WRITE(NP,10005)
      WRITE(NP,10006)    (MAP(J,31),J=1,50),SLMPOP
      WRITE(NP,10002)    ((MAP(J,I),J=1,50),I=32,36)
      WRITE(NP,10007)
      WRITE(NP,10006)    (MAP(J,37),J=1,50),TOTPOP
      WRITE(NP,10002)    ((MAP(J,I),J=1,50),I=38,40)
      WRITE(NP,10008)    (MAP(J,41),J=1,50),B
      WRITE(NP,10009)    (MAP(J,42),J=1,50),F
      WRITE(NP,10010)    (MAP(J,43),J=1,50),R
      WRITE(NP,10002)    ((MAP(J,I),J=1,50),I=44,45)
      WRITE(NP,10011)
      WRITE(NP,10012)    (MAP(J,46),J=1,50),(POPCNT(1,JJ),JJ=1,2)
      WRITE(NP,10013)    (MAP(J,47),J=1,50),(POPCNT(2,JJ),JJ=1,2)
```

(continued)

349

TABLE C.2 (continued)

```
      WRITE(NP,10014)   (MAP(J,48),J=1,50),(POPCNT(3,JJ),JJ=1,2)
      WRITE(NP,10015)   (MAP(J,49),J=1,50),(POPCNT(4,JJ),JJ=1,2)
      WRITE(NP,10016)   (MAP(J,50),J=1,50),(POPCNT(5,JJ),JJ=1,2)
      RETURN
10000 FORMAT('1',102X,'TYPE COUNT PERCENT'/)
10001 FORMAT(('  I ',50(A1,1X),'I ',A1,3X,I4,2X,F5.2))
10002 FORMAT(('  I ',50(A1,1X),'I'))
10003 FORMAT('+',104X,'TYPE  POPULATION')
10004 FORMAT(('  I ',50(A1,1X),'I   ',A1,2X,I10))
10005 FORMAT('+',104X,'HOUSING NEEDS')
10006 FORMAT(('  I ',50(A1,1X),'I   ',I10))
10007 FORMAT('+',104X,'TOTAL POPULATION')
10008 FORMAT('  I ',50(A1,1X),'I BUS.  ',I10)
10009 FORMAT('  I ',50(A1,1X),'I FAC.  ',I10)
10010 FORMAT('  I ',50(A1,1X),'I REC.  ',I10)
10011 FORMAT('+',104X,'POPULATION CENTERS')
10012 FORMAT('  I ',50(A1,1X),'I RESIDENCE  ',2I4)
10013 FORMAT('  I ',50(A1,1X),'I BUSINESS  ',2I4)
10014 FORMAT('  I ',50(A1,1X),'I FACTORY  ',2I4)
10015 FORMAT('  I ',50(A1,1X),'I RECREATION',2I4)
10016 FORMAT('  I ',50(A1,1X),'I COMMERCIAL',2I4)
      END
```

```
      SUBROUTINE SLMBLD(COUNT,CHAR,ISW)

C     BUILDS SLUMS
C
      INTEGER COUNT(1),CHAR(1)
      DO 1000 II = 1,3
      NT = COUNT(II)/50
1003  IF(NT) 1000,1000,1002
1002  CALL LOCATE(II,II,J,I,CHAR,1,ISW)
      CALL BUILD(J,I,II,4,COUNT,CHAR)
      NT=NT-1
      GO TO 1003
1000  CONTINUE
      RETURN
      END


      SUBROUTINE EXPT(TOTPOP,RATE,EXPECT,PERHSE,GRATE)

C     CALCULATES EXPECTATIONS FOR NEEDS OF EACH TYPE OF SPACE,
C     BASED UPON NEW POPULATION AND PERCENTAGES OR SERVICING
C     RATES.  UPDATES TOTPOP.
C
      INTEGER EXPECT(1),RATE(1),TOTPOP
      DIMENSION PERHSE(1)
      TOTPOP = TOTPOP*(1.0+GRATE*0.01)**10
```

(continued)

TABLE C.2 (continued)

```
      DO 1000 I = 1,4
1000  EXPECT(I) = TOTPOP*PERHSE(I)/RATE(I)/100.0+0.5
      DO 1001 I = 5,7
1001  EXPECT(I) = FLOAT(TOTPOP)/RATE(I)+0.5
      RETURN
      END

C
C     SUBROUTINE NEEDS(NEED,EXPECT,COUNT)
C
C     DETERMINES NEEDS AS THE DIFFERENCE BETWEEN EXPECTATIONS AND
C     TOTAL ON HAND FOR EACH TYPE OF SPACE.
C
      INTEGER NEED(1),EXPECT(1),COUNT(1)
      DO 1000 I = 1,7
1000  NEED(I) = EXPECT(I)-COUNT(I)
      RETURN
      END

C
C     SUBROUTINE PLANER(III,PRIORT,K)
C
C     RETURNS NEXT NEED TO BE FILLED.
```

```
      INTEGER PRIORT(1)
      DATA IKP/0/
      K = 2
      IF(IKP-7) 1000,1001,1001
 1000 IKP = IKP+1
      III = PRIORT(IKP)
      RETURN
 1001 IKP = 0
      K = 1
      RETURN
      END

      SUBROUTINE LOCATE(III,JJJ,J,I,CHAR,K,ISW)

C     FINDS AND RETURNS A LOCATION.

      INTEGER MAP(50,50),ROTOT(50,9),COTOT(50,9),CHAR(1),POPCNT(5,2)
      COMMON /SPACE/MAP,ROTOT,COTOT,POPCNT

C     ARGUMENTS TO LOCATE

C     III = TYPE OF NEED TO BE FILLED (CHARACTER TO LOOK FOR)
C     JJJ = TYPE OF CELL TO BE DESTROYED (SEARCH MAP FOR THIS)
C     J   = RETURNED ROW LOCATION
C     I   = RETURNED COLUMN LOCATION
C     CHAR= CHARACTER ARRAY
```

(continued)

353

TABLE C.2 (continued)

```
C     K   = RETURN SWITCH (2=NORMAL)
C     ISW = 1 TO USE MODAL ROW AND COLUMN TO START SEARCH
C         = 2 TO USE MEAN ROW AND COLUMN
C
C     PICK THE APPROPRIATE STARTING POINT
C
      GO TO (1000,2000),ISW
C
C     PICK MODAL ROW AND COLUMN
C
1000  K = 2
      JKEEP = 1
      IKEEP = 1
      ITEST = ROTOT(1,III)
      JTEST = COTOT(1,III)
      DO 1001 II = 2,50
      IF(ITEST-ROTOT(II,III)) 1002,1003,1003
1002  ITEST = ROTOT(II,III)
      IKEEP = II
1003  IF(JTEST-COTOT(II,III)) 1004,1001,1001
1004  JTEST = COTOT(II,III)
      JKEEP = II
1001  CONTINUE
      IF(ROTOT(IKEEP,III)) 3100,3100,1005
```

```
1005 IF(COTOT(JKEEP,III)) 3100,3100,1006
1006 J = JKEEP
     I = IKEEP
     GO TO 2500
C
C   USE APPROPRIATE POPULATION CENTER TO START SEARCH
C
2000 K = 2
     ITYPE = 1
     IF (III.LE.4) GO TO 2001
     ITYPE = III-3
2001 J = POPCNT(ITYPE,1)
     I = POPCNT(ITYPE,2)
     JKEEP = J
     IKEEP = I
C
C   IF FIRST TRY IS OK, RETURN
C
2500 IF(MAP(J,I).EQ.CHAR(JJJ)) GO TO 4000
C
C   OTHERWISE, START A CONCENTRIC SQUARES SEARCH ROUTINE
C
     DO 3000 INC = 1,49
     MINC = JKEEP-INC
     MAXC = JKEEP+INC
     MINR = IKEEP-INC
```

(continued)

355

TABLE C.2 (continued)

```
      MAXR = IKEEP+INC
      JMIN = MAXO(MINC,1)
      JMAX = MINO(MAXC,50)
      IMIN = MAXO(MINR+1,1)
      IMAX = MINO(MAXR-1,50)
      IF(MINR) 3003,3003,3001
3001  I = MINR
      DO 3002 J = JMIN,JMAX
      IF(MAP(J,I).EQ.CHAR(JJJ)) GO TO 4000
3002  CONTINUE
3003  IF(MAXR-50) 3004,3004,3006
3004  I = MAXR
      DO 3005 J = JMIN,JMAX
      IF(MAP(J,I).EQ.CHAR(JJJ)) GO TO 4000
3005  CONTINUE
3006  IF(MINC) 3009,3009,3007
3007  J = MINC
      DO 3008 I = IMIN,IMAX
      IF(MAP(J,I).EQ.CHAR(JJJ)) GO TO 4000
3008  CONTINUE
3009  IF(MAXC-50) 3010,3010,3000
3010  J = MAXC
      DO 3011 I = IMIN,IMAX
      IF(MAP(J,I).EQ.CHAR(JJJ)) GO TO 4000
3011  CONTINUE
3000  CONTINUE
```

```
C      END OF SEARCH ROUTINE
C
C      CANNOT LOCATE.   SET SWITCH AND RETURN.
C
3100   K = 1
4000   RETURN
       END

       SUBROUTINE DESTRY(J,I,III,COUNT,CHAR)
C
C      CONVERTS A FILLED SPACE TO AN EMPTY ONE AND ADJUSTS TOTALS.
C
       INTEGER MAP(50,50),ROTOT(50,9),COTOT(50,9),CHAR(1),COUNT(1),
     * POPCNT(5,2)
       COMMON /SPACE/MAP,ROTOT,COTOT,POPCNT
       ROTOT(I,III) = ROTOT(I,III)-1
       COTOT(J,III) = COTOT(J,III)-1
       ROTOT(I,9) = ROTOT(I,9)+1
       COTOT(J,9) = COTOT(J,9)+1
       COUNT(III) = COUNT(III)-1
       COUNT(9) = COUNT(9)+1
       MAP(J,I) = CHAR(9)
       RETURN
       END
```

(continued)

TABLE C.2 (continued)

```
      SUBROUTINE PRIO(JJJ,III,DESPRI,COUNT,K)

C     DETERMINES TYPE OF SPACE TO BE DESTROYED NEXT.
C
      INTEGER DESPRI(1),COUNT(1)
      K = 2
      DO 1000 I = 1,7
      JJJ = DESPRI(I)
      IF(JJJ-III) 1001,1003,1001
 1001 IF(COUNT(JJJ)) 1000,1000,1002
 1002 RETURN
 1000 CONTINUE
 1003 CONTINUE
      K = 1
      RETURN
      END


      SUBROUTINE BUILD(J,I,JJ,III,COUNT,CHAR)

C     PUTS SOMETHING IN AN EMPTY SPACE AND ADJUSTS TOTALS.
C
      INTEGER MAP(50,50),ROTOT(50,9),COTOT(50,9),CHAR(1),COUNT(1),
     *  POPCNT(5,2)
```

```
COMMON /SPACE/MAP,ROTOT,COTOT,POPCNT
ROTOT(I,III) = ROTOT(I,III)+1
ROTOT(I,JJJ) = ROTOT(I,JJJ)-1
COTOT(J,III) = COTOT(J,III)+1
COTOT(J,JJJ) = COTOT(J,JJJ)-1
COUNT(III) = COUNT(III)+1
COUNT(JJJ) = COUNT(JJJ)-1
MAP(J,I) = CHAR(III)
RETURN
END
```

are short and simply structured. LOCATE could have been divided into two routines easily, by placing the starting point algorithm and the search itself in two subroutines.

Input and Output

A total of 55 cards or imput records must be supplied for CITY. All of them are described in detail in the listing of CITY's main program and illustrated in Table C.3. The first card provides two important parameters and the overall title for the run. The second input record gives the characters to be used in representing the various land uses. The first character is for dwellings, the second for apartments, and so forth. The following set of symbols and their meanings was employed in the CITY runs described in this book.

    D Dwelling unit
    A Apartment
    H High rise apartment unit
    G Ghetto area
    $ Business and Commercial Area
    F Factor or manufacturing (U in the Boulder runs to indicate the
        University of Colorado)
    * Recreation and parks
    + Boundary or other unbuildable area
  blank Vacant land

Following the array of characters, 50 cards give the initial map of the city. Each card represents a single row in the map and should contain only those characters defined on Card 2.

The map is followed by three additional input records. The first gives the densities (how many people served by) for all of the kinds of property specified previously except vacant space, an annual growth rate expressed as a percentage, and the total starting population of the city.

The next card gives two priority arrays, for building and for destruction. Some care should be exercised in preparing this card because confusion can cause disastrous errors in operating the program. The entries in each array are two-digit numbers, each standing for a kind of property. The numbers correspond to the order in which the properties have been identified earlier; 01 means dwelling, 05 means business, and so forth. The order in which the numbers appear in the priority arrays governs their priority. For example, to specify that dwellings are to be built first, followed by business, and then ghetto, the record would be

$$010504...$$

because 01 is a dwelling, 05 a business, and so forth. The destroy priorities follow the building priorities on the card according to the same rule.

TABLE C.3
Example CITY Input

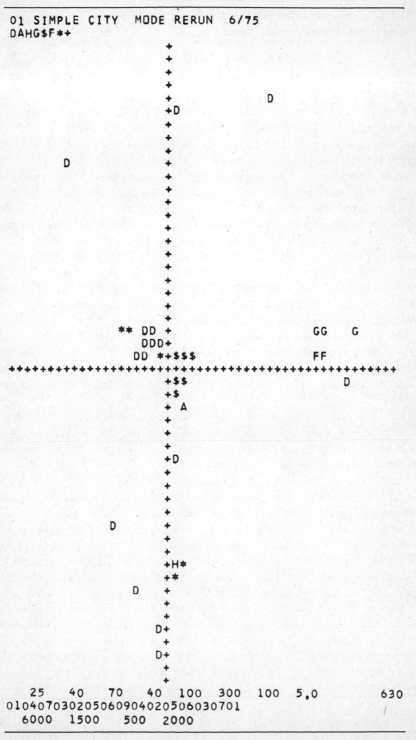

```
01 SIMPLE CITY  MODE RERUN  6/75
DAHG$F*+
                        +
                        +
                        +
                        +
                        +              D
                        +D
                        +
                        +
                        +
           D            +
                        +
                        +
                        +
                        +
                        +
                        +
                        +
                        +
                        +
                        +
     **  DD +                    GG   G
         DDD+
         DD *+$$$                 FF
+++++++++++++++++++++++++++++++++++++++++++++++
         +$$                        D
         +$
         + A
         +
         +
         +
         +D
         +
         +
         +
         +
    D    +
         +
         +
         +H*
         +*
    D    +
         +
         +
         D+
         +
         D+
         +
         +
   25    40    70   40   100  300  100  5.0           630
0104070302050609040205 06030701
   6000   1500   500  2000
```

The final card gives the percentages of the population to be housed in each kind of residential unit. A card reading

50.00 30.00 10.00 10.00

would require 50% of the population to be in dwellings, 30% in apartments, and 10% each in high rises and ghettos.

A complete set of input for CITY is shown in Table C.3. This set of inputs has been used to produce one of the series of runs with the simple crossroads city that begins with a very small population and grows slowly (see Table C.4). The spatial distribution of the units is governed primarily by two elements of the input, the priorities and the search mode. The location of the starting point in a search has a major effect on the form of the final city, whereas the priorities have their impact on a more fine-grain analysis of the maps.

The two procedures for selecting a starting point in CITY's spatial search are designated the "mean" and "modal" algorithms in the program listing. In the modal approach, if a location for a dwelling unit is to be found, the search begins at the intersection of the row and column that contain the most dwellings. In the "mean" approach, average row and column numbers are maintained for several groups of property. To locate the starting point for a dwelling search, for example, the "residence" row and column values in the population center array are used. This array contains center of gravity information so that the search begins in the center of density of the class of property being searched. The mean or center of gravity location procedure results in a very compact city; the modal approach gives a city that is somewhat more dispersed.

The effect of changing priorities can be seen in a detailed look at the structure of the final city maps. Although the overall pattern of the city is the same for both mode and mean runs, when the priorities are changed different buildings are seen in the same locations. This is a function of the order in which properties are built. The search pattern always proceeds in the same way but the symbol placed at a selected location is governed by the input building priorities. The two "mean" runs of the simple city show the effects of priority very clearly.

The second urban map given to CITY was an actual city. Several runs have been based on Boulder, Colorado, and the results, although complex, are interesting. Boulder has a constraint not found in the crossroad community — it is bounded on the West (the left of the maps) by mountains and protected "greenbelt" areas. The mountains, as well as the final pattern of streets, are included in the initial map because the program has no provision for increasing the boundary (unbuildable) areas. Because the major employer in Boulder is the University of Colorado, the symbol F for factory was replaced by a U.

In the first series of CITY maps, shown in Table C.5, priorities similar to those apparently employed by Boulder were used. The set is characterized by low-build and high-destroy priorities for ghettos and a high value is given to

TABLE C.4
Simple CITY Output

(a) Years 0–40, Using the Modal Search Procedure

MAP LEGEND --

CATEGORIES	HOUSE	APARTMENT	HIRISE	GHETTO	BUSINESS	FACTORY	RECREATION	BOUNDARY	VACANT LOT
SYMBOLS	D	A	H	G	$	F	*	+	
RATES	25	40	70	40	100	300	100		
PERCENT	60.00	15.00	5.00	20.00					

PRIORITIES --

ORDER	BUILD	DESTROY
1	1 D	9
2	4 G	4 G
3	7 *	2 A
4	3 H	5 $
5	2 A	6 F
6	5 $	3 H
7	6 F	7 *
8		1 D

CURRENT POPULATION   630   GROWTH RATE   5.00 PERCENT PER YEAR
THE MODE WILL BE USED TO DETERMINE THE STARTING POINT FOR LOCATE

(continued)

TABLE C.4a (continued)

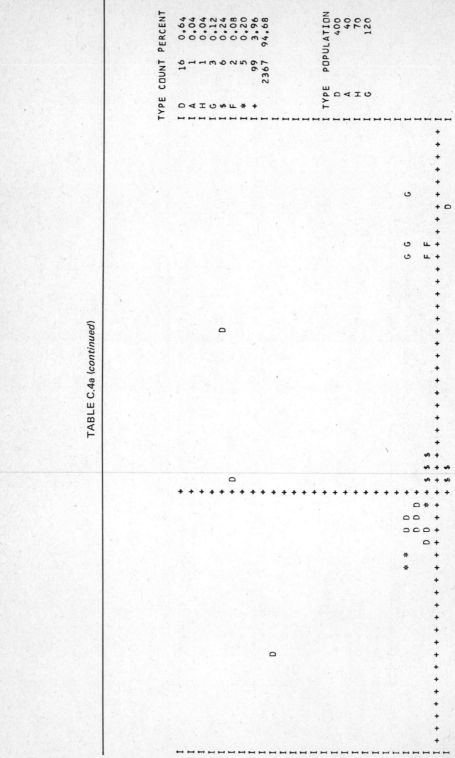

TYPE	COUNT	PERCENT
D	16	0.64
A	1	0.04
H	1	0.04
G	3	0.12
$	6	0.24
F	2	0.08
*	5	0.20
+	99	3.96
	2367	94.68

TYPE	POPULATION
D	400
A	40
H	70
G	120

```
I
I  HOUSING NEEDS
I       0
I
I
I
I  TOTAL POPULATION
I       630
I
I
I
I  BUS.        600
I  FAC.        600
I  REC.        500
I
I  POPULATION CENTERS
I  RESIDENCE   25  27
I  BUSINESS    22  26
I  FACTORY     40  25
I  RECREATION  19  30
I  COMMERCIAL  31  25
```

(continued)

```
              A
         $              D                    H *
+ + + + + + + + + + + + + + + + + + + + + + + + + + + +
                                        D +   D +
                         D

               D
```

YEAR 0 FOR SIMPLE CITY MODE RERUN 6/75

TABLE C.4a (continued)

TYPE	COUNT	PERCENT
D	25	1.00
A	4	0.16
H	1	0.04
G	5	0.20
$	10	0.40
F	3	0.12
*	10	0.40
+	99	3.96
	2343	93.72

TYPE	POPULATION
D	625
A	160
H	70
G	200

HOUSING NEEDS
-29

TOTAL POPULATION
1026

BUS.   1000
FAC.   900
REC.   1000

POPULATION CENTERS
RESIDENCE   24 26
BUSINESS   22 25
FACTORY   40 24
RECREATION   16 26
COMMERCIAL   31 24

(continued)

$ A A
A

D

H *
*

D

D

D

D

YEAR 10 FOR SIMPLE CITY MODE RERUN 6/75

TABLE C.4a (continued)

TYPE	COUNT	PERCENT
D	40	1.60
A	6	0.24
HG	1	0.04
$	8	0.32
$	17	0.68
F	6	0.24
*	17	0.68
+	99	3.96
	2306	92.24

TYPE	POPULATION
D	1000
A	240
H	70
G	320

```
I
I HOUSING NEEDS
I        41
I
I
I
I
I
I TOTAL POPULATION
I       1671
I
I BUS.      1700
I FAC.      1800
I REC.      1700
I
I POPULATION CENTERS
I RESIDENCE    22  23
I BUSINESS     22  23
I FACTORY      39  24
I RECREATION   15  23
I COMMERCIAL   30  23
```

```
I  $ A A
I    A A
I
I        D
I
I
I
I
I
I
I
I
I              H *
I                *
I
I
I
I
I
```

```
+ + + + + + + + + + + + + + + + + + + + + +
                          D           D
                                D
                    D
```

YEAR 20 FOR SIMPLE CITY MODE RERUN 6/75

(continued)

TABLE C.4a (continued)

TYPE		COUNT	PERCENT
I	D	65	2.60
I	A	10	0.40
I	H	2	0.08
I	G	14	0.56
I	$	27	1.08
I	F	9	0.36
I	*	27	1.08
I	+	99	3.96
I		2247	89.88

TYPE	POPULATION
D	1625
A	400
H	140
G	560

370

HOUSING NEEDS
-4

TOTAL POPULATION
2721

BUS.   2700
FAC.   2700
REC.   2700

POPULATION CENTERS
RESIDENCE   23 21
BUSINESS   22 21
FACTORY   38 25
RECREATION 14 21
COMMERCIAL 30 23

YEAR 30 FOR SIMPLE CITY MODE RERUN 6/75

(continued)

371

TABLE C.4a (continued)

TYPE	COUNT	PERCENT
D	106	4.24
A	17	0.68
H	3	0.12
G	22	0.88
$	44	1.76
F	15	0.60
*	44	1.76
+	99	3.96
	2150	86.00

TYPE	POPULATION
D	2650
A	680
H	210
G	880

```
                                          HOUSING NEEDS
                                                12

                                          TOTAL POPULATION
                                                4432

                                          BUS.      4400
                                          FAC.      4500
                                          REC.      4400

                                          POPULATION CENTERS
                                          RESIDENCE    22  17
                                          BUSINESS     22  18
                                          FACTORY      37  25
                                          RECREATION   13  17
                                          COMMERCIAL   29  21
```

(continued)

YEAR 40 FOR SIMPLE CITY MODE RERUN 6/75

TABLE C.4

Simple CITY Output

(b) Year 40, Using the Mean Search Procedure

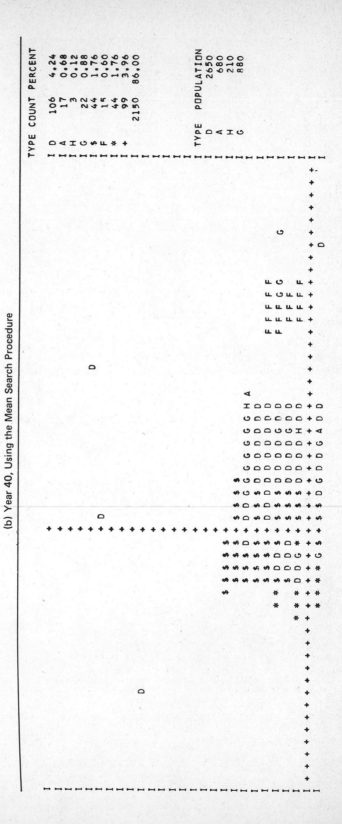

TYPE	COUNT	PERCENT
D	106	4.24
A	17	0.68
H	3	0.12
G	22	0.88
$	44	1.76
F	15	0.60
*	44	1.76
+	99	3.96
	2150	86.00

TYPE	POPULATION
D	2650
A	680
H	210
G	880

```
HOUSING NEEDS
        12


TOTAL POPULATION
        4432


BUS.      4400
FAC.      4500
REC.      4400

POPULATION CENTERS
RESIDENCE    26  27
BUSINESS     20  21
FACTORY      38  23
RECREATION   17  29
COMMERCIAL   29  22
```

YEAR 40 FOR SIMPLE CITY   MEAN RERUN 6/75

(continued)

TABLE C.4
Simple CITY Output

(c) Year 40, Modal Search with Changed Priorities

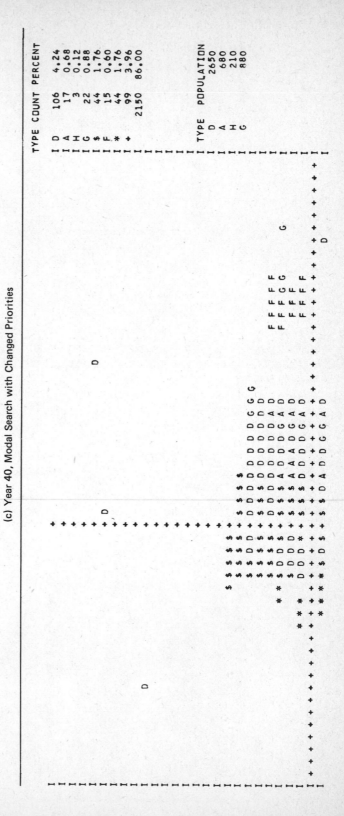

TYPE	COUNT	PERCENT
D	106	4.24
A	17	0.68
H	3	0.12
G	22	0.88
$	44	1.76
F	15	0.60
*	44	1.76
+	99	3.96
	2150	86.00

TYPE	POPULATION
D	2650
A	680
H	210
G	880

YEAR 40 FOR SIMPLE CITY MEAN RERUN 6/75 REVISED PRIORITIES

```
I I I I I I I I I I I I I I I I I I I I I I I I I I I I I I I I
```

```
                    D D D D D
                    G G D D D
                D G G H A A D
              G D G D D D A D
          A A G D G D D D D D
          D D D D D D D D D
        G D A A D D D D D
   $ G A A G G D D D D D
   $ D A A D D D D G H
   $ D D D D D D G
   + + + + + + + + + + + + + + + + + + + + + + H * + + +
   $ * * * * D D D                    D   H *
   * * * * * D D G G               D   + + +
   * * * * * * G G G
   * * * * * *            D
   * * * * * *
   * * * * * *
   * * * * *         D
```

```
I                    HOUSING NEEDS
I                    12
I
I
I                    TOTAL POPULATION
I                    4432
I
I                    BUS.    4400
I                    FAC.    4500
I                    REC.    4400
I
I                    POPULATION CENTERS
I                    RESIDENCE   26  27
I                    BUSINESS    20  21
I                    FACTORY     38  23
I                    RECREATION  16  29
I                    COMMERCIAL  29  22
```

(continued)

377

TABLE C.4
Simple CITY Output

(d) Year 40, Mean Search with Revised Priorities

TYPE	COUNT	PERCENT
D	106	4.24
A	17	0.68
H	3	0.12
G	22	0.88
$	44	1.76
F	15	0.60
*	44	1.76
+	99	3.96
	2150	86.00

TYPE	POPULATION
D	2650
A	680
H	210
G	880

HOUSING NEEDS
12

TOTAL POPULATION
4432

BUS.   4400
FAC.   4500
REC.   4400

POPULATION CENTERS
RESIDENCE   22 17
BUSINESS   22 18
FACTORY   37 25
RECREATION 13 17
COMMERCIAL 29 21

YEAR 40 FOR SIMPLE CITY MODE RERUN 6/75   REVISED PRIORITIES

TABLE C.5
Boulder CITY Output

(a) Years 0–40, Using the Mean Search Procedure

MAP LEGEND --

CATEGORIES	HOUSE	APARTMENT	HIRISE	GHETTO	BUSINESS	FACTORY	RECREATION	BOUNDARY	VACANT LOT
SYMBOLS	D	A	H	G	$	U	*	+	
RATES	20	350	2000	100	300	400	500		
PERCENT	30.00	40.00	20.00	10.00					

PRIORITIES --

ORDER	BUILD	DESTROY
1	1 D	9
2	2 A	4 G
3	3 H	5 $
4	7 *	2 A
5	6 U	3 H
6	5 $	6 U
7	4 G	7 *
8		1 D

CURRENT POPULATION 10680 GROWTH RATE 2.00 PERCENT PER YEAR
THE MEAN WILL BE USED TO DETERMINE THE STARTING POINT FOR LOCATE

(continued)

TABLE C.5a (continued)

TYPE	COUNT	PERCENT
D	169	6.76
A	12	0.48
H	1	0.04
G	11	0.44
$	41	1.64
U	34	1.36
*	16	0.64
+	356	14.24
	1860	74.40

TYPE	POPULATION
D	3380
A	4200
H	2000
G	1100

HOUSING NEEDS
0

TOTAL POPULATION
10680

BUS.   12300
FAC.   13600
REC.   8000

POPULATION CENTERS
RESIDENCE   23 26
BUSINESS   17 22
FACTORY   21 28
RECREATION   12 30
COMMERCIAL   19 25

YEAR   0 FOR   BOULDER, COLORADO: MEAN RERUN 6/75 STANDARD PRIORITIES

(continued)

TABLE C.5a (continued)

TYPE	COUNT	PERCENT
I D	195	7.80
I A	15	0.60
I H	1	0.04
I G	13	0.52
I $	43	1.72
I U	33	1.32
I *	26	1.04
I +	356	14.24
I	1818	72.72

TYPE	POPULATION
I D	3900
I A	5250
I H	2000
I G	1300

HOUSING NEEDS
568

TOTAL POPULATION
13018

BUS.   12900
FAC.   13200
REC.   13000

POPULATION CENTERS
RESIDENCE   22 25
BUSINESS   17 22
FACTORY   21 28
RECREATION   11 30
COMMERCIAL   19 25

YEAR 10 FOR BOULDER, COLORADO: MEAN RERUN 6/75 STANDARD PRIORITIES

(continued)

385

TABLE C.5a (continued)

TYPE	COUNT	PERCENT
D	238	9.52
A	18	0.72
H	2	0.08
G	16	0.64
$	53	2.12
U	40	1.60
*	32	1.28
+	356	14.24
	1745	69.80

TYPE	POPULATION
D	4760
A	6300
H	4000
G	1600

HOUSING NEEDS -792

TOTAL POPULATION 15868

BUS. 15900
FAC. 16000
REC. 16000

POPULATION CENTERS
RESIDENCE   24 28
BUSINESS   17 21
FACTORY   21 29
RECREATION 11 29
COMMERCIAL 19 25

YEAR 20 FOR BOULDER, COLORADO: MEAN RERUN 6/75 STANDARD PRIORITIES

(continued)

TABLE C.5a (continued)

TYPE COUNT PERCENT
I D   290   11.60
I A   22   0.88
I H   2   0.08
I G   19   0.76
I $ 64   2.56
I U   48   1.92
I *   39   1.56
I +   356   14.24
I   1660   66.40

TYPE POPULATION
I D   5800
I A   7700
I H   4000
I G   1900

HOUSING NEEDS
-58

TOTAL POPULATION
19342

BUS. 19200
FAC. 19200
REC. 19500

POPULATION CENTERS
RESIDENCE   24 27
BUSINESS   17 20
FACTORY   20 30
RECREATION   11 29
COMMERCIAL   18 25

YEAR 30 FOR BOULDER, COLORADO: MEAN RERUN 6/75 STANDARD PRIORITIES

(continued)

TABLE C.5a (continued)

TYPE	COUNT	PERCENT
D	354	14.16
A	27	1.08
H	2	0.08
G	24	0.96
$	79	3.16
U	59	2.36
*	47	1.88
+	356	14.24
	1552	62.08

TYPE	POPULATION
D	7080
A	9450
H	4000
G	2400

HOUSING NEEDS
647

TOTAL POPULATION
23577

BUS.   23700
FAC.   23600
REC.   23500

POPULATION CENTERS
RESIDENCE   23 27
BUSINESS   17 19
FACTORY   19 30
RECREATION   10 29
COMMERCIAL   18 24

YEAR 40 FOR   BOULDER, COLORADO: MEAN RERUN 6/75 STANDARD PRIORITIES

(continued)

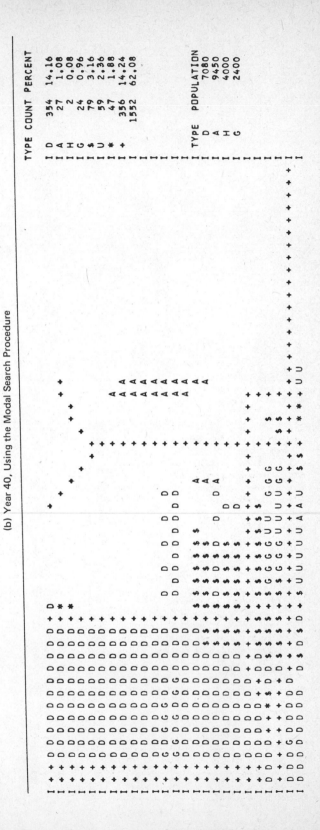

TABLE C.5
Boulder CITY Output

(b) Year 40, Using the Modal Search Procedure

TYPE	COUNT	PERCENT
D	354	14.16
A	27	1.08
H	2	0.08
G	24	0.96
$	79	3.16
U	59	2.36
*	47	1.88
+	356	14.24
	1552	62.08

TYPE	POPULATION
D	7080
A	9450
H	4000
G	2400

```
                                              POPULATION CENTERS
                                              RESIDENCE   22 20
HOUSING NEEDS    TOTAL POPULATION  BUS. 23700  BUSINESS    16 20
        647              23577     FAC. 23600  FACTORY     21 27
                                   REC. 23500  RECREATION   6 38
                                              COMMERCIAL  18 23
```

YEAR 40 FOR   BOULDER, COLORADO: MODE RERUN 6/75 STANDARD PRIORITIES

(continued)

TABLE C.5
Boulder CITY Output

(c) Year 40, Modal Search with Revised Priorities

TYPE	COUNT	PERCENT
D	354	14.16
A	27	1.08
H	2	0.08
G	24	0.96
$	79	3.16
U	59	2.36
*	47	1.88
+	356	14.24
	1552	62.08

TYPE	POPULATION
D	7080
A	9450
H	4000
G	2400

```
HOUSING NEEDS
    647

TOTAL POPULATION
    23577

BUS.      23700
FAC.      23600
REC.      23500

POPULATION CENTERS
RESIDENCE    22  20
BUSINESS     16  21
FACTORY      21  27
RECREATION    6  38
COMMERCIAL   18  24
```

YEAR 40 FOR   BOULDER, COLORADO: MODE RERUN 6/75 REVISED PRIORITIES

(continued)

TABLE C.5

Boulder CITY Output

(d) Year 40, Mean Search with Revised Priorities

TYPE	COUNT	PERCENT
D	354	14.16
A	27	1.08
H	2	0.08
G	24	0.96
$	79	3.16
U	59	2.36
*	47	1.88
+	356	14.24
	1552	62.08

TYPE	POPULATION
D	7080
A	9450
H	4000
G	2400

```
HOUSING NEEDS
647

TOTAL POPULATION
23577

BUS.        23700
FAC.        23600
REC.        23500

POPULATION CENTERS
RESIDENCE    23  25
BUSINESS     16  19
FACTORY      20  31
RECREATION   10  29
COMMERCIAL   18  25
```

YEAR 40 FOR   BOULDER, COLORADO: MEAN RERUN 6/75 REVISED PRIORITIES recreational areas. Of this series the modal search has resulted in the final map most resembling Boulder at present; the University expands in roughly the way it actually has and apartments blossom in the Northeast section. Neither the mean nor the mode search resulted in an increase in housing units in the Southwest – the actual case. The mode procedure produced a very dense housing area in the Northwest – correct – but not to the extent indicated by CITY.

A second series of CITY maps was based on a very different set of priorities than those Boulder actually seems to employ. As has been the case with the simple city, the overall pattern of the city is not changed significantly but specific building locations are. With different priorities, therefore, a close analysis of the final maps reveals vastly different "neighborhoods," where different classes of housing appear together in one map whereas they are not adjacent in another.

GENERAL REFERENCES

Abelson, R. P. Simulation of social behavior. In G. Lindzey & E. Aronson (Eds.), *The handbook of social psychology.* Vol. 2. *Research methods.* (2nd ed.) Reading, Mass.: Addison-Wesley, 1968.

Ahrens, J. H., & Dieter, U. Computer methods for sampling from the exponential and normal distributions. *Communications of the ACM,* 1972, 15, 873–882.

Ahrens, J. H., Dieter, U., & Grube, A. Pseudo-random numbers: A new proposal for the choice of multiplicators. *Computing,* 1970, 6, 121–138.

American National Standards Institute, Inc. (ANSI) *USA Standard FORTRAN (ANSI X3.9-1966).* New York: ANSI, 1966.

American National Standards Institute, Inc. (ANSI) *Flowchart symbols and their usage in information processing (ANSI X3.5-1970).* New York: ANSI, 1970.

American Psychological Association. (APA) *Publication Manual of the American Psychological Association.* (2nd ed.) Washington, D.C.: APA, 1974.

Anderson, J. R., & Bower, G. H. *Human associative memory.* Washington, D.C.: Winston, 1973.

Apter, M. J. *The computer simulation of behaviour.* New York: Harper & Row, 1970.

Apter, M. J. The computer modelling of behaviour. In M. J. Apter & G. Westby (Eds.), *The computer in psychology.* London: Wiley, 1973.

Bachrach, A. J. *Psychological research: An introduction.* New York: Random House, 1962.

Barr, D. R., & Slezak, N. L. A comparison of multivariate normal generators. *Communications of the ACM,* 1972, 15, 1048–1049.

Bobrow, D. G., & Raphael, B. A comparison of list-processing computer languages. *Communications of the ACM,* 1964, 7, 231–240.

Bobrow, D. G., & Raphael, B. New programming languages for artificial intelligence research. *Computing Surveys,* 1974, 6, 155–174.

Booth, T. L., & Chien, Y. T. *Computing: Fundamentals and applications.* Santa Barbara, Calif.: Hamilton, 1974.

Boothroyd, J. Algorithm 201: Shellsort. *Communications of the ACM,* 1963, 8, 445.

Brown, P. J. Programming and documenting software projects. *Computing Surveys,* 1974, 6, 213–220.

Carnahan, B., & Wilkes, J. O. *Digital computing and numerical methods (with FORTRAN-IV, WATFOR, and WATFIV programming).* New York: Wiley, 1973.

Colby, K. M. Simulations of belief systems. In R. C. Schank & K. M. Colby (Eds.), *Computer models of thought and language.* San Francisco, Calif.: Freeman, 1973.

Colby, K. M., & Gilbert, J. P. Programming a computer model of neurosis. *Journal of Mathematical Psychology,* 1964, **1,** 405–417.

Colby, K. M., Hilf, F. D., Weber, S., & Kraemer, H. Turing-like indistinguishability tests for the validation of a computer simulation of paranoid processes. *Artifical intelligence,* 1972, **3,** 199–221.

Dahl, O. J., Dijkstra, E. W., & Hoare, C. A. R. *Structured programming.* New York: Academic Press, 1972.

Day, A. C. *Fortran techniques: With special reference to non-numerical applications.* Cambridge, England: Cambridge University Press, 1972.

Duke, R. D. *Gaming-simulation in urban research.* Ann Arbor: Institute for Community Development and Services, University of Michigan, 1964.

Dutton, J. M., & Starbuck, W. H. The plan of the book. In J. M. Dutton & W. H. Starbuck (Eds.), *Computer simulation of human behavior.* New York: Wiley, 1971.

Feigenbaum, E. A. The simulation of verbal learning behavior. In E. A. Feigenbaum & J. Feldman (Eds.), *Computers and thought.* New York: McGraw-Hill, 1963.

Feldman, J. Simulation of behavior in the binary choice experiment. In J. M. Dutton & W. H. Starbuck (Eds.), *Computer simulation of human behavior.* New York: Wiley, 1971. [Also in E. A. Feigenbaum & J. Feldman (Eds.), *Computers and thought.* New York: McGraw-Hill, 1963.]

Forrester, J. W. *Industrial dynamics.* Cambridge, Mass.: M.I.T. Press, 1961.

Friedman, D. P. *The Little LISPer.* Chicago: Science Research Associates, 1974.

Frijda, N. H. The problems of computer simulation. *Behavioral Science,* 1967, **12,** 59–67. [Also in J. M. Dutton & W. H. Starbuck (Eds.), *Computer simulation of human behavior.* New York: Wiley, 1971.]

Gelernter, H. Realization of a geometry-theorem proving machine. In E. A. Feigenbaum and J. Feldman (Eds.), *Computers and thought.* New York: McGraw-Hill, 1963.

Griswold, R. W., Poage, J. F., & Polonsky, I. P. *The SNOBOL4 programming language.* (2nd ed.) Englewood Cliffs, N. J.: Prentice-Hall, 1971.

Guetzkow, H. *Simulation in social science: Readings.* Englewood Cliffs, N. J.: Prentice-Hall, 1962.

Gullahorn, J. T., & Gullahorn, J. E. The computer as a tool for theory development. In D. Hymes (Ed.), *The use of computers in anthropology.* The Hague: Mouton, 1965.

Hamming, R. W. *Numerical methods for scientists and engineers.* (2nd ed.) New York: McGraw-Hill, 1973.

Hanson, D. R. A simple technique for representing strings in Fortran IV. *Communications of the ACM,* 1974, **17,** 646–647.

Harrison, M. C. *Data-structures and programming.* Glenview, Ill.: Scott, Foresman, 1973.

Henshaw, R. C., & Jackson, J. R. *The Executive Game.* Homewood, Ill.: Irwin, 1966.

Hintzman, D. Explorations with a discrimination net model for paired-associate learning. *Journal of Mathematical Psychology,* 1968, **5,** 123–162.

Hunt, E. B., Martin, J., & Stone, P. J. *Experiments in induction.* New York: Academic Press, 1966.

IBM, *System/360 continuous system modeling program (CSMP)* (360A-CX-16X). White Plains, N.Y.: IBM, 1967. (a)

IBM, *General purpose simulation system/360, user's manual* (H20-D326-0). White Plains, N.Y.: IBM, 1967. (b)

Kaiser, H. F., & Dickman, K. Sample and population score matrices and sample correlation matrices from an arbitrary population correlation matrix. *Psychometrika,* 1962, **27,** 179–182.

Knuth, D. *The art of computer programming.* Vol. 1. *Fundamental algorithms.* Reading, Mass.: Addison-Wesley, 1968.

Knuth, D. *The art of computer programming.* Vol. 2. *Semi-numerical algorithms.* Reading, Mass.: Addison-Wesley, 1969.

Knuth, D. E. *The art of computer programming.* Vol. 3. *Sorting and searching.* Reading, Mass.: Addison-Wesley, 1973.

Knuth, D. E. Structured programming with go to statements. *Computing Surveys,* 1974, 6, 261–302.

Lehman, R. S. Simulation and modeling in the classroom. In Bailey, D. E. (Ed.), *Computer Science in Social and Behavioral Science Education.* Englewood Cliffs, N. J.: Educational Technology Press, 1977.

Lehman, R. S., & Bailey, D. E. *Digital computing.* New York: Wiley, 1968.

Lehman, R. S., Starr, B. J., & Young, K. C. Computer aids in teaching statistics and methodology. *Behavior Research Methods and Instrumentation,* 1975, 7, 93–102.

Lehmer, D. Mathematical methods in large-scale computing units. *Annals of the Computer Laboratory* (Harvard University), 1951, 26, 141–146.

Lewin, K. *Field theory in social science.* New York: Harper, 1951.

Lindsay, P. H., & Norman, D. A. *Human information processing: An introduction to psychology.* New York: Academic Press, 1972.

Loehlin, J. C. *Computer models of personality.* New York: Random House, 1968.

Main, D. Toward a future-oriented curriculum. *American Psychologist,* 1972, 27, 245–248.

Markowitz, H., Hansner, B., & Karr, H. *SIMSCRIPT.* Englewood Cliffs, N. J.: Prentice-Hall, 1964.

Martin, W. A. Sorting. *Computing Surveys,* 1971, 3, 147–174.

Maurer, W. D., & Lewis, T. G. Hash table methods. *Computing Surveys,* 1975, 7, 5–19.

McCarthy, J. (Ed.), *LISP 1.5 programmer's manual.* Cambridge, Mass.: M.I.T. Press, 1963.

McPhee, W. N. Note on a campaign simulator. *Public Opinion Quarterly,* 1961, 25, 184–193.

McPhee, W. N. *Formal theories of mass behavior.* London: Free Press, 1963.

Naylor, T. H., Balintfy, D. S., Burdick, D. S., & Chu, K. *Computer simulation techniques.* New York: Wiley, 1966.

Newell, A. (Ed.). *Information processing language-V.* (2nd ed.) Englewood Cliffs, N. J.: Prentice-Hall, 1964.

Newell, A., Shaw, J. C., & Simon, H. A. Elements of a theory of human problem solving. *Psychological Review,* 1958, 65, 151–166.

Newell, A., & Simon, H. A. GPS, A program that simulates human thought. In E. A. Feigenbaum and J. Feldman (Eds.), *Computers and thought.* New York: McGraw-Hill, 1963. (a)

Newell, A., & Simon, H. A. Computers in psychology. In R. D. Luce, R. R. Bush, & E. Gelernter (Eds.), *Handbook of mathematical psychology.* Vol. 1. New York: Wiley, 1963. (b)

Newell, A., & Simon, H. A. *Human problem solving.* Englewood Cliffs, N. J.: Prentice-Hall, 1972.

Pool, I., Abelson, R. P., & Popkin, S. *Candidates, issues, and strategies: A computer simulation of the 1960 presidential election.* Cambridge, Mass.: M.I.T. Press, 1964.

Popper, K. *The logic of scientific discovery.* New York: Basic Books, 1959.

Pugh, A. *DYNAMO user's manual.* (2nd ed.) Cambridge, Mass.: M.I.T. Press, 1963.

Rajecki, D. W. *EXPER SIM.* Ann Arbor: Department of Psychology, University of Michigan, 1972 (mimeographed).

Reitman, W. R. *Cognition and Thought: An Information Processing Approach.* New York: Wiley, 1965.

Restle, F. Sources of difficulty in learning paired associates. In R. C. Atkinson (Ed.), *Studies in mathematical psychology*. Stanford, Calif.: Stanford University Press, 1964.

Sakoda, J. M. The checkerboard model of social interaction. *Journal of Mathematical Sociology*, 1971, **1**, 119–132.

Sands, W. A. A computer program for the generation of score vectors from a multivariate normal distribution with a specified mean vector and variance-covariance matrix. *Educational and Psychological Measurement*, 1973, **33**, 719–722.

Schank, R. C., & Colby, K. M. (Eds.) *Computer models of thought and language*. San Francisco: Freeman, 1973.

Scheuer, E. M., & Stoller, D. S. On the generation of normal random vectors. *Technometrics*, 1962, **4**, 278–281.

Schultz, R. L., & Sullivan, E. M. Developments in simulation in social and administrative science. In H. Guetzkow, P. Kotler, & R. L. Schultz (Eds.), *Simulation in social and administrative science: Overviews and case-examples*. Englewood Cliffs, N. J.: Prentice-Hall, 1972.

Sedelow, S. Y. The computer in the humanities and fine arts. *Computing Surveys*, 1970, **2**, 89–110.

Selfridge, O. Pandemonium: A paradigm for learning. In *Symposium on the Mechanization of Thought Processes*. London: Her Majesty's Stationery Office, 1959.

Shell, D. L. A high speed sorting procedure. *Communications of the ACM*, 1959, **2**, 30–32.

Simon, H. A., & Feigenbaum, E. A. An information-processing theory of some effects of similarity, familiarization, and meaningfulness in verbal learning. *Journal of Verbal Learning and Verbal Behavior*, 1964, **3**, 385–396.

Simon, H. A., & Hayes, J. R. The understanding process: Problem isomorphs. *Cognitive Psychology*, 1976, **8**, 165–190.

Simon, H. A., & Newell, A. Models: Their uses and limitations. In L. D. White (Ed.), *The state of the social sciences*. Chicago: University of Chicago Press, 1956.

Starbuck, W. H., & Dutton, J. M. The history of simulation models. In J. M. Dutton & W. H. Starbuck (Eds.), *Computer simulation of human behavior*. New York: Wiley, 1971.

Turing, A. M. Computing machinery and intelligence. *Mind*, 1950, **59**, 433–460. [Also in Feigenbaum, E. A., & Feldman, J. (Eds.), *Computers and thought*. New York: McGraw-Hill, 1963.]

Uhr, L. *Pattern recognition, learning, and thought*. Englewood Cliffs, N. J.: Prentice-Hall, 1963.

Vandeportaele, D., & Garside, D. R. *CITY – A model of city growth based on a rigid set of priorities*. Research Triangle Park, N. C.: North Carolina Educational Computing Service, Document #CEG-SOC-04, 1972.

Volkart, H. (Ed.) *Social behavior and personality*. New York: Science Research Council, 1951.

Wampler, R. H. A report on the accuracy of some widely used least squares computer programs. *Journal of the American Statistical Association*, 1970, **65**, 549–565.

Wherry, R. J., Naylor, J. C., Wherry, R. J. Jr., & Fallis, R. F. Generating multiple samples of multivariate data with arbitrary population parameters. *Psychometrika*, 1965, **30**, 303–313.

Wilde, D. U. *An introduction to computing: Problem-solving, algorithms, and data structures*. Englewood Cliffs, N. J.: Prentice-Hall, 1973.

Author Index

Subject Index